A Greek Island Cos...

A Greek Island Cosmos

Kinship & Community on Meganisi

Roger Just

Senior Lecturer
in Anthropology
University of Melbourne

James Currey
OXFORD

School of American Research Press
SANTA FE

James Currey
73 Botley Road
Oxford OX2 0BS

School of American Research Press
Post Office Box 2188
Santa Fe, New Mexico 87504-2188

Orders in Australia from:
Bushbooks
PO Box 1958
Gosford
NSW 2250

Publication of this book was assisted by
a publications grant from the University of Melbourne

British Library Cataloguing in Publication Data

Just, Roger
  A Greek island cosmos : kinship and community on Meganisi.
  - (World anthropology)
  1. Anthropology - Greece 2. Kinship - Greece - Meganisi
  3. Greece - Civilization
  I. Title
  301'.09495

ISBN 0-85255-268-8 (James Currey paper)
ISBN 0-85255-267-X (James Currey cloth)

Library of Congress Cataloging-in-Publication Data

Just, Roger.
  A Greek island cosmos : kinship & community on Meganis / Roger Just.
     p. cm.
  Includes bibliographical references and index.
  ISBN 0-933452-72-1 (cloth) -- ISBN 0-933452-73-X (pbk)
  1. Kinship--Greece--Meganisi. 4. Meganisi (Greece)--Social life and customs. I. Title: Kinship
& community on Meganis. II. Title.

GN585.G85 J87 2000
306.83'09495'5--dc21   00-059644

Typeset in 10/11 pt Monotype Photina
by Long House Publishing Services, Cumbria, UK
Printed and bound in Great Britain
by Woolnough, Irthlingborough

To John Campbell

Contents

Illustrations

PHOTOGRAPHS

MAPS

TABLES

FIGURES

Preface & Acknowledgements

This book has been long in the making, and the debts I have accumulated are many. Their acknowledgements must therefore be brief. I would like to thank my sometime peers: Malcolm Chapman, Paul Dresch, Tim Jenkins, Maryon McDonald, Keith Patching, Roger Rouse and Sandra Ott, who in the 1970s made the Institute of Social Anthropology at Oxford an exciting place to be; and there were others. When I went to Greece, I received hospitality, friendship and intellectual support from Michael Herzfeld, Maria Couroucli, Akis Papataxiarchis and the late John Peristiany, to all of whom I remain deeply grateful. I owe an enormous debt to the British School at Athens which provided me with a home away from home and a necessary retreat from fieldwork, but particularly to its then director, Hector Catling, and his wife, Elizabeth Catling, not only for their material generosity but for their intellectual liberality. Many people have read and commented on this book in its various incarnations. I would like to thank Tim O'Meara, Rohan Bastin, Charles Stewart, Michael Herzfeld (again), Sharon Macdonald, Yanna Rider and, particularly, Peter Loizos, who has had to deal with my manuscript for almost as long as he has known me. All remaining errors, infelicities and misdirections are, of course, those they could not save me from. The book would not have been completed without the opportunity to spend four months out of the line of fire in the Department of Anthropology at the University of Amsterdam. I would like to thank Leontine Fischer and Jojada Verrips for that opportunity. I would also like to thank Gerd Baumann and Peter van der Veer for letting me try out a portion of the book at the Amsterdam School for Social Science Research Staff seminar, and for the valuable comments that seminar provided. Over the last eight years I have been sustained by the comradeship of my anthropological colleagues, past and present, at the University of Melbourne: Rohan Bastin (again), Peter Dwyer, Peter and Elizabeth Koepping, Douglas Lewis, Monica Minnegal, Tim O'Meara (again), Mary Patterson and Thomas Reuter, friends and colleagues who, through collectively difficult times, yet made (and make) it a pleasure to come to work. Special thanks are due to Chandra Jayasuriya, cartographer in our Department of Geography and Environmental Studies, who meticulously redrew my clumsy maps and diagrams, and to John Lord, a friend of thirty years' standing (and still the most literate man I know), whose editorial advice was invaluable. I would also like to acknowledge the financial support during fieldwork of the Philip Bagby Trust, Oxford, and the British Social Science Research Council.

Like all ethnographers, I could have achieved nothing without the goodwill and generosity of those whom I had the impertinence to study. I could not disguise their island, and I could not disguise their village, but I have changed all personal names and I have attempted to mask all personal identities. My many friends and hosts must therefore be thanked anonymously; but to the people of Meganisi and to the villagers of Spartokhori as a whole, let me express my profound gratitude. Their lives became an important part of mine, and for me they will always be a *kalos kosmos*.

Finally, I dedicate this book to John Campbell, for the work on which it is based would never have been undertaken, and the book itself would never have been written, were it not for his support, his advice and encouragement, his friendship, and above all the example that he set me and the generations of scholars that have now followed (wittingly and sometimes unwittingly) down the paths that he marked out.

Roger Just
Department of Geography & Environmental Studies
The University of Melbourne

Introduction

This book is about kinship and family in a relatively small, relatively isolated, Greek village. More specifically it is about the part played by kinship and family in generating and sustaining the practices, values and sentiments that make a Greek village into a community, and that provide its inhabitants with that complex sense of 'belonging' that underwrites their collective identity and solidarity (Cohen 1982), in short, that makes of them an 'us' distinct from (though not necessarily opposed to) the larger identities of nation and state. At one level, then, this book examines one of the most conventional topics in the anthropology of Greece and of Europe (and in much of anthropology elsewhere), the village community, and it examines it through one of the more conventional means, the study of kinship and family. Yet I think there are reasons to consider afresh both the value of village studies and the role of kinship in the maintenance of local solidarities, reasons connected not with a defence of a venerable tradition, or with some attempt to 'fill in the ethnographic map', but with the salient role of 'place and space' in people's construction of their collective selves (Fog Olwig and Hastrup 1997).

It is true that no accumulation of village studies, however numerous, will yield a comprehensive understanding of Greece, much less of the Mediterranean or Europe (Stewart 1991: 137–9). What is parochial remains parochial. More importantly, what is parochial operates subject to forces (historical, political, economic, ideological) that lie outside its bounds, and whose domain becomes as large as the field of enquiry one chooses to consider. It is also true that over the last 40 years a high proportion of the rural populations of southern Europe has emigrated overseas or been absorbed into the industrialized north, while at the same time Greece and other southern European countries have themselves become transformed into predominantly urban nations. For these reasons an anthropological predilection for 'village studies' in Europe has seemed to many to be out of step with reality – at best, a little quaint, at worst, a ferreting out of pockets of the exotic by a discipline seeking to recapitulate its third-world past. I believe such reasoning to be wrong, and on two grounds, one general, one more specific.

First, the small-scale community – whether it be village, neighbourhood, quarter or street – is what, experientially, most people actually know, and to what, with varying degrees of self-deception, romanticism and occasional perspicacity, they remain loyal. The much vaunted 'face-to-face' society of anthropological tradition may have been something of an expedient fiction inasmuch as

1

it sought to distinguish one class of societies from another ('simple' from 'complex', 'traditional' from 'modern'), and inasmuch as it legitimated the reduction of a field of inquiry to an area of fieldwork, but in the end we all live in face-to-face societies, even those of us who move from one academic common-room to another around the world. Our social experience is an experience of people, not of 'society'. Migration, urbanization, transnationalism, globalism, all the movements that (quite rightly) preoccupy our current reflections on society should not let us lose sight of the fact that wherever people are, and however they have got there, their daily lives are still made up of personal encounters, individual relationships and local events in a local setting, not of the large-scale processes that frame and perhaps ultimately determine those encounters, relationships and events. Indeed, studies of contemporary migration, urbanization, transnationalism and globalism seem only to confirm that people adhere to small-scale communities wherever they are, and (thanks now to technology) hark back to those from which they have come. If ethnography is not to abandon its heritage of close empirical studies of how people live their lives, then in a quite radical way it remains wedded to the local wherever that is found.

Second, if for me the small-scale community happened to be a village in Greece, at the time of my first fieldwork the village also held a special place in Greek society, for although the demographic changes of the postwar years had transformed Greece from a rural to an urban nation, the very rapidity of those changes also meant that the distinction between urbanite and villager was anything but clear. This is not to suggest that life in the city and life in the village were the same. Indeed, the two were constantly contrasted, only people were able to contrast them precisely because they constantly shifted between the two. 'Villagers' and 'urbanites' were often the same people (Dubisch 1977). Moreover, in the case of the village of Spartokhori with which this book is primarily concerned, migratory movements between the village and Athens were matched not only by overseas emigration, but also by the extensive peregrinations of the majority of the adult male population as seamen in Greece's then burgeoning merchant marine. What this promoted was not so much a dissolution of the village community as a sharpened awareness of what it meant to be a villager.

But if the village of Spartokhori was alive and well during the period of my fieldwork, it was, as I have intimated, alive and well in a complicated way – or rather, it was alive and well as an active participant in national and international events, not as some bounded, self-sufficient and isolated world unto itself. Somewhat naively, that was not quite what I had expected, for when towards the end of 1976 I set out for Greece, I still entertained the notion of studying a 'traditional village'. Quite what I meant by that I cannot now say, most probably because I was never able to formulate it in the first place. I suspect Foucault is right: the idea of the 'traditional' serves only to contrast in some indeterminate fashion what appears to have been the way of things 'in the past' with the present and observable changes of the present (1972: 21). The concept has little real content. But it does has have tremendous allure, and if I could not formulate what I meant by a 'traditional village', I nevertheless felt sure that I would recognize one when I saw it. Besides which, it was remarkable how lightly in those days (and still) the phrase dropped from people's lips. I recall my quest with some embarrassment, but romanticism dies hard, and in 1976 I did not want to study a suburb in Athens or the tourist trade at some beach resort, both of which, by the way, would have made excellent research topics, as some people were already saying, and as others' works have subsequently proved.[1] Instead I travelled with my rucksack in search of the Platonic Form of the Village, which was always over the next mountain or on the next island.

I thought I had found it several times, first, on a mountain on the island of Mitilini. But within a couple of weeks I was hauled in by the local police and interrogated. My notes were examined and my passport temporarily confiscated. Mitilini was a border area and had a large Greek army presence. There were rumours circulating at the time of Turkish spies masquerading as Americans (though not, I think, Australians). My interrogation was understandable, but the police's action left the villagers embarrassed, and me uneasy. Besides, it had begun to snow and I was very cold. I sailed back to Athens. I also found my village in what might seem an unlikely location, Corfu, one of the greatest tourist islands of them all. But Corfu is also agriculturally productive, and tourism is largely confined to the coast. Inland there were a number of villages that corresponded to my dreams, one of which now forms the subject of an outstanding ethnography by Maria Couroucli (1985) who, unbeknownst to me, was working there at the time. I selected one Corfiot village, then a second, and travelled out daily from Corfu town on a rented motor-scooter. In both cases I met with the same reaction. The villagers were friendly, but, they explained, there was no hotel in their village. I pointed out that I did not want to stay in a hotel; I wanted to rent a house or a room. There were no rooms or houses to rent in their village, they said. Why, they did not even have running water. It was no place for a tourist. But I was not a tourist, I protested. I didn't care about running water. I wanted to stay in a village just like theirs. But they smiled and directed me back to the coast. There were lots of cheap hotels there, they explained, and, as some of the younger men pointed out, there were also lots of foreign girls. I would be much happier on the coast.

I sulked in Corfu town, watching my time and my money run out. I had been in Greece for nearly three months and I had still not found my village. And then, at the instigation of a Corfiot family who befriended me, I decided to try the island of Lefkadha, where the family had relatives. In fact, back in Oxford, Lefkadha had been my initial choice, but on arriving in Athens I was advised by Professor John Peristiany to look elsewhere, for another anthropologist was already working there (Kalafati-Papagalani 1985, 1989). Personally I had thought that Lefkadha was large enough for more than one anthropologist; nevertheless I had taken Professor Peristiany's advice and avoided it. Now I felt I had nothing to lose. My Corfiot friends made a telephone call and I set out again. My friends' relative graciously drove me round a large part of Lefkadha. It looked interesting, and there were plenty of villages, but somehow my enthusiasm was not aroused. Besides which, for all the help I was now being given, the problem still remained of how to gain entry to a village. I was sitting in a coffee-shop in Lefkadha

---

[1] See for example Stott (1985), Hirschon (1989), Zinovieff (1991), Kenna (1993), Galani-Moutafi (1993, 1994).

pondering this when a young Englishman entered and remarked on the relatively obvious. 'You're not Greek, are you?'

'No,' I replied, and we fell into conversation.

He and his partner, an English-language teacher, had been living in Lefkadha for some months. He asked me if I had been to Meganisi, a tiny island off the east coast of Lefkadha. I said I had never heard of it. He told me he had stayed there once with friends. He said it was 'different', and suggested it might be worth a visit. There was a caique that sailed there from Lefkadha town a couple of times a week. I should go to the village of Spartokhori and ask for someone called 'Nick the Greek' who ran a coffee-shop there. I decided to give it a try.

I arrived on Meganisi on 25 April 1977 and, in the politely curious company of the other caique passengers, walked up the steep path to the village of Spartokhori. I found 'Nick the Greek's' and ordered a coffee. The village looked wonderful, exactly what I thought I had been searching for: quaint, utterly 'traditional' in appearance, and certainly pretty much out of the way. Nick spoke rapid if erratic English, for he had lived in Canada for five years. Cautiously, I asked if there was anywhere I could stay. Nick had a room for rent – how long did I want it for? Possibly for quite some time, I hesitantly replied. Perhaps even for six months. That was no problem, said Nick. I could stay for as long as I liked. The room was only about ten feet long and six feet wide, just big enough for a single bed and a small table, and it had no window. Nor was it, strictly speaking, part of Nick's house. Rather, it was one of two rooms that Nick had built on top of his café/bar, as he called it. I ended up living in that room for over two years. It was cold and damp in winter; hot and stuffy in summer. But it was mine. I couldn't believe it. I had found my village and the village would have me.

In the light of my previous experiences I was, of course, puzzled that gaining entry to Spartokhori had proved so easy. It certainly was not a tourist village, and it was off the beaten track. And yet the notion that I, a single thirty-year-old male at the time, should wish to stay there for so lengthy a period seemed to cause no particular surprise or arouse any particular concern. Fieldwork, I suspect, is much guided by the accidental. I gradually discovered that I owed the ease of my entry to the activities of a somewhat mysterious character known around the Ionian Islands as 'Alekos', a Scotsman in his early forties who had served in the British army in Cyprus and then dropped out to become a sort of latter-day hippy, travelling the islands with his red bandanna, his guitar and sketch-book, and making a living as best he could. He was large, gregarious, a mighty drinker, and, to the amusement (and perhaps envy) of many of Spartokhori's younger men, always arrived with a new 'wife'. He was the Spartokhoriots' visiting eccentric, and they loved him. He was also very useful, for he was a bricklayer by trade, and for payment in food, drink and shelter he had helped in the construction of a number of the village's new houses. The Spartokhoriots assumed I was another of the same. Nick the Greek told me from the start that if I wanted to find work, there were a number of people whom I could 'help'. On that score I must have disappointed the Spartokhoriots. On several desperate occasions the local builder did draft me into house construction as a labourer, but I had no great talent for it. For two summers I also 'worked with the nets' for a fisherman, Alkis, and until the village's internal politics put

an end to that, it was one of the most enjoyable and profitable activities of my
stay. In general, however, I became Nick's 'boy', that is to say, it was assumed I
was under his patronage and that I worked for him as part of his household. And
so I did. I continued to rent my room, but bit by bit I was absorbed into the
running of Nick's establishment, becoming part-time cook and dish-washer, and
when flotillas of yachts started to call in during summer to spend an evening at
Nick's café/bar, polyglot waiter and general adviser on intercultural affairs.
Meanwhile, I also tried to be an anthropologist, and to learn everything I could
about the village and its inhabitants.

John Peristiany once remarked to me that anthropologists study 'what is'.
That may be a limitation, but it is also a saving grace. I had wanted to study a
traditional village, and had gone to some lengths to find one. The irony was that
having travelled from Australia to England, and from England to Greece, I found
myself amongst a people some of whom could talk quite knowledgeably about my
own home town of Geelong. But that my notion of a traditional village was
hopelessly misconceived (not because everything had changed, but because
everything is *always* changing) in the end mattered little, for if this book is about
a relatively small, relatively isolated, Greek rural community, part of my purpose
now is to show that such communities are, and always have been, anything but
removed or isolated from the large-scale social processes that have shaped, and
continue to shape, the contemporary world. My contentions nevertheless remain
twofold: first, that it is a concentration on the local setting (on ethnography) that
best demonstrates the connectedness of the local with the global; second, that it
is to the local setting that people's feelings of identity are most securely anchored.

The particular idiom within which those feelings are conceived and expressed,
and the particular institutions and practices which sustain them, are, of course,
matters for empirical investigation, although I suspect the range of possibilities is
finite. My claim for Spartokhori, like Strathern's for the English village of Elmdon
(1981, 1982), is that kinship was at the core. That, of course, is a suspiciously
conventional claim. But when I set out to do fieldwork in Greece, one of the
things I did not want to study was kinship and family, which may be the only
way I can ever pride myself on ever having emulated Professor Evans-Pritchard,
who similarly did not want to study witchcraft among the Azande, or cattle
among the Nuer (1976: 242). Like him, I had to be guided by those whom I was
studying. This perhaps requires a note of explanation.

Through the writings of a generation of scholars in the 1960s and early
1970s – for Greece, notably John Campbell and John Peristiany – two topics had
come to dominate Mediterranean anthropology. 'Honour and shame' was one;
'kinship and family' the other. For my generation, new ground needed breaking
if only to claim a patch, and persuaded by contemporary wisdom, I thought there
were other more relevant issues. I wanted to study 'class', 'economics', 'politics',
the cut and thrust of conflict and vested interest. Besides which, not only did
there not seem to be a lot left to say about Mediterranean kinship, but within
anthropology as a whole, kinship studies appeared to be nearing their end. Once
the discipline's sacred cow, by the 1970s kinship looked ready for pole-axing.
Needham's magisterial essay (1971) brilliantly summarized three-quarters of a
century of scholarship, but he also seemed to be sounding the death knell of the

topic to which he had devoted much of his scholarly life. Kinship, we were told, did not exist.

'Class' in Spartokhori proved to be a complicated issue, but there was plenty of economics and politics and conflicts of interest. Only it did not take me long to discover that it was impossible to understand much about any of these without first understanding something about kinship and family. My mentors had been right. Kinship and family provided the framework within which village economic and political life operated; even more so, they provided the idiom in which just about all human relations were understood and discussed. Ironically, I found that it was only through an investigation of kinship and family that I could approach the issues that from the start I had deemed desirable. It is true that this book could have been written from a number of other perspectives: from, say, that of economic change, or of moral values, or of political alliance, or of categories of inclusion and exclusion, or even (to pay homage to a recently resuscitated trope) of the confrontation between 'modernity' and 'tradition'. Yet to choose kinship and family is not to reject any of these, but to choose what participates in them all (which was really what Needham was saying: kinship is not a discrete topic), and if I have used kinship and family as a net to cast over the greater part of what I was able to observe, at least it has the singular merit of corresponding to the Spartokhoriots' own construction of events.

Admittedly, kinship did go into significant eclipse for nearly twenty years. But as Parkin now suggests, 'a feeling has arisen in some quarters ... that to neglect kinship is to disregard a good deal of what any society explicitly recognizes' (1997: ix).

> Moreover, quite a number of anthropologists, refusing to be either seduced or browbeaten by the insistence of some of their colleagues that there is no such thing as kinship, have persisted in developing traditional approaches, with many fruitful results. Some recent conferences have indicated that their twilight world is steadily becoming a new dawn (Parkin 1997: x).

This book is thus intended as a contribution to a topic that has proved to be far from exhausted.[2] More specifically, I would also like to see it as answering a call made long ago by Leach (1961) and Freeman (1968) for more detailed studies of bilateral (or cognatic) kinship systems, whose importance is still, I think, neglected.[3]

One final point. It was impossible not to be aware of the fact that I was observing the island of Meganisi and the village of Spartokhori at a very particular time. I confess in the Epilogue that Meganisi has changed since I left it in 1980. It had also changed a great deal before I got there. And since history has no halts, that is hardly remarkable. But the changes Meganisi was undergoing while I was there were fundamental, for they concerned the entire nature of its economy and demography. The late 1970s were, I suspect, a crucial period in the island's history. And whether or not the changes were more profound than at any other time, they were certainly changes of which the population itself was acutely

---

[2] Parkin's own work (1977) testifies to the renewed interest in kinship, as does that of others: Holy (1996), Stone (1997), Carsten (1997), Schweizer and White (1998). As Peletz concludes in his review of the field, 'the study of kinship is alive and well and still vital to the discipline, though often carried out under other rubrics and aliases' (1995: 367).

[3] As both Leach (1961: 6) and Freeman (1968: 271) point out, that neglect was in some large part the result of Radcliffe-Brown's quite extraordinary declaration that '[c]ognatic systems are rare, not only in Africa but in the world at large' (Radcliffe-Brown 1950).

aware. Social change, economic change, demographic change were part of the lived experience of the villagers. In my description of the 'present', I cannot, therefore, help but cast my accounts of kinship, family, inheritance, dowry, household composition, economy and so on as part of a historical process. That is how I found them. That is also one reason why, in a book that from my own point of view has been lamentably long in the writing, I have chosen, like Mary Douglas (1963), to employ the past tense.

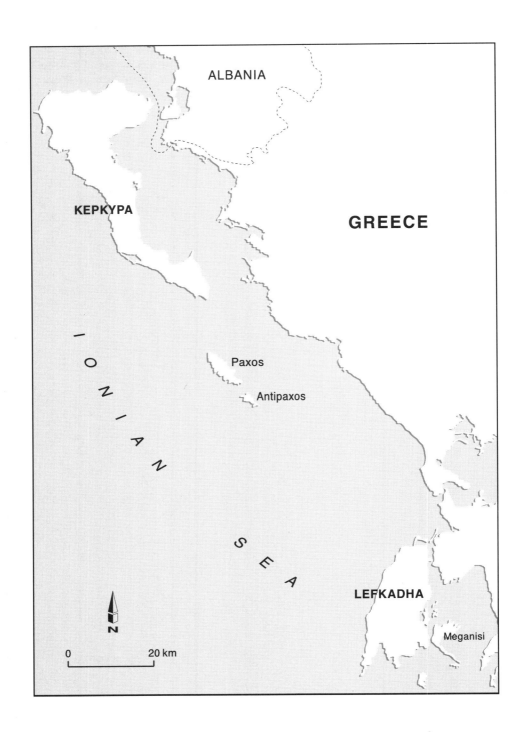

Map 1.1 The Ionian Islands

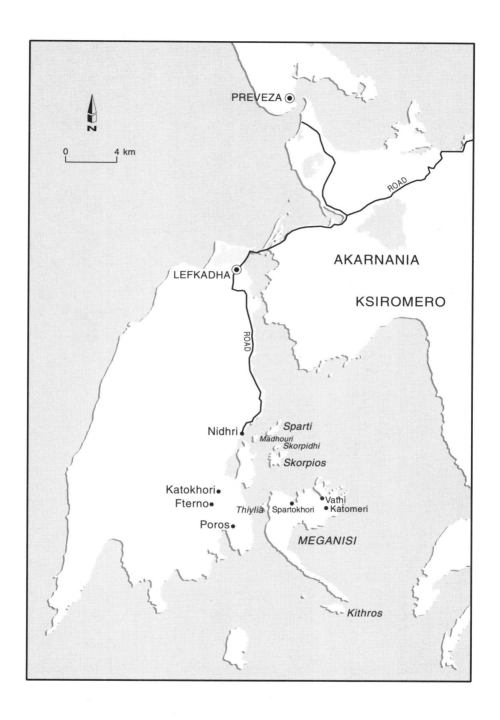

Map 1.2 Lefkadha & Meganisi

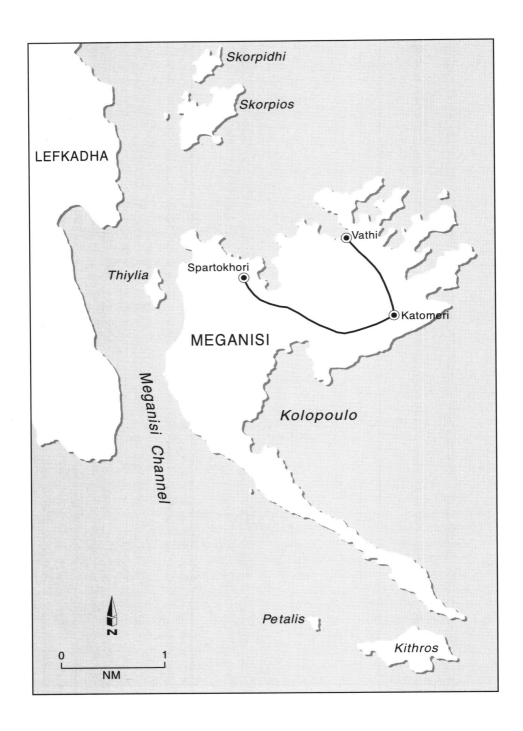

Map 1.3 Meganisi

1
Orientations

Approaching a village

Meganisi is only twenty square kilometres in area, but it is the largest (hence its name – *mega*, meaning large) of a scattering of islands, most of them uninhabited, that lie between the southern half of Lefkadha and the coast of mainland Greece (see Map 1.2). It is also an extremely beautiful island. Its long, thin tail, the crest of a submerged mountain ridge, sweeps down in an arc to create an open bay, the Kolopoulo, where the Meganisiot fishermen lay out their nets; its coastline is indented with inlets, coves and beaches, most of them inaccessible by land; its hills and valleys are terraced and thickly planted with olive trees, amongst which it is suprisingly easy to become lost. And from a vantage point at the centre of Meganisi one can look out over the sea to mainland Greece and the mountains of Akarnania, finely etched against the clear sky in winter, shimmering in the heat haze and humidity of summer; to the islands of Skorpios (the late Aristotle Onassis's Xanadu), Thiylia (owned by a number of Meganisiot families), and Madhouri (once the home of Lefkadha's great nineteenth-century poet, Aristotelis Valaoritis); and behind Madhouri to the bare mountain ridges of Lefkadha. The view is a symphony of blues, of sea and of mountains that climb straight out of it, broken here and there by the islands' patches of vivid green. The natural beauty of the place is something on which, after a while, one no longer remarks; but people know that it is there, and in conversation with a stranger the Meganisiots will proudly point to their surroundings just as, like rural Greeks everywhere, they will argue the superiority of their climate or the freshness of the air (Hart 1991: 86 n.8). Self-esteem demands as much, but the Meganisiots' contentions are still largely true.

At the time of my first fieldwork (carried out between 1977 and 1980) Meganisi was not difficult to get to, but it was still remote and little visited by outsiders whether foreigners or Greeks. Communications were just inconvenient enough to keep most people away, and '*Ekhoume isihia edho*' ('We have peace and quiet here') was a phrase continually rehearsed for my benefit as part of a litany of the island's virtues, although in dourer moods, and especially in winter, the islanders would complain of their seclusion. Two wooden-hulled caiques operated a ferry service to Lefkadha, but they left before dawn, arrived in Lefkadha town shortly before 8.00 am, and sailed back from Lefkadha at about quarter past two. In summer the service was daily; in winter it was reduced to two or three times a week, weather permitting. But though this caique service was of little use to tourists, it was vital to the island. The caiques brought the mail, transported meat, livestock, fresh fruit and vegetables, tinned goods and other supplies for the island's general stores, and allowed the Meganisiots to frequent Lefkadha town where they carried out their major transactions and where all the facilities of a provincial capital were available: government offices, banks, lawyers, doctors, a hospital, post office, telecommunications centre, and a variety of shops and stores.[1] Most importantly, however, the caiques allowed the Meganisiots to reach the bus station from where they could travel to Athens, some seven hours away on the other side of Greece,[2] and ferried back from Lefkadha those Meganisiots whose return from Athens for the summer holiday period nearly doubled the island's population. But if one missed the caiques, or they were not running, or one simply did not know about them (for their existence was very much a matter of local knowledge), then the only way to get to the island was to journey by bus or taxi down the coast of Lefkadha to Nidhri (see Map 1.2) and there to hire a small boat, a costly affair. And even if 'foreigners'[3] did make the effort to get to Meganisi, there were few places for them to stay. In the village of Spartokhori, one of the coffee-shop owners had two small windowless rooms for rent above his newly constructed coffee-shop and bar. Somewhat euphemistically these were referred to as the *ksenodhohio* (hotel), and visiting dignitaries, public service technicians, or commercial travellers selling *psilika* (haberdashery and cloth) occasionally stayed the night there. It was one of these rooms that I permanently rented. In the small port settlement of Vathi, two coffee-shop proprietors again had a few rooms for rent to the occasional yachtsperson who might wish to stay overnight. In the other main village of Katomeri, slightly inland from Vathi, there was nowhere at all for foreigners to lodge, although for the last two months of my fieldwork I stayed in the house of an old widow, for by that time I was no longer a stranger.

On the whole, however, in 1977 Meganisi was still a rural retreat. It was, to use a cliché I shall be at some pains to qualify, 'remote'. Certainly tourism was not something much affecting the lives of most islanders, although that began to change over the period of my stay. During the first summer I spent in Spartokhori a flotilla of small four- and five-person yachts started to cruise the Ionian waters as part of a British package-tour holiday, and every second week they called in to Spartokhori with thirty or forty tourists to eat and drink at the bar, an event much anticipated by its owner. By the summer of 1980 there were fourteen flotillas operating in the area and the café/bar was full almost every night. But these tourists did not stay on the island. They ate and drank in the village, slept

---

[1] In 1981 the population of Lefkadha town was 6,694. Few facilities were available on Meganisi itself. A government-appointed doctor was supposed to be stationed there, but for over a year the position went unfilled.

[2] Although Lefkadha is an island, it is directly linked by road to the mainland and thence to Athens. At the time of my fieldwork Lefkadha was joined to the mainland at its northeast tip by a pulley-bridge that connected with a road built across the tidal swamp. A permanent bridge has now replaced the pulley-bridge.

[3] The term used in Greek is *kseni*, which may denote not only non-Greeks, but anyone (Greek or otherwise) 'foreign' to the local community. I have generally translated it by the more neutral term 'outsiders'.

Plate 1.1 The *stefani*

in their boats and sailed off the next morning with their hangovers. Spartokhori began to appear on the tourist map, but from the villagers' point of view 'tourist attraction' still had a reverse meaning. It was the tourists who were the attraction, and the old men of the village adopted the custom in the evening of pulling up their chairs outside the café/bar to drink their wine and watch, comment on and ferociously discuss what even to me began to seem the curiouser and curiouser antics of my quasi-compatriots. All this, however, was strictly seasonal. For eight months of the year we did have *isihia*, 'peace and quiet', and even in summer the only foreigners besides myself who stayed on the island for any length of time were a number of hardy (and by then early-middle-aged) members of the 1960s Dutch alternative society who camped with their children on the beaches.

As for the village of Spartokhori, in 1977–80 it conformed to the archetype of what tourist brochures routinely label 'unspoiled' (Kenna 1993: 78). It sat high on a cliff overlooking a bay, where thirty or so small fishing boats were regularly moored, and an olive grove where the Spartokhoriots spread out their fishing nets to dry. A zigzag concrete road constructed during the period of the Junta and replacing an older, more direct, but extremely precipitous track, climbed up the fifty metres of cliff-face to a balcony, the *stefani* (crown), and the village's entrance marked by an ikon of its patron saint, Ayios Yeoryios (St George). Within the village the majority of houses were handsome stone-built two-storey buildings of a type once common throughout mainland Greece and the Peloponnese. Some were whitewashed; others were left plain stone. All had steeply pitched tile roofs and heavy wooden shutters to their windows. Most adjoined each other, forming terrace rows separated by narrow unpaved lanes. Unfortunately (at least from the point of view of the visiting foreigner) some had been 'modernized' by the addition of concrete balconies and cement rendering over the stonework, and a few new houses had been built in a style distressingly common throughout Greece in the 1970s: concrete frames filled with hollow brick, cement-rendered and brightly painted. But the village as a whole was not only 'quaint' (as every second yachtsperson remarked), it was also extraordinarily neat and clean. As the Spartokhoriots proudly remarked, '*Lambi* (It shines).' Nor did any traffic disturb the scene. Spartokhori's schoolmaster owned a car (never used) as did Katomeri's schoolmaster and schoolmistress (a married couple who lived in Spartokhori and commuted daily across the island's solitary and unsealed road), but the only other vehicle in the village was a truck owned by Alkis, a fisherman who made a second income from general haulage. Sometimes, when there was a wedding or a baptism or a festival in Katomeri or Vathi to which Spartokhoriots were invited, Alkis's truck doubled as a bus.

But although the village might have appeared idyllic to a foreigner, it did not possess many of the amenities that the Spartokhoriots themselves had come to consider the necessities of a comfortable life. Electricity (and hence street lighting) came belatedly to the village in 1973, although by the time of my arrival almost all houses had been connected and refrigerators were common possessions. The coffee-shops and a few private houses also had television. During my first six months in Spartokhori there was only one hand-operated telephone set in the village operated by the 'postman', which meant that calls were anything but private. When telephone cables were laid down in 1977, the Spartokhoriots were quick to take advantage of them, and by 1980 roughly half of Spartokhori's homes had their own telephone. But what was most complained of was the absence of a water supply. For domestic purposes Spartokhori's residents had constructed concrete storage tanks beneath or adjoining their houses to collect rainwater,[4] but this still had to be brought inside by bucket, for only a few of the most recently built or renovated houses had installed electric pumps. In any case water was always scarce in summer, and the Spartokhoriot women were obliged to stagger down the steep cliff road with rugs, carpets, clothes and sheets piled on top of their heads to pound their washing in the brackish water that seeped from an underground stream into the bay.[5]

Spartokhori's houses, too, were simply equipped. Very few had a *saloni*, a sitting room or 'best room' with the soft furnishings and display cabinets filled with photographs and ornaments that had long become ikons of familial pride in most parts of rural Greece (cf. du Boulay 1974: 23–4; Hart 1991: 63–4). Hardly any possessed a bathroom, and most older homes had no kitchen. Either a small outhouse had been constructed for cooking, or else a corner of a room had been made into a cooking area by the addition of a sink, a small water tank hung on the wall and a gas-ring set up on a table or bench. Many families cooked in the open fireplace, although most houses still possessed a brush-fired stone-built oven in the backyard where bread was baked and the large midday meal cooked. Those who did not have such an oven or who could no longer be bothered to use it bought their bread from the village baker, who for a small fee would also cook their midday meal. Some domestic modifications had nevertheless become standard. As in most parts of rural Greece the ground floor of the houses had once sheltered livestock as well as serving as a storeroom for wine, oil, cheese, cereals and agricultural implements (cf. du Boulay 1974: 15–17; Hart 1991: 58–9; Clark 1988: 228). By 1977 no one kept animals within the house, partly because this was already regarded as 'backward' and 'peasantish', partly because with the demise of agricultural pursuits few Spartokhoriots possessed livestock. In most cases the ground floor had been divided into two or more living areas, but only by the addition of internal frames and hardboard partitions. Similarly the interior stone walls had often been covered with hardboard, usually painted a bright gloss blue or green. Painted hardboard was also pinned to the rafters to form a ceiling, and the flagstone floors were covered with plastic. A table and a number of wooden chairs completed most houses' furnishings.

The size of the village in 1977–80 is a complex question to which I shall return, but in terms of houses Spartokhori comprised 252 dwellings in good repair. This made it a substantial village, but it was still very much a village. The only public

---

[4]Even this was an innovation dating from the 1960s. Previously rainwater had been collected and stored in large earthenware containers and used only for drinking.

[5]Two wells had also been sunk close to the shoreline, but the water was not considered fit for human consumption. The underground stream flows from the rocks into the bay just below sea level, creating an eddy of brackish water. This explains the curious observation of a French military officer, C. P. de Bosset, who visited Meganisi in the early nineteenth century and stated: 'In dry seasons the sheep and goats of this rock are known to drink salt water' (C.P. de Bosset 1821: 370 ff.). Sheep and goats will not drink salt water. The misconception was repeated in Norrie & Co.'s *New Piloting Directions* (1831: 194).

buildings were the church of Ayios Yeoryios (and outside the village, the cemetery church of Ayios Nikolaos), the village's primary school and a recently constructed office for the village president and his council (which also housed a doctor's surgery). Nor were there any grand private houses with their intimations of a transplanted urbanity. There was not even a village square properly speaking, merely a widening in the main street where the village's four coffee-shops and two of its general stores were located. This area, referred to as *ta magazia*, 'the shops', was the centre of public life, but in contrast to, say, the sort of Italian rural town described by Silverman (1975) – which was actually smaller than Spartokhori[6] – there was no feeling of *urbs in rure*, no vaunting of any equivalent to *civilta* (civilization/culture/urbanity). On the contrary, when the Spartokhoriots complained (as they often did) about the lack or lateness of the amenities of civilization, of *politismos*, they were inclined to add resignedly, 'Well, what do you expect? It's a village (*khorio*), isn't it? *Dhen ekhoume oute toualettes edho* (We don't even have toilets here).' For the Spartokhoriots, this last plaint, though not quite accurate, served as a salient index of their backwardness.[7]

What for the foreigner, however, could most conjure up the illusion of a different and forgotten world secluded from the rush of history and modern strife was less the village's architecture – its stone and whitewashed houses, its alleys and winding streets – than the appearance of its inhabitants, human and otherwise. Chickens scrabbled in the streets balefully eyed by the tribes of semi-feral cats that lived on society's fringe,[8] while at any hour of the night one might be woken by the harrowing cry of a donkey which could be seen next day stepping daintily out to the fields, its master or mistress perched side-saddle on its back. The older men were usually attired in a motley of patched and darned garments, city suits worn threadbare, old jumpers, black business shoes worn without laces or socks.[9] The oldest men wore knitted singlets of raw homespun wool, never dispensed with even in the summer's fiercest heat. Most men wore a cloth cap. Some, with nautical pretensions, affected the stiff-peaked blue variety. Only one man, Spartokhori's last remaining full-time shepherd, sported the luxuriant moustache familiar from nineteenth-century illustrations (and it was considered a prodigy), but almost all men wore a tuft of hair directly beneath their nostrils or a thin line along their upper lip. Such masculine vanities became

[6] In 1960 the total population of the commune of Montecastello di Vibio in central Italy stood at 1,885, but of those only 345 individuals (or 112 households) lived within the town walls. Nevertheless this tiny town boasted walls, a number of imposing palazzi, a football field, an elementary school, public gardens, three piazzas, a church with its famous bell tower, a town hall containing a tax office and a medical centre, a post office, a police barracks, a pharmacy, a number of cafés and bars, 27 permanent places of commercial activity and even a theatre (Silverman 1975: 15–20). According to the Greek national census of 1961, Spartokhori's population was 834; in 1981 it was 561.

[7] Many Spartokhoriot families had installed bowled toilets in an outhouse. Deep shafts allowed the sewage to seep away into the ground beneath the village. For toilets (or latrines) as a sign of urbanization as early as the mid-1950s, see Friedl (1964a: 42).

[8] Greeks are disinclined to dispose of cats, which together with dogs, horses and donkeys are considered to be 'rational' animals (*loyika zoa*). For the profusion of cats in Athens, see Faubion (1993: 50).

[9] For the male Greek villager's tendency to wear old city clothes and shoes rather than specifically designed work wear, see Freidl (1964a: 5, 44). For an elaboration of the significance of wearing shoes as part of men's public role, see Herzfeld (1986: 228–9).

Plate 1.2 The 'boys'

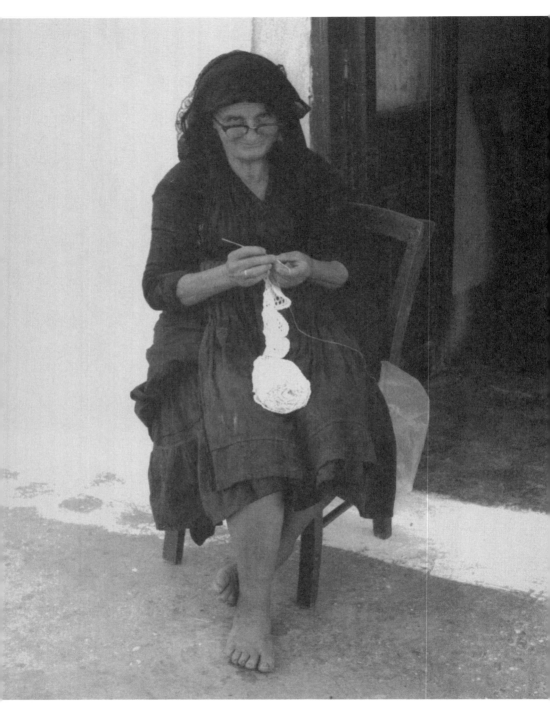

Plate 1.3 Women's dress

less distinct as the week progressed, for shaving was a Sunday affair. All younger women wore 'European' dress,[10] but, like their sisters in Lefkadha, most Spartokhoriot women of middle age or over still wore traditional costume:[11] a full skirt to mid-shin gathered at the waist in hundreds of tiny pleats; a tight bodice cut low beneath the breasts and fastened with hooks and eyes; a modest *mandili*, or kerchief, folded into a triangle, drawn around the shoulders, and pinned together at the throat with its two long ends pulled down and tucked into the bodice's tight waist. Another mandili always covered the head, and an apron with one small pocket outside to hold a handkerchief and another larger one inside to hold money completed the attire. In winter a crocheted woollen shawl was added, and numerous underskirts. Even in summer one underskirt was always worn, for when the women were working (which was always) their pleated overskirt was drawn up at the front and rolled back over the hips to be fastened behind like a bustle.

To arrive, then, by caique on Meganisi (often in the company of some unhappily trussed sheep or pig), to walk through the olive grove where fishermen sat mending their nets stretched tight by a dexterous toe, to climb the steep road up the cliff-face to the village entrance and to view the whitewashed houses, the little church, the grizzled elders sipping ouzo in the shops, the women walking past in village dress, the chickens ranging freely in the street, the donkeys parked resigned beside some gate – all this might have been to imagine, in quite romantic vein, that one had discovered the 'real' Greece. And Spartokhori was quite real, as real as Athens with its 3.5 million inhabitants, its high-rise apartments, its traffic jams, smog, department stores, discotheques, soft-core pornography and haute couture fashion. But for all Spartokhori's contrast with the capital, for all its frankly picturesque charm, the mistake would have been to believe that the village and the metropolis were separate worlds; that Spartokhori was some sort of self-contained rural retreat whose 'authenticity' as an 'unspoiled Greek village' entailed its separation and isolation from Athens and, thereby, from Greece's integration with Europe and the rest of the world. Athens and Spartokhori were, of course, both part of modern Greece, both part of the same political unity, and in the end the remote village and the metropolis have always been connected by all the ties of national history, national politics, national bureaucracy, and national commerce. But beyond the overarching structures and constraints of a single state and the overarching ideals and sentiments of an 'imagined community' (Anderson 1983), by the late 1970s Spartokhori was also bound to Athens quite directly through the movements and activities of its population. And beyond Athens lay Melbourne and Sydney and Montreal and New York and Johannesburg, cities with which the Spartokhoriots maintained familial connections, but of which many also had direct experience (as others did of Hong Kong, Rio de Janeiro or Kinshasa). Spartokhori was a remote village in Greece, but from another perspective it was the centre of the world.

[10]There is an ambivalence in Greece as to whether Greece is, or is not, part of Europe. For an extensive treatment of this topic, see Herzfeld (1987a: 41–2 and *passim*). In certain quite mundane contexts, the term *Evropaiko* (European) thus refers to what is held to be not traditionally Greek.
[11]Herzfeld (1987a: 98–9) again connects this gendered difference to men's public role and women's association with the domestic and the intimate.

The interconnectedness of 'remote' rural communities with national and international centres requires some comment, for it has been precisely recognition of that interconnectedness (though less often its exploration) that has prompted much of the criticism of anthropological studies of Greece, the Mediterranean and Europe in general. Some anthropological history is at this point required.

Rural, urban and global

From its beginnings in the 1950s and 1960s the anthropology of Europe, and especially of the Mediterranean, has been written largely as an anthropology of villages and small-scale rural communities. As Delamont notes in her recent review of European anthropology, it has been written in terms of villages just such as Spartokhori (1995: 106–7).[12] Specifically urban studies have been rare, and nowhere has the rural bias been more clearly evident than in the case of Greece. As late as 1983 Vermeulen could state that 'up to now no published urban monograph exists on Greece' (1983: 109) and that '[o]nly four anthropologists have reported on research that took the city as the sole or primary locus of study, mainly in the form of theses ...' (1983: 117).[13]

Since the early 1980s the balance of ethnographic research (and, as importantly, its publication) has shifted, and a number of monographs have appeared that focus on Greek urban or at least semi-urban communities (Hirschon 1989; Cowan 1990; Herzfeld 1991, 1997; Sant Cassia and Bada 1992; Panourgia 1995; Sutton 1998) while a much longer list of books, papers and articles could be cited that incorporate some substantial discussion of urban or semi-urban life. Most ambitiously, Faubion has tackled aspects of Athens' intellectual elite, although the status of his book as an 'urban ethnography' is something he modestly (or perhaps polemically) disclaims (1993: 14–15). The appearance of such works, however, does little to rebut the charge that overall anthropologists of Greece (and generally of the Mediterranean and Europe) have been preoccupied with what Herzfeld (himself a defender of rural studies) nicely terms 'the examination of obscure, peripheral communities' (1985: xvi).

Criticism of Mediterranean anthropology's rural focus nevertheless mounted steadily from the 1970s onwards, and interestingly as much from within the discipline as without it. The charges have taken various forms – partly theoretical, partly methodological, partly political – but they converge on a number of issues: a concentration on the marginal and the 'exotic' at the expense of the mainstream and the representative (e.g. Cowan 1990: 31; Crump 1975; Davis 1977: 7–8; Faubion 1993: 105–7);[14] a failure to study the links between rural

[12]It must be admitted that some of the small-scale rural communities studied by anthropologists were rather less small-scale and rural and than others. The agro-towns of Spain and Italy that received attention (for example, Blok 1974, Brandes 1980, Corbin and Corbin 1983, 1987; Davis 1973; Gilmore 1980; Schneider and Schneider 1976) were not of the same order as the more frequently reported hamlets of the Mediterranean and particularly of Greece, differing not only in size, but, importantly, in terms of social complexity: a greater division of labour, an indigenous class structure and, accordingly, the possession of many of the pretensions of urban life.

[13]Vermeulen cites Gutenshwager (1971), Hirschon (1976), Sutton (1978) and Vermeulen (1970).

[14]For a subtle analysis of the pervasive problem of exoticism in anthropology and of its particular

and urban populations and to situate studies of rural communities within their national (and international) contexts (Davis 1977: 7–8; Boissevain 1975, 1979); a neglect of comparison and of history (Davis 1977); and a failure to take up such wider issues as state formation, nationalism, urbanization, bureaucratization, class conflict and commercialization (Grillo 1980: 5; Mouzelis 1978: 68–70; Freeman 1973; Goddard, Llobera and Shore 1994: 22). Parallel with these charges runs the argument that a fetishization of fieldwork and of participant observation has been responsible for the preponderance of village and community studies (Boissevain 1975; Crump 1975; Davis 1977: 6; Grillo 1980; Llobera 1986; Goddard, Llobera and Shore 1994: 22), while the related ambition (or pretence) of presenting holistic ethnographic accounts has led to the depiction of rural communities as bounded, self-contained and internally coherent isolates (Boissevain 1975; Davis 1977; Cowan 1990; Llobera 1986; Goddard, Llobera and Shore 1994: 14). In Boissevain's blunt words, village studies 'tribalized Europe' (1975: 11; 1994: 41).

Again, a number of works have responded to these criticisms,[15] but for anyone in the 1990s presenting yet another village study the charges must be taken seriously, for it can no longer be assumed that the study of a small rural community is the appropriate undertaking for an anthropologist of Greece, and there are some scholars who would deem it to be quite inappropriate. The tradition requires justification. But two very different issues emerge that must be carefully distinguished: first, whether the choice of a rural village or community as an object of study is a legitimate choice; second, if it is a legitimate choice, what the appropriate approach to its study might be. These are different orders of question. The first is prescriptive and involves an attempt to define what anthropologists of Europe ought (and ought not) to be studying on criteria of social relevance. In essence it is political. The second question merely raises the obvious problem of all scholarly investigation – how does one properly study what one has chosen to study? How does one get it right? That question is essentially methodological, but since its answer relates to the empirical nature of what is being investigated, criticism of how anthropologists of Greece, the Mediterranean and Europe have gone about their work has tended to become conflated with criticism of where they have chosen to work.

Here some understanding of the historical context within which earlier studies of Greek rural communities were made is important. As Cowan has suggested, it is almost certainly the case that anthropology's historical predilection for studying the remote and the rural in Greece expressed 'both theoretical priorities (the desire to record 'traditional' or 'dying' ways of life) and methodological proclivities (towards holistic studies of face-to-face communities using participant-observation)' (Cowan 1990: 31 n.1; Llobera 1986). The extraordinarily rapid social, economic and demographic changes experienced by Greece in the wake of

[14] (cont.) bearing on the anthropology of Greece, see Herzfeld 1987a.
[15] For Greece and Cyprus, see, for example, Loizos (1975a and 1981) for politics and nationalism; Herzfeld (1982a) for history and nationalism, (1991 and 1992) for bureaucracy, commercialisation, and class, and (1997) for the nation state; Stewart (1991) for religion; Faubion (1993) for 'modernization'; Danforth (1989) for Greece's contribution to European and American 'New Age' mysticism, and (1995) for nationalism and ethnicity in a transnational context.

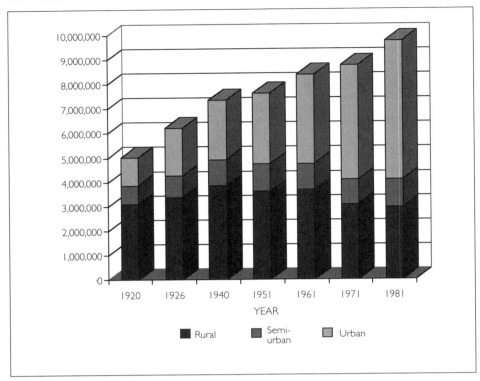

Figure 1.1 Rural, semi-urban and urban population of Greece, selected years, 1920–81

Table 1. 1 Rural, semi-urban and urban population of Greece, selected years, 1920–81

Year	Rural	Semi-urban	Urban	Greece
1920	3,108,048	760,500	1,148,341	5,016,889
1926	3,373,281	899,466	1,931,937	6,204,684
1940	3,847,134	1,086,079	2,411,647	7,344,860
1951	3,622,619	1,130,188	2,879,994	7,632,801
1961	3,674,592	1,085,856	3,628,105	8,388,553
1971	3,081,731	1,019,421	4,667,489	8,768,641
1981	2,955,342	1,125,547	5,659,528	9,740,417

the Second World War centred on the twin phenomena of internal migration from rural areas to Athens and international migration from rural areas to other European and overseas centres (Evelpidis 1968; Moustaka 1968; Kayser 1968; Kayser, Pechoux and Sivignon 1971; Baxevanis 1972; Tsaoussis 1976; Friedl 1976; McNeill 1978; Vgenopoulos 1985), and as Greece's rural population started to decline, it is hardly surprising that some anthropologists should have felt a degree of urgency in recording ways of life that seemed destined to disappear or to be substantially transformed (see especially du Boulay 1974: 3–7). But in spite of the rapid social and demographic changes that began to reshape Greece in the post-war years, it is worth questioning just how obscure and peripheral village communities were in the 1960s and 1970s. A glance at national statistics is helpful (see Fig. 1.1 and Table 1.1). It was not until 1951, only a few years before the first two foreign ethnographers of Greece, John Campbell and Ernestine Friedl, conducted their fieldwork (in 1954–5 and 1955–6 respectively) that the rural population of Greece (defined by the Greek Statistical Service as populations living in villages of less than 2,000 inhabitants) fell below 50 per cent of the nation's total.[16] In 1961, five years before Juliet du Boulay commenced her fieldwork, Greece's rural population still accounted for 43.8 per cent of the total.[17] Not until 1971 did the majority of Greece's population become urbanites, with 53 per cent of the population living in cities and 35 per cent classified as rural. In the light of Greece's historical demography, whatever anthropology's 'theoretical priorities' and 'methodological proclivities' the choice of rural fieldwork sites in the 1960s and 1970s was hardly perverse. Greece was a substantially rural nation.[18]

As Cowan suggests, however, anthropologists did not choose village settings in Greece simply because of the size of the rural population (or even the prospect of its decline). The practical (and quite mundane) advantages of working in a small-scale rural community for the transference to a European context of anthropology's traditional method of participant observation were made quite explicit by Friedl in the first published foreign ethnography of Greece: two fieldworkers (Friedl and her husband) could expect to know everyone in a community of only 216, and one of the village's families was willing to have them live in their house near the village's centre (1964a: 4). There can be little doubt that several generations of anthropologists (myself included) continued to choose to work in villages on much the same grounds, for as Delamont (1995: 111) notes, the scale and complexity of urban centres force different strategies on researchers if their

---

[16]At the same time a further 14.8 per cent of the population was classified as 'semi-urban', which might as well mean semi-rural, since the category is defined by the Greek Statistical Service as the '[p]opulation of those municipalities or communes in which the largest population center has 2,000–9,999 inhabitants' (*National Statistical Service of Greece*, 1979: 12).

[17]The 'semi-urban' population accounted for 12.9 per cent of the total.

[18]Those who criticize European anthropology's focus on small-scale rural communities on the grounds that they are not representative of their respective nation-states need *ex hypothesi* to take account of basic demographic data. The Greek case is simply not comparable with that of Italy, where, in the light of anthropological studies of marginal rural communities, Crump could justifiably complain, 'Where on earth do the Italians, with the world's seventh largest industrial economy, hide their industry?' (1975: 22). Though astute, Crump's essay, 'The context of European anthropology: the lesson from Italy', might have been better subtitled 'The lesson *for* Italy'.

studies are to be manageable: the circumscription of a particular neighbourhood, which is then treated as an 'urban village'; the isolation of a particular set of people (recent immigrants, trade unionists, religious devotees), who are then studied as a class; the selection of a particular institution or organization (a hospital or factory), which is then taken as an urban microcosm. But in the end such strategies are still only methodological expedients to isolate and bound a particular segment of the urban population so that it too can be approached in much the same manner as a village;[19] and if urban villages (neighbourhoods, local communities, particular organizations) are simply substituted for rural communities, the shift from rural to urban studies does not in itself address many of the perceived failings of Mediterranean and European anthropology; it merely relocates them.[20] The charge of exoticism may be avoided and some comfort derived from the dubious proposition that if the majority of a nation's population are urban-dwellers, then an urban study must be more representative than a rural one, but little else, for in the view of European anthropology's more radical critics (Llobera 1986, 1987, 1994; Goddard, Llobera and Shore 1994: 33–5) the real reason why anthropologists would be advised to stop 'pussyfooting around the verandahs of their village "communities"' (Llobera 1994: 109) is so that they might take on in conjunction with sociologists, historians and social theorists the study of those large-scale social processes that have moulded contemporary Europe and concentrate on 'higher-level socio-cultural units (be they districts, regions, ethnonations, nation-states, multinational states, federations, world-system or wider social and cultural manifestations and traits)' (Goddard, Llobera and Shore 1994: 34). In terms of this argument, hanging out on urban street-corners would be no advance on pussyfooting around rural verandahs. As Llobera makes clear (1986), for him it is ethnography itself – the micro-study of a particular group of people – that is the problem.

But should it be? The investigation of large-scale social processes is certainly necessary for an anthropology of Europe (or of anywhere else), and it is being pursued.[21] But it would be a curious irony if an overriding concern with 'higher-

[19]Hirschon's study of a refugee community in Piraeus (1989) was in many ways ground-breaking, but though the study was certainly an urban one, the inhabitants of Yerania constituted a quite well-defined community that Hirschon could treat very much in the fashion of a village study. By contrast, more recent (and more radical) anthropological studies of the Greek capital (Faubion 1993; Panourgia 1995) present a deliberately fractured collage of observations and ruminations, a tactic that has its own problems if anthropology is still to be thought of as a systematic study of the social.

[20]As Driessen comments, 'Anthropologists seem to have a special predilection for studying marginal phenomena. *This is certainly true for what is called urban anthropology, much of which consists of studies of ethnic, predominantly marginal enclaves in metropolitan society.* So even when anthropologists eschew the periphery and choose urban centres for their fieldwork, they mainly work in the fringes' (1992: 5–6; my emphasis).

[21]Llobera (1994) cites with cautious approval Gellner's (1983) and Dumont's (1986 and 1991) studies of European nationalism, but other anthropologists of Europe have also tackled the wider issues of nationalism, ethnicity, bureaucracy, etc even if they have sometimes done so from a particular regional base. See, for example, Chapman (1978 and 1992); McDonald (1989 and 1996); Macdonald (1993); Hastrup (1985 and 1990); Herzfeld (1992 and 1997). It should be noted that Dumont and Pocock's criticism of village studies in India (1957) and Dumont's subsequent brilliant attempt to grasp the character of Indian society as a whole (1970) foreshadowed much of the debate about the failings of European anthropology, a point elaborated by Stewart (1991: 137–9).

level socio-cultural units' and 'wider social and cultural manifestations and traits' were to eclipse detailed ethnographic studies at precisely the time when sociologists, social-historians and social theorists are themselves turning towards fieldwork, participant observation and ethnography in the attempt better to ground their studies in experiential reality. In retrospect it is possible to accept that in confining themselves to the study of small-scale face-to-face communities – and thereby predominantly rural communities – the vision of anthropologists of Greece, the Mediterranean and Europe was sometimes a limited one (at least when set against the ambitions of their critics);[22] but it was one compensated for by remarkably detailed accounts of values, sentiments, roles and institutions as they operated at the local level (Herzfeld 1980; Pina-Cabral 1989; Loizos 1992). The real problem lies not with fieldwork or participant observation (or with rural studies as opposed to urban studies) but with how to relate the micro-events of ethnographic observation (wherever they are located) to the wider social and historical contexts in which they occur, and, importantly, of which they are also an integral part (Driessen 1992: 5). Abandoning participant observation and small-scale ethnographic settings in favour of the study of higher level socio-cultural units does not necessarily resolve the problem. As Barth (correcting Boissevain) cogently argued twenty years ago:

> Large-scale society also takes place between people. By insisting on this fact, we avoid a trap into which anthropologists easily fall: that the study of local communities is the study of small-scale systems, while large-scale society somehow exists only outside these loci and is to be discovered in the *interconnections between* communities in a region, between regions in states and supra-national alliances (Boissevain, 1975). No such hierarchy in fact obtains, and small-scale communities do not aggregate hierarchically into large-scale systems: the events of large-scale systems are there, under our very noses, if only we can recognize the significant contexts for these events: an exchange between neighbours may well require the context of a world market to be understandable, while a love-letter remains an event in a small-scale system, no matter how much postage is required for it to reach its destination. (Barth 1978: 256; original emphasis)

The question of the interconnections between local communities, regions and states was nevertheless the dominant form in which early criticisms of European community studies were couched (see particularly Boissevain and Friedl 1975), and among Davis's major complaints in his 1977 overview of Mediterranean anthropology was that village-based studies had largely failed to explore the links between rural populations and urban ones 'even though every Mediterraneanist makes an obligatory reference to the fact that peasant societies are part societies, encapsulated in nation states' (1977: 8). How warranted this charge was in the case of Greece is perhaps a matter of opinion, for in 1983 Vermeulen qualified his own comments about the lack of urban anthropology in Greece by noting that although anthropologists had preferred to work in small-scale rural communities, in many studies attention had been paid to rural–urban links (1983: 117), a

---

[22]Goddard, Llobera and Shore suggest, reasonably enough, that part of the agenda for Mediterranean anthropology implied by Peristiany's 1965 edited volume (to which most of the leading Mediterraneanists of the time contributed) was that the focus would be on 'small-scale, face-to-face and relatively bounded social units: the community' (1994: 6–7).

point also admitted by Mouzelis (1978).[23] In this respect the works of the three most influential earlier ethnographers of Greece (Friedl, Campbell and du Boulay) are prime examples. Friedl's ethnography (1964a) was securely village-based, but a series of articles she published both before and after her ethnography (1959, 1964b, 1976) were all attempts to show the degree to which urban values (or what were perceived by Greek villagers to be urban values) defined rural aspirations. Campbell's classic study (1964) of rural (and very remote) Greek life went out of its way to point out not only the role that, ideologically, the transhumant Sarakatsani of mountain Epiros played in the intellectual (and political) definitions of the scope of Hellenism,[24] but more importantly the extent to which, practically, the Sarakatsani negotiated with and were dependent on urban-based merchants, brokers and bureaucrats. And even though du Boulay's ethnographic commitment was avowedly to document a 'traditional' and 'dying' way of life (1974: 3), for that very reason she could not ignore the effects on her village community of migration to urban centres, a theme she later quite specifically developed (du Boulay 1983). And what can be said of the works of Friedl, Campbell and du Boulay applies to the majority of ethnographic writings on Greece during the 1960s and 1970s.[25] The focus was securely rural, but most ethnographers were well aware of the manifold ties and connections – ideological, cultural, economic and political – that in the end united their village communities with urban centres and the state.[26]

By the early 1980s, however, demographic changes in Greece had approached the stage at which, I would argue, it was no longer possible to recognize merely connections between rural communities and urban centres. Overseas and urban migration from the rural areas of Greece had continued unabated throughout the 1970s, and by 1981 Greece's urban population had reached 58 per cent of the total and the rural population had declined to 30 per cent (see Fig. 1.1 and Table 1.1). Here Cowan's further observation that the choice of small, remote villages as field-sites in Greece 'continued *even after* the majority of Greece's population had migrated to the cities and abroad' (Cowan 1990: 31 n. 1, my emphasis)[27]

[23]Davis cites as exceptions the work of Corbin and Stirling (1973) for Spain, and of Khuri (1976), Nader (1965), Peters (1972) and Gilsenan (1973) for Lebanon. Anthropologists of Greece, it seems, were culpable. Referring specifically to the study of rural–urban links in Greece, however, Vermeulen cites Campbell (1964), Siegel (1973), Dubisch (1977), Friedl (1976) and Kenna (1977). Of these Dubisch and Kenna were too late to have been taken account of by Davis. Mouzelis (1978: 69), making a point similar to Vermeulen's, also includes Lineton (1971) and Friedl (1959 and 1964a).

[24]The ethnic affiliations of the Sarakatsani were a matter of some dispute. Romanian scholars claimed them to be Hellenized Koutsovlachs, i.e. erstwhile Romanian-speakers, while Greek scholars, and the Sarakatsani themselves, had no doubt that they were Greek (Campbell 1964: 1–6).

[25]It is worth noting that in the original cyclostyle publication of the proceeding of the 1963 Mediterranean Sociological Conference edited by Peristiany, *Mediterranean Rural Communities and Social Change* (1963), of the thirteen contributions dealing with Greece and Cyprus, nine dealt in some way with rural migration overseas or to urban centres, or with the connections between rural and urban communities.

[26]Mouzelis, too, accepted this point. His basic argument was that rather than looking at the connections between rural communities and urban centres from a 'village-outward' perspective, anthropologists would have been better served by adopting class as a concept 'more sensitive to the importance of larger configurations' (1978: 69).

[27]Cowan's claim is misstated. 'The majority of Greece's population' never migrated to the cities, abroad, or anywhere else. Presumably Cowan means that as a result of migration to the cities and abroad, the rural population of Greece no longer represented the majority of the nation.

does seem to imply some ethnographic perversity, and to raise once again the spectre of anthropology as a discipline dedicated to the marginal and the exotic. But again, such a charge rests on an espousal of 'representativeness' as a criterion of anthropological relevance, and on the assumption that by the 1980s to study a Greek rural community was thereby to misrepresent 'Greece'. Surely, however, the question of representativeness could now (or should now) be dismissed as an overriding theoretical (and methodological) concern, along with the very notion of culture itself as any sort of neatly bounded unity (whether ethnic, regional, national or supra-national). It is, after all, precisely this realization that has freed anthropology in general from its preoccupation with attempting to account holistically for 'a people' and enabled it to embark on studies at once more fine-grained and more fluid of contemporary social life whether in the developing world or the heart of the metropoles. It would be something of an irony if a latter-day concern with representativeness in Greek or Mediterranean studies should result in a new stipulation of the cities as the proper field of study.

But such general objections aside, the very rapidity of Greece's postwar urbanization and the capital's 'cancerous' rate of growth (McNeill 1978: 4) need to be carefully considered. In 1951 the population of Athens was 1,378,586. Over the next decade it increased by 34 per cent to 1,852,709. Between 1961 and 1971 it grew by a further 37 per cent to reach 2,540,241. Between 1971 and 1981 the percentage increase slowed to 19 per cent, but in absolute numbers the increase was still nearly 500,000 to 3,027,331, in a country whose total population was less than 10 million. Thus by 1981 Greater Athens officially accounted for 31 per cent of Greece's population (and unofficially for a great deal more).[28] In 1951 it had accounted for 18 per cent. Athens had nearly doubled its size in thirty years, and almost exclusively as a result of internal migration.[29] But although this is precisely the demographic shift that might appear to render village studies suspect, its consequences can be viewed in a very different light, for one result of the rapidity of Athens' growth is that true Athenians, old Athenians, those who can claim their roots in the city for several generations, are a rare breed (Faubion 1993: 61–2). By the 1970s Athens was already a city of erstwhile country folk and their immediate descendants (Burgel 1976: 13–14). Today this is evident every summer and Easter or on any major public holiday.[30] The capital is deserted. To be sure, the richest Athenians are going to country homes and beach houses, residences they have acquired or built. Others may

[28]The growth of Athens now appears to have slowed. The 1991 census recorded a figure of 3,072,992 for Greater Athens (National Statistical Service of Greece 1994b). Census figures are not, however, a totally reliable guide. The number of people who regularly live in Athens is probably closer to four million.

[29]All figures presented above are taken from the *Statistical Yearbook of Greece, 1978* (National Statistical Service of Greece 1979), *Statistical Yearbook of Greece, 1990-91* (National Statistical Service of Greece 1994a). For more detailed accounts of Greece's urbanization and the growth of Athens, see Kayser, Pechoux and Sivignon (1971), Burgel (1976), Buck Sutton (1983) and Vermeulen (1983).

[30]Even more so on census day, or when local elections are being held (the latter instituted in 1994). The Greek state has been obliged to declare these public holidays to enable urban migrants to return to their rural places of origin where they may still be registered.

escape to hotels and resorts. But in general the Athenian's second home (unlike, say, the Parisian's) is more often a legacy than an acquisition. People are returning whence they or their parents came, to 'their village', and not only to visit aged grandparents or country cousins but to resume their place in a community to which they still belong (Buck Sutton 1983: 240–2). Conversely, from a village-based perspective it was no longer necessary by 1980 to talk of the dependency of rural areas on urban centres of power, or of patrons and clients and brokers and mediators and the whole apparatus of ties and connections that in the final analysis have always bound village communities to the state and to the political and economic interests of an urban ruling class, in order to grasp the village's place in the wider national (and international) order. The connections between village and city had become much more basic, for just as Athens consisted largely of transplanted country folk, so too villages were inhabited, albeit intermittently, by people who regularly lived in the city (Kolodny 1974: 245–6; Dubisch 1977), and not only in the Greek capital, but in cities throughout the world. Perhaps fortuitously, but nevertheless on good grounds, it could now be argued that rural-based studies are vital for an anthropology of Greece not because Greece is any longer an agrarian society, but because the nature of Greece's urbanization has created a situation in which urban and rural life are so intertwined that the one cannot be understood without reference to the other.

But let us return to the island of Meganisi and to that 'obscure, peripheral community', Spartokhori, for if the choice of a village as a fieldwork site can be justified as still relevant, even particularly relevant, to an understanding of contemporary Greece, its study nevertheless raises methodological problems.

Community

A more experienced traveller than myself might have noted from the outset that Spartokhori was a little too neat and clean, a little too carefully tended. At all events I soon discovered that Spartokhori was a wealthy place even if its wealth had been quite recently acquired. It may have been no more than a village, but it was no longer a peasant village. Its economy was securely linked to an international world, for the majority of Spartokhoriot men of middle age or younger were sailors. Some were captains or crew on the ferries that ran between Italy and Patras or Crete and Piraeus; some travelled the Mediterranean on tramp-steamers; some worked on large cargo ships that sailed to China, Japan, Mexico or Brazil; some worked on tankers that transported North Sea oil, but all were in receipt of substantial wages or salaries. The Spartokhoriots' wealth was based on their employment in shipping; and it was, incidentally, the Spartokhoriots' work *sta karavia*, 'on the ships', that explained why I was never able to rent a house in the village despite the fact that many were unoccupied during my stay. On the one hand, the Spartokhoriots could afford to be not much interested in the small amount of rent I could pay (at least not when set against the worry of having a 'foreigner' take over their house). On the other hand, though many houses were empty during my stay, they had not been abandoned. Spartokhori's more well-to-do sailors and their families had taken up residence in Athens, but either they intended to return to the village when their children had finished their secondary or tertiary studies, or else they returned regularly to the village for three or four months each summer. And it was not just sailors and their families who were continually coming and going. A small but growing group of professionals (doctors, lawyers, school teachers, even one university professor) lived in Athens but returned to the village whenever they could for a few days or a week or a month at a time. Finally there were the 'emigrants' – people who over the period of my stay returned to the village after having spent two or three or ten years in America or Canada or Australia or South Africa, while others departed for their first, second or third time *sto eksoteriko*, 'overseas'. Whatever Spartokhori's appearance, it was not quite the remote rural enclave it seemed. It was the core of a community that stretched across the world. And importantly, it was not a core that had separated from its extensions. There was no neat division between 'emigrants' and 'villagers'. Indeed a great number of the Spartokhoriots who seemed to me at the time of my fieldwork to be archetypical 'villagers' were much more widely travelled and had a much greater experience of the world (whether as sailors or as sometime migrants) than most people to be found in an Australian country town or a suburb of London or, for that matter, an Oxford college. Certainly they had a wider experience of it than did I, who could not casually talk of having run a store in the Belgian Congo or having fished for prawns in the Arabian Gulf.

Admittedly that experience was sometimes construed within the somewhat unaccommodating perspective of Greek villager (people in Australia or America 'don't have families';[31] 'anyone can speak Arabic since it has so few words'),[32] but this was not always the case. Spartokhori's sailors were sailing the world and its emigrants establishing themselves in Johannesburg, Montreal or Melbourne, between which cities and the village they shifted as circumstances dictated, but the money they earned was being invested in the education of their children. Spartokhori's students, the *fitites*, were growing up half in the village and half in Athens, while others were studying overseas. They were well on their way to becoming members of Greece's newly emergent middle class. And while on the whole they were less well travelled than their seafaring fathers and brothers, their views were considerably more informed. Spartokhori did not lack its sophisticates, and as a result it had a curious double visage, a disconcerting conjunction of the rustic and the cosmopolitan that can perhaps best be conveyed anecdotally.

Within my first few months in the village I was invited to attend a baptismal celebration for two little girls, a pair of first cousins. Their fathers, two brothers who had prospered as sailors to the extent of becoming ship-owners in their own right, lived in Athens, but they were back in the village every few months, and the celebration that night took place in the courtyard of their father's old, but

[31]Divorce rates in America, Australia and 'Europe' were always mentioned, as was the practice of placing the elderly in old-age homes, a particular horror. In general it was also claimed that outside Greece family members maintained no ties with each other. See Vernier (1991: 128), who reports that on Karpathos it was believed that the French were unaware of physical family resemblances because they were so sexually promiscuous.
[32]By contrast, Greek was considered to be the most difficult language, for not only did it have a grammar, but unlike all other languages it had 'many words for the same thing'. See Just (1995a).

quite substantial, village house. Large trestle tables had been set up and well over a hundred guests were in attendance. A few men were smartly attired, but most were dressed much as they would be on any day of the week: patched trousers, frayed shirts, no socks and scuffed business shoes without laces. Some Athenian ladies could be picked by their elegant dresses and careful coiffures, but the majority of the women were in traditional dress, the black-shrouded grand-mothers nestling quietly in the corners, the brown-clad matrons swinging robustly through the crowd with enormous platters of food balanced on their heads. The tables were laden with lobster, fish, baked lamb, cheese, salad, fruit and melons. The cheese, it was pointed out to me, was *ap'to spiti*, 'from the house', made from the milk of sheep and goats that the brothers' old father still kept. As always, the preferred festive drink was commercially bottled beer, but the wine served was also *ap'to spiti*, made the year before in the village. On every table, however, there was also a large bottle of Scotch whisky (Chivas Regal, no less) for those who had acquired the taste.[33]

A record player was screaming the high-pitched wailing *klarino* songs of mountain Epiros and the dancing started: first the young unmarried girls in a circle, next mixed groups of men and women. Then, as the night wore on, the dancing became more excited as groups of young sailors took over. Their lead-dancers slowly gyrated, arched their backs and slapped their heels, oblivious to all around them as they hung suspended from the handkerchief of the next in line before finally leaping into the air in an explosive demonstration of their virile prowess. Plates, bottles, bowls (full or empty – anything that would smash) were hurled into the air in appreciation of the music while the dun-coloured matrons bustled forth from the shadows busily applying their brooms to sweep away the more dangerous of the wreckage. I sat watching the little girls' grandfather in his place of honour at the head of the main table. He was white-haired, bristly-cheeked, in his eighties. He nodded back and forth smiling to himself. An old cloth cap sat on his head and his much-washed white shirt was open to reveal his hand-spun raw wool singlet. He was an illiterate shepherd (and some said sheep-rustler) originally from Lefkadha who had married and settled in Sparto-khori some fifty years before. He looked very happy as he surveyed the scene. My companions assured me that he was very happy. He had all his *pedhia*, all his 'children', all his descendants, arrayed before him, some twenty-five of them or more: four sons, two daughters, and their respective wives, husbands and children. (It was they who were the smartly dressed Athenians). And I wondered, as I drank more of the wine 'from the house', whether I would be able to remember enough of the scene the next day to describe it. It would, I thought, make a good vignette of 'village life'. In many respects it was precisely what I had imagined 'traditional' Greece would be. Certainly for me on that summer's night it was all exotic enough: the music, the flying plates, the dancing, even the braying donkey parked behind a wall. Perhaps the bottles of Chivas Regal ought to have alerted me to some departure from the purely bucolic, but it was not until I fell into conversation with the man sitting next to me that I was properly jolted from my rural reverie.

[33]For the growing consumption of whisky in Greece, and not only by the elite, see Stewart (1991: 126).

My neighbour was from Meganisi's 'other' village, Katomeri, but he was related by marriage to the Spartokhoriot brothers who were holding the party. He spoke perfect English (or rather perfect American) for he was a surgeon who had trained in the United States and had worked there for fourteen years. Now he worked in a hospital in Athens, but he returned to Meganisi every summer. He asked me if I enjoyed golf and whether perhaps I would like to go water-skiing; he also began to tell me about village life. Personally he thought the practice of throwing plates somewhat barbaric, but he assured me that everyone would be happy if I joined in (and certainly the man seated next to him, a paediatrician from Athens, seemed to have few reservations about the custom). A little disconcerted by these urbane intrusions I turned to Vassilis who had brought me to the party. Vassilis, I knew, made a meagre living from growing olives and operating the olive-oil mill he had inherited from his father. He had also worked on the ships for a few years as a deckhand in order to make ends meet. His wife was one of the women in village dress padding barefoot from the house to the courtyard with yet more food and drink. Vassilis and his wife, I felt, were 'real' villagers. But then Vassilis introduced me to his brother (ten years younger than he) whose daughter, herself only about six years old, had been the sponsor, the godmother, of one of the little girls baptized that day. Vassilis's brother, like Vassilis himself, spoke no English. He did, however, speak German, for he had gained his doctorate in philosophy from Heidelberg. We spoke together in Greek. I tried to explain what I was doing and he expressed interest. He told me that if I had any questions about religion I should talk to his wife (who came from the village of Katomeri and was the sister of the American surgeon). She had a degree in theology and would be able to answer all my questions.

It was at this stage (or rather, the next morning) that my feelings of unease (which had been growing for some time) began to crystallize. Every time I attempted to formulate a sentence which went anything like 'The Spartokhoriots think/believe/say/do the following,' I found myself committing a solecism, for who were 'the' Spartokhoriots? Who were 'the villagers' whose collectively held beliefs, attitudes and practices I aspired to describe? Or, to put the question another way, in what spheres of discourse and practice was it legitimate to refer to the Spartokhoriots as a whole? Surely it was reasonable to question what body of assumptions and what particular outlook on the world might be shared by a university student studying economics in Athens, by a professor's wife who herself held a degree in theology, by a shop-owner who had spent ten years in North Carolina, by a sailor as familiar with the waterfront pubs of Glasgow as with the bars of Rio de Janeiro, and by a farmer or fisherman or *nikokira* (housewife) whose lives on Meganisi had been interrupted only by a period of military service or an occasional visit to see children in Athens. It was equally reasonable to reflect on what form of analytic framework might be employed to present a coherent account of Spartokhoriot village life without either artificially selecting as the 'true' Spartokhoriots only those members of the older generation whose lives had been totally encompassed by the village or, worse, idealizing as Spartokhoriot 'social structure' or 'culture' a body of seemingly traditional ideas and practices regardless of the fact they no longer informed, or informed in any systematic way, the lives of the majority of the community. Was Spartokhoriot cosmology represented by the old man who told me that the televised footage of American astronauts landing on the moon was a fake, a piece of CIA propaganda designed to frighten Greeks into thinking that they were continually being watched, since self-evidently the moon was far too small for anyone to stand on, or by his grandson who was studying physics at the University of Athens?

These were problems for me in 1980. I think they continue to be the sort of problems that vex anthropology today despite much of the current talk about contested values and practices and the realization that few societies or cultures are or ever were homogeneous or entertained a singular understanding of their world. Part of the attraction of studying small-scale societies or communities was the assumption that their value system, beliefs, way of life, or, broadly speaking, culture, though certainly not without divisions of gender, status and class, could nevertheless be grasped as some sort of distinct and reasonably coherent whole, that, as Driessen puts it, they were 'well-ordered' communities (1992: 6). Nowadays that assumption is considerably less secure, and in an increasingly fluid and increasingly interconnected world, and especially (though not at all exclusively) in Europe, it must be asked in what sense it is possible to see small-scale societies or local communities as possessing a shared way of life rather than being just collections of people who happen to be living in the same place at the same time but whose experiences, allegiances, beliefs, values and forms of knowledge might cohere in no particular way with those of their neighbours but perhaps much more notably with those of their professional or educational or occupational colleagues and peers throughout the world. In short, what sense does a Greek village actually have a way of life that makes it, if not a unique social entity, at least a distinct social entity? For a discipline whose object of study is neither the individual human being nor humanity in general but the variety of the forms of human sociality, it needs to be asked whether a village in Greece any longer provides a viable unit of study.

I shall argue that it does. But I shall also argue that it can no longer be assumed that a village constitutes a ready-made social entity, the anthropological task being then to describe and analyse its attributes. Rather, it must be queried from the outset in what sense or senses (and they may be limited) a village does have a particular form of sociality, in what way or ways it does possess a coherent form of collective life. This is perhaps only a shift in emphasis, but the idea of community, often so casually invoked (Baumann 1996: 14–15), must itself be problematized so that rather than its existence being taken as the starting point of investigation, its creation and perpetuation over time becomes an explicit object of enquiry.[34] And in an increasingly fluid and increasingly interconnected world, this may mean (amongst other things) considering people's quite conscious commitments to the preservation of local identity despite mobility, dispersal, diversity and active participation in creating change.[35] Here the idea of

[34]The concept of 'community', however, has certainly not gone unscrutinized. For a valuable review, see Cohen (1985).

[35]The conscious revival and celebration of 'localism' in a wide variety of forms appears as one of the notable developments in Europe since the 1960s, corresponding, perhaps paradoxically, with Europe's growing economic and political unification. At one extreme this may involve the political assertion of ethnic distinctiveness; at another the resuscitation (and reinvention) of local 'cultural' events. See Macdonald (ed.) (1993) and Boissevain (1991, 1992).

a community – the notions that people have about themselves, about the nature of their collective identity, about the forms of their solidarity, about their distinctiveness as a group – may be quite as important as any catalogue of empirical commonalities: not just, for example, people's 'shared values', but the positive evaluation that people place on the *notion* of their values being shared   (Macdonald 1993: 21; McKechnie 1993: *passim;* McDonald 1993: 228).[36] In short, the rhetoric of community must itself be seen as partly constitutive of community. Let me revert to the description of Meganisi and Spartokhori with which I commenced.

Self-realizations

In the opening section of this chapter I deliberately presented a sketch of Spartokhori that emphasized its remoteness from the metropolis (both culturally and geographically) and its quaintness (at least to urban or foreign eyes). Not only might I therefore be accused of having chosen to study yet another 'obscure peripheral community'; worse, I might be accused of exoticizing it in the process, of constructing a distanced other which, through denial of its coevalness with the modern world, becomes no more than the romantic foil of metropolitan dissuasions, a charge sometimes levelled not just against anthropologists of Europe but against anthropology as a whole (Fabian 1983; Herzfeld 1987a; Torgovnick 1990). To a scholar such as Faubion, already 'on the margins of Europe' by having arrived in Athens (1993: 12), I might indeed appear a latter-day pastoralist, concerned only with Greece's 'living "traditionals"' and promoting my own favourite 'tribe' (1993: 105). But as Herzfeld has argued,[37] it is precisely such communities as the Cretan mountain village which he studied (and, I would claim, the maritime village with which this book is concerned) that 'lie at the very core of the self-image that Greeks collectively present to the outside world' and that have played 'a vital role in the formation of national self-stereotypes' (Herzfeld 1985: xvi).

It should be noted, however, that Herzfeld's observation has little to do with representativeness in any strictly empirical sense. Rather it draws attention to the fact that an indigenous Greek language of exoticism and simultaneously of authenticity (together with Faubion's pastoralism) clothes the centre's descriptions of its peripheries which become at once the other and the quintessence of self.[38] As I have mentioned, in 1977 the island of Meganisi was little visited by outsiders. In 1993, however, it was 'discovered' by *To Vima*, one of Athens' most respected newspapers. *To Vima* waxed predictably lyrical, but it did so in a quite particular mode:

> we found ourselves on Easter Thursday on as yet unspoiled Meganisi ... Meganisi ... is unrivalled, almost virginal, at least before midsummer comes and Greeks and foreigners

---

[36] This position has now become virtually orthodox. It still owes much, however, to Barth's seminal article (1969) on ethnicity, which stressed the importance of self-perceived differences between groups as opposed to any empirical checklist of cultural *differentia.*

[37] Faubion, with reservation, also concedes this point (1993: 105).

[38] The tendency, however, is by no means uniquely Greek. See Ardener (1987), Chapman (1978, 1993) and McKechnie (1993).

arrive with their yachts. That's how we saw it the morning of Easter Thursday as we woke with tingling fingers; and as the holy day progressed between the olives and the sea, green from the pine-trees and cypresses, the inhabited and the deserted places sketched their names: Vathi, Katomeri, Atherinos Spartokhori and Ayios-Yannis; finally, towards evening, Spilia. And what we didn't see we heard: how, for example, the cave of Polyphemos, who, as we know, travelled from Limnos to Sicily, also nested [*sic*] on Meganisi; how the rock which the enraged Cyclops threw to crush Odysseus when he substituted the negative pronoun for his real name is still here. From here on the associations become easy, especially if you carry with you, half-translated, Odysseus' rhapsody on the same topic, that little island in front of the beach of the Cyclopes who denied all civilisation, which Odysseus and his comrades trod not knowing in the middle of the black night what their eyes would encounter in the morning. But the poet, who knows everything, has already described it in admirable fashion ... (D.N. Maronitis, 1993; my translation)

It is a particularly Greek mode, for Meganisi's exoticism and its remoteness from the modern world are made continuous and identical with Homer's classic antithesis of 'civilization', the island of the Cyclopes. But at the same time the very poetic bridge that is employed, the invocation of Homer and the Odyssey, also assures Greek connoisseurs of culture that Meganisi is one with the very font of Hellenism. The island is both exquisitely other and irrevocably Greek; a paradigm of the primitive recalled through the epitome of civilization.

Day to day, of course, there is nothing particularly exotic about the island of Meganisi or the village of Spartokhori for those whose lives are normally or intermittently lived there, and one might be inclined to say that *To Vima*'s historical romance was its own problem. Certainly it is no part of this book's intention to romanticize village life, but rather to report on its complex mundanity. Yet as Herzfeld again suggests, local self-perceptions are not immune from intellectual discourse, or at least from being partly constructed as a bricolage of others' sentiments and opinions (1985: 33–4). Hence, to an extent, a local rhetoric that dwells on the island's natural beauty, its temperate climate, the freshness of its air. Hence, to an extent, the emphasis on *isihia*, 'peace and quiet'. Hence, to an extent, even the attention drawn to the shepherd's prodigious moustache. A local vaunting of otherness has become a national legacy to which the Spartokhoriots, along with Greece's country folk in general, have willy-nilly been made heir (see Herzfeld 1982a; Danforth 1984). Yet the force of this form of discourse is only partly responsible for promoting the Spartokhoriots' sense of themselves as distanced from the metropolis and of their way of life as distinct from it. Another and more important factor intervenes. And here it is necessary once more to consider the social consequences of demographic change. For in fact it is the very merging of Greece's urban and rural populations that has prompted for many of its citizens a sharper awareness of the contrast between city and village. The same people may in the course of their lives be both urbanites and villagers, but urban life and village life remain decidedly different. Athens is not Spartokhori, whatever the demographic overlap, and much of village discourse dwells on that fact. For many if not most Spartokhoriots it is a contrast enabled by first-hand experience. The old grandmother who carries a cauldron of water back from the well on her head and who cooks her midday meal on the hearth may be doing what she has done all her life, but not so her

Plate 1.4 A sheep to Meganisi

daughter who may have lived ten years in Athens, Patras, Sydney or Toronto, or who may currently be an urban resident for eight months of the year but still counts herself (and is counted by others) to be a member of the village. The old man who singles out the bowled toilet as an ikon of civilization is not disputing some bucolic daydream of the Athenian intelligentsia but deploring the lack of what he personally considers a necessary accoutrement of urban life. And if the vision of a sheep or a pig being hauled on to a caique might provoke some wry comment from the average passenger on the Athenian underground, so it does from the caique's Spartokhoriot passengers, for they too are sometime Athenian commuters – even if they may also be the *vlahi*, the 'bumpkins', whom Faubion's elite coterie deride (Faubion 1993: 61–2). Just as Hart comments for the village of Richia in the Peloponnese: 'If there is a local "collective reality", it is the collective knowledge of ... heterogeneity. What went on in the village did not go on apart from this fact but occurred as a result of, and against a background of, the possibilities of life in other places.' (Hart 1991: 5)

A sense of Spartokhori's remoteness, a sense of its difference, were integral to the Spartokhoriots' own estimation of their location. And if they could praise the village where they were born for not being the city where they sometimes lived, they could equally condemn it for being in their own eyes 'backward'. There was plenty of fresh air, but in 1980 there was still no running water. There was 'peace and quiet', but there was also the feeling of being 'fenced in like sheep'. It was a healthy place to live, but getting proper medical attention was not always easy. Comparison and contrast with conditions in the city or overseas were a recurrent theme of village conversation, and the conclusion, whether proud or resigned, was always to remark that here it was after all just a village. To emphasize Spartokhori's remoteness is thus only to remain true to the Spartokhoriots' own perceptions.

Physical conditions, material amenities, even customary oddities provided, however, only the most obvious contrasts within a local reflection on village life and its alternatives. At the core was a form of comparative sociology; not quite an objective one, to be sure, for its purposes were often strategic and self-justificatory, but not an imaginary one either, for it arose from experience. It was remarkable how often in conversation not only with one of Spartokhori's educated elite (the doctor or the lawyer or the ship's captain who lived most of the year in Athens) but also with the coffee-shop proprietor or the sailor or the fisherman or the farmer (who were normally resident in Spartokhori) 'we' was replaced by 'they' as soon as village affairs were discussed. Doubtless my presence prompted a realignment of pronouns: 'we' were myself and my companion of the moment; 'they' were the other Spartokhoriots. But if such a shift – the temporary distancing of self, the temporary objectification of one's own – is an almost inevitable consequence of the invitation to self-commentary, it was nevertheless entered into with a legitimacy that did not derive solely from conversational context. It derived from a genuine ability to adopt an external stance towards the village supplied by first-hand knowledge of a world outside it. At the same time, however, and because of that same objectification, the Spartokhoriots' form of comparative sociology still centred on the nature of 'us'. It was about community (and its absence) or, to adopt the imagery securely in place, the likeness of the village (in contrast to the city) to 'all one family', to a place where everyone knew one another, where everyone was related to one another, where everyone cared for one another, where each person's joy was everyone's joy, one person's sorrow a collective sorrow. Moreover, this was a rhetoric translated into fact. Expectant mothers might travel from the island two hours by caique and six hours by taxi to give birth in a hospital in Athens, the only place where they believed 'proper' medical facilities were available; but equally, young couples and their families would return in force from Athens to celebrate their weddings in the village, the only place where this could 'properly' be done – for they were Spartokhoriots marrying Spartokhoriots in a ceremony that both required the participation of *i dhiki mas*, 'our own people', and further created a people who were 'their own'. And though Spartokhoriots might often die in Athens, they were usually buried in the village.

The idea of the village as 'all one family', as a place where everyone knew each other, where everyone was related to each other, where everyone cared for each other, where one person's joy was everyone's joy, one person's sorrow a collective sorrow, was integral to a continual and conscious contrast of Spartokhoriot life with life in Athens and overseas. It was, of course, an ideal. It blandly papered over the cracks and fissures of day-to-day animosities, resentments and competition. And like most ideals it could be, and was, turned on its head. Difference could be re-evaluated. One young sailor swore to me that when he married he would never live in the village; nor as a bachelor was he happy to be there more than a few months at a time. As he pointed out, if he had a fight with someone in Athens and told them to get fucked, that was the end of it. If it happened in the village, then his brothers and his father and his uncles and everyone else would be involved and there would be a *megali fasaria*, a 'great to-do'. It was the city's anonymity that gave him his freedom. Similarly, the old man of seventy who had returned to the village after fifteen years in Australia to live out his retirement in the village of his birth, 'to look after his olive-trees' as he put it, angrily confided to me (as perhaps he could confide to few others) that he was going crazy in Spartokhori. Everybody was watching him. Everyone was gossiping, asking why he bothered with his olives, suggesting that perhaps he had gone broke overseas. 'You know, Rogeri,' he said to me, 'it's not like that in Australia. People leave you alone there.'

Studying community

An exploration of the Spartokhoriot 'us', of the nature of the Spartokhoriot community and the form of its cohesion, forms the substance of this book. It takes, therefore, that indigenous comparative sociology of which I have spoken as its starting point and also, in part, as its subject matter. Following the ethnographic lead of the contributors to Macdonald's collection of essays (1993), it takes seriously Ardener's premise that when it comes to questions of identity 'the "people" themselves play the part of theoreticians in this field' (Ardener 1989b: 67, cited Macdonald 1993: 6). True to the Spartokhoriots' theorizing, it thus explores the creation and maintenance of village sociality largely through the

idiom of kinship and family. I have not, however, limited myself to a phenomeno-
logical approach to kinship and family, and I have had no hesitation in objectiv-
izing family structures and familial relationships and in going well beyond, or
questioning, what any (or many) Spartokhoriots would or could say about such
matters. As Bourdieu (himself the most reasoned critic of objectivism) observes, 'If
it is to be more than the projection of personal feelings, social science necessarily
presupposes the stage of objectification'. (1990: 11)

Beyond, then, the Spartokhoriots' rhetoric of kinship and family, beyond indeed
their rhetoric of solidarity and community (neither of which should be seen as
either cynical or contrived, but as the sincere expression of values) I shall attempt
to specify the conditions in which that rhetoric operates and by which it has been
reproduced and the strategies to which it is directed. In so doing I shall follow a
double path: historical and, as it were, deconstructive on the one hand; sociological and constructive on the other. For historically Spartokhori is not an
ancient community. Its origins can be dated fairly securely to the late seventeenth century. Nor has it been a stable community. Its history has been one of
constant immigration and emigration according to the dictates of political and
economic circumstance, of which the present population's dispersal to the cities
and overseas constitutes only the most recent phase. Its cohesion and solidarity
as a community do not, therefore, stem from ancestral continuities; rather they
have been created and recreated in the face of continual mobility. And they have
been created through one of the commonest mechanisms of assimilation, namely
marriage – but marriage strategically employed and aided by a particular form of
kinship reckoning to which it gives rise. From an historical perspective
Spartokhori has always fragmented; from a sociological one it continues to unite.

2
Delineations of History

One evening I was sitting with the men in one of Spartokhori's coffee-shops when, for no particular reason, everyone got *kefi* (high spirits)[1] and decided to dance. The stereo was turned up to pain level with the *klarino* music of Epiros, everyone bought each other beer and wine in great quantities, encouragement was shouted to all those demonstrating their skills ('Go to it, Uncle Thomas!' 'Bravo, cousin mine!') and yet another boisterous night was in the making.

I was sharing a table with Andonis, a strong, good-looking man in his early thirties who had arrived in Spartokhori from the village of Kharia on Lefkadha some six years before to profit from the spate of house-building generated by the money the Spartokhoriots were beginning to make as sailors. Andonis was doing well. He had plenty of work, and he had married a pretty young woman from Spartokhori with whom he had two small children. He ought to have been a happy man. After half an hour, however, I noticed that Andonis was weeping. He sat silently watching the performance while tears flowed down his face. Concerned, I asked what was wrong. He assured me all was well. He was well; his family was well; there was nothing the matter at all. He claimed he did not even know he had been crying. 'Well,' he eventually said, 'some people get happy; others weep. That's the way it is.' But then, after a pause, he added, 'Ah, Rogeri, but if you were to see me in Kharia ... then you would see me laugh.'

Perhaps not too much should be pinned on the transitory emotions of an individual. Doubtless Andonis was in the passing grip of that sort of self-pity most of us feel when forced to watch others enjoying something from which we are excluded. Nevertheless, Andonis did have a real problem: he was a *ksenos*, a 'foreigner', an 'outsider', from Lefkadha. The Spartokhoriots treated him fairly. Most people were pleasant enough to him. But his exchanges with them were of a commercial nature. The Spartokhoriots employed his services; he profited from their needs. But he had little place in their lives. He dealt with the village and the village dealt with him, but it never embraced him, and when a dispute arose he was without support, and without access to that elaborate system of pressures, checks, balances, threats and cajolements that is always at work in the village and through which every villager works. Andonis was an individual. The village was a community. They faced each other on those unequal terms.

[1] See Papataxiarchis (1991: 170–2) for an account of the meaning and etymology of *kefi*. As Papataxiarchis notes: 'The spirited body of the man who dances solo, a body animated by an all-embracing desire and elevated beyond earthly, material concerns into communitas proper, captures the aesthetics of *kefi*.'

It is, however, precisely the notion of community that must be at issue, for if it was easy impressionistically to register the sense of corporate identity that made the village a community, and that made each person who belonged to it a Spartokhoriot and not simply a Greek who happened to be living in Spartokhori (and emphatically not a Katomeriot or a Vathiot), it was still difficult to specify with precision what the nature of 'community' was. 'Belonging', 'cohesion', 'identity', 'solidarity' – these are difficult things to pin down, for though they may be continually expressed in action and implied in speech, their ultimate reference is not to any specific set of acts or remarks but to the less tangible sentiments by which those acts and remarks are inspired. As I have already mentioned, in their attempts to express to me their sense of community the Spartokhoriots readily resorted to sentimental terms: the claims that in the village everybody 'knew' each other, everybody 'cared' for each other, everybody 'trusted' each other, that one person's sorrows were the village's sorrows, one person's joy their collective joy. Set against the gossip, strife, malice, quarrels and petty animosities that filled out daily life, such a description was idealized to say the least, and largely rehearsed for the benefit of outsiders such as myself. Generalized goodwill was not the basis of daily interaction. Nevertheless, the limits (if not the nature) of community were made apparent by the bounds within which virtue, however idealized, was automatically asserted; equally, they were made apparent by the bounds beyond which vice was automatically presumed. The Spartokhoriots' relationship with the inhabitants of their neighbouring village, Katomeri (no more than an hour's walk away), provides a particular case in point. What I had initially taken to be a more or less jocular rivalry between the two villages was gradually revealed as something altogether more serious, and when towards the end of my stay I announced that I intended to spend three months in Katomeri, I was taken aside by many friends and seriously advised to reconsider, for I should not find the Katomeriots *filotimi* (honourable), nor *filokseni* (hospitable), nor *kirii* (gentlemanly), nor *eksipiretiki* (helpful) – in short, I should not find them all the things that the Spartokhoriots collectively held themselves to be. I should find the Katomeriots wastrels, drunkards and louts (and it was even whispered to me that they were syphilitic). I hasten to add that I found the Katomeriots to be none of these things (while for their part the Katomeriots held reciprocal and equally unflattering views about the Spartokhoriots). But even though some individual Spartokhoriots had friends (and a very few had relatives) in Katomeri whom individually they would defend, it was clear that collectively the Katomeriots were beyond the pale.[2]

If, however, the Spartokhoriots' sense of community gave rise to a sort of moral universe of inclusion and exclusion, on what grounds were its borders constituted – mere location? Around whom and against whom were they set: those who lived in the village as opposed to those who did not? No doubt continual proximity, the fact that many Spartokhoriots had lived most of their lives in each other's company and throughout all the crises both collective and individual that

---

[2] Hostility between neighbouring villages is, however, characteristic of much of southern European rural society. See du Boulay (1974: 43–51) and Herzfeld (1985: 36–9) for Greece, and Pitt-Rivers (1954: 8–12) for Spain.

those lives entailed, did contribute towards a sense of community. Affections, friendships, hatreds – at the very least an intimate knowledge of each other – bound the older Spartokhoriots together. And inasmuch as the intimacies of one generation were passed on to the next, they affected even those Spartokhoriots who had moved to Athens or who had spent decades overseas. To delve into the storehouse of one's elders' memories, or simply to recall the anecdotes of childhood, was to enter into a collective realm of shared experience that defined the village and its inhabitants. The fact remains, however, that so many Spartokhoriots were living in Athens or had spent decades overseas. Their ties to the village, or, more importantly, their recognition as villagers by the village, were not maintained by daily intercourse. Their Spartokhoriot identity was dependent on neither continued nor continual village residence. Rather, it was something automatically granted and reassumed the moment they returned to the village, for wherever they went and however long they were away they remained *ta pedhia mas*, 'our children', a phrase whose expression of *collective* parenthood was, I think, no less telling than its adversion to kinship as the grounds upon which the Spartokhoriots' sense of community was constructed. Andonis remained a *ksenos*, in contrast to the village's *pedhia*, not because he had spent only six years in Spartokhori, but because he was not related by family connections to the rest of its inhabitants. That was the basis of his exclusion, for as I shall show in Chapters 4 and 5, the Spartokhoriots' claim to being 'all one family' was not only a metaphorical assertion of mutual concern and mutual intimacy; it was also very close to being literally the case. One way or another almost every Spartokhoriot could trace a series of overlapping genealogical ties and connections to almost every other Spartokhoriot, and in the end the village could be seen in terms of a single, complex, genealogy that connected almost all its members. However important the consequences of everyday familiarity for promoting a sense of community and of belonging might be, in the end familiarity had to be underwritten by kinship in order to count.

Andonis, however, was far from being the only resident of Spartokhori not to have been born in the village and to have immigrated there for economic reasons. At least fifteen other men and forty women amongst Spartokhori's population had similarly arrived and settled in the village over the preceding two or three decades, yet they considered themselves, and were considered by others, to be *poli Spartokhorites*, 'very much Spartokhoriots'. Indeed, Spartokhori's history (and the history of the island of Meganisi as a whole) had been as much one of continual immigration as of emigration. Its population over the last few centuries had been anything but stable. Playing counterpoint to the Spartokhoriots' claim of being 'all one family' was a rather more peculiar saying: '*Imaste oli kseni edho* (We are all foreigners/outsiders here).' On the face of it, the saying seems paradoxical, for basically *kseni* (plural of *ksenos*) is a category of exclusion. It refers to 'them', to all those who are not part of whoever in a given context constitute 'us', and it regularly contrasts with *dhiki mas*, 'our people', whether they be 'our nation', 'our village' or, significantly, 'our family'.[3] Indeed, it was against the very assumption of community conceived of as a family that the Spartokhoriots'

[3] For the the of the *dhiki mas/kseni* distinction in Greece and its context-sensitive application, see Campbell (1964: 38); Herzfeld (1987a); Buck Sutton (1988: 206); Stewart (1991: 170); Just (1992).

assertion that they were all really 'foreigners' gained the quality of a slightly *risqué* public secret, often related in a tone of wry confidentiality as if it might be expected to shock. But almost every Spartokhoriot could claim a parent, grand-parent or great-grandparent who had originally come from the mainland or Lefkadha or from one of the other Ionian Islands, and even the popular (though etymologically doubtful) derivation of their village's name was that its inhabitants had once been *sparti*, 'scattered'.[4]

In neither contemporary nor historical terms was Andonis's status as an immigrant thus unusual. His real problem, his singularity, lay with his marriage, for his wife, too, was a *kseni* (fem.) despite her village birth. Her father, old 'Uncle' Stathis, had arrived in Spartokhori from the mainland some twenty-five years earlier with his wife, numerous children and a team of horses to do a season's work on the road that was then being constructed across the island. Somehow, as he remarked to me, he had never got round to leaving. He stayed on in rented accommodation and did whatever labouring jobs were available. One by one all his children emigrated overseas except for his youngest daughter born after his arrival in Spartokhori, who married Andonis, the immigrant builder from Lefkadha. Andonis, his wife and his parents-in-law thus constituted a sort of genealogical isolate. Andonis was a foreigner *married* to a foreigner, and thus within the village no one's brother-in-law, no one's son-in-law, no one's nephew, cousin or uncle. It is perhaps worth noting that Andonis did have one kinship connection with the community, for he had taken good care to see that both his children were baptized by Spartokhoriots, an elderly couple, and this relationship he courted assiduously. Alas it was eventually frustrated, for shortly before my departure his god-relatives left to join their children in North Carolina. As for his father-in-law, old Uncle Stathis, it was perhaps a sign of his partial acceptance by the village that he was universally addressed as 'Uncle', but he still lived on the margins of society, and when I once enquired his family name, no one could remember it. In the end the Spartokhoriots shrugged their shoulders and said, 'Well, he's a *ksenos*.' After more than twenty years of residence, his surname was still an irrelevancy because it was shared by no one else, and signified relatedness to no one else.

In this context village solidarity cannot be seen as a consequence of long-term population stability. Rather, the village's cohesion was the result of an active process. Through marriage, and through a particular reckoning of the kinship ties created by marriage, Spartokhori had continuously incorporated immigrants into the overarching kinship system that defined its community and allowed its population to talk of one family. Movement, however, had gone on in both directions, and over the whole of Meganisi's relatively brief history, Spartokhori and the other villages of Meganisi (Katomeri and Vathi) had also been subject to emigration and the dispersal of their populations, of which the postwar migration to Athens and overseas was but the latest phase. In short, the cohesion of the

---

[4] This is not the only folk etymology. The original name of the village was Vayenospilia, but the name Spartokhori occurs in a document as early as 1839 (Palmos 1992: 104–5). Palmos lists three further possible derivations for the name Spartokhori: 1. the villagers were farmers and 'sowed/scattered' (*espernan*) the soil; 2. the village was notable for a type of tree, the *sparta*; 3. the village's houses were *sparti* (scattered). All four etymologies were cited by Spartokhoriots.

village in terms of kinship and family masked, or rather continually mended, both its continual fragmentation and its continual augmentation. What appeared to be, and genuinely was, a tightly-knit village community was the product of a quite dynamic and unstable past, and persisted despite an equally dynamic and unstable present. As Buck Sutton (1988) has shown, such instability has been quite common for rural Greece, but its ethnographic import has not always been fully realized.[5]

Over this chapter and the next I shall therefore present the outlines of Meganisi's settlement and of the growth of Spartokhori, for only when population movements (and the economic and political factors that promoted them) are taken into account can the cohesion of the village community through the structures of kinship and family be properly appreciated. It is not my intention, however, to offer a history of the island or of the village. That lies beyond the scope of this book. Nevertheless an understanding of the present presupposes some excursus into the past: not history for history's sake, but the tracing of those trajectories that have resulted in existing social forms and existing social values. Comprehension of the features of contemporary life on which this book focuses would be incomplete (if not quite mistaken) without some knowledge of their historical delineations. As this book progresses, I hope increasingly to offer what Geertz (1973) has popularized as 'thick description'; what I offer for the moment, however, is a 'thin' account of the past not intended as a piece of historical ethnography, yet still presented as something more than historical background.

First settlements

The three villages of Meganisi – Spartokhori, Katomeri and Vathi – are not ancient settlements. Apart from a possible identification of Meganisi and its neighbouring islands with the Homeric islands of the Taphoi (which is about as likely or as unlikely as any other Homeric identification) and a brief British archaeological survey of the island conducted in 1925 which showed evidence of settlement from Neolithic through to Roman times (Benton, 1934; Leekley and Noyes 1975: 8), the earliest evidence about Meganisi comes from the writings of the Florentine ecclesiastic, Christopher Bondelmonti, who travelled throughout the Greek islands in the first half of the fifteenth century.[6] At the end of his brief description of Santa Maura, that is, Lefkadha, Bondelmonti adds: 'Finally, to the east, appear some uncultivated islands once inhabited by monks (Patres), but which as a result of pirate attacks have now become deserted.' (Bondelmonti 1824: 56; my translation).[7]

---

[5] Buck Sutton synthesizes the work of social and economic historians, geographers and demographers of Greece to show the extent of population mobility from the Ottoman period onwards. As she notes, relatively few ethnographic studies have explored the demographic history of particular villages over long periods of time (1988: 188-9). To the exceptions that Buck Sutton cites (Aschenbrenner 1976; Bialor 1976; Vermeulen 1976) should be added Couroucli (1985), Seremetakis (1991), and Karakasidou (1997).

[6] For an account of of Bondelmonti and his *Librum*, see Turner (1987).

[7] Bondelmonti's somewhat quaint Latin reads:'Ad orientam denique insulae incultae propalantur, in quibus olim habitevere Patres, nunc tandem propter insidias piratarum ad desolationem devenere' (Bondelmonti 1824: 56).

The first, and passing, post-classical reference to Meganisi (for geographically the islands referred to must be Meganisi and its neighbours, Skorpios, Skorpidhi, Thiylia, Arkoudhi etc) thus declares it uninhabited. It also adverts to a related matter continually associated with Meganisi up to the nineteenth century in both historical sources and the oral tradition: namely, piracy.

In fact the history of Meganisi's modern settlements spans only 300 years, during which time its population was forged out of diverse groups who came to the island driven by a variety of political and economic circumstances. As Buck Sutton has argued for rural Greece in general, once a wider historical framework is adopted, 'False assumptions of a stable village base only recently disrupted by external systems give way to the recognition that the rural Greek population has quite literally been in motion for centuries' (1988: 187). Most Spartokhoriots, however, did not dwell on their origins. (There was little reason why they should.) As a matter of local pride they were, of course, insistent that they 'had a history', and certain facts relayed by school-teachers and local scholars were widely known: that the great Greek revolutionary hero, Kolokotronis, had passed through Meganisi on his way to fight the Turks in Lefkadha (Kouniakis 1974); that one of the *kapetani* (guerrilla leaders) of the War of Independence, Dhimos Tselios, had been a Meganisiot (Tertsetis 1967: 20–21; Palmos 1992: 112). Such matters related, after all, to Greece's national struggle and to the stuff of national history. To these 'historical facts', the Spartokhoriots could, of course, add their collection of family anecdotes and tales, some of which went back to the late nineteenth century. On the whole, however, local historical knowledge was shallow. One day, bemused by being so often told that the Spartokhoriots were all really 'foreigners', I broached the subject in the *kapnopoulio* (tobacco-shop), where many of the older men regularly gathered to talk. I wanted to know which families had first come to the island. Discussion started amicably enough, but clearly this was the first time the question had been publicly debated. Half an hour later I left not very much the wiser, but with the tobacco-shop in uproar as a dozen old men thumped the counter and yelled at each other in furious dispute.

On one point, however, there was consensus. The Spartokhoriots were insistent that their village (and equally the villages of Katomeri and Vathi) had scarcely existed before 1830. This they attributed to the threat of piracy, although they also dwelt with relish on another version of their history in which it was they who had been the pirates – bandits and thieves who had taken refuge on the island. 1830, however, is a somewhat magical date, for it coincides roughly with the formation of the modern Greek state, though not, it should be noted, with the inclusion of the Ionian Islands within that state.[8] To an extent I suspect the Spartokhoriots were superimposing national history on local history, viewing the foundation of their village and the foundation of modern Greece as contemporaneous. But documentary evidence confirms that up to the nineteenth century the population of Meganisi remained small, and that it was not until the

---

[8]The Greek War of Independence commenced in 1821 and was effectively concluded by 1827. The Kingdom of Greece (complete with Bavarian monarch) was officially instituted in 1832. The Ionian Islands (including Lefkadha), which had become a British Protectorate under a Lord High Commissioner in Corfu (Kerkyra) in 1814, were ceded to The Kingdom of Greece by Great Britain in 1864. For convenient accounts of the political history of the period, see Dakin (1972), Clogg (1979) and Svoronos (1985).

late nineteenth century that its villages grew to any size. Moreover, before the expulsion of the 'Turks'[9] from mainland Greece, piracy in what was effectively a no-man's-land (or rather, sea) between British- and Ottoman-controlled territories would certainly have made habitation of the island dangerous,[10] while documentary evidence also suggests that there was, indeed, a considerable overlap between Meganisi's population and the pirates who threatened the area's security. To an extent, however, the Spartokhoriots underestimate their antiquity.

Meganisi may have remained uninhabited throughout the period of Lefkadha's Ottoman rule (1479–1684). From the Venetian conquest of Lefkadha in 1684 onwards,[11] however, documents show that Meganisi became the recipient of three different groups of immigrants:[12] first, 'sufficient families' for its cultivation brought across from the island of Ithaki in 1691 by one of the Venetians' Greek clients, 'Count' Anastasios Metaxas;[13] second, refugees or settlers from the Ottoman-ruled mainland who appear to have made their own way to Meganisi and whose presence on the island was noted with some dismay by the Venetian authorities in 1760;[14] and third, villagers from southeastern Lefkadha who had

[9]Thus they were (and are) called, for 'Tourkos' was synonymous with Muslim. In the nineteenth century, however, the area of northwestern Greece down to the Gulf of Preveza (which formed part of the Pashadom of 'Albania') had a mixed population of 'Turks', 'Albanians' and 'Greeks', that is to say, it was divided between Muslims and Christians, and all three languages (and some others) were spoken.

[10]For the instability of island populations as a result of piracy, see Buck Sutton (1988: 190–1), Kolodny (1974: 149–70) and Vacalopoulos (1976: 70–100).

[11]After a period of Frankish rule during the Middle Ages, most of the Ionian islands were in Venetian hands by the beginnings of the sixteenth century. Lefkadha was the exception, having fallen to the Turks in 1479. They subsequently lost it to the Venetians in 1502, but recaptured it the next year. Lefkadha then remained under Ottoman control until 1684, when it was taken by the Venetian general, Francesco Morosini.

[12]My account of the early settlement of Meganisi is based largely on information contained in Mahairas (1951), who quotes (in Greek translation) a number of Venetian documents relevant to Meganisi's history that were housed in the National Archives in Venice and in the Lefkadha Archives. I was unable to locate in the Lefkadha Archives many of the documents translated by Mahairas, but I was able to supplement them with some that he does not cite. For the Venetian period, Rondoyiannis' compendious history of Lefkadha (1980, 1982) largely repeats Mahairas.

[13]Letter from Francesco Grimani, Proveditor General da Mar, to the Venetian Senate, 1706, quoted in Mahairas (1951: 214). It is clear that the Venetian Senate never ratified Metaxas' appropriation of Meganisi, for Grimani's letter (fifteen years after the event) is an attempt to regularize Metaxas' possession of it by suggesting an annual rent. The Senate did not take up this suggestion, and in 1716 the island was made over to its 'few inhabitants' for an annual rent to the public treasury (Mahairas 1951: 214).

[14]Letter from Francesco Grimani, Proveditor General da Mar, to the Venetian Senate, 1760, quoted in Mahairas (1951:137). Grimani observes that 'some Greek families from Kseromero [the mainland] have come to the island of Meganisi and have constructed two small villages consisting of about one hundred huts, and they are likely to become more'. He goes on to suggest that it would be advisable to appoint some reputable Lefkadhiot as governor of the island, a suggestion not taken up. The two letters signed 'Francesco Grimani' cited, one dated 1706 and the other 1760, are both quoted in Greek translation from Mahairas (1951:214 and 137 respectively). The originals, written in Italian (or Venetian), are (or were) housed in the Venetian State Archives before the second world war. It is possible that Mahairas made a mistake in transcription, and that both letters date from 1706. If, however, the date 1760 is an error, it is one repeated by Rondoyiannis (1980: 553–4), and a good reason for accepting two different dates for the two letters is that their respective contents appear to fit the narrative of events. It is nevertheless unlikely that both letters were written by the same person. The Grimanis were an important family within the Venetian oligarchy, and in all probability there were two Francesco Grimanis (perhaps grandfather and grandson) who at different times held the same office of Procurator General da Mar in Lefkadha.

property rights on Meganisi recognized by the Venetians in 1684.[15] For a time, from 1719 to approximately 1750, the Venetians also made over the island of Meganisi to a group of refugee Catholic families from the Island of Hios, though there is no evidence that the Hiots actually lived on Meganisi.[16]

The available sources provide an incomplete and confused picture of Meganisi's early history, but a number of general points emerge. First, despite the Sparto-khoriots' belief that most of their ancestors came to the island after 1830, the names included in Venetian records make it highly probable that many of the families now resident in Spartokhori are the descendants of those southern Lefkadhiots who were landowners on Meganisi as early as the seventeenth century.[17] Church records further show that some of them were actually living on the island by the mid-eighteenth century.[18] Second, affairs on Meganisi from the Venetian period through to the nineteenth century and the Greek War of Independence (1821–8) appear to have been more than a little unruly. Situated between the Ottoman-controlled mainland and Lefkadha (ruled variously by the Venetians, French, British, and for a brief period constituted as part of the Septinsular Republic under Russian and Ottoman protection)[19] Meganisi gained

[15]Edict issued by Francesco Morosini, 7 October 1684. The edict (handwritten in Venetian and located in the Lefkadha Archives) is concerned with upholding the rights of certain 'vechiardi' 'seniors', from the villages of Poros and Fterno in southeastern Lefkadha, whose lands on 'un scoglio detto Mega Nisi' (an island called Big Island) were being molested by certain people from the islands of Ithaki and Kefalonia. Morosini imposes penalties on anyone disturbing the island, or trespassing on it with animals without the permission of the vechiardi. A further edict (also located in the Lefkadha Archives) was issued by Lefkadha's Proveditor Estraordinario, Pietro Bragadin, on 18 December 1703 in response to complaints lodged by a certain Micco Palmo from the village of Poros in Lefkadha. It refers back to Morosini's edict of 1684, and again upholds the property rights on Meganisi of villagers from southeastern Lefkadha.

[16]Hios fell to the Turks in 1695, and a number of the Hiots, mostly Roman Catholics of Italian origins, made their way to Venice where they were supported at public expense. The Venetians eventually found the financial burden too great, and dispatched the Hiots to Lefkadha, where lands on Meganisi were made over to them for their support. Of the twenty-two Hiot families that came to Lefkadha in 1719, however, only seven remained by 1750, the others having left variously for Istria, Dalmatia, Corfu and Venice. For the edict of 1719, see Mahairas (1951: 138–44). For a more extensive history of the Hiot refugees, see Svoronos (1940b). See also Rondoyiannis (1980: 553–4).

[17]An edict (located in the Lefkadha Archives) upholding the rights on Meganisi of landowners from the villages of Poros, Katokhori, and Fterno was issued in 1720 by Antonio Morosini, Proveditor Estraordinario di Santa Maura. Attached to it was a list of 126 land owners and the amounts of their holdings entitled Cattastico de' Benni tutti ch'esistono nel Scoglio di Mega Nisi formato per Pubblico Comando nell'anno 1720. (List of all property that exists on the island of Mega Nisi made by public command in the year 1720). Between them, the landowners bear a total of thirty-two family names. Of those thirty-two family names, eleven were carried by Meganisiot families in 1980.

[18]A book of handwritten church records headed Vivlion Ay. Yeoryiou, Meganision (Book of [the church of] St. George, Meganisi) refers to payments made in 1731 for work done on the church, and lists the adhelfi (church 'brothers'), who contributed. Most came from villages in southeastern Lefkadha and from Ithaki, but sixteen are listed as coming from Meganisi itself (nine of whom bore family names common in Spartokhori in 1980). A second list, dated 1757, again includes adhelfi from villages in Lefkadha (and from Lefkadha town), but sixteen are listed as coming from Meganisi itself. Finally, a folder of handwritten pages in the Lefkadha Archives headed simply 'Meganisi' records baptisms for the years 1757–90, and it is likely (though not certain) that the children baptized were born on Meganisi.

[19]Lefkadha and the other Ionian Islands were 'liberated' from Venetian rule by the French Republic in 1797. In 1798 the French were driven out by a combined Russian and Turkish force, and in 1800 the Ionian Islands were constituted as the Septinsular Republic under Russian and Ottoman protection. In 1807 they passed back into French control. The British then captured them during

some notoriety as a haunt for refugees and 'klefts'[20] – outlaws, pirates and brigands – from both the Ionian Islands and the mainland.[21] As one nineteenth-century French observer commented:

> From its situation between the Ionian states and the main land [*sic*], this island has always been exposed to the insults of the Turks, and the predatory adventurers who infect the neighbouring sea. Although these outrages have become less frequent since the islands were placed under British protection, yet it is still found necessary to keep a detachment of British troops at Meganisi, to protect it against the frequent incursions and depredations of Ali Pasha's subjects ... (de Bosset 1821: 370)

Indeed, as early as 1684, and again in 1703, the Venetian authorities had been obliged to protect the property owned on Meganisi by Lefkadhiot villagers from the depredations of islanders from Kefalonia and Ithaki. In 1760 they were also troubled by the settlement on Meganisi of 'undesirables' from the mainland. And such undesirables continued to be a problem for all Lefkadha's subsequent rulers, for a degree of complicity, or more probably of simple overlap, between Meganisi's inhabitants and the pirates and brigands who supposedly attacked it becomes evident.[22] Twice, in 1800 and 1802, the authorities of the Septinsular Republic were forced to send a force to Meganisi proclaiming to the Meganisiots that 'the sword of justice is at your throats' and threatening the direst of consequences if the Meganisiots continued to harbour and shelter brigands and outlaws from the mainland.[23] Not many years later, both the French and the

[19] (cont.) the course of the Napoleonic wars. In November 1815 Great Britain, Prussia, Austria and Russia agreed that the Ionian Islands should be an independent state under the protection of Great Britain, and governed by a Lord High Commissioner.

[20] 'Kleft' (Greek *kleftis*) means simply 'thief', but it was also the term used for the bandits who controlled much of the Greek countryside during the Ottoman period. Since (under such famous 'captains' as Kolokotronis) they bore the brunt of the fighting during the Greek War of Independence, they were subsequently canonized as national heroes.

[21] Thus Goodisson: 'During the time that these islands were under the Venetian republic, this place [Meganisi] was the haunt of pirates and assassins, most of them escaped or outlawed from Albania' (1822: 83). The waters of Lefkadha as a whole appear to have been infamous for piracy. See, for example, Lacroix: 'Up to 1684, under Ottoman rule, Santa Maura [Lefkadha] was known only as a retreat of the dreadful pirates who laid waste the Archipelago, the islands, and the neighbouring coasts' (1853: 625, my translation). See also de Saint-Vincent: 'also the customs [of the Lefkadhiots] predisposes them towards the inclination which has led them to piracy. More than once the inhabitants of the neighbouring islands have been forced to unite in order to repress their brigandage' (1823: 353, my translation).

[22] As Gallant emphasizes, 'far from being lone wolves, most Greek bandit gangs were composed of kinsmen who operated in well-defined social networks; rather than being removed from peasant society, bandit gangs were an integral part of it' (1988: 272). The klefts of Akarnania on the mainland regularly made strategic withdrawals to Lefkadha, Ithaki and Kefalonia, where they settled their families for safety (Rondoyiannis 1982: 108–56), and given Meganisi's out-of-the-way location between Lefkadha and the mainland, much of the island's population probably consisted of the families and kin of these klefts. See Goodisson (1822: 83) cited above.

[23] The Russo-Turkish alliance (which had resulted in the establishment of the Septinsular Republic) placed the government of the Ionian Islands, and particularly the authorities in Lefkadha, in a difficult position. The klefts who operated on the mainland and who withdrew to the Ionian Islands were well known to the Islands' Greek authorities, and well equipped with friends and sympathizers there. Indeed, with the collapse of the Russo-Turkish alliance the klefts contributed to the defence of Lefkadha which, in 1806, appeared ready to fall to the infamous Ali Pasha of Albania, who had long coveted it. On the other hand, since the government of the Septinsular Republic was bound by treaty to the Ottoman Empire, it was also obliged to respect the wishes of Ali Pasha, nominally the Sublime Porte's vassal, who from 1799 onwards continually demanded the prosecution and repatriation of the klefts and their families (Svoronos 1940a; Rondoyiannis 1982: 108–56).

Table 2.1 Population of Meganisi, 1691–1834

Year	Population	Source
Before 1691	Uninhabited? Used by villagers from SE Lefkadha	Bondelmonti, 1824. Inference from Venetian edicts
1691	'Sufficient families' imported by Metaxas from Kefalonia	Francesco Grimani, 1706. (Mahairas 1951)
1720	126 landowners from Poros, Fterno and Katokhori. Not resident?	Census ordered by Morosini, 1720. Lefkadha Archives
1731	Church of Ayios Yeoryios in existence (Spartokhori). 16 *adhelfi* from Meganisi.	Church records. Lefkadha Archives
1757	16 *adhelfi* from Meganisi	Church records. Lefkadha Archives
1760 (?)	Two villages amounting to 100 huts. Population from Kseromeno (mainland)	Francesco Grimani 1760. Venice Archives (Mahairas 1951)
1765	Meganisi pop. 249	Venice Archives (Partsch 1889)
1819	Meganisi pop. 300	de Bosset 1821
1821	Meganisi pop. 600+	Goodisson 1822
1824	Meganisi pop. 500	Davy 1842
1831	Meganisi pop. 517	Census, Lefkadha Archives
1832	Meganisi pop. 532	Census, Lefkadha Archives
1833	Meganisi pop. 536	Census, Lefkadha Archives
1834	Meganisi pop. 636	Census, Lefkadha Archives

[23] (cont.) Moreover, despite the heroic mythology, many klefts were common criminals. On both political and moral grounds, therefore, the attitude of the Ionian Islands' authorities towards the klefts was not clearcut. In 1800, in an attempt to appease Ali Pasha, a campaign was launched against the klefts by land and sea, as part of which the governing body of Lefkadha sent an armed force to Meganisi with a strongly worded edict 'to all workers of Meganisi' advising them that the only way to avoid capital punishment was to take up arms against the klefts and rigorously to prevent the landing on Meganisi of any boat from the mainland (edict of 15 April 1800, quoted in Rondoyiannis 1982: 118–19). The campaign was a limited success, and most of the klefts fled by sea. Complaints from Ali Pasha continued, however, and in 1802 a further campaign was organized by the government of the Septinsular Republic. As before, a pronouncement was made to the 'workers' of both Lefkadha and Meganisi demanding their cooperation in combating brigandage. Later the same year Lefkadha's governing body ordered a mobilization of the peasantry and, in the case of Meganisi, demanded that the inhabitants sign a declaration that on pain of imprisonment, the burning of their houses and the confiscation of their property, they would not welcome brigands and would expel the families of brigands. Further to this declaration, a list of Meganisi's inhabitants was drawn up and signed by the heads of the island's villages (Rondoyiannis 1982: 148). Presumably this latter measure was an attempt by the authorities to distinguish true Meganisiots from mainland klefts, but its very necessity betrays the uncertainty of the distinction.

British in turn felt obliged to station garrisons on the island[24] to protect it from the Ottoman-controlled mainland, but equally to restrict the activities of the Meganisiots themselves. As the British Resident of Lefkadha, Rear-Admiral William Henry Smyth, remarked: 'Among the dependent islets [of Lefkadha], Meganisi (Aspalathia) holds the first place, as its name imports; but since, in the insurrection of 1819 it became a station for spies, I was under the necessity of disarming the inhabitants, and, for a time, restricting intercourse with neighbours.' (Smyth 1854: 53)[25]

The constant association in the late eighteenth and early nineteenth centuries of Meganisi with pirates, brigands, outlaws and 'spies' is, of course, inextricable from the broader political situation: Greek revolutionary resistance to Ottoman rule on the mainland, and a desire for union with a newly formed Greek state among the population of foreign-controlled Lefkadha.[26] Piracy and banditry merged with political struggle in a context in which most outlaws could be seen as 'primitive rebels' (Hobsbawm 1959). And in those turbulent years Meganisi's location made it an obvious refuge for those escaping either Ottoman oppression on the mainland, or local justice on Lefkadha.

Growth

Those troubled times also kept the island's population small. Available figures vary (see Table. 2.1), but by the 1820s Meganisi still had a population of no more than five or six hundred, and conditions there were regularly reported as wretched. In 1824 the admirably thorough Dr Davy, British Army Surgeon for Lefkadha, visited the island. His brief description is typical of the period:[27]

> The first night we stopped on Meganisi, and had an opportunity of seeing a considerable portion of that poor and barren island with a population of about five hundred

[24]For the British garrison, see de Bosset (1821: 370) cited above. The French had also placed a small garrison on Meganisi which was taken in 1810 by klefts from the mainland under the leadership of Kolokotronis with the assistance of the British navy preparatory to the British capture of Lefkadha (Rondoyiannis 1982: 231; Kouniakis 1974).

[25]The 'insurrection' of 1819 was caused by the British's attempt to levy a tax on all villagers in Lefkadha to pay for the dredging of a canal through the salt-flats that effectively joined Lefkadha to the mainland at its northeastern tip. For an account of the insurrection (or riot) see Goodisson (1822: 81 n. 4); Mahairas (1940: 50–61); Jervis-White Jervis (1852: 213–14); Gallant (1990). Since the insurrection took place not on Meganisi, but outside the village of Sfakiotes on Lefkadha, Smyth's particular attention to Meganisi in the wake of the insurrection seems to mark the Meganisiots as amongst the usual suspects whenever there was trouble.

[26]As Gallant (1990) notes, 'The already severe problems faced by the Colonial Office concerning civil control [in the Ionian Islands] were compounded by the establishment of the Kingdom of Greece in 1832. Ionian islanders had always considered themselves members of a Greek 'nation', a point even the British conceded... The creation of a territorially-based Greek nation-state provided a context in which the islanders could define more precisely their own national identity and it provided a coherent ideology for action: unification with Greece.' (1990: 489)

[27]See also Goodisson: 'This rocky island becomes more impoverished every year, the soil being continually washed away by the rains, and there are no vallies [sic] to arrest its progress to the sea' (1822: 83). De Bosset similarly relates, 'There are about three hundred inhabitants, under the presidency of a magistrate, who find great difficulty in procuring a scanty subsistence from some arid tracts of land, and from the produce of their sheep and goats, which feed upon the brush-wood, the chief vegetation of the island. It is destitute of any sweet water except that which falls from the clouds, and hence the inhabitants are obliged to send abroad for a supply.' (1821: 370)

Table 2.2 Population of Meganisi and villages 1865-1991

Year	Meganisi (Tafos)	Spartokhori	Katomeri/Vathi*
1865	778	353	425
1870	928	not given	514
1879	1,095	495	600
1889	1,104	500	604
1896	1,460**	666	747/30
1907	1,684***	770	869
1920	1,657	747	897
1928	1,640	749	891
1940	2,075	856	1,198
1951	2,139	887	900/333
1961	2,008	822	888/286
1971	1,664	682	756/215
1981	1,619	561	588/197
1991	1,246	511	523/211

* Census figures for Katomeri and Vathi are variously combined and separated.
** Includes Madhouri (9) and Skorpios (8).
*** Includes Madhouri (21), Sparti (9), Skorpios (11), Skorpidhi (2), Ayios Nikolaos (2).
Sources: 1865–1907, Khouliarakis (1973); 1920–91, National Statistical Service of Greece.

souls, collected in three villages, in ruder conditions than the inhabitants of the wilder parts of the mountainous district of Zante [Zakynthos], generally poor, squalid, and dirty, the men said to be very indolent, the women laborious and overworked; without cisterns, and depending for water on two wells close to the sea-shore, at some distance from the villages (Davy 1842: Vol I, 199).

From the latter half of the nineteenth century, however, Meganisi suddenly experienced a quite remarkable population growth (see Tables 2.1 and 2.2). The beginnings of this growth were noted by the German geographer, Joseph Partsch, who visited the island in 1888. Partsch had consulted the archives in Venice and states that in 1765 Meganisi had a population of only 249. In 1831 the British census gave the island a population of 517.[28] By 1879, however, it was 1,095, and by 1907 it had reached 1,639 (Kolodny 1974: 791). In short, Meganisi's population more than tripled in roughly seventy-five years, the increase accelerating towards the end of the century. Like the Meganisiots themselves, Partsch (who was struck by the increase from 249 in 1765 to 1,095 by 1879, which he calculated as 340 per cent in 114 years) attributed the island's population growth to the decline of piracy (Partsch 1889: 28–9). But while Partsch was no doubt partly correct, Meganisi's startling growth towards the end of the nineteenth century and into the twentieth requires further explanation.[29] The decline of piracy is only one part of the story. Aspects of the local economy form the other.

From at least the nineteenth century and roughly up to the Second World War Meganisi's economy was based on three interlocking activities: pastoralism,

[28]Increasing to 536 for both 1833 and 1834. Figures are from the *Stato Annuale di Battezzati, Sposati, Morti, nella Citta e Isola de Santa Maura* for the years 1831, 1832, 1833 and 1834, Lefkadha Archives.
[29]Partsch notes that the population of Lefkadha as a whole also increased by 96 per cent from 11,737 in 1765 to 23,083 in 1879 (Partsch 1889: 28). Nevertheless, Meganisi's population growth was out of all proportion to Lefkadha's.

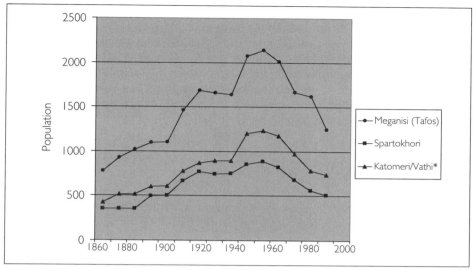

Figure 2.1 Population growth of Meganisi and villages, 1865–1991

agriculture and maritime pursuits (both fishing and trading). Their relative balance shifted over time, but of the three it was pastoralism that most contributed to Meganisi's growth. Elderly Meganisiots were unanimous that 'in the old days' (that is, before the Second World War) Meganisi had been 'all sheep and goats';[30] but they also told a tale which, from individual to individual, was remarkably consistent. A father, grandfather, great-grandfather or great-great-grandfather (at all events a male ancestor) had been in the practice of coming annually to Meganisi from one of the villages of Lefkadha (or in some cases from the mainland) in search of winter pasture for his flocks. Then one year he saw a Spartokhoriot girl, fell in love, married, and settled permanently on the island. Thus he and his descendants became Spartokhoriots.

The romantic gloss given these stories does not lessen their credibility, and well within living memory the population of Meganisi and its villages was still increasing as the result of the gradual absorption into the community via marriage of shepherds and goatherds whose annual migrations brought them to the island.[31] If the transportation of flocks by caique seems an arduous way of securing pasturage, it must be recognized that the mountain regions of Lefkadha are snow-covered in winter, while its narrow plains on the southeast coast opposite Meganisi have long been planted with olive trees and other crops which, as elsewhere in Greece, made sheep and particularly goats unwelcome visitors (Campbell 1964: 21; Hart 1991: 68). Meganisi, too, was planted with olive trees from at least the late nineteenth century, and cereals were grown up to the 1950s; but the island's highest areas are still well below the winter snow-line, and the island has large tracts of rocky land unsuitable for anything except the

---

[30]Travellers' accounts indicate much the same for the nineteenth century. See de Bosset, 1821: 62; Goodisson 1822: 83; *New Piloting Directions for the Mediterranean Sea* (1831: 194).
[31]See also Hart 1991: 57–8 for a similar pattern of settlement by itinerant shepherds in the Peloponnese.

pasturage of sheep and goats. Given the regional ecology, seasonal migration from the mountains of Lefkadha to Meganisi was worth the effort.

Given the tales of love at first sight, it might seem that for some shepherds it was worth the effort in other respects too, and so, perhaps, it was; but more than the chances of personal infatuation must be considered. Many of the older Sparto-khoriots knew that their immigrant male ancestor or his family had already owned land on Meganisi before settling there (and, as I have mentioned, the property rights on Meganisi of villagers from southern Lefkadha were recognized by the Venetians as early as the seventeenth century). The island romances of itinerant shepherds should not, therefore, be construed simply as the arrival of some likely lads who happened to woo and win a local bride. Rather, it is much more likely that such shepherds were following in the footsteps of their own village compatriots who had already shifted residence from Lefkadha (or the mainland) to Meganisi. The convergence of kinship connections, material interests and mutual family knowledge essential to the formation of marital alliances in rural Greece were probably already in place. In a sense, newly settled shepherds were still marrying within their own community.[32]

Thus if Partsch was correct in attributing the rapid growth of Meganisi during the nineteenth century to the decline of piracy and to the advent of more stable political conditions, settlement on the island was probably still less a case of straightforward immigration than of the gradual transference of populations to a location that had for long been their seasonal outpost. Given the exponential growth of Meganisi's villages in the late nineteenth century, it is also plausible to suggest that something like a critical mass was reached, let us say (somewhat arbitrarily) Spartokhori's 353 inhabitants in 1865 (see Table 2.2), after which the villages took off by constituting viable communities in their own right. For those shepherds who came annually to the island to graze their flocks or to cultivate land their families already owned, a point was reached when Meganisi's settlements presented themselves as attractive alternatives to their natal villages. Thus while the total population of Meganisi increased steadily from 437 in 1808 to 778 in 1865, it doubled its size to 1,663 between 1865 and 1907, an important factor in this process of consolidation and growth – a factor which, as the oral tradition suggests, determined the decision of many individual shepherds to settle on the island – being the availability of local brides and hence the possibility of integration into the newly forming communities through the ties of kinship and family.[33] And what I have described by way of an historical reconstruction actually continued in an attenuated form up to the time of my fieldwork. In 1979 and 1980 several families from Lefkadha who had relatives on Meganisi were still bringing their flocks of sheep and goats to the island in winter, while the four families in Spartokhori who owned the largest flocks of sheep and

[32] It is worth noting that in the nineteenth and earlier part of this century intermarriage between the villages of Meganisi and those of southern Lefkadha was common, and Poros (on Lefkadha) and Spartokhori (on Meganisi) were so closely allied that both villages contributed to the upkeep of the small chapel of Ayios Ioannis on the west coast of Meganisi facing Poros (Palmos 1992: 40).

[33] Meganisi's rapid population increase was by no means unique in Greece towards the end of the nineteenth century. Many other rural areas also became the recipients of new migrant populations, and Buck Sutton notes that 1880–1920 'was the period of maximum village creation in recent Greek history' (1988: 199–200). Cf. Couroucli (1985: 30) for a comparable population growth in Corfu.

Table 2.3 Agricultural production figures, Spartokhori, 1961/2–1978/9

Year	Trees	Oil (kg)	Sheep	Goats
1961/2	31,600	281,250	2,250	550
1962/3	29,500	unknown	1,170	880
1963/4	32,600	343,200	1,180	440
1964/5	unknown	unknown	unknown	unknown
1965/6	33,100	150,000	unknown	unknown
1966/7	33,100	6,000	unknown	unknown
1967/8	unknown	unknown	365	125
1968/9	33,100	unknown	490	156
1969/70	33,500	130,000	370	71
1970/71	33,500	280,000	250	250
1971/2	33,500	56,000	400	480
1972/3	32,000	300,000	420	530
1973/4	33,600	20,000	200	530
1974/5	33,800	64,000	200	530
1975/6	35,000	150,000	320	580
1976/7	35,200	70,000	540	480
1977/8	35,200	75,000	370	355
1978/9	unknown	150,000	510	340

Sources: 1961/2–1963/4 Statistical Bureau, Lefkadha; 1964/5–1978/9 Agricultural Bureau, Lefkadha.

goats were all relatively recent immigrants who had settled on the island between 1930 and the late 1960s. What must be stressed, however, is that such late-comers were emulating a pattern of movement and a way of life already abandoned by the bulk of Meganisi's population.

The decline of agriculture and the reformation of class

The elderly may have been unanimous that in the old days Meganisi had been all sheep and goats (and many of them had been shepherds and goatherds in their youth), but by the late 1970s pastoralism played only a marginal role in the island's economy. In 1978/9 the Agricultural Bureau of Lefkadha recorded the village of Spartokhori with a total of 510 sheep and 340 goats (see Table 2.3), and during my stay only one man, assisted by his young son and an aged uncle, was still working as a full-time shepherd, maintaining a flock of 150 milking ewes. Up to 1980 another elderly man, the proprietor of a general store, also kept a flock of about forty ewes minded by a shepherdess. The rest of Spartokhori's livestock (approximately a hundred sheep and a few goats) were owned in twos and threes and served only to supply households with fresh milk and enough cheese for domestic consumption.[34] The majority of the older Meganisiots

[34]The higher livestock figures recorded by the Agricultural Bureau derive from the activities of the four immigrant families from Lefkadha. Three bought land on the island's rocky tail, some distance from the village and virtually inaccessible by land, where they kept several hundred sheep and goats.

nevertheless still considered themselves *aghrotes* (farmers), a category which includes both agriculturalists and pastoralists and which was also their official classification for receipt of the government's non-contributory pension. Inasmuch as the classification related to present (rather than past) occupations it concerned exclusively olive cultivation, for olives were Meganisi's sole commercial crop, and olive cultivation was the only form of agriculture that seriously occupied a section of the population, the oldest. In 1977/8 Spartokhori alone had 35,200 olive trees, and some people were still planting new trees during my stay; but the majority of the island's trees were unworked, and most families produced only enough oil to satisfy their household needs or the needs of their close relatives. The surplus, sold to merchants from Lefkadha, provided some elderly couples with a modest income, but it was still one that required supplement, and olive-oil production was in steep decline.[35]

In fact olive cultivation had a relatively brief history on Meganisi. Nineteenth-century accounts make no mention of olive trees and the Meganisiots themselves were insistent that the majority of the island's trees were planted this century.[36] In the depressed rural economy of prewar Greece, a simple priority, 'to feed the children', had determined a concentration on cereals as subsistence crops, and the terraces on which the olive trees now grow were originally constructed for barley and wheat. In the early part of this century flax, too, was grown for home-spun clothes, and there were extensive vineyards on the island.[37] By 1980, however, no grain was grown on Meganisi, and flax was a vague memory. A few families still had small patches of vineyard, but grape-growing was considered laborious work not worth the effort. Garden produce (onions, garlic, potatoes, beans, lettuce, pears, plums, almonds, lemons) and poultry for eggs, still played an important part in the household economy, but in market terms the produce was insignificant. In short, and despite appearances, by the late 1970s the Meganisiots were no longer in economic terms agriculturalists.

The history of the demise of Meganisi's agricultural economy is also, however, the history of the demise of economic inequalities that related to the ownership of land, and thus raises the question of social class, a complex question in rural Greece. From a national perspective, Greece has always been a class society (Mouzelis 1978), but it is notable that class has not featured prominently in most anthropological accounts of Greek rural communities. In the light of Bennett's

[34](cont.) The other kept a large flock of goats on the tiny island of Kithros off the end of Meganisi's tail. These flocks were not regularly milked, but kept for meat.

[35]When I arrived in Spartokhori in 1977 there were four olive-oil mills in operation: three privately owned and one belonging to the village's agricultural cooperative. Ten years earlier there had been six mills. By the winter of 1980 only two mills were operating. Statistics (see Table 2.3) show extraordinary fluctuations in oil production: 300,000 kg, for example, in 1972/3, followed by 20,000 kg in 1973/4. This is explained by the fact that most of Meganisi's olive trees fruit fully only every second year, which results in a two-year cycle of good and bad crops (see Couroucli 1985: 35 for biannual olive crops).

[36]See Rondoyiannis (1982: 642–3) who points out that Lefkadha's major cash crop at the turn of the century was grapes. Hart (1991: 69) similarly points out the late popularity of olives in the south-eastern Peloponnese.

[37]Most of these were owned by wealthy absentee landlords in Lefkadha, for grapes became an important cash crop in Lefkadha (and generally in Greece) after the phylloxera blight destroyed France's vineyards in 1869 (Rondoyiannis 1982: 615–16).

recent work (1988) which, exceptionally, does examine a class-based rural Greek community,[38] it might now be suggested that to an extent this omission has been due to the accidents (or choices) of fieldwork location,[39] but certainly it was not the result of ethnographic blindness. Most Greek rural communities that have been studied by anthropologists simply have not shown the obvious manifestations of class as they have been recognized for the rest of the southern Europe,[40] nor, in 1980, did Spartokhori.

Gross differences of individual wealth certainly existed, but in Spartokhori there were no latifundia, there were no absentee aristocratic or bourgeois landowners, there was no proletariat of landless labourers, and certainly there were no *pallazzi* nor even particularly distinguished private houses or public buildings: none of that provincial microcosm of class distinction as evident in buildings as in bank balances that Silverman (1975), for example, describes for an Italian town no bigger than an average Greek village, or that Gilmore (1980) saw as the most salient feature of life in a Spanish agro-town. On the whole, Spartokhori in the late 1970s conformed to the socio-economic pattern described for most rural Greek communities that have been studied. It was culturally homogeneous; it was deeply imbued with a spirit of competitive egalitarianism; it was a community in which no group's claim to established superiority was recognized, but in which the assertion 'we are all just people (*anthropi*)'[41] was endlessly repeated as part of a continual jockeying for material and moral advantage in a world in which cleavages and animosities related to the relatively impermanent successes and failures of individuals and their families (Bennett 1988: 219; Campbell 1983).[42] Nevertheless, the Spartokhoriots' recollection of the past was not of equality,

[38]Bennett's article is concerned with the farming community of Lehonia on the Pilion peninsula near Volos, whose population 'is differentiated into landowners and labourers'. See also Karakasidou (1997) for a good historical account

[39]As Bennett comments, 'Lehonia's internal class structure sets it apart from most of the villages represented in the ethnography of Greece', although, as she notes, some class distinctions have been recorded in the countryside (Hoffman 1976: 330–1; McNeill 1978; Dimen 1979; Schein 1970, 1974), 'class differences in Greece have been observed primarily within the city, or between the rural and urban sectors', and 'completely missing from the picture of rural Greek society is a description of the social and cultural structures in communities where there are, or were, landowners who lived without doing agricultural work and labourers who lived without owning any land' (1988: 218–20).

[40]It is instructive to compare ethnographies of Greece with their counterparts in rural Italy, Spain and Portugal, for the differences are staggering, and cannot be attributed merely to the ethnographer's adoption or rejection on ideological grounds of 'class' as an analytic tool. Friedl (1964a), Campbell (1964), du Boulay (1974), Allen (1976), Herzfeld (1985), and, if we may include Cyprus, Peristiany (1965) and Loizos (1975a & b) – to name but the best-known names – did not encounter the sort of social and economic differentiation described by Pitt-Rivers (1954) and Gilmore (1980) for rural Spain, or Cutileiro (1971) and O'Neill (1987) for Portugal, or Blok (1974) and Silverman (1975) for Italy. These authors represent, of course, only a random selection from the ethnography of southern Europe, but the differences between Greece on the one hand and rural Spain, Portugal and Italy on the other is abundantly clear.

[41]For use of the identical phrase in the southeastern Peloponnese, see Hart (1991: 172).

[42]If the Spartokhoriots had a notion of class – and, since most of them supported either KKE (Greece's Communist Party of the Exterior) or PASOK (Andreas Papandreou's Panhellenic Socialist Movement), most of them did – they applied it not to relations within the village, but to their relationship as villagers with external forces of oppression and evil somewhat vaguely designated as 'the rich', 'the big people', 'the capitalists', 'the bureaucracy', 'the government', 'the politicians', and last but by no means least, the United States and the CIA. See Herzfeld (1985: 19–33) for similar attitudes amongst Cretan villagers.

economic or otherwise. As Bennett remarks on the history of rural Greek communities, 'A pattern appears to emerge: localized structures of class differentiation disappeared or diminished as they became more firmly integrated into the Greek nation and the international economy' (1988: 219–20), or, as Spartokhori's village president rather more simply put it (in a manner strikingly reminiscent of Bennett's informants), there was now much more 'democracy' than in the past, for 'the rich have become poor and the poor have become rich'.[43] This, the president explained to me (and it is perhaps worth noting that he had been a lifelong communist) was 'a sort of natural law'.

What the president was talking about when he referred to wealth, poverty and democracy was, at least in the first instance, the ownership of land. In 1980 nearly everybody in the village owned their own land; 'in the past', he told me, 'before the war', it had been a different matter. Half the villagers had been landless and had had to work as labourers and sharecroppers for the 'wealthy'.[44] But the 'wealthy' of the past referred to two distinct, though occasionally interconnected, groups: first, a class of absentee landlords from Lefkadha who possessed considerable holdings on Meganisi during the nineteenth and early twentieth centuries; second, a number of village families whose wealth was based on the ownership of a disproportionate amount of Meganisi's land up to the late 1950s.

The details of the island's appropriation by absentee landlords during the nineteenth century has not been thoroughly studied,[45] but it seems that during the period of British rule (1810–64) the opening up and liberalization of trade throughout the Ionian Islands created a new mercantile class in Lefkadha whose members, allying themselves with Lefkadha's traditional elite, invested their fortunes in land, their accumulation of property being aided by the high interest rates which, as merchants, they exacted on loans made to the peasantry. The Meganisiots' own version of events was simpler. Certain people on Lefkadha became 'friends of the British' and therefore whatever they wanted they got – it was merely a matter of influence and patronage. Such an account probably betrays as much about how many older Meganisiots assumed the world to work as it does about the political and legal processes of land acquisition under British rule; nevertheless, large tracts of Meganisi were certainly owned by notable Lefkhadiot families (and cultivated as vineyards)[46] during the nineteenth and

[43]Bennett's informant stated, 'The poor have much more money', the title of her article.
[44]The president's estimation of the current situation was roughly borne out by available statistics. A sample of 111 Spartokhoriot households gave an average holding of 37 *stremmata*, and most families had holdings close to that average. (One *stremma* equals one-tenth of a hectare, or approximately 0.25 acres.) Fourteen households owned less than ten *stremmata*, and a very few families, most of them recent immigrants, owned no land. At the other end of the scale, one family, again recently arrived, owned 200 *stremmata* used for sheep and goat grazing, and the largest landowner possessed 524 *stremmata*. Those few families who had no land had non-agricultural occupations, and no one worked as an agricultural labourer for any one else except by way of a favour to a kinsman or (on advantageous terms) to help out an old widow or widower. The sample was obtained from the records of the Lefkadha branch of the Agricultural Bank.
[45]*Pace* Rondoyiannis's (1982) inclusion of a considerable amount of economic data in his history. A short publication by the late Dhimos Malakasis (1982), public notary for Lefkadha at the time of my stay, does document the rise and fall of the 'merchant-landowner' class from 1820 to 1920. The general points I make here derive from conversations I had with Mr Malakasis.
[46]Amongst those most frequently mentioned by villagers were the family of Lefkadha's great poet, Aristotelis Valaoritis (whose house on the neighbouring island of Madhouri is now a museum); the

early part of the twentieth centuries. It should be stressed, however, that these Lefkadhiot landowners were precisely *absentee* landowners. This division between a peasantry and what might be termed a landed gentry was not one internal to the Meganisiot population itself. Interestingly, however, the detailed Greek Government census of 1870 (*Ipouryion Esoterikon* 1872: 192–3) does contain information that might well be construed as evidence for *internal class* divisions among the island's nineteenth-century population.

The 1870 census breaks down the total population of 928 persons (492 males and 436 females) for the deme of Taphos, that is, Meganisi, into five landowners (*ktematiai/ propriétaires*),[47] fifty-six manufacturers (*viomekhanoi/industriels*), six merchants (*emboroi/commerçants*), 190 farmers (*georgoi/ agriculteurs*), fifty-five 'shepherds' (*poimenes/bergerers*), three female 'workers' (*ergatriai/ouvrières*) (but notably no male workers), three male servants (*uperatai/domestiques*) (but notably no female servants), one priest, and eight local and government functionaries. A further 521 individuals are classified as 'occupation unknown'. The categories, given in both Greek and French, are not always easy to interpret, and the intro-duction to the census itself describes the difficulties and ambiguities encountered in assigning Greece's population to particular occupational categories (*Ipouryion Esoterikon* 1872: kd–lb). No elaboration, however, is given of the distinction made between landowners and farmers. Was this distinction on Meganisi simply quantitative, perhaps with landowners being those rich enough not to have to work their own land? Or is it possible that in 1870 only five men on Meganisi owned their own land, and that the other 190 farmers (and the fifty-five shepherds) rented their land, or were sharecroppers, or worked for the five land-owners? Further, what Meganisi's fifty-six manufacturers were engaged in remains somewhat mysterious. It is likely there were carpenters, boat-builders, perhaps a stonemason and a blacksmith on the island, but fifty-six seems too large a number. As the introduction to the census admits, however, *viomekhanoi* was a broad category and overlapped with other occupations, including agricul-tural work. Those who owned and/or operated olive-oil presses or flour mills on Meganisi may have been classified as manufacturers, but it is also notable that no male workers (*ergatai*) are included among Meganisi's population, and it is possible that men who found seasonal work in the oil-presses and flour mills, or who perhaps assisted in grape-pressing and wine-making, were classified, or chose to classify themselves, as manufacturers rather than workers.[48] It is also odd that no one on Meganisi was listed under the census category of 'sailors' (*nautikoi/marins*), since, as we shall see, the Meganisiots were well known as

[46](cont.) family of the historian Konstandinos Mahairas (who were merchants and shipowners in the mid-nineteenth century); the aristocratic Fetsis family from Lefkadha town; and the Stamatopoulos family (again merchant ship-owners in the mid-nineteenth century). See Rondoyiannis (1982: 513–5) and Palmos (1992: 55, 105, and 112).

[47]I use here a 'classical' transliteration of the Greek terms here in order to preserve the specificity of the nineteenth century *katharevousa* (refined Greek) categories. Census material of the period was published bilingually in both Greek and French. Nowadays it is published in Greek and English.

[48]There is one other possible explanation. Ansted (1863: 197) noted that Meganisi 'is remarkable for quarries of excellent stone … [which] is exported to various islands and the mainland, besides being almost exclusively used for the newer buildings of the town of Santa Maura'; but I could find no one on Meganisi who knew anything of this, nor could I find anything that resembled a quarry. Palmos (1992: 70), however, mentions stone as cargo on Spartokhoriot vessels.

sailors in the nineteenth century. It would, of course, be tempting to think that some proportion of Meganisi's sailors (and fishermen), and of its landless workers, were accounted for by the largest section of the island's population (521 people) listed as 'occupation unknown'; however, as the introduction to the census explains, this category was largely composed of women and children. One thing, however, does becomes quite clear from the census: Meganisi's population in 1870 was stratified: five landowners at one end of the scale, three male servants at the other. Somebody (or bodies) was rich enough to have a servant or servants; three men were poor enough to be them.

The oral tradition does not extend back to 1870, but the Spartokhoriots remembered well enough the inequalities of wealth that existed up to and beyond the Second World War, and which may have paralleled those of the earlier period. Older Spartokhoriots frequently cited the names of individuals and families for whom in their youth they had worked, and who, they also claimed, had owned half the island. The general drift of accounts (often vague and sometimes contradictory) was that these local landowners were either the political clients of Lefkadha's ruling elite (the absentee landlord class) whom they served as political party bosses on the island, and by whom they were generously rewarded,[49] or else that they were immigrants who came to the island with sufficient wealth to establish themselves in advantageous positions. Moreover, it should not be forgotten that with a system of high interest loans it was possible even at the local level for individuals to create small fortunes. Shop-keepers and others who were able to accumulate surplus produce could extend credit for goods (largely foodstuff) that resulted in a spiral of indebtedness for the less fortunate – and owning an oil mill, owning a flour mill, a general store or a trading and transport caique were all occupations that could profitably be pursued in conjunction with agriculture and the accumulation of land.

But although inequalities of wealth and land-ownership on Meganisi earlier this century are not to be doubted, whether the island's local landowners constituted a separate class seems much less certain. Bennett, for example, takes three conditions as necessary and sufficient to constitute a system structured by class relations: 'systematic and permanent differences in control of critical resources among groups in the population, social barriers between these groups, and an awareness by the participants of common interests within each group and different interests among them' (1988: 218). By all accounts, the differences in wealth on prewar Meganisi appear to have not been systematic, permanent, or between groups separated by social barriers or possessing a self-conscious aware-ness of their group interests. Those who were wealthy are perhaps better described as rich peasants, local landowners, entrepreneurs and brokers who were able individually to profit at the expense of their neighbours, but who remained culturally identical with them and structurally incapable of repro-ducing and consolidating their collective advantage over time. One of the names regularly cited by villagers in connection with the wealthy families of the past was Malamas. A recently published work on Meganisiot place names by Kostas

---

[49]It was common in Greece up to the second half of this century for politicians to be able to secure the block vote of whole villages through the activities of their *kommatarhes*, or party-bosses, local men who dispensed money or favours on their behalf.

Palmos, himself a Meganisiot, is revealing. Palmos relates that the first Malamas, a ship-owner from Kalamata, was forced by bad weather to put in at Meganisi on his way to Italy. Malamas liked Meganisi, married a local woman and settled on the island permanently. The Malamas family became the richest on Meganisi, continuing with their shipping business, as well as becoming large landowners employing Meganisiot labourers.[50] Palmos continues: 'As I have heard from the descendants of these people, they [the Malamas family] helped their workers and were not usurers. They even took children of their workers as sons-in-law' (Palmos 1992: 82; my translation).

There is a note of local patriotism (and possibly a reflection of Meganisi's currently egalitarian ethos) in Palmos's specific denial that the Malamas family ever practised usury; but his mention of the Malamas family's intermarriage with their workers coincides with everything I heard about the rich. Social barriers were not erected, and a preference for local marriage partners would itself have militated against the establishment of discrete classes.

Nevertheless, given the economic inequalities that existed on Meganisi and the generally depressed state of Greece's rural economy (Rondoyiannis1982; Mouzelis 1978: 19-20; Buck Sutton 1988), it is not surprising that in the first decades of the twentieth century poorer Meganisiots (like so many other Greeks) should have resorted to emigration.[51] I was told that 'about a hundred' men had emigrated to America from the village of Spartokhori in the early years of this century, and a similar number from Katomeri,[52] sufficient to explain the hiatus in Meganisi's growth that appears between the census figures of 1907 and 1920 (see Table 2.2). The irony is that emigration should have started so soon after the island's rapid population increase. It seems that some Meganisiots were leaving for the United States while shepherds and goatherds from Lefkadha, the fathers and grandfathers of many of the island's present population, were still settling on the island. But as Hart has commented for Richia in the southeastern Peloponnese (where in the late nineteenth century a remarkably similar process of simultaneous settlement by shepherds and overseas migration by villagers took place), 'This is perhaps less odd than it seems if we think in terms of family subsistence strategies rather than individual strategies' (Hart 1991: 69). As part of such family subsistence strategies it should be noted that emigration from Meganisi during the early 1900s was an almost exclusively male affair. Men set off to seek their fortune overseas, leaving their wives, sisters and daughters at home. Not all returned. Some died. Others disappeared and were generally believed to have entered into bigamous relationships with foreign women and to

[50]Interestingly, Palmos says: 'The Malamas family had in their employment Meganisiots, from the villages of Lefkadha and Ithaka' (1992: 82). Presumably they hired Lefkadhiot and Ithakan labourers who subsequently became Meganisiots in the manner described above.
[51]Overseas emigration was a panhellenic phenomenon, and it is estimated that between 1890 and 1914 some 350,000 Greeks, or nearly one-sixth of the country's population, departed to the United States (Clogg 1979: 93). As Mouzelis notes, despite rural unemployment, peasants preferred to emigrate to the United States rather than become proletarians in Greece's urban centres. 'Thus the number of Greeks who left for the United States every year was greater than the total number of workers employed in the Greek industry.' (1978: 21)
[52]Kouniakis (1937: 84 cited Rondoyiannis 1982: 616 n. 4) gives a figure of 1,495 male emigrants from the whole of Lefkadha between 1900 and 1910, of which 210 came from Meganisi, thus confirming the Spartokhoriots' rough estimates.

have forgotten their families. A number of old men bitterly related that they never knew their father, and that as children they had been left destitute and orphans.[53] The majority of emigrants, however, regularly sent back remittances to support their families, for the real purpose of emigration was the accumulation of capital – capital that would provide dowries for daughters or an education for a son, but most importantly that would buy land on Meganisi on their return. Men embarked on emigration not to start a new life, but to improve their family's lot in their old one.

'Uncle' Andonis from Katomeri provides a good illustration of this situation. He was one of eleven siblings (eight brothers and three sisters) from a near landless family. One of his brothers emigrated to America, and a few years later, in 1910, Andonis (who was thirteen years old at the time) followed with his father, leaving the rest of the family behind in the village. Andonis stayed ten years in America before returning first to Greece, and eventually to Katomeri where, at the late age of forty-two, he finally married. In America he travelled widely and lived half a dozen to a room with fellow migrants, working variously as a shoeshine boy, a house painter, a factory piece-worker and even, despite his diminutive stature, as a professional wrestler. In 1980 he used to relate his adventures to the somewhat condescending amusement of the younger generation: how he first saw an aeroplane; how he first saw an Afro-American and asked how he had gained so dark a suntan. But the point is that between them Andonis and his father sent back a fortune to Meganisi, roughly US$8,000, with which his father was able to buy land.

Importantly, however, Andonis's father was able to buy land not only because he had made the money to do so, but because Lefkadha's absentee landlords were willing to sell it. In the 1920s Greece's economy was in the process of substantial reconstruction (Mouzelis 1978: 22–7), and prompted by the low returns from agriculture, a general fear of social unrest and the growing opportunities for the redeployment of wealth in the national and international economy, Lefkadha's notable families were moving on.[54] By the mid-1920s virtually the entirety of Lefkadha's landed elite had left, and by the 1930s all of Meganisi's land was in the hands of local inhabitants.[55] The disappearance of absentee landlords from Lefkadha did not, however, put an end to economic inequalities amongst the Meganisiots themselves – in fact it may well have aggravated them. It was rich peasants and local entrepreneurs who were in a position to take advantage of the availability of land, while landlessness for a large section of the community, and a local system of credit, loans, sharecropping and indebtedness, persisted. What overturned this situation was a rather more complex matter.

In some cases I was told that rich families had, like Lefkadha's 'aristocrats',[56]

[53] The term *'orfanos'* (orphan) is commonly used in Greece to refer to anyone who has lost his or her father, regardless of whether the mother is still alive.

[54] Major shifts in the structure of Greece's economy followed in the wake of the disastrous Asia Minor defeat, the loss and destruction of Smyrna, and the influx of nearly 1.6 million refugees into Greece. See Mouzelis (1978: 22–7).

[55] I again express my gratitude to Lefkadha's public notary, Dhimos Malakasis, who consulted his ledgers on my behalf. The departure of Lefkadha's elite is also briefly discussed by Rondoyiannis (1982: 618).

[56] Or so the Meganisiots called them. Strictly speaking they were a landed gentry. See Bennett (1988: 230) for a similar usage.

sold out and gone to Athens. More commonly, when I enquired about the fate of wealthy families of the past I heard tangled tales of an excess of daughters (and hence of dowries) or simply of an excess of children, or in some cases of no children at all, or of wastrel sons who 'ate' their fathers' fortunes and bequeathed to their children only a fraction of what they had themselves inherited. In short, I got life-histories about the decline and fall of individual families, of which the Malamas family (mentioned above) was but one. As the Meganisiot saying goes, 'A man may last a hundred years, but not his wealth.' But while such stories may explain why the so-and-sos who were once rich are no longer so (and while they again suggest that differences of wealth and land-ownership on Meganisi were not tantamount to differences of class), they do not explain the end of the system of inequality itself. Taken as a whole, however, these individual life-histories do reflect a quite profound structural change in the economy of the island in the postwar years, for those who were once wealthy on Meganisi were wealthy because of the land they possessed and/or because they owned the means of production (olive and flour mills) or the means of distribution (village shops with credit facilities, caiques for transport) of an essentially agricultural economy. By the late 1970s land was worth little – at least in terms of what it produced[57] – and, as I have suggested, the Meganisiots were no longer really agriculturalists. It is here that the president's 'natural law' comes into play. At the time of my fieldwork Spartokhori's single largest landowner, a man in his early sixties, possessed 524 *stremmata* of land, of which all but eight *stremmata* he had inherited from his father, in his time one of Spartokhori's richest men. Owing to his father's wealth he had received an education and become a primary schoolmaster, indeed *the* village schoolmaster, a position of considerable status in the 1950s. As an educated man he could not lower himself to engage in manual labour, and up to the late 1950s his land was worked by other villagers for payment either in cash or in kind. He had enjoyed both the power of a local magnate and the respect owed to a man of learning. By the 1970s his fortunes had been reversed. He was no longer considered a wealthy man, and certainly he was not to be numbered amongst Spartokhori's prosperous, for even supposing that he could have found anyone willing to work for him, a day's labour picking olives was reckoned at 1,000 drachmes (plus food), whereas his schoolmaster's salary was only about 20,000 drachmes a month. The high price of labour (indeed the unavailability of labour) and the low price received for oil simply meant that it was not economic for him to work his land (Bennett 1988). Thus his olive trees remained uncultivated, his land unproductive, and his income little more than his schoolmaster's salary. (Moreover, by the 1970s the position of village schoolmaster no longer commanded much respect, even from the illiterate.) In 1978 he received a promotion to headmaster at a primary school on the mainland and did not return during my stay.

Numerous parallel examples could be recounted. Those whose wealth had been based on the workings of an agricultural economy – on the ownership of land, trees, flocks, or an olive-oil mill or a flour mill – had been historically over-taken, the form of their investment rendered obsolete. However much land they

[57]Meganisiots were nevertheless reluctant to sell land, and by the late 1970s many were beginning to discern its potential value if tourisism developed, which by 1994 it had (see Epilogue).

owned, families could cultivate only that for which their own labour sufficed, and agricultural production was thus limited to home consumption. What changed Meganisi's economy fundamentally from a peasant economy to a cash economy in which the rich became poor, and the poor became rich, might be seen simply as part of Greece's postwar modernization, for from the 1950s onwards Greece as a whole experienced profound economic and demographic changes that resulted in the decline of its peasant class (Bennett 1988: 217; Mouzelis 1978: 118–25), and on Meganisi, as in many other areas of Greece, the changes took two distinct, but connected, forms. One (common to rural Greece as a whole) was renewed international emigration;[58] the other (common to many of Greece's island and coastal communities) amounted to the development and transformation of what I have referred to as the last aspect of Meganisi's traditional economy, namely, seafaring.[59]

[58] See Vgenopoulos for Greek postwar migration. Between 1949 and 1969 the number of permanent emigrants was 1,179,076, and of temporary emigrants, 966,744, although the figures are not completely reliable (1985: 42-8).

[59] It could be argued that Greece's modernization in the 1950s amounted to no more than a move away from a peasant economy and the development of a consumer economy fuelled by overseas remittances and the growth of the Greek shipping industry (most of which lay outside Greek state control). Investment in industry and manufacturing remained low. For Mouzelis, who notes the parallel effects of emigration and shipping (1978: 120), it was thus more a case of underdevelopment than of modernization.

3
The Advent of Wealth

Ask anyone in Lefkadha in 1980 about the island of Meganisi, and the first thing they were likely to have said to you was that the Meganisiots were a *plousios laos* and a *naftikos laos*, a 'wealthy people' and a 'seafaring people'. The two attributes were closely connected, and by popular repute Lefkadha's banks overflowed with the money the Meganisiots earned as sailors. Due allowance must be made for exaggeration, but it remains true that by the standards of most Greek rural communities at the time the Spartokhoriots were wealthy, and the immediate source of their wealth lay in their employment *sta karavia*, 'on the ships'. Even the Meganisiots were pleased to admit their collective prosperity, though in a society committed to secrecy, the extent of anyone's personal fortune remained purposefully vague.

The past, as we have seen, was a different matter and the consensus of memory was insistent on the point. *Ftohia* (poverty), *dhistihia* (misery), *halia* (wretchedness) were words that littered recollection of a time when 'we lived like animals, not like men'. The popular dating for Meganisi's change of fortune was the war. For most Meganisiots history divided at this point: there was 'before the war' and 'after the war'; 'in the old days' and 'nowadays'; 'poverty' and 'wealth'. And it divided at this point because in the immediate postwar years two things began to happen for the Meganisiots: their employment 'on the ships', and renewed overseas emigration – this time not only to America, but also to Canada, Australia and South Africa. As my old friend and protector Mikhalis put it, 'Before the war where could we go? There were no ships. There was no Australia or Canada or Africa.'[1] And though, as Mikhalis emphasized, the war had been a terrible thing since so many of 'the boys' had been killed, nevertheless he considered it the work of God who looked down on Meganisi, saw its misery and suffering, and brought the war to change all that. Mikhalis's theology may have been a little idiosyncratic, but his view serves to underscore events that by many were perceived as near-miraculous.

Those who were younger and who had participated in the making of the change (rather than simply observing it and benefiting from its wonder) were inclined to refine the dating. Though employment on the ships commenced in the

---

[1] No Meganisiots had emigrated to Germany, the largest recipient of Greek postwar migration (Vgenopoulos 1985: 43), though many Lefkadhiots had. The Meganisiots disarming explanation was that there had been no need to emigrate to Germany since they had emigrated to Australia, Canada and the United States.

immediate postwar years, it was not until well into the 1960s that its real economic benefits began to be felt. Similarly, though postwar emigration to Australia, Canada, South Africa and the United States commenced in the 1950s, it was not until the late 1960s that the venture began to yield domestic returns. In concert, however, work on the ships and overseas emigration radically changed life on Meganisi. And, like migration, the Meganisiots' employment on the ships had its historical antecedents.

Although an island, Lefkadha was not noted for its maritime tradition. Its villagers were a landed peasantry distrustful of the sea. Only the inhabitants of the coastal villages of eastern and southern Lefkadha could be counted as exceptions, and, of course, the inhabitants of Meganisi, Lefkadha's tiny island dependency, for one could hardly survive on Meganisi without some familiarity with and knowledge of the sea.[2] On Meganisi fishing used to be the seasonal alternative to agriculture and herding. Before the war a degree of village specialization obtained: the Katomeriots (and Vathiots) had the greater reputation as fishermen; the Spartokhoriots were mostly agriculturalists. To an extent this was still so in 1980, for in Spartokhori there were only half a dozen boats whose crews could be deemed to fish commercially (that is to say, who attempted to derive some substantial part of their annual income from fishing), while in Katomeri those who still classified themselves as *psarades*, fishermen, operated over forty boats during the height of the season.[3] There is, however, a difficulty in giving precise figures either for commercial boats or for commercial fishermen, for fishing was always pursued in conjunction with some other activity, whether that activity was confined to the village (olive cultivation, shop-keeping) or took place outside it (like employment on the ships). The distinction between a fisherman and a villager who happened to own a boat and go fishing was a fine one. Even in Spartokhori there were more than forty small boats moored in the bay, and the Katomeriots possessed close to a hundred. When fish were plentiful everyone fished; when they were not, fishing was a pleasant and occasionally profitable way to pass the time of day. Catches were sold if they were sufficiently large; if not, the fishing was *mono yia fayito*, 'just for food', food that nevertheless made a welcome contribution to the household economy. Historically this had always been the case. Fishing had been both a part-time and seasonal occupation for a people who did what they could to get by. If by 1980 fishing, like agriculture, appeared to have become part of a residual economy, this was not so much because the nature of fishing had undergone a substantive change, but because the entire peasant economy of which it had once formed a part had become subordinated to wage (or salaried) labour. Within a historical perspective, however, the importance of fishing lies in the fact that it helped prepare the Meganisiots for the transition from that peasant economy to the particular form of wage labour on which their wealth in the postwar years was based, for

---

[2] See Rondoyiannis (1982: 502-15) for Lefkadha's shipping industry for 1841-64. There were only seven sizeable boats (owned by merchants from Lefkadha town), and most of the captains of the larger boats were not Lefkadhiots. But see Kendrick, who claims that 'a major part' of Lefkadha's population were 'mariners' (1822: 65), and Bory de Saint-Vincent who says of the Lefkadhiots that 'ils ont été de tout tems [*sic*] fort adonnés á la marine' (1823: 353).

[3] Fishing was mostly for *palamidhia* (bonito), a shoal fish that appears irregularly between May and August.

Plate 3.1 Fishing

whether from Spartokhori, Katomeri or Vathi, almost every older man had at some stage 'worked with the nets' on his own or someone else's boat. The Meganisiots knew the sea.

But the Meganisiots' involvement in maritime pursuits had not been limited to fishing. During the nineteenth century and up to the Second World War wooden-hulled caiques provided the major form of transport between the Ionian islands and along the mainland coast. In Lefkadha the Meganisiots owned or operated the greater share of these caiques. From all three villages – Spartokhori, Katomeri, Vathi – caiques plied between Lefkadha and the other Ionian islands, even travelling as far afield as Italy to the west and, of course, the Piraeus and Athens to the east. They provided a local passenger service. They carried Lefkadha's major exports: salt and wine. They brought its major imports: grain and manu-factured articles. And Meganisi's caique-owners also acted as merchants in their own right, selling oil, salt, wine and cheese as well as shoes, clothes and utensils along the coastal villages of the mainland and between the islands.[4]

The imposing ruins of quite a large house on the bay below Spartokhori was testimony to the importance of this prewar commerce and the Meganisiots' role in it. The house was a solitary building and, standing apart from the compact village on the cliffs above, something of an oddity. Its owner, an old widow, had long since moved into the village of Spartokhori, but the house had been built for her early in the century by her father, a prosperous merchant in Lefkadha town, as dowry, in itself a peculiarity since both on Meganisi and in Lefkadha residence was traditionally virilocal, and dowries generally modest. But as a merchant her father had built this house on Meganisi in order to secure the services of a Meganisiot son-in-law, that is to say, the services of a competent sailor who could transport his goods. As the old woman remarked to me, where else could he have found one? So she, as a bride of eighteen, had been despatched to Spartokhori as part of a commercial compact that married her father's business interests to the available means of transport. To judge by the remains of the house it was no cheap compact. Such a combination of mercantile and maritime interests appears to have been common before the war. Richer peasants who owned a mill or a shop often also owned a caique. Again it must be stressed that people pursued several occupations. Caique operations were seasonal, and fair-weather sailing preferred. Besides, in winter there were the terraces to be dug and the olives to be gathered. A man could be both sailor and agriculturalist. Where there was a degree of specialization it often occurred within a family enterprise. One or two brothers would operate a caique with the assistance of a crew of relatives and friends, while other brothers and their father would stay at home with the women to work the family's land.

These caiques, of varying size but up to seventy or even a hundred tons, originally powered by sail but later by engine, continued to operate from Meganisi up to the 1950s. According to local estimate there were between thirty and forty caiques of reasonable size based in Meganisi before the war. The 1950s, however, spelt the end of the island's caique operations. The development of

---

[4] Palmos (1992: 70) relates that the small boats or ships that used to be moored in Meganisi's harbours were of three types: 1) vessels of. 6–12 tonnes used for carrying stone; 2) vessels of 13–38 tonnes used by Meganisiots for trading their produce (potatoes, onions, wheat, oil, etc); 3) vessels of 39–64 tonnes that were chartered by non-Meganisiots to carry merchandise.

Greece's road system meant that increasingly short-distance transport of goods and people began to be effected by land rather than by sea, while at the same time the rapid growth of Greece's merchant marine meant that steel-hulled vessels operating from Piraeus and Patras replaced small wooden-hulled caiques for longer-distance transport. Concomitant with these changes was the general demise of local trade networks and their replacement by national (and international) commercial links. Increasingly goods and people moved between Athens and Greece's rural areas, not between those areas themselves.[5] In this context Meganisi's 'captains' sold their caiques, but in many cases only to return to sea, for the same developments that spelt the end of Meganisi's caique operations also opened up a new and lucrative form of employment for which the Meganisiots were ideally suited. Greece's postwar shipping boom, the development of its international mercantile fleet, meant that there were jobs for those prepared to risk a life at sea. It would, of course, be unwise to equate fishing in coastal waters and trading around the Ionian islands with serving aboard cargo-ships and oil-tankers sailing to Europe, Japan, South America and the Middle East; but at least as islanders and seafarers the Meganisiots were prepared for the opportunities that Greece's shipping industry provided.

By the time of my fieldwork there were few able-bodied men on Meganisi under sixty years of age who had not spent at least some years working on the ships. It did not follow, however, that everyone who had been to sea had prospered. The Meganisiots' transition to working on the ships was not over-night: nor, for many, was it permanent. In the early years, in the 1950s, it was still necessary to have *meson* (influence) to secure work even as a deckhand, and wages were not high, although (an important fact) they were at least *wages*. Many Meganisiot men went to sea for only a few years in order to save money for a specific purpose: the education of a son, the marriage of a daughter, or to buy land on Meganisi. Much like the temporary emigration of the early 1900s, a period of work aboard ship was something that presented itself to Meganisiot men when they faced some particular crisis or had some pressing need. Once that need had been met, such sailors reverted to a life of agriculture.

Meganisi's male population – or at least its older male population – did not, therefore, divide up neatly into sailors and non-sailors (farmers, fishermen, store-keepers etc). A rough gauge of the extent of employment on the ships is provided by Figure 3.1, which shows the occupations of the village's permanent male residents as they were in 1980. The light gray areas represent by age groups those Spartokhoriots who were actively employed as seamen; dark gray areas represent by age group retired sailors who had served sufficiently long in the merchant marine to be officially classified as *naftiki* (seamen) and to be in receipt of pensions from the merchant seamen's contributory pension fund, the Naftiko Apomahistiko Tamio (Sailors' Retirement Fund) always referred to by the acronym 'NAT'.[6] The number of men officially classified as retired seamen

---

[5] It is perhaps worth noting that according to Ansted (1863: 134) an Austrian Lloyds steamer left Corfu every Saturday night and arrived in Lefkadha town on Sunday morning. However, in 1980 there was no sea connection between Corfu and Lefkadha, or, for that matter, between Lefkadha and any of the other Ionian islands. All inter-island connections involved back-tracking by road to Patras or Preveza, and then sailing out.

[6] Figures for the number of pensioners were provided by the Meganisiot branch secretary of NAT.

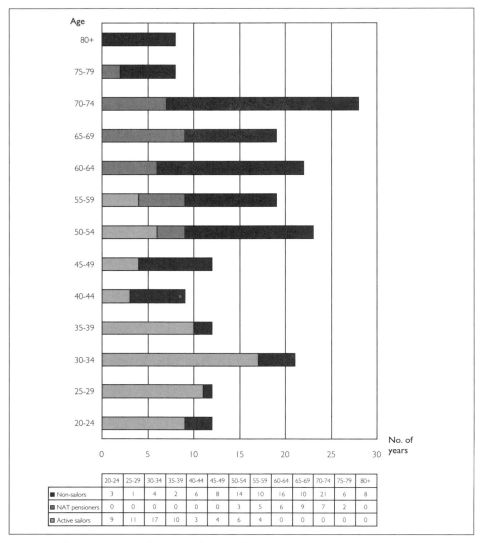

	20-24	25-29	30-34	35-39	40-44	45-49	50-54	55-59	60-64	65-69	70-74	75-79	80+
■ Non-sailors	3	1	4	2	6	8	14	10	16	10	21	6	8
▨ NAT pensioners	0	0	0	0	0	0	3	5	6	9	7	2	0
▨ Active sailors	9	11	17	10	3	4	6	4	0	0	0	0	0

Figure 3.1 Maritime employment of Spartokhoriot male core population, 1980

nevertheless underrepresents the older generation's maritime employment, for a minimum of 15 years' service was required for entitlement to a NAT pension. Thus although the count of those receiving a pension provides a ready index of ex-sailors, it ignores those who had served only a few years aboard ship, and even some who had served ten or more years before deciding that loss of their pension rights was preferable to a continued life at sea. But almost all the older Spartokhoriot men resident in the village (regardless of whether or not they were classified as ex-sailors in terms of their pension rights) were also engaged in olive cultivation, whose economic importance to them was more or less inversely proportional to their age; that is, the older they were and the fewer years they had served at sea, the smaller their NAT pensions and the greater the role that agriculture continued to play in their lives. Finally, it should be noted that some of Spartokhori's ex-sailors in the oldest age groups (65 years and above) derived their pension entitlement not from having worked on the ships, but from having operated caiques – if, that is, they had had the foresight to contribute to NAT.[7]

In short, the older generation was a transitional one for whom agriculture had been interspersed with periods at sea, and for whom agriculture had become the renewed occupation of their retirement. But most of Meganisi's younger men had become fully professional sailors, and it was they who were profiting from the high wages being paid to Greek crew by the late 1970s (as were a number of older men in their fifties who had been young enough when they committed themselves to a maritime career to rise through the ranks by training and experience). The bulk of this last category, however, does not appear in Figure 3.1, since, for reasons to be discussed, they were no longer *permanent* village residents.

In spite of its historically uneven receipt amongst individuals, the influx of wealth into the community as a result of employment on the ships was, in comparative terms, vast. By 1980 the lowest paid of Meganisi's seamen, those still employed as deckhands, earned 30,000 drachmes a month while at sea (or approximately £330). Deckhands, however, were in the minority. Most of Meganisi's younger seamen had become ship's officers or specialists of one sort or another (bosuns, cooks, electricians, mechanics), while a number of them held the rank of first or second captain. Bosuns and cooks earned (with overtime) upwards of 50,000 drachmes a month, and first mechanics and captains could earn 100,000–150,000 drachmes a month. At an exchange rate of roughly 90 drachmes to £1 in 1980, this gave the latter category a monthly salary of £1,100–600. Moreover, for those sailors whose homes were permanently in the village, salaries came on top of what were the still functioning remnants of a subsistence economy. Houses and property on the island were inherited, and sailors were thus free of the encumbrances of rent and mortgages; and in the 1970s and early 1980s there were no rates or service charges to be paid. Moreover, as a result of their own occasional labour and that of their wives, but most frequently as a result of the activities of the older generation, they were supplied with many of their daily needs without financial outlay: vegetables, milk, cheese, eggs, fish and, most importantly, oil.

The high wages paid to sailors over and above most of their subsistence requirements substantiated opinion in Lefkadha that the Meganisiots were a *plousios laos*, a 'rich people'. Indeed, those sailors who were frank enough to discuss the matter with me revealed that they did maintain impressively high bank accounts.[8] And even if not all Meganisiots, and certainly not most of the older Meganisiots, were individually well off, an awareness of the island's general prosperity informed the opinions even of those who had not themselves directly

[7] Self-employed maritime workers could contribute on a voluntary basis to NAT.
[8] Sailors left their savings in bank accounts partly because forms of investment were limited and bank interest rates were high, up to 16 per cent. The major reason for retaining such nest-eggs, however, was simply the inadequacy of social services. In effect, savings functioned as personal insurance funds.

benefited from maritime employment, for they saw their children and their grandchildren earning sums that in their youth would have seemed fantastical, and they knew them to be enjoying comforts, amenities and prospects that in their day would have been, if not unimaginable, certainly only to be imagined. Nevertheless, by the late 1970s relative disparities of wealth on Meganisi were acute. The overall standard of living had risen greatly (as it had everywhere in Greece in the decades following the war). No one was threatened by starvation or suffered real physical deprivation. But the gap between rich and poor was actually widening, if only because employment on the ships, which had brought the wealth, was in turn creating further opportunities that not everyone was able equally to exploit. Meanwhile the earnings of those still engaged in fishing or agriculture seemed in comparison with the sailors' wages to be derisory.

In this context the president's observation that 'the rich had become poor and the poor had become rich' deserves further elaboration. On the whole, those who were first to take advantage of employment on the ships, and who persevered with a life at sea rather than returning to agriculture once their extraordinary needs had been met, were the island's poorest, those whose family landholdings were small, and for whom the rejection of agriculture was therefore small loss. Barefoot boys who went to sea at twelve years of age in the 1950s had in some cases achieved a captain's ticket and were earning over 100,000 drachmes (£1,100) a month by 1980. There were even a dozen Meganisiot families who had become small-scale ship-owners in their own right, and who owned between them approximately twenty-five vessels, tramp steamers and small cargo vessels of about 1,000 tons (Rondoyiannis 1982: 622). The village of Spartokhori's two ship-owning families consisted of two sets of matrilateral first cousins. They owned seven ships between them. Their income was not something I was ever in a position to determine, but by anyone's standards they were wealthy men, and certainly they were Spartokhori's wealthiest men. They did not, however, come from rich families. The father of one set of brothers had been an caique captain in his day – but he had had an excessive appetite for drink, and by the brothers' own account they had grown up in extreme poverty. The father of the other set, a man in his eighties, was an illiterate shepherd who had settled and married in Spartokhori before the war. Conversely (much as in the case of the schoolmaster), those whose wealth had lain in the traditional form of land and trees, and who for that reason had chosen to continue with agriculture as their primary means of livelihood, had seen their positions eroded. By the 1970s the scions of those once wealthy families who owned 500 trees and over 100 stremmata (ten hectares) of land (and who in addition perhaps ran a store or owned a mill) had seen their families' investments rendered nearly worthless. Employment on the ships had acted as an economic equalizer.

By 1980, the situation was changing yet again. The majority of young Meganisiot men were still becoming sailors (though often with specific training and with qualifications as a ship's electrician or mechanic or officer), and, as the older generation readily observed, when they themselves died there would be no one at all working the olive trees. Agriculture had become a thing of the past, but so too, at least as an ambition, had work on the ships. Those middle-aged men who had already profited from their years at sea had grander plans for their children, and a considerable number of younger Meganisiots (both male and female) were receiving a tertiary education in Athens or elsewhere in law, medicine or economics on the proceeds of their fathers' employment in the merchant marine (though as we shall see, there were other paths to professional training and status). This, too, was recognized by the older Meganisiots who proudly summarized their progress: 'First we were *aghrotes* (agriculturalists); then we were *naftiki* (sailors); now all the *pedhia* (young people) *kseroune grammata* (know letters, that is, are educated).' But of course this was not quite true. What was emerging in 1980 from Meganisi's economic transformation was the beginnings of a new class structure whose differentiations were set to be greater, and certainly more complex, than ever before, since they related to the entry of some, but only some, of the younger generation into Greece's new urban bourgeoisie where matters of taste, manners, aspirations and, most importantly, access to those social (rather than strictly economic) means of reproducing and consolidating advantage would increasingly separate them from their compatriots. Education and the possibilities for advancement that it heralded were paving the way for new divisions among the Meganisiot population of a sort perhaps more difficult to overcome than those that had once existed within an agricultural economy, for what was being accumulated was now as much 'cultural capital' (Bourdieu 1984) as financial capital.

It should, nevertheless, be stressed that in 1980 a class analysis of Meganisiot society would have been premature. An egalitarian ethos was subscribed to by all, and in general the acute differences of individual wealth that existed within the community can be better understood in terms of a generational model, for those differences (and the very economic history of the island) were still compressed within the confines of individual families. It was the older generation of agriculturalists (and short-term seamen) who were 'the poor'; it was their sons and grandsons, the *naftiki*, who were 'the rich'. And then an older brother might be a ship's cook, while his younger brother was studying electronics. 'Older' and 'younger' generations did not, of course, neatly divide. But in broad terms a division of the community into an impoverished older generation and a highly paid younger generation represented the economic structure of Meganisi's population in 1980, a structure that (as we shall see later) substantially inverted the traditional relationships of power within the family.

Emigration

If work on the ships provided many Meganisots with an escape from poverty to a life of comparative riches, and opened the way for a growing number of the next generation to enter Greece's new middle-class, postwar emigration to Australia, Canada and South Africa (as well as renewed emigration to the United States) was the alternative route to social and economic advancement. Again, like work on the ships, it attracted the poorest Meganisiots, those who had the least to leave behind.

No records are available for postwar Meganisiot emigration, and precise quantification proved to be an impossibility. The number of individuals can only be guessed at, but amongst Meganisi's population in 1980 there was scarcely a person who did not have some close relative or relatives living overseas, and it was generally believed that from the 1950s onwards about ninety to a hundred families had left from each of the island's two main villages.[9] Indeed, unlike the emigration that had taken place in the early part of the century, postwar emigration was predominantly a family affair. Husband, wife and children departed together from Meganisi (though seldom with their aged parents); alternatively, single men would make the first step, waiting some years until they were financially secure before sending back to the village for the women to whom they were already engaged, or requesting that their family negotiate an arranged marriage and send them out a bride. But whatever the details, emigration was no longer solely male with women remaining as guardians of the house and land. Inasmuch as that task was necessary, it was relegated to the older generation left behind. For that generation, the economic benefits of their children's emigration was often considerable, and in 1980 my older friends in the village usually assumed that a letter from overseas meant a cheque (as I discovered through the continual enquiries made about the contents of my own mail). Of course the amounts remitted to the elderly varied greatly in accordance with their needs, the success of their overseas children and their children's generosity. Some aged couples I knew regularly received $1,500–2,000 (Australian, Canadian or American) a year; others were sent nothing. My old friend Mikhalis received 15,000 drachmes (approximately £160) a month from his children in Australia: 10,000 drachmes for himself and his wife, 5,000 drachmes for his youngest son, a bachelor who still lived at home and who was the only one of Mikhalis's children not to have emigrated. This supplemented an annual income from the sale of oil of approximately 150,000 drachmes (£1,600), but Mikhalis was always keen to stress that it was his overseas *pedhia* who supported him, for this demonstrated both his children's filial piety and the respect in which he, their father, was held. 'Children,' he would proclaim, 'are a man's wealth.' Under the circumstances it was difficult to know whether the statement was intended metaphorically or literally.

But money from remittances, important though it was for the older generation, was the lesser portion of the wealth that came to Meganisi as a result of emigration, for the new and renovated houses that interspersed Spartokhori's older or unmodified dwellings were built or modernized not only by sailors whose incomes allowed such luxury, but also by returned migrants. As in the earlier period, overseas migration was often undertaken for the benefits it would yield at home. Although many Meganisiots had settled permanently in South Africa, Canada and the United States, residence in these countries was still frequently seen as a temporary expedient embarked on only to improve a family's eventual

---

[9] It was possible to gain from the island's present inhabitants the number of their children and close relatives living overseas, but children born overseas were not usually distinguished from those born in Greece. Moreover, if someone said that he or she had five *pedhia* in Australia, that inclusive term might refer to overseas-born grandchildren as well as children. Both sets of village grandparents would also count the same grandchildren as their own, thus creating overlaps. Such complications could be sorted out for individual cases, but accurate quantification of the overall number of emigrants from Meganisi was virtually impossible. In any case, in some instances entire families had left for overseas, or the older generation had died since their childrens' emigration.

situation in Greece. South Africa was a particular case, for in the late 1970s fear of a 'black revolution' had prompted many Meganisiots who had emigrated there to return to Greece. Emigration to South Africa, however, was slight compared with emigration to Canada and America, and here the provisional nature of the venture was clear. The Meganisiots often remarked, 'America is a good place to work, but not to live,' and families would emigrate there for five or ten years specifically to 'economize', to accumulate sufficient overseas savings to enable them to enjoy a better life in Greece.

But although overseas emigration was often undertaken with a view to coming back to Greece, the aim of postwar migrants was no longer to buy land on Meganisi. For the majority of Meganisi's returned migrants overseas emigration was instead a stepping-stone from peasantry to membership of the urban bourgeoisie. Money that had been saved in the United States or Canada or South Africa was invested in setting up a small business in Athens. Alternatively families would spend sufficient time in the United States or Canada to enable their children to gain overseas tertiary qualifications which gave them an advantageous entry into the Athenian professional world. The standard pattern of movement was from the village to overseas, and from overseas to Athens. Importantly, however, ties with the village were seldom severed. Returned migrants constructed and renovated houses in the village regardless of whether or not they intended to live there permanently, partly because a new house was a tangible demonstration of success to the community in which their reputation continued to be of personal account, partly because they envisaged a pattern of life that included periodic village residence. In the end no clear distinction could be made between emigrants and village residents. For those who had invested their overseas savings in Athens, the village became their summer home, while for those who had seen their children enter the professions as a result of their overseas education, the village became their place of retirement (often supported by an overseas pension). A number of case histories may illustrate the complexities of these movements.

The Canadian chemist

In 1977, during the first year of my stay in Spartokhori, an elderly couple returned to the village with their two adult children, a son and a daughter. The family had been resident in Montreal for more than ten years. The father had been over fifty years of age when he emigrated to Canada where he had worked in a factory. He spoke little English (and no French). The two children, who had both been educated in Canada, were fluent English speakers, and the son, whom I shall call Labros, was a university graduate in chemistry.

The family stayed on Meganisi most of the summer of 1977, and reoccupied their village house which had been closed for a decade. The family had returned, however, only to accompany Labros who hoped to find employment in Athens as a chemist in a government laboratory or in the private sector (an ambition he subsequently achieved). His parents and his sister were then all to depart for Canada once more, where Labros's sister, who was married to a Greek-Canadian, intended to remain permanently. The parents' return to Canada, however, was again to be temporary, for the father had only *a few more years to work before he was entitled to a Canadian old-age pension as well as to a Canadian war-service pension. Once these pensions were secured, the parents intended to return to Spartokhori where they would live out the remainder of their old age. In short, a period of approximately fifteen years' overseas work undertaken in middle age meant for Labros's parents a secure retirement in the village of their origin, while for Labros it supplied entry into Athenian middle-class professional life. Only for his sister was it to result in permanent overseas settlement.*

It should be noted, however, that while the sort of temporary, or perhaps better transitional, migration described above was commonplace for Meganisiots during the 1970s and 1980s, it could not have been effected without the assistance of Meganisiots who had become permanent overseas residents, for some form of sponsorship was required by most host countries, and the sponsorship of one brother by another, of parents by children, or indeed of villagers by any number of kinds of relative, was standard practice. Permanent overseas residents constituted a sort of beach-head that allowed relatives who did not wish to emigrate permanently the opportunity to spend sufficient time in a foreign country to achieve their immediate ends. Not surprisingly, in some cases sponsorship connected postwar migration with the migration that had taken place in the early part of the century.

Babis's brother

Old Babis, a villager in his seventies, had an older brother who had emigrated to the United States in the 1920s. This brother eventually settled in Indiana where he became a house-painter. His business prospered, and over the years he had acted as sponsor (and sometimes employer) for a number of his relatives. Sotiris, for example, a villager in his late forties who at the time of my stay was earning his living as a fisherman and farmer, had spent fifteen years on and off in the United States before his marriage working for Babis's brother, who by Meganisiot reckoning was his 'uncle' (his patrilateral first cousin once removed). During this same period Babis's own two sons both emigrated to the United States, again sponsored by this same uncle. They, however, both settled permanently in the United States, and both married American women – one of Greek extraction, the other of German origin. Again, they had both initially worked for their uncle. In fact the Indiana house-painting business and its family connections with Spartokhori were still operating in 1977, for shortly after my arrival in Spartokhori a young man in his late twenties returned after nearly five years in the United States. He was an affinal relative of Babis (Babis's wife's sister's husband's brother's son), and he too had been working in Indiana as a house painter.

Neither Sotiris's overseas ventures, nor that of the above-mentioned young man, had been particularly successful, which, of course, is why they both resettled in the village rather than making the move to Athens. Some few men, however, had deliberately decided to continue with a village-based life, and, leaving their wives and children in Spartokhori, temporarily migrated overseas to improve their situation within the village or to meet some immediate domestic demand.

Their pattern of migration thus closely reduplicated what had taken place in the early years of the century. Two complex examples will illustrate this variation.

Christos and his brothers-in-law

Christos was in his late forties when I was first in the village. Technically he was a sailor and stood in due course to receive an NAT pension. In fact the extent of his seafaring was to have owned and operated a caique in the 1960s that ferried villagers between Meganisi and Lefkadha. This caique had been sold some ten years before my arrival and Christos was farming land he owned jointly with his aged father who (with his second wife) lived in the same household as Christos and his wife. In 1979 Christos purchased a new caique in partnership with his wife's brother, the owner of one of Spartokhori's coffee-shops. The caique was equipped for fishing, an occupation into which the two brothers-in-law intended to diversify, but it could also be used for general haulage, thus allowing Christos to increase his eventual NAT pension. Significantly, however, the purchase of the new caique had followed Christos's return to Spartokhori after nearly six years of periodic absences in the United States where he had worked as a barman, since Christos had a son who was studying hotel management (an MA in Business Administration) at an American state college. Christos had in fact emigrated to the United States a year before his son's departure in order to qualify as a tax-payer to reduce the cost of his son's education. He then continued to work there to support his son, who planned to return to Greece when his studies were completed. And Christos himself had been sponsored (and employed) by a relative who was a permanent resident in the United States, namely his wife's other brother, the brother of the coffee-shop proprietor with whom he had purchased his new caique. The whole venture, which drew on the resources of several family members, was thus envisaged from the start as a temporary measure both to take advantage of the American educational system and, in the process, to accumulate some capital for investment within the village. Since this was the case, Christos had left both his wife and his unmarried daughter at home in Spartokhori under the protection of his father, with whom he shared his house.

The second example concerns a set of four brothers whose movements virtually cover the range of Meganisiot migratory practices in the 1970s.

The Four Brothers

The four brothers were aged between forty and fifty years at the time of my fieldwork. All four had emigrated to Canada in the 1960s, leaving their elderly parents in the village. In Canada they found highly paid work as tradesmen on pipeline and dam constructions in the far north. One of them subsequently married in Canada, opened a restaurant, and settled permanently overseas. The other three were all in various ways 'semi-migrants'.

The oldest, who was already married to a Spartokhoriot woman when he emigrated, returned with his wife to Greece in 1977 after nearly fifteen years in Canada where their two children had been born. He was a frequent visitor to the village, but had opened a carpentry business in Athens where he was normally resident (and where he had family connections, since his wife's brother, the son of an old caique captain, had become a successful Athenian doctor). Again, he had returned to Greece because he wanted his children to grow up Greek, and his story was the standard one: a relatively lengthy, but still temporary, period of overseas migration that allowed him, the son of a poor agriculturalist, to become an independent tradesman and small businessman in Athens, while as Canadian citizens his children had the option of overseas education (and residence) should that prove advantageous.

The youngest brother, Yerasimos, was an unusual case. At forty years of age he was still unmarried, and in 1979 he too returned to Greece, but to Spartokhori rather than to Athens. This he did partly to care for his aged parents, but also because he entertained the romantic notion of leading a simple and carefree life as an agricultural peasant (though whether this notion would prove durable was doubted by many, not least by his brothers). In short, Yerasimos belonged to a small class of men who self-consciously opted to carry on with what they perceived to be a traditional (and superior) life-style, as Yerasimos put it, that of 'the Greeks'. Indeed, Yerasimos's decision amounted to a rejection of the West (as he had experienced it in Canada) and of the modern (as he saw it in Athens). Even his decision to look after his parents in their old age (however noble) was part of a deliberate embracing of tradition, for ideally in Spartokhori it had always fallen on the youngest son to fulfil that role, although it was a role that few felt obliged to take up.

The remaining brother was perhaps the most interesting case, for his pattern of migration was unique. On his return from Canada he married a young woman from Lefkadha, and she and their three small children lived in a large and newly constructed village house in Spartokhori. For roughly six months of the year he too lived in the village, tending his olives and working his land; for the other six months he returned to the north of Canada where he was employed as a contract tradesman on pipeline construction. The high wages he received during this period allowed his annual retirement back to the village and his family. He was in effect a seasonal migrant. But though this pattern of overseas work made his an exceptional case, in terms of periods of residence in and absence from the village his life differed little from that of Spartokhori's sailors.

Case histories such as the above could be multiplied to cover the migratory movements of members of almost every Spartokhoriot family. The particular details varied, and there were notable successes and notable failures, but a common pattern emerges whose general features and whose overall effects ran parallel to the social and demographic changes caused by the Meganisiots' employment in shipping. In terms of individual life-histories or the histories of particular families, these parallels were often close indeed, for both presented themselves as alternative routes to essentially the same ends: immediate economic advancement, escape from the life of an agricultural peasant, and the possibility for the next generation of entry into the urban and professional world whose advantages in Greece have always been extolled.

Education and migration

For most semi-migrants the return to Greece was necessarily a return to Athens rather than to the village, since Spartokhori offered little scope for the productive investment of their overseas savings. More importantly, for the overseas-educated youth it was only in Athens that they could find employment to match their training and skills. This did not preclude village residence for some part of each year, or the building or renovation of village houses, but in the end the route to social and economic advancement led always to the capital. Only the oldest generation of returned migrants resettled permanently in the village, and for the educated *pedhia* the village was becoming their holiday home.

In the end, employment on the ships led in the same direction, but it must be stressed that in 1980 it was also employment on the ships that was arresting the sort of wholesale rural depopulation common to many other areas of rural Greece. Unlike the bulk of Greece's non-agricultural workforce, sailors were not constrained by their employment to live in the city, for in most cases negotiations for a voyage could be made by a telephone call, or by spending a few days in Piraeus. The types of ships on which the Meganisiots worked and the terms of their employment varied considerably. Some men were crew on domestic shipping lines or on ferries between Greece, Italy and other Mediterranean ports. Others sailed on supertankers between Europe, the Middle East, China, Japan and South America. The majority worked on cargo-ships in European waters or on the transatlantic run. Those who held high rank were sometimes on permanent contract and paid a retainer when not at sea, but most sailors arranged their contracts on an *ad hoc* basis. Some would be at sea at regular intervals for a few weeks at a time. For others a single voyage might keep them at sea for over a year. But whatever the arrangement there was seldom any need for Meganisiot sailors to shift their normal place of residence to Athens. Moreover, they were largely free to determine the periods they would spend at sea and the periods they would spend resting in the village. Again, the length of such rest periods varied greatly according to the terms of employment and individual financial needs, but it was not uncommon for Meganisi's sailors to work six months on and six months off, or even to spend an entire year in the village after a particularly lengthy voyage. Earnings aboard ship were sufficiently high to allow these periods of recuperation, but it should be noted that during such intervals most sailors also reverted to village-based employments: helping tend the olive trees that were the older generation's continual concern, and making up the crews on fishing boats. To this extent employment on the ships was slowing the island's depopulation. Meganisi remained a viable base from which sailors could operate, and most sailors professed a preference for a village-based existence. They were, however, more ambitious for their children, and few sailors positively encouraged their sons to follow them to sea. Increasingly they also recognized that daughters, too, were not content to become village housewives. Education was seen (as it has been seen throughout Greece) as the answer, but though Spartokhori, Katomeri and Vathi each had a village primary school, there were no facilities on the island for secondary schooling, mandatory by 1980 for both boys and girls. This was a lack which became a major political issue for the Meganisiots.[10]

There were, of course, secondary schools on Lefkadha, and some students from Meganisi attended them, but local schools were generally believed to be inferior, and it was held that only in Athens were proper educational facilities to be found. This prejudice (if prejudice it was) coincided with practical difficulties. It was impossible to commute daily by caique to Lefkadha, and unless one had willing relatives there with whom children could board, schooling in Lefkadha was almost as difficult to arrange as schooling in Athens. Furthermore, unless economic circumstances forced the issue (as they did for those few younger Meganisiot couples still basically reliant on agriculture or fishing), most Meganisiots were notably unwilling to see their children board even with relatives. This, it should be noted, applied as much to tertiary students as it did to children of secondary-school age, and as much to males (who were considered quite incapable of looking after themselves) as it did to females (who were thought to require strict parental supervision and protection). The upshot was that the desire to educate children usually resulted in a wholesale family relocation to Athens.

It was, then, education rather than employment that forced a form of urban migration on Meganisiot sailors and their families. But it was a quite particular form. On the one hand it tended to be seasonal, for since employment did not tie the sailors to Athens, they and their families were free to return to the island for their children's summer holidays. On the other hand, migration also tended to be cyclical, for most Meganisiot sailors protested that they had no intrinsic desire to live in Athens, and complained continually of conditions there (cf. Allen 1980 & 1986). Most stated firmly that as soon as their children's educational requirements had been met, they would return to the island, and in the late 1970s and early 1980s it seemed that many were remaining true to their words. Urban migration appeared to be part of the domestic cycle: young families stayed in the village where their children attended primary school; when children reached

---

[10]The establishment of a secondary school on Meganisi was one of the prime objectives of *O Mendis*, the island's Athenian-based association. The degree of feeling aroused by the issue can be judged from the following letter published in the Athenian newspaper *Vradhini*, and reproduced in the island association's monthly paper, *Meganisiotiki Andilali* (Meganisiot Echoes):

> In the Ionian Sea, near Lefkadha and opposite Onassis's Skorpios, exists one of the most beautiful islands in Greece, Meganisi, with a population of 3,000 inhabitants, which is gradually becoming deserted. The chief reason for its depopulation is the lack of a high school.
>
> Each year, the ten-year-olds who have finished primary school there, together with their families, take the road of departure and arrive in the suburbs of Piraeus and Athens, carrying with them this great perplexity: why, on the opposite shores of Lefkadha and Akarnania, does every village have its own high-school ... while our own island, which is cut off because the sea surrounds it, a sea which in winter grows wild, has no high-school?
>
> Applications and entreaties have been many – even a question in parliament – for the foundation of a high school, but the relevant educational authorities reply that we must collect a hundred pupils.
>
> If this is so, then why do high-schools operate with less pupils than their teachers' fingers ... Certainly those high-schools have been created out of necessity. Yes, but the same necessity, and to a greater degree, exists also on Meganisi. For that reason, we beseech the Minister for Education that when next year he establishes new high-schools, he should not forget MEGANISI, Lefkadha. (*Meganisiotiki Andilali*, Year 4, no. 17, March 1980; my translation)

secondary-school age the family relocated to Athens; once educational ambitions had been fulfilled, parents retired back to the village.

In 1980 it was difficult to predict how long this pattern would persist. The Meganisiots fondly believed that the establishment of a secondary school on the island would immediately halt the island's gradual depopulation, for some families were not returning (and in any case Meganisi's villages were sadly depleted in winter). But local patriotism notwithstanding, there was little doubt that for many families, and especially for those who were well off, Athens held its own attractions. Moreover, unlike their parents, the younger generation who had gained an education on the proceeds of their fathers' work aboard ship or their families' overseas migration were not going to have the option of staying in the village. A pattern of migration that appeared at the time as part of the domestic cycle was set to become the beginnings of a permanent population shift.

The constitution of a community

In 1980, however, the question of 'who was a villager', or perhaps 'when was a villager', seemed curiously problematic. Admittedly, the dispersal over time of a population (and its descendants) through various forms of movement and migration is a common enough process around the world, and increasingly so, and it would be absurd to attempt to define a community in Greece (or anywhere else) by tracing all those people who had at some time lived in some particular place. Let us allow as a practical limit that the village community consisted of no more than those people who at the time of my stay made up its population, and consign the claims of absent friends and kith and kin to the realms of the merely potential (for no doubt all the while I was in Spartokhori there were people in Melbourne or Durban or Toronto whose hearts were still in Spartokhori, and others who were contemplating their return there). The point remains that even from a rigorously village-based perspective, it was impossible without committing a substantial ethnographic violence to exclude from Spartokhori's community in 1980 those whose lives had not been, or were not, or would not be confined to the village on the grounds that they were no longer true villagers. In Spartokhori the authentic villager was as likely to have been someone who had lived in Sydney, or who was living on and off in Athens, or was about to live in Johannesburg, as to be someone who had never left Meganisi's shores. Whether counted or discounted for the purposes of some particular demographic or statistical representation, the recurrent presence in the village of urban-dwellers and overseas migrants, and the recurrent absences of those whom I had at first taken to be simply villagers, was part of Spartokhori's reality. The village stood at the centre of a far-flung world, and the Spartokhoriots continually moved between that centre and the extremities they had colonized, for as Hart perceptively comments, 'One of the ironies of the current world scene in Greece is that the more remote the village, the more severe the struggle for a livelihood, the more likely it is to have been, in the course of at least the last century (and probably since the early nineteenth century), implicated in cosmopolitan trajectories of upward mobility' (1991: 70).

But the question of who was a villager, for all its complexity – indeed, precisely because of its complexity – was not something that I thought could be simply abandoned. It still seemed an obvious preliminary task to establish certain basic facts about Spartokhori's population: its number, age, sex and marital status, its distribution amongst households, employment and so forth. In short, it seemed necessary to define what constituted the object of my study: who the people *were* about whose social structure and moral values I would be writing. But because this could not be done in any way that would yield simple, straightforward results (the sort of paragraph of no particular consequence, but of unquestionable authority, that starts, 'Spartokhori is a small agricultural village of 561 inhabitants, situated ...'), I also began to realize that instead of being a preliminary question, the empirical definition of the community was a substantive one, and that instead of being capable of answer in precise quantitative terms, it was a question that hinged on a complex of social definitions and historical outcomes. In short, the attempt at mensuration led inevitably to matters of classification (Ardener 1989b), and to a properly anthropological undertaking and not merely the prelude to one. The attempt to determine the size of the village, the number of its inhabitants, their distribution amongst households, etc turned into an investigation of what it was that could be understood as a village, a villager or a village community in Greece in 1980. The first part of that investigation, couched in quantitative terms that will require continual qualification, is set out in the remainder of this chapter; but directly or indirectly, and for the most part descriptively, it will be the recurrent concern of this book.

Population

According to official statistics the population of Meganisi and its villages has been in decline since 1951. At that date, the census recorded the village of Spartokhori with a population of 887. In 1961 Spartokhori's population was still 882. By 1971, however, it had dropped to 682. The census of 1981, conducted shortly after my departure, recorded a population of 561 (see Table 2.2). Like all census figures, however, those of the Greek Bureau of Statistics are concerned only with who was where on a particular night, in the last case, the night of 5 April 1981. Inevitably the measure of the size of a community such as Spartokhori's is not so simple.

In 1979 I approached the village president, the *proedhros* of Spartokhori, in the hope that an accurate count of the community could be determined from the *dhimotoloyio*, the village registry, in which all births, deaths and marriages are supposed to be recorded. The president was unwilling to give me free access to these records, but obligingly consented to work through them himself and to answer any questions I might have. Thereupon, and in my presence, he counted all the males listed in the registry, excluding those who had emigrated overseas, and a number of other men whom he considered to have left the village permanently; at the same time he included many men who lived most of the year in Athens, Piraeus, Patras and elsewhere, but whom he considered still to be Spartokhoriots. The figure arrived at was 494. This, the president pronounced with some satisfaction, was the number of *ta pedhia mas,* 'our boys'.[11]

I was not so satisfied. Naturally I wanted all females counted, but the president was unwilling to go through the records again, claiming that the number of Spartokhoriot women would 'of course' be the same as the number of Spartokhoriot men. I thought this was unlikely to have been quite the case, but on the assumption of an equal sex ratio, then, on the president's figure, the total Spartokhoriot population in 1979 would have been approximately 988. This, it should be noted, is a 76 per cent increase on the official 1981 census figure of 561, but given the number of men who may have been away at sea on census day, and the number of families who may not have been able or willing to return to Spartokhori for the census, as an estimate the president's figure was probably reasonably accurate. It should be stressed, however, that it was still an estimate, and what made it pointless to argue about precise numbers (and to continue to demand figures for women) was that I was more than a little unsure about the criteria of inclusion and exclusion the president was using. So, I think, was he, for there was considerable hesitation over a large number of names in the registry, and then, with a shrug, another individual was either added to, or omitted from, the tally.

I hasten to add that the apparent arbitrariness of the count was not the result of any indifference or lack of cooperation on the part of the president. Rather, it followed from genuine difficulties that I ought to have foreseen in establishing any precise criteria for village membership. What I had originally hoped to obtain from the records were two, or possibly three, clearcut figures: (a) the number of people permanently resident in the village, that is, those who at the time I still hoped to define as the villagers; (b) the number of Spartokhoriots who had emigrated to, and were resident in, Athens and other urban centres; and (c) the number of Spartokhori's overseas migrants, though I had already realized that this last figure would be difficult to ascertain. But, given the Spartokhoriots' mobility, any division of the population into villagers and urban migrants was unworkable, and I realized that the president had wisely abandoned the attempt and was basing his count partly on a subjective assessment of whether a man was frequently or infrequently in the village, and (a point of some significance) partly on whether or not a man owned, or stood to inherit, a house in the village. The president's 494 (male) Spartokhoriots thus included both those men who were normally resident in the village, and some who lived for the greater part of each year in Athens or Patras; it did not include all men born in Spartokhori, even if they were still resident in Greece and occasionally visited the village. Even the president's criterion of house-ownership or inheritance (which may seem objective enough) was not consistently applied, for a question of intention intervened. The president, for example, excluded from the tally his own son, who by unbreachable custom would inherit his father's house (to the exclusion of the president's daughters and sons-in-law, some of whom were resident in the village) on the grounds that his son was a doctor in Patras whose busy practice prevented his ever staying in the village for more than a few days at a time, and who would never live for any length of time in his father's house.

[11]The dictionary meaning of the term *pedhi* (pl. *pedhia*) is not sex-specific, that is, 'child'. In village usage it tends to refer to males; hence my gendered translation, which is true to the president's intent.

In the ensuing discussion (in which I found myself becoming as confused as evidently I was making the president), I continued to maintain that surely it was possible to establish at least the village's core population, that is to say, the number of its permanent residents. The president remained dubious. At all events, he claimed, the figure could not be derived from the village registry. I would have to make my own house-by-house count. And even then, he said, should students whose families remained in the village be included? They were certainly members of the village, and members of its constituent households. Normally they were resident in the village for at least three months of the year. But given their education, they were unlikely to remain so. And in general, residence for what portion of the year constituted village residence? What about families whose house was in the village but who were renting in Athens while their children studied? And residence for how many years in Athens, or even overseas, distinguished the emigrant from the villager? In the end he threw his hands in the air, laughed politely, and said, 'Anyway, you know as well as I do; it all depends on which day of the year we're talking about.'

In the end I took the president's advice and over the period of my stay in Spartokhori I gradually compiled a record of household compositions, genealogies, overseas and urban migrations, and, in general, attempted to discover the histories of all those connected with the village, some few of which I have already presented. Nor was the president's opinion about the difficulties of the enterprise unfounded. There were practical problems: people's memories were often short, and even with people I came to know well a variety of social inhibitions often prevented their giving full accounts of their relatives' activities and whereabouts. But there were always and at every point problems of classification. General patterns emerged, but individuals' histories and their place(s) of residence could not be allocated to a neat series of rubrics, let alone a threefold division into the categories of villager, urban migrant and overseas migrant. In this chapter I have therefore approached matters much as they would be approached by the Spartokhoriots themselves, for I have taken not the individual, but the household, the *spiti*, as the basic unit of the village (cf. Peristiany 1965; Pina-Cabral 1992). For the president, ownership of a village house or membership of a village household were prime considerations in determining membership of the village community, regardless of whether or not a person's normal place of residence was the village. And this was a view shared by most villagers. If pressed, the Spartokhoriots could attempt a guess at the population of their village (usually quite wide of the mark), but their natural inclination was to estimate the village's size not in terms of people, but in terms of the number of its constituent households. Here again their estimations of the total number of households usually proved unreliable (for they had never had cause to count them), but they were able accurately to enumerate households one by one, referring to each by the name of its owner or senior male resident. The exact composition of each household and the present whereabouts of its members were things I had slowly to discover for myself.

Table 3.1 Household composition of core population, Spartokhori 1979/80

66 houses uninhabited or seasonally occupied	18 empty year-round 48 seasonally occupied	
186 houses with at least one year-round resident	30 houses with one year-round resident	21 widow 5 widower 2 unmarried woman 1 deserted wife 1 deserted husband
	11 houses with widow or widower plus unmarrie dadult(s)	2 widow and unmarried daughter 3 widow and unmarried son 1 widow, daughter and daughter's daughter 1 widow, two unmarried husband's brothers 1 widow, two unmarried sons and two unmarried daughters 1 two widows (husband's mother and son's wife) 2 widower and unmarried daughter
	61 houses with elderly married couples	58 married couple only 2 married couple and husband's unmarried sister 1 married couple and unrelated unmarried woman
	nuclear families ⟶	46 married couple with children
	84 houses with younger married couple — 16	1 married couple as yet without children and husband's father 2 married couple with children and husband's father 12 married couple with children and husband's mother 1 married couple with children, husband's father and wife's mother
	38 stem families 22	3 married couple as yet without children and husband's parents 10 married couple with children and husband's parents 2 married couple with children and wife's parents 5 married couple with children, husband's parents and husband's unmarried brother 1 married couple with children, husband's parents and husband's father's mother 1 married couple with children, husband's parents, husband's father's mother and husband's father's unmarried sister

Households

As stated in Chapter 1, Spartokhori consisted of 252 houses. In fact the number of the village's habitable dwellings was greater than this, for three quite recently built houses had never been lived in,[12] and during my stay another four houses were in the process of construction. Moreover, of the village's fifteen 'shops' – four coffee-shops, six general stores (two of which doubled as drinking houses), a bakery, a draper's store, an electrical appliance store and two butcher's shops – six were separate buildings that I have not included in the 252 *spitia* (pl.), while the other nine were all in various ways integral to inhabited dwellings, being built either beneath or adjoining them. A further three freestanding shops were closed up, either because their owners were no longer interested in running them, or because they were absent from the village. The number 252, then, might better be understood as the number of Spartokhori's households rather than as the number of its physical dwellings, though the term *spiti* was used to cover both (du Boulay 1974: 18): the house and the family that goes with it. In 1979–80 I conducted a census of these 252 households. The results are set out in Table 3.1 and analysed below.

Of Spartokhori's 252 *spitia*, eighteen were empty, but they were not abandoned, and they were still referred to by the names of their heads of household. The members of six of these eighteen households were overseas, and the members of the other twelve were in Athens, Preveza, the Peloponnese and Lefkadha. In some cases their houses had been empty for five, ten or even fifteen years, but it was to one such house that the Canadian 'emigrant' family and their chemist son returned temporarily in 1977. Some of these eighteen houses were actually vacated during my stay as entire families moved to Athens or overseas, but in most cases it was assumed that some family members would be returning once the children's education had been completed or overseas savings accumulated. (Indeed, a number of houses not included in the above eighteen were reopened during my stay by people who had been absent from the village for some years.) Legitimately, then, all of these eighteen *spitia* could still be considered (and were considered by the Spartokhoriots) to be village households rather than empty houses. It was merely the case that, given the mobility of the Spartokhoriot population, all of their constituent members happened to be absent over the period of my census. A further forty-eight houses were occupied seasonally during the summer period, but stood empty for nine or ten months of the year. Of these, thirty were owned by sailors who, with their families, were resident for most of the year in Athens or Piraeus. The remaining eighteen were owned by men and women also employed in Athens and other urban centres whose occupations ranged from factory worker or hospital gate-attendant to university academic and heart specialist. All in all, then, at the time of my census sixty-six village households had no year-round residents.

[12]One was a holiday home (into whose construction I was unwillingly drafted) owned by a French academic. The second had been built by a young man just before he emigrated to the United States. On his return he moved in with his aged parents. The third was built on the bay beneath the village and was to be occupied by a young sailor and his wife and children. In the end they remained resident with the sailor's parents.

Analysis of the remaining 186 households makes it possible to determine what could perhaps be referred to as Spartokhori's core population, that is to say, the number of its inhabitants who were resident year-round in the village, and who had no other normal place of residence. Once again, however, it should be stressed that this core population relates to the situation only as it stood in 1979–80. People returned to the village during my stay; it was known that others were soon to depart. My isolation of a core population is thus very much a matter of analytic convenience, and provides only a snapshot located quite specifically in time. In fact the core population cannot be taken as a distinct section of the Spartokhoriot community (villagers as opposed to migrants), for while it is true that many of the older generation (farmers, shepherds and a great number of the older women) had never left the village for more than a few days (or, in the case of men, for the period of their military service), many other members of the core population had previously been migrants, while in a few years' time others would be forced to become so. For the purpose of counting the core population, I have also excluded students boarding in Athens and elsewhere whose parents remained in the village, for although the Spartokhoriots considered such students still to be members of their parents' households, the village was no longer their permanent place of residence, and it was unlikely ever to be so. In any case they numbered only about twenty-five, since, as I have mentioned, it was the more normal practice for the family as a whole to remove itself to Athens for the duration of children's education. But I have included in the core population all sailors normally resident in the village with their wives and children, for though the sailors themselves might be away at sea for a year or more at a time, the village was nevertheless their only home.

For these 186 houses that in 1979–80 contained at least one year-round resident, household compositions were as follows. Thirty were occupied year-round by one person only: twenty-one by widows (mostly elderly); five by widowers (again elderly); two by unmarried women, both aged; one by an elderly married woman whose husband had left her; one by a man in his fifties whose wife had similarly left. A further eleven households were again headed by widows or widowers, but included some other member or members of their family. Two consisted of a widow with an unmarried daughter; three of a widow with an unmarried son; one of a widow with her middle-aged daughter and grand-daughter; one of a widow and her deceased husband's two unmarried brothers; one of a widow with her four adult but unmarried children (two sons and two daughters); one of two widows (mother-in-law and daughter-in-law) and two of a widower with an unmarried daughter. Another sixty-one households consisted of middle-aged or elderly couples whose children were not normally resident with them. In two cases these households also contained the husband's unmarried sister, and in one case the household included an unrelated unmarried woman.

This left a remainder of eighty-four households that contained a younger married couple with children (or a recently married couple without children), that could, in short, be considered to account for the village's economically active population rather than its population of aged. Of these households, forty-six consisted of a married couple and their children, that is, nuclear families. Sixteen households also included a widow or widower grandparent (usually the husband's father or mother, and in one case the husband's father and the wife's mother). Twenty-two households contained two generations of married couples, in some cases with the addition of an unmarried child of the senior couple as well as the children of the younger couple. Importantly, these larger extended family households were all stem families, for in no cases did married siblings cohabit. Two of these households actually contained four generations of the same family: a paternal great-grandmother, a senior couple, a junior couple and the junior couple's children.

To summarize, sixty-six, or just over a quarter of the village's 252 houses, stood empty or were occupied only during summer and holiday periods. Thirty had only one year-round resident. A further eleven were occupied year-round by widows or widowers with the addition of some other single or separated adult person or persons. Sixty-one, or just under a quarter of the village's houses, contained only elderly or late middle-aged couples as their permanent residents, though sometimes with the addition of an unmarried adult woman. Only eighty-four, or approximately a third of the village's households, contained a younger married couple with children, or a newly-wed married couple.

The 'core' population

Viewed from this perspective, the demographic effects of urban and overseas migration seem severe (Figure 3.2). The total number of individuals accounted for by my core population amounted to only 551 (263 males and 288 females), an even smaller population than the 561 recorded by the government census of 1981. Discounting the sixty-six uninhabited or seasonally inhabited *spitia*, the average household size was less than three people. Moreover, the average age of Spartokhori's core population was high: 43.5 years for men and 45.4 years for women (although these averages conceal a bimodal distribution of the population around both the very young and the old), and men and women above fifty years of age constituted a disproportionately large section of the village's population in comparison with the national profile. Those people most notably absent from the core population were men between the ages of forty and fifty years (Spartokhori's male migrants), women between thirty-one and forty years (their wives), and young people between eleven and twenty years (their children, for the most part Spartokhori's secondary, and in some cases tertiary, students) (Allen 1973: 53–63). But men in their early middle age (between thirty-one and forty years old) were quite well represented, as were small children. The men were the younger professional sailors still resident in the village with their families, whose wives appear for the most part in the twenty-one to thirty years age group, and children in the zero to ten grouping.

Some idea of the degree of migration from Spartokhori, and also of the urban/rural distribution of the Spartokhoriot community, can also be gained by superimposing the male half of the core population (as defined by my census) on to the corresponding configuration derived from the president's figures for 'our boys', though of course no account is thereby taken of women, of permanent overseas migrants, or of men whom the president considered to be 'no longer

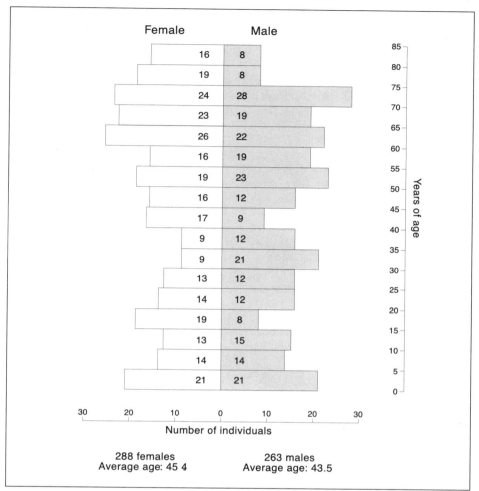

Figure 3.2 Age/sex distribution of core population, Spartokhori, 1980

Spartokhoriots' (see Figure 3.3). Again, the majority of men between thirty and fifty years of age who were counted by the president as Spartokhoriots, but who appear outside the village's core population, were sailors resident with their families in Athens.[13] According to the collective deliberations of Spartokhori's president and his council, 'our boys' also included about forty Spartokhoriot men established in Athens and elsewhere in Greece as professionals, nine of whom were doctors, the others variously lawyers, teachers, civil servants, technicians and one university academic. A number of less successful migrants had entered

[13]While there were in 1980 sixty-four active sailors numbered amongst the core population (and thirty-two retired sailors in receipt of NAT pensions), the total number of Spartokhoriot sailors stood at approximately 135 (with forty-five pensioned sailors) (NAT president, Meganisi, personal communication).

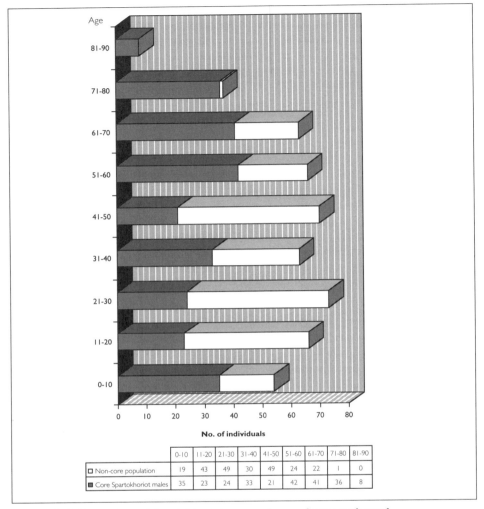

	0-10	11-20	21-30	31-40	41-50	51-60	61-70	71-80	81-90
□ Non-core population	19	43	49	30	49	24	22	1	0
■ Core Spartokhoriot males	35	23	24	33	21	42	41	36	8

Figure 3.3 Comparison of Spartokhoriot core male population with total male population, 1980

the urban workforce, and others had established themselves in Athens and other towns and cities as tradesmen or in small businesses.

The effects of this depopulation did not go unremarked by the villagers. In winter, when the village was reduced to its core population, the Spartokhoriots (like villagers in many parts of rural Greece) would lament their demographic fate: '*Efiye o kosmos* ('everyone has left'). Now there are only *emis i yerondes* (we the old folk) here. Look at all the *spitia*; they're all one-two, one-two. All widows and old men' (cf. Hart 1991: 71).[14] As we have seen, however, a third of the

---

[14]In Richia (Peloponnese), people commented in winter that their village had become nothing but a *yerokomio* (old people's home).

village's houses did contain younger married couples (even if husbands were often away at sea), and in 1979 there were over forty children between the ages of five and twelve attending the village primary school, with as many infants below school age also in the village. Moreover, the fact that so many elderly widows, widowers and couples were living on their own was not the result solely of emigration. In many cases the domestic isolation of the older generation had resulted from a growing preference among the young for neolocal residence on marriage rather than continued residence within the paternal home. Many widows, widowers and elderly couples did have children (and grandchildren) still resident in the village, but in separate households. These qualifications aside, however, a sense of loss pervaded the village in winter, and the emotional effects of emigration were real enough. Houses that the elderly remembered once to have held a dozen people were now occupied by them alone. Their children and children's children were in Athens or Preveza or Patras, and though they might see them frequently, for much of the year they were separated. Worse, their children and grandchildren might be in America or Canada or South Africa or Australia (cf. Hart 1991: 4).[15] One old widow, whose eight children had all settled overseas, rehearsed her tearful obsession for anyone who would listen: 'I made so many children, and now I'm alone. And I don't know letters, so I can't write. And my grandchildren can't speak Greek when they telephone. But I kiss the ikon, and St Yerasimos comes to me at night and says, "Don't worry, Stathoula," and ....' The young people she addresses become embarrassed and try to leave, commenting afterwards that after all she is a *ghria* (old woman), so what can you expect: '*Etsi ine i zoi* (such is life),' or at least, such it had become for many.

Reunion

Migration and depopulation had resulted in plenty of other similar personal tragedies, but despite what is shown by government census figures, despite what my own household census revealed, and despite permanent losses to the village's population through overseas emigration, in 1980 Spartokhori was still not in rapid decline. Of the sixty-six houses that had no year-round resident, eighteen, as I have mentioned stood empty, but the remaining forty-eight were regularly reoccupied over Easter and sometimes at Christmas, and more importantly they were occupied for the duration of the summer school and university holidays. In most cases their entire family complement returned for this three-month break, since thirty of the forty-eight houses were owned by sailors whose employment allowed them to determine their non-working periods. And if the head of the household happened to be at sea, the rest of the family was still at liberty to return to the village. The owners of the other eighteen houses, whether they were professionals or members of the urban workforce, were more constrained, but the very fact that Spartokhori had not become a mere depository for the aged, and that friends and relatives were known to be returning there for

---

[15]Hart estimates the population of Richia (Peloponnese) to have been 'about a hundred residents in winter, and several times that number in summer' (1991: 54).

Plate 3.2 Family Easter

summer, meant that they too made every effort to spend as long in the village as possible. And again, if heads of household were unable to spend more than one continuous month in the village, most contrived to allow their families to spend the full period there. Much the same applied to those thirty houses that were occupied year-round by only one person, for nine were occupied by what might best be described as a family caretaker, the oldest family member, usually a widowed grandmother, who remained in the village while her children and grand-children were in Athens, but who was reunited with them over the summer months. Similarly, of the eleven houses that contained only a widow or widower plus some other unmarried adult(s), four had family members who regularly returned to the village from Patras and Athens. In the same fashion many of the sixty-one households that consisted of middle-aged or elderly couples became full in summer when children and grandchildren returned. Indeed these sixty-one households accounted for a total of twenty-four young unmarried men and women aged fifteen to twenty-five, the majority of whom were students boarding with relatives in Athens. By village reckoning these twenty-four *pedhia* were certainly still members of their respective households, since they were still unmarried. Finally, even those eighty-four houses that contained something approaching a full complement of members in winter accounted between them for another thirteen unmarried individuals studying or working in Athens, who again were seen by the villagers as belonging to their respective households, and who regularly returned to them. As the Spartokhoriots remarked, 'when the *fitites* (students) return', a phrase that had become a virtual synonym for 'summer', the size of their village doubled, and there might be in excess of 1,000 people at home.

If this annual reunion is considered in conjunction with the continual arrivals (and departures) of overseas migrants, and with the temporary (though often quite long-term) dislocations of residence that had become part of the domestic cycle, it becomes apparent that the population of Spartokhori was not dis-appearing, it was merely in perpetual motion. And what must again be stressed is that such perpetual motion both effectively dissolved the distinction between villager and emigrant, and substantially retarded the development of divisions of class. Outside the village, the lives, experiences and achievements of individual Spartokhoriots varied radically, and within the village considerations of status and/or education distinguished the behaviour of some Spartokhoriots from their compatriots. The heart-specialist or the university academic were not likely to be found gathering olives or working in the olive mill, but then neither were the schoolmaster and schoolmistress who were continuously in the village. For the most part, however, Spartokhori's non-permanent population melted back into the community. Fishing boats were crewed in summer by those resident year-round in the village, and by those who had returned to it. Olives were gathered in winter by those who had managed to escape the capital for Christmas, and by those who usually saw out the lonely season on their own. During school and university holidays the coffee-shops were filled without discrimination by students and sailors, by agriculturalists and returned migrants, by those who knew only the village and by those who could compare it to the world. The doctor drank with the bosun, the fisherman with the lawyer, the agriculturalist with the mathematics graduate. Nor could it have been otherwise, for in the village,

village morality held sway, and ties and obligations were recognized that external variations of experience, status and wealth could not dispel. The doctor was, after all, the bosun's son-in-law; the fisherman was the lawyer's brother; the mathematics graduate was the agriculturalist's nephew. The return to the village was not just the return to a location; it was the reabsorption into a community and into a family.

4
Terms of Kinship

Such, in brief, was the history of Meganisi, this remote and tiny island so seemingly sheltered from the concerns of the outside world. Such too was the history of Spartokhori, the traditional village into which I had entered, with its whitewashed houses, its gnarled fishermen, its grizzled elders, its quaintly attired women, its donkeys and chickens and sheep and goats and all the sights and sounds that prompt the sense of having discovered a different, unchanging and forgotten world – but a history, in fact, of continual comings and goings, arrivals and departures, congregations and dispersals which, by the time of my fieldwork, linked the island and the village not only to Greece's capital, but to cities, ports and country towns around the globe. Nor were the links merely those of constant communication between people who had left, and people who had been left behind; rather, they were links formed by the continual passage of people whose own lives encompassed urban residence, overseas migration, village retreat or a voyage from China to Peru.

That history and that dynamism were all too easy to forget. Spartokhori's atmosphere could seduce the senses, but it could also lull the mind, and I admit to being surprised one day when I was addressed in the coffee-shop in quite passable English by a diminutive octogenarian whose name was Herakles, who wore a week's stubble, a peaked sailor's cap, shoes without laces or socks, a homespun wool singlet and battered trousers and jacket that might once have been a suit, and who, it transpired, had emigrated to the United States in 1909, returned for the Balkan war in 1912, gone back to America in 1919, returned to the village briefly in 1926, run a liquor store in Yugoslavia for ten years, and then returned to Spartokhori in 1938 finally to marry and settle down. But in the end what most brought home to me to the realities of Meganisi's connectedness with the rest of the world was to be embraced by a man in Katomeri who had lived longer in the Australian provincial town of my family and birth than I ever have.

Yet for all its cosmopolitan connections the sense that Spartokhori conveyed of being an enclosed, self-contained community was not entirely illusory. Nor did that sense derive solely from architecture and ambience, the degree to which, physically, the village's sum of buildings, inhabitants and surroundings approximated to the romantic vision of an untouched enclave. Spartokhori was indeed a tight-knit community and not just an agglomeration of people drawn together to live out their lives in accidental proximity. Despite both the historical and actual mobility of its population, the village was welded together by a sense of corporate identity evidenced as much by exclusion as inclusion. As the fate of Andonis the builder has already illustrated, there were Spartokhoriots and non-Spartokhoriots, *ta pedhia mas* (our boys) and others, *i dhiki mas* (our people) and *kseni* (foreigners/outsiders). That sense of corporate identity is difficult to convey in summary manner, for it was expressed throughout the hundreds of daily exchanges that cumulatively made up village life. But in order to grasp at least the basis of what made Spartokhori a community and not simply a settlement, of what made someone a Spartokhoriot and not simply someone who lived in Spartokhori, of what provided the framework for the complex of loyalties and prejudices, affections and animosities that constituted the villagers' sense of belonging, it seems reasonable to explore what the Spartokhoriots themselves always singled out in their own expressions of solidarity: namely, kinship and family. 'We are all foreigners here' may have been close to a historical truth, but in village discourse the phrase gained its impact because it ran counter to another and seemingly contradictory pronouncement, 'We are all one family here', a pronouncement that not only approached the empirically verifiable, but also proclaimed a moral certainty.

The statement's moral content must be stressed. Although I shall argue that notions of kinship and family were central to the Spartokhoriots' sense of community, it has to be remembered that kinship and family are themselves complex phenomena, not analytic bedrock. Community, identity, solidarity could not be explained in terms of kinship and family were it not also the case that in Spartokhori (and generally in Greece as well as throughout much of the world) kinship and family act as prime moral *loci*, as repositories of the most deep-seated values and sentiments. To discover the genealogical intricacies of the Spartokhoriot community, the ties of consanguinity, affinity and spiritual parenthood that linked its members one to another, would be to discover nothing about the construction of community were it not also the case that those ties were morally valued. Thus, though I shall spend considerable time in this chapter and the next describing the Spartokhoriot kinship system (the forms of relationship that were recognized, the terms by which those relationships were specified, the rules that governed their generation), in so doing I shall be describing only the foundation upon which was erected an essentially *moral* system that asserted not simply that X was Y's cousin by virtue of a certain form of genealogical reckoning, but that X and Y should cherish each other *because* they were cousins. Without such a moral evaluation, the kinship system is a meaningless set of relations. In short, I shall be explaining one moral and emotive category, community, by reference to another, kinship and family, or at least I shall be arguing that in the case of Spartokhori they were largely congruent.

To claim that kinship and family were what made the village a community is not, therefore, to assume *a priori* that kinship and family constitute some sort of universally privileged domain of relationships that is automatically of sociological consequence (Schneider 1984). Ties of kinship and family have first to be ideologically valued by the social actors they empirically relate to if they are to play any part in social life. I shall argue that they were so valued in Spartokhori, for the Spartokhoriots themselves regularly construed the contingencies of amity (or animosity), the experience of village familiarity, the events of a lifetime, in terms of kinship and family, so that for them kinship and family constituted not a set of genealogical connections that happened to relate them to each other, but rather a public morality and a mode of mutual evaluation. This was so even when communal life was scarcely in accord with the Spartokhoriots' public protestations of harmony. In the final analysis kinship divided as much as it conjoined, and communal life was as much about conflict as cohesion, for like most moral systems, the values of kinship and family also provided the grounds for mutual condemnation. But again, like many moral systems, kinship and family also defined who might judge, and who was worth judging. The real measure of moral exclusion was simply disregard (cf. Pitt-Rivers 1965; Jamous 1981).

In this and the following chapters, I shall try to substantiate my broad contention that the Spartokhoriots' sense of community was congruent with their notions of kinship and family, but in so doing I shall be engaged in a double project: first, to describe the Spartokhoriot kinship system in terms of its structure; second, to explore the morality by which that that structure was informed.

Greek kinship in perspective

Greek kinship, or rather the ethnography of Greek kinship, presents us with a paradox. As Loizos and Papataxiarchis observe, 'Greece has been described by anthropologists as a society largely based on kinship. Investigators have singled out familism as the most important orientation in Greek life, thus justifying the priority that most ethnographers have given to kinship' (1991: 3). Yet while this is undoubtedly true, neither the ethnography of Greece, nor of the Mediterranean in general, ever featured greatly in the heyday of kinship studies. As Davis commented:

> It is a curiosity of kinship studies that they have not have achieved the same depth of analysis and subtlety in the Mediterranean as they have elsewhere. So far as the bilateral Mediterranean is concerned, kinship studies have suffered from the all-too-easy assumption that a kinship system so familiar requires no further exploration and writers have been tempted, and have often succumbed, to elaborate the themes of what kinship and relationships are for, even what kinship relations are like, without paying the proper preliminary attention to what the system is (Davis 1977: 198).

That 'proper preliminary attention' to the system is what I now wish to pay. Since the publication of Davis's overview of Mediterranean anthropology, the study of kinship and family in the Mediterranean has considerably progressed (Goddard 1994). Nevertheless, the general problem to which Davis refers, the apparent familiarity of Mediterranean (and Greek) family and kinship structures to both ethnographers and their readers alike, does remain an obstacle. The 'bilateral family' (which in 1965 Peristiany took to have been standard throughout Greece's history)[1] appears in its general structure, and in the terminological

---

[1] Peristiany was discussing the village of Alona in Cyprus, but clearly his observation was intended to have general application: 'The Greek family is, and so far as we know has always been, bilateral with, I believe, a stress on patrilineality expressed, in Alona, with the greater formalism related to agnation, with the moral ascendancy of the male and with the surname, a recent innovation, which follows the paternal line' (1965: 179).

classifications it employs, to be unproblematic to most natives of, say, the United Kingdom, the United States, or France. Greek families (at least in the sense of domestic units) normally consist of husband, wife and unmarried children (sometimes with the addition of a grandparent or grandparents); Greek kinship terms for the most part label the familiar categories of uncle, aunt, nephew, niece, first, second and third cousins and so on (Aschenbrenner 1986: 47). Most importantly, kinship in the Mediterranean often appears to boil down to no more than the family or to an extension from the family (Goddard 1994: 57–8), so that the distinction once made (particularly by Africanists) between kinship as a mode of social or political organization involving corporate groups (clans, lineages, sublineages, etc), and family as the realm of private and domestic life, appears largely inappropriate (Harris 1990: 1–2). Inasmuch as one can talk about kinship as opposed to domestic relations in the Mediterranean, then one is usually (but not always) talking about the bilateral kindred. Campbell's classic essay on the Sarakatsani nicely exemplifies the point:

> *Kindred relationships are considered by the Sarakatsani to be extensions from the family.* Naturally, it is always a member of a man's elementary family who mediates his various relationships in the kindred, parents providing the links with grandparents, uncles, aunts, cousins, siblings those with nephews and nieces. *And although the kindred is a system of personal relations while the family is a corporate group,* the systematic character of the former, and the structure of the latter, are necessarily interdependent and consistent. (Campbell 1963: 76; my emphases)

Here not only is the kindred an extension from the family, but it is the family, *not* the kindred, that provides the only candidate for a recognizable corporate group. Thus while familism may, as Loizos and Papataxiarchis suggest, have been considered 'the most important orientation of Greek life', and while Greece may have been described by ethnographers as a society 'largely based on kinship', as a mere extension of the family the actual structure (as opposed to the 'importance')[2] of Greek kinship seems at first sight relatively uninteresting. Indeed, as Pitt-Rivers (speaking of the Mediterranean as a whole) summed up the situation as he saw it in 1977: 'The relative autonomy of the nuclear family – together with the absence of a clear rule of marriage[3] – has made the Mediterranean an area of little interest to the theoreticians of kinship'. (1977: 72; see also Goddard 1994: 57–8)

Since the 1970s, however, a steady accumulation of ethnographic data has begun to make it possible more fully to appreciate the degree of variation to be encountered within the seemingly all too familiar cognatic kinship systems of Greece and the Mediterranean, and for Greece alone there is now sufficient

---

[2] Herein lay the imprecision of which Davis complained. As he remarks, 'It is often said – indeed, there is scarcely a study from the northern shore which does not say it – that "the family" is overwhelmingly important in the social organisation of Mediterranean communities ... on the other hand, the only study which attempts to discuss the importance of the family in a precise way is by Farsoun (1970) and it is not comparative. Otherwise the articles and monographs are loose and vague'. (1977: 167)

[3] It is important to remember that for functionalists marriage rules articulating the relationship between clans, lineages, moieties, etc were fundamental to the study of kinship, and, indeed, were often definitional of such corporate groups. Moreover, the entirety of alliance theory, deriving from the work of Lévi-Strauss (1949), hinged on the rules of marriage (or rather, the exchange of women) between groups.

information for both Couroucli (1985: 13–14) and Loizos and Papataxiarchis (1991: 8-10) to have attempted broad taxonomies of that variation. Admittedly their taxonomies are not purely structural but, consonant with contemporary trends in kinship studies, include consideration of the forms of domestic and economic organisation that underlie each type. Thus Couroucli (who suggests a fourfold regional taxonomy) classifies Greek kinship types according to differing forms of subsistence, as follows.

1. Pastoral communities of continental Greece, characterized by 'patrilocal residence, inheritance down the agnatic line, and the predominance of households composed of patrilateral extended families'.

2. Agricultural communities of continental Greece, in which 'residence still remains patrilocal, but there is a total absence of *ménages du type frérèche* [i.e. households composed of co-resident brothers and their families] and in which men inherit house and land, but some fields are given to daughters as dowry'.

3. Island agricultural communities (especially of the Ionian Islands) where one finds 'the fragmented plot mode of production' and a strictly nuclear family organisation.

4. Fishing and maritime communities of the Aegean 'characterized by strong manifestations of a matrilineal tendency (land and houses inherited down the female line, matri-neolocal residence) and by the predominance of nuclear families' (Couroucli 1985: 14; my translations).

For their part, Loizos and Papataxiarchis (1991) suggest a threefold taxonomy which similarly takes into account forms of residence, household composition, and inheritance and dowry, but which is not explicitly linked to geographic regions, and which emphasizes degrees of gender equality and inequality rather than forms of economic activity, as follows.

1. '[C]ommunities in which married sons reside in the immediate vicinity of their natal households, usually after a short period of coresidence with their parents', and in which there is a strong agnatic emphasis in kinship, a marked degree of male dominance and of female subordination, and the transfer of male-controlled property, names and reputations from father to sons.

2. At the opposite pole, uxorilocal communities where 'women's dowries are houses built near their natal homes, so that neighbourhoods tend to be clusters of matrilaterally related women (and their male kin). Property and names are transferred through gendered lines, from mother to daughters and from fathers to sons, and women often get the lion's share of family property and dominate in the administration of these properties as well as the arrangement of marriages. A matrilateral bias characterizes kinship in these societies.'

3. Finally, between these two poles there is a third and intermediate type in which 'the representation of kinship as fully bilateral, with only rather small areas of life where men can argue for their superiority as a sex, and small and rather unimportant areas of behaviour organized to stress male–male links or

anything resembling agnatic descent. These systems tend to neolocal marital residence and full partible inheritance of land'. (Loizos and Papataxiarchis 1991: 9–10)

Despite the somewhat different principles of classification, there is a fair degree of congruence between the two taxonomies, and Spartokhoriot kinship falls quite squarely within Couroucli's second type (despite the fact that Meganisi is part of the Ionian Islands, not continental Greece) and Loizos and Papataxiarchis's third type:

1. The representation of kinship in Spartokhori was fully bilateral, and agnatic groupings were no more than nominal.

2. Inheritance of houses and land was fully partible, but both houses and land were transmitted from father to sons with daughters taking a relatively small proportion of land as dowry.

3. Residence was ideally patrilocal, but married brothers never cohabited, so that on marriage all but one of a set of brothers would live neolocally.

But while Spartokhoriot kinship was thus by no means unusual, it possessed two related structural features that warrant particular attention, for they significantly contributed to the ability of kinship to weld the village's population into the single family of which the Spartokhoriots continually spoke. In brief, these were:

1. An extremely extensive and fluid reckoning of kinship connections that allowed kinship to be strategically invoked between individuals whenever it was advantageous, and which could thus be used to substantiate the Spartokhoriots' claim that everyone in the village was related to everyone else.

2. An extreme form of 'bilateral' reckoning which not only made no distinction between patrilateral and matrilateral relatives, but which also assimilated relatives by marriage to consanguineous relatives so that affinity effectively collapsed into consanguinity and marriage provided the means of potentially more than doubling the number of a person's kin.

Two further features of Spartokhoriot kinship are effectively entailed by the above, and are in any case common to cognatic kinship systems (Freeman, 1968). They nevertheless deserve emphasis.

3. The degree of overlap that inevitably occurs between individuals' personal kindreds in a bilateral system was greatly increased as a result of the Spartokhoriots' extended form of kinship reckoning.

4. Kinship did not in itself provide the basis for permanent divisions of the population into discrete all-purpose groups. On a day-to-day basis, kinship solidarity manifested itself at the level of the individual household, which was defined by co-residence rather than by any particular configuration of kin. On the other hand, neither ideologically nor practically were the ties of recognized kinship limited to, or reducible to, the household (or the nuclear family or the elementary family), as has sometimes been suggested for the Mediterranean

(Peristiany 1965; Pitt-Rivers 1977). Beyond the household, cooperation between kin was often the result of contingent factors (friendship, common interests, political sympathies), but such cooperation always invoked kinship. More importantly, despite the overlapping and fuzzy-edged nature of bilateral kindreds, for a variety of particular purposes, notably marriage and godparenthood, kinship did structure relations between groups.

To these features of Spartokhoriot kinship must be added one final consideration, not in itself a structural feature, but a practice on which the full effect of kinship as the basis of community cohesion depended: namely, a strong tendency towards village endogamy.

These are features of Spartokhoriot kinship that I shall describe in detail, and which I shall examine within a comparative context. But a word of warning is necessary, for although I shall argue, for example, that the Spartokhoriots were bilateral to an extreme, and that in contrast to recent accounts given of some other rural Greek communities (Herzfeld 1985, Couroucli 1985, Vernier 1991, Makris 1992), agnatic groupings played little or no part in Spartokhoriot social organization, the meaning of such terms as 'bilateral', 'agnatic', etc are often less than self-evident, and their ascription to particular communities depends to some degree on what factors the analyst cares to consider or to emphasize. This is an old anthropological story, but not one that looks like becoming a closed book. Indeed, the current shift in the study of kinship and family away from social structure and towards gender relations, although in itself quite warranted, seems to have resuscitated rather than resolved some classificatory problems. In 1964, for example, Campbell presented Sarakatsani kinship as thoroughly bilateral, although he certainly had no hesitation in describing what nowadays would be called the Sarakatsani's androcentric ideology. In 1991 Loizos and Papataxiarchis situate the Sarakatsani (as described by Campbell) as a classic example not of bilaterality, but of the type of Greek kinship that places 'an agnatic emphasis' on kinship as a result of virilocality, male cooperation in pastoralism and the value put on maleness and male–male relatedness.[4] Thus while there can be no doubt about the existence of a considerable degree of regional variation in Greek kinship systems and family organization, the language used to describe that variation – a language, be it noted, necessitated by the very attempt to talk about the variation (Parkin 1997: 7–8) – can be confusing. After all, on the face of it bilaterality and agnation would seem to be opposed.

Misunderstandings, therefore, are always a risk. In some recent accounts of rural Greek communities that show a strong agnatic bias there is, for example, renewed talk of lineages, sub-lineages (Couroucli 1985, Vernier 1991, Seremetakis 1991, Makris 1992) and, more cautiously, patrigroups (Herzfeld 1983, 1985). Yet Loizos and Papataxiarchis note, with respect to earlier writings on Greece that similarly spoke of lineages, etc:

> Extreme concern with kinship has given rise to an over-application of descent theory and the 'discovery' of lineages where they did not exist. For example, there has been discussion of 'patrilineal emphasis,' 'patrilines,' and 'lineages' (Aschenbrenner 1976:

---

[4] Greek scholars, too, have seen Sarakatsani social structure as fundamentally agnatic. See Herzfeld (1987a: 58–9) for a shrewd discussion of the socio-political implications of their categorization (and of Campbell's).

216–17) where the reality was just a matter of surnamed groups, and 'dual patrilineal and matrilineal descent lines' (Hoffman 1976: 333) where men and women simply inherited names and property through the father's and the mother's side respectively (Loizos and Papataxiarchis 1991: 3 n.2).

Loizos and Papataxiarchis's admonitions should be taken seriously, for there is always the possibility that ethnographers of Greece may be in danger of reduplicating the sorts of muddles in the models that occurred when Africanist concepts were transferred to New Guinea and the Pacific (Karp 1978; Barnes 1962; Kuper 1988: 204–9). Classifications always simplify (that is why they are classifications), but they can also misdirect. Even in the cases cited by Loizos and Papataxiarchis, however, it must be recognized that surnamed groups do constitute a form of patrilineal emphasis (as Peristiany remarked),[5] and that where men and women 'simply inherited names and property through the father's and the mother's side respectively' surely it is not illegitimate to talk of this form of inheritance in terms of dual patrilineal and matrilineal descent lines, simple (that is to say, commonplace) though it may be. The real problem is that the terms 'patrilineal', 'matrilineal', 'agnatic', etc cannot be taken as classifications that immediately and unambiguously specify types of social structure and organization in their totality (Leach 1961: 11). Rather they refer, more or less provisionally, to certain aspects of social structure and organization. So, importantly, does my own use of the word 'bilateral', for as we shall see, the Spartokhoriot kinship system possessed many of those same features that have prompted other ethnographers of Greece to talk of lineages and patrigroups. In the end (as always) it is for ethnographic description to flesh out the provisionality of classifications and to render them meaningful. With this in mind, I start with a brief account of what for the Spartokhoriots was their most central kinship concept: namely, *ikoyenia* or family.

The meaning of family

The term *singhenis* is the ordinary everyday word in Greek for a relative, and certainly it was a word used by the Spartokhoriots, but by far the commonest way of expressing relatedness between people in Spartokhori was to make reference to a shared *ikoyenia*, or family (cf. Dubisch 1991). Thus, for example, someone might say, '*O Pavlos ky'egho, imaste ikoyenia* (Pavlos and I, we are family).' It is important to realize, however, that *ikoyenia* in Spartokhori was not a technical or well-defined term. Its meaning was quite as imprecise and fluid as its standard English translation, and what was being referred to as family varied according to both the context and the intention of the speaker. Spartokhoriot usage was not exceptional in this, but it was, perhaps, slightly idiosyncratic in that there is a strong tendency in many Greek communities to use the term *ikoyenia* as a virtual synonym for the household, the *spiti*, and then to refer to more distant relatives, or those who are not coresident, as *singhenis*, 'relatives', or as *soi*, 'kin' or members of the kindred, the latter particularly if the *soi* is bilaterally defined.

[5] See note 1 above.

In Spartokhori, too, the term *ikoyenia* most commonly referred, implicitly at least, to the members of a household or *spiti*. In practice that usually meant husband, wife and children, that is, a nuclear family. Alternatively, and depending on actual domestic arrangements, it could mean the nuclear family with the addition of a grandparent or grandparental couple (usually the husband's parents) and possibly one or more other co-resident unmarried adults (usually siblings of the husband, more rarely those of the wife), that is, a stem family. I say implicitly, however, because if the question were put to a Spartokhoriot whether, for example, parents who happened to be living in another household, or married brothers and sisters who had their own households, were or were not family, then the answer would be emphatically that they were. For many practical purposes *i ikoyenia mou*, 'my family', might refer to the domestic unit, but as soon as the definition of family became subject to conscious reflection, it became more extensive (cf. Clark 1988: 189–95). As we shall see in Chapter 6, except *statistically* the household represented no particular configuration of kin, and no Spartokhoriots would have considered their mother or father or brothers or sisters to be outside their family just because they happened not to be co-resident with them. Important though the household was as a social, economic and moral unit, it could not be made to yield the definition of family, which always overflowed the household's bounds, for the household was essentially a *de facto* consolidation of kin whose unity, though based on kinship, was defined by co-residence (cf. Clark 1988: 40, 189).

Given, then, that the definition of family regularly escaped the boundaries of the household, a more extensive definition might be sought in terms of all those people who were normally addressed by and referred to by means of a kinship term. In practice this tended to mean all of a person's bilateral *and* affinal relatives up to, and including, second cousins. Indeed such a grouping had some practical significance. When, for example, a family celebration was held – an engagement, wedding or baptismal party – it was conventional automatically to invite the members of this group. Moreover, such a definition was also in rough accord with the limits of the incest prohibition, which can be seen to constitute an important boundary for the definition of family, since it was only when 'the blood has changed (*ehi alaksi to ema*)' that a relative might be taken in marriage. Nevertheless, even the incest prohibition (or the rule of exogamy) did not provide a definition of family for the Spartokhoriots in the same way as it did for the Sarakatsani, where it neatly circumscribed the *soi*, the bilateral kindred, so that the collateral limits of the *soi* and the collateral limits of the incest prohibition were reciprocally defined, both being set at second cousins (Campbell 1964: 42-58). In Spartokhori, day-to-day reckoning of family similarly stopped at second cousins, and, like the Sarakatsani (and the Ambeliots), the Spartokhoriots were inclined to say that third cousins were not really family (Campbell 1964: 107; du Boulay 1974: 145). But the Spartokhoriots' interpretation of the Orthodox incest prohibitions was such that they nevertheless forbade marriage between third cousins. In short, the relationship of third cousin was in most respects on the margins of what was normally considered family, but it was still clearly recognized to constitute an impediment to marriage, so that the incest prohibition and the working definition of family were not entirely congruent. Thus, like membership of the household or *spiti*, the incest prohibition did not so much define family as define a particular grouping of relatives in connection with a particular regulation (those who might not marry as opposed to those who might), and, much as Clark has argued for Laikotera (1988: 192), I would suggest that in the end the definition of family was always situational, an elastic concept with no fixed and precise limits.

This elasticity is of some significance, for although second cousins provided the rough limits of socially recognized kinship in Spartokhori, when the Sparto-khoriots said 'We are all one family', the remark was not intended to be purely (or simply) metaphorical. The village was, of course, thought to be like a family in terms of the mutual concern, mutual obligations, and sense of solidarity that ideally bound its members together, but the Spartokhoriots were happy to acknowledge the possibility that lines of kinship might be followed out from any individual more or less *ad infinitum* to third, fourth or fifth cousins and thence into a realm where any precise knowledge of relationships was wanting, but where the possibility of relatedness could still be entertained (cf. du Boulay 1974: 145-6; 1984: 536).[6] Family in this sense – and for the Spartokhoriots it was a quite legitimate sense – came to include everyone with whom any kinship con-nection could be traced, or with whom a kinship connection could be presumed to exist. Thus the assertion that the whole village constituted a single family had a meaning that was more than metaphorical, for almost every Spartokhoriot was in one way or another related to almost every other Spartokhoriot. Indeed, as I tried to sort out the villagers' tangled genealogies, my confusions would be met with laughter, and repetition of the comment that (sentiment aside) the Spartokhoriots were indeed all one family.

I stress the imprecision and fluidity of the term *ikoyenia* as it was employed in Spartokhori, but no contradiction was felt between its various usages. When a Spartokhoriot referred to his or her family and to his or her brother's family as separate entities, it posed no problem that from another point of view, or in another context, both sets of relatives might be taken to constitute a single family. Similarly, the truth of almost all Spartokhoriots being related to one another, and therefore constituting a single family, was not controverted by the fact that in daily life Spartokhoriots might bitterly oppose each other as families. Context would always dispel the apparent contradictions of meaning. Context alone, however, would not disentangle contradictions of feeling, for if family was a vague and portable word in terms of what it denoted, it nevertheless retained constant moral connotations. Indeed, Bloch has argued that in general kinship terms do not so much *denote* kinship roles as form 'part of the process of defining a role relation between speaker and hearer' and are thus best looked at in terms of the place they hold in the system of values and from the point of view of which tactical uses they can serve (Bloch 1971: 80). In short, kinship terms are morally indexical, and for the Spartokhoriots, family consisted of those to whom loyalty

---

[6] Du Boulay states that in Ambeli the kindred, the *soi*, 'is a clearly defined category of blood relations which ... includes ... collateral relations outwards to second cousins' (1984: 534). She goes on to argue, however, that 'there exists also an opposing understanding according to which the blood of kinship extends into the wider society far beyond the bounds of the canonical kindred'. But such an understanding is only opposed if one takes the incest prohibition as setting the limits of kinship in the first place.

was owed; family consisted of those who owed one loyalty; family consisted of those with whom one was identified and with whom one identified oneself; family was *i dhiki mas,* our people, as opposed to outsiders. Ideologically this was not open to doubt, and family as a moral concept had a fixity in defiance of its particular application to particular individuals or groups. It had the peculiar characteristic of being a term whose real content was both emotional and immutable, whilst at the same time seeming to refer to a group of actual individuals who ought to be definable but who were in fact subject to continual redefinition. And much of the tension of village life was accountable in terms of the difference between family as a moral concept and family as a definable group. It was, after all, well recognized that not all of those who could be counted family could be counted on to behave as family. But the morality of family and the mutual obligations it entailed were still not disputed. The question was only whether or not certain people lived up to their obligations. 'Family' thus tended to become a negotiable entity. Whether or not one claimed relatedness to someone else became as much a matter of mutual regard as of fact, and of strategy and circumstance as much as of genealogical definition (cf. Bourdieu 1990: 160). This will be more fully explored in Chapter 6. In practice, however, it was difficult if not impossible ever to escape identification with, minimally, those with whom one cohabited – and that alone, I think, explains the anthropological tendency (with which Clark 1988: 26–30 has taken issue) to equate household and family in Greece, and to assume its internal cohesion and solidarity (Friedl 1964a: 87; Campbell 1964: 148, 1983: 184–5; du Boulay 1974: 17; Dimen 1986: 53–4; Clark 1988: 26-30). In fact family reached not its definition, but its irreducible limit, with the *spiti,* and however internally divided the household might be by disputes, quarrels and longstanding grievances (cf. Clark 1988: 382–413), in its dealings with the outside world it always presented a united front. With the household, family as a moral concept and family as a definable group were required publicly to coincide.

For the Spartokhoriots to assert that the village was all one family was thus to take the moral unity of the household (integral to its public definition) and to translate it to the village as a whole. In this sense the move was metaphorical. It employed the most powerful (since it was the most irreducible) example of a moral unity to convey a sense of the village's unity. But the very imprecision of family as a term of reference also meant that what could be seen as metaphorical could equally be argued to have a basis in fact; that is in the extensive and recognized ties of consanguinity, affinity and godparenthood that united the Spartokhoriot community into a single genealogical unit. That factual basis was in turn a consequence, in part at least, of the terminology, classifications and rules that constituted the Spartokhoriots' kinship system.

The classification of kin

The Spartokhoriots' kinship terminology is bilateral and does not differ greatly with respect either to the actual terms employed or the classifications of relatives those terms entail, from the bilateral terminology found throughout most of the Greek-speaking world (Herzfeld 1983: 157; Andromedas 1957). I shall comment only briefly on the terminology's general features. What I shall argue, however, is that in Spartokhori the bilateral nature of this more or less standard terminology was taken to an extreme so that, coupled with a correspondingly thorough-going cognatic ideology, the Spartokhoriot classification of kin allowed the possibility of the entire village being seen as a single kinship unit.

Each Spartokhoriot stood at the centre of a bilaterally defined group of kin, referred to simply as his or her *ikoyenia*, or family. Since this kindred was ego-centred, no two individuals (with the exception of a pair of same-sex unmarried siblings) had exactly the same set of kin, or referred to and addressed them by exactly the same terms. By the same token, however, each individual's kindred substantially overlapped with the kindreds of numerous other individuals (cf. Freeman 1968). This is a general feature of bilateral kindreds, exaggerated in the Spartokhoriot case since the limits of the kindred were not precisely defined and could be seen to extend collaterally beyond even second or third cousins.

In common with standard Greek kinship terminology, no distinctions were made between patrilateral and matrilateral relatives. Degrees of cousinhood were also reckoned according to a standard Greek pattern (similar to the English system) with first cousins (*prota ksadherfia*), second cousins (*dheftera ksadherfia*) and third cousins (*trita ksadherfia*), etc. It is worth noting, however, that Greek (and Spartokhoriot) terminology departs in one minor respect from the English system in its expression of the relationships between cousins of different generational levels. In English these relationships are clumsily referred to as removes of cousins. In Greek they become relationships between uncles or aunts and nieces or nephews. Thus Ego's FBSS (Ego's 'first cousin once removed') is in Greek a nephew, a logic that does, of course, appear in English folk, as opposed to official, usage.[7] The major differences between the Greek (and Spartokhoriot) kinship terminology and the English terminology all occur with the classification of affines. These deserve special note.

The generic term for an affine is *simpetheros* (fem. *simpethera*). The term is constructed by the addition of the prefix *sin* (together, with) to the term for father-in-law (*petheros*) or mother-in-law (*pethera*). The paradigmatic relationship is thus between the two sets of co-parents-in-law, who are reciprocally *simpetheri*. A great many other people, however, may call each other *simpetheri*, and in Spartokhori the category was both ill defined and, like that of *ikoyenia* itself, extensive. In theory any two people who could trace an affinal link between them could call each other *simpetheri*, and on occasion they did so. In practice, those who regularly recognized each other as *simpetheri* constituted a more limited, but still indeterminate, set. The gloss invariably supplied by the Spartokhoriots was simply, 'If a boy marries a girl, then the two families are *simpetheri*.' The formula turns out to be vague because of the very fluidity of those who might be considered family. On the one hand, some quite close affinal relatives were regularly referred to simply as *simpetheri*, for no more specific kinship term was available. Thus the siblings of Ego's son-in-law or daughter-in-law were his or her *simpetheri* (DHB/Z or SWB/Z). Similarly Ego's brother's wife's brother (BWB),

[7] Such terms as 'second cousin once removed' are seldom used by English-speakers outside of specialist contexts, and many English-speakers are uncertain about their denotation. In folk practice they are often replaced by 'uncle/aunt' or 'nephew/niece' on the basis of relative age.

or sister's husband's brother (ZHB), were both Ego's *simpetheri* (though it should be noted that these relationships were the result of two marriages, not one). On the other hand, the term *simpetheri* was also used to denote all collateral extensions of the paradigmatic relationship between co-parents-in-law. Thus people might address their siblings' parents-in-law as *simpetheri* (BWM/F or ZHM/F), and even two people whose respective siblings were co-parents-in-law might address each other as *simpetheri* (eg BSWFB and BDHFB, or BSWMZ and ZDHFB). After that, collateral usage of the term would fade out, and people would be unlikely to call their cousins' parents-in-law *simpetheri*. But the set of people who could be designated *simpetheri* still remained extensive.

One interesting point that emerges, however, is that although *simpetheros* is the generic term for an affine or relative by marriage(s), in no case was it actually used in Spartokhori to designate any of the immediate relatives of Ego's own spouse (as opposed to the relatives of his or her siblings' spouses, or his or her children's spouses). The relatives of Ego's own spouse, although collectively *simpetheri*, were individually referred to either by a set of specific affinal terms, or else they became terminologically assimilated with Ego's own blood relatives. I shall return to this latter point in due course, because it is of some significance. For the moment, however, it should be noted that with respect to affines, Greek in general expresses a series of genealogical distinctions not recognized in English between varieties of brother- and sister-in-law (Friedl 1964a: 71). In brief, the fundamental distinction is between a spouse's siblings, and siblings' spouses. Thus Ego's wife's brother (WB) is his *kouniadhos*, while Ego's sister's husband (ZH) is his or her *ghambros*, both of whom in English would be without differentiation brothers-in-law. Similarly Ego's husband's sister (HZ) is her *kouniadha*, while Ego's brother's wife (BW) is his or her *nifi*, both of whom in English would be without differentiation sisters-in-law. A further two terms are then used to express the reciprocal relationship obtaining between two people of the same sex whose respective spouses are (a) a pair of sisters, or (b) a pair of brothers. Thus two men who have married a pair of sisters are each other's *badzanakis* (pl. *badzanakia*) (WZH), and two women who have married a pair of brothers are each other's *sinifadha* (HBW) (pl. *sinifadhes*), literally 'co-bride'. Again, in English, they would be simply brothers-in-law and sisters-in-law – if, indeed, they were considered to be relatives at all. Finally, in the descending generation, the term for sister's husband (ZH), *ghambros*, also applies to daughter's husband (DH), son-in-law. Similarly, *nifi*, the term for brother's wife (BW), also applies to a son's wife (SW), daughter-in-law. No verbal distinctions are made between these different genealogical specifications, and the meanings of the terms *ghambros* and *nifi* must be disambiguated by context. At this point it should be noted that the root meanings for *ghambros* and *nifi* are 'groom' and 'bride'. It is thus tempting to translate, or at least to gloss, *ghambros* as 'man-who-has-married-into-our-family' and *nifi* as 'woman-who-has married-into-our-family', thus dispensing with any reference to genealogical levels (Friedl 1964a: 71).[8]

---

[8] Given not only the above terminological assimilations between brother's wife and son's wife and between sister's husband and daughter's husband, but also the terminological distinctions between siblings' spouses and spouse's siblings, it is also tempting to view the whole affinal terminology as reminiscent of a wife-giver/wife-taker exchange system. For several reasons, such an interpretation

Ego's close affinal relatives, then, are designated by specific terms: husband's or wife's father (*petheros*); husband's or wife's mother (*pethera*); brother's wife (*nifi*); sister's husband (*ghambros*); wife's brother (*kouniadhos*); husband's sister (*kouniadha*); son's wife (*nifi*); daughter's husband (*ghambros*); a further two specific terms designate the particular relationship between two men who are married to a pair of sisters (reciprocally *badzanakia*) and between two women who are married to a pair of brothers (reciprocally *sinifadhes*). The generic term for affines, *simpetheri*, is left to designate the relationship between co-parents-in-law, and then an ill-defined but extensive set of other relationships between people that result from the marriages of their respective relatives. But the generic term for affine and the specific terms for affines by no means account for all those relatives that people acquire through marriage, for in general Greek kinship terminology possesses another feature quite common amongst contemporary European bilateral termi-nologies, which is a degree of terminological assimilation between affinal relatives and consanguineous relatives. In Spartokhori this assimilation was taken to an extreme, and in two ways. First, with the exception of those close affinal kin mentioned above, all of Ego's spouse's collateral relatives were terminologically assimilated with Ego's own consanguineous relatives, and in Spartokhori could be referred to and addressed as 'uncle', 'aunt', 'cousin', 'nephew', 'niece', etc. Second, not only were Ego's spouse's relatives terminologically assimilated with Ego's own consanguineous kin, but so too were the both the spouses of Ego's relatives, and the spouses of Ego's spouse's relatives (cf. du Boulay 1984: 552).

The simplest way of grasping this situation is to take the case of first cousins, and to contrast Spartokhoriot and English classifications. Four distinct genea-logical specifications of relatives of each sex are grouped in English by the covering term 'cousin', which (for analytic purposes) kinship theory standardly distinguishes as patrilateral parallel cousins (FBS/D), matrilateral parallel cousins (MZS/D), patrilateral cross-cousins (FZS/D) and matrilateral cross-cousins (MBS/D). Greek also standardly groups all four genealogical specifications of cousin for each sex under the same term, '*ksadherfos*' (masc.) and '*ksadherfi*' (fem.). In Spartokhori, however, it was not just these four genealogical specifications for each sex that became without distinction 'cousins' (*ksadherfia* n. pl.), but sixteen. First, Ego's spouse's four types of cousin were considered to be without distinction Ego's own cousins, thus making a total of eight genealogical specifications for first cousins of each sex (FBS/D, MZS/D, FZS/D, MBS/D and then H/WFBS/D, H/WMZS/D, H/WFZS/D, H/WMBS/D). Second, the spouses of all those eight types of cousin were in turn considered to be Ego's cousins, making sixteen genealogical specifications for first cousins of each sex (FBS/D, MZS/D, FZS/D, MBS/D; then FBSW/DH, MZSW/DH, FZSW/DH, MBSW/DH; and then H/WFBS/D, H/WMZS/D, H/WFZS/D, H/WMBS/D, H/WFBSW/DH, H/WMZSW/DH, H/WFZSW/DH, H/WMBSW/DH). To take an extreme case, Ego's spouse's mother's brother's

---

[8] (cont.) cannot be sustained. First, as will be seen in due course, the rules of consanguinity and affinity prohibit most forms of repeated marriage between families. No idea of regular intermarriage between descent groups can thus be entertained. More fundamentally, the very notion of descent groups between which marriages could be regularly contracted is sociologically inappropriate (at least in Spartokhori), because, as will be shown, the recognition of kinship is fundamentally bilateral. Finally, the terminology itself reverts to complete bilateral symmetry after the asymmetries to be found with the varieties of brother- and sister-in-law.

daughter's husband was called Ego's first cousin in just the same way as his or her mother's brother's son or daughter. In short, the number of genealogical specifications for a first cousin of each sex increased, in comparison with the English terminology, by a factor of four (or of two by two), and what applied in the case of cousins applied equally in the case of all other collateral classifications. Ego's spouse's nephew was also Ego's nephew, and Ego's niece's husband and Ego's spouse's niece's husband were also both Ego's nephew. Spartokhoriot kinship reckoning thus involved a systematic terminological collapse of affinity into consanguinity, which in practice rendered the distinction between kin and affines largely inapplicable. To put the matter in a slightly different way, Spartokhoriot kinship terminology was bilateral not only in making no distinctions between relatives on the father's side and relatives on the mother's side, but also in making few distinctions between relatives on Ego's side and relatives on Ego's spouse's side, or between any of those relatives and their respective spouses.

The systematic and thorough-going nature of what I shall call affinal assimilation within the Spartokhoriot kinship terminology needs to be underscored, for as I have suggested, a degree of terminological assimilation between affinal and consanguineous relatives occurs commonly in European kinship terminologies, and is certainly part of the standard Greek terminology. Thus there is little doubt that, for most English-speakers, the husband or wife of Ego's (consanguineous) uncle or aunt is automatically considered to be an uncle or an aunt. On the other hand, I think that for most English-speakers it would be a moot point whether the husband or wife of their niece or nephew was a nephew or niece, or whether the spouses of their cousins were cousins, though it is not implausible (Bloch 1971). Moreover, I think it fairly unlikely that most English-speakers would refer to their spouse's nephews, nieces, uncles, aunts and cousins as their own nephews, nieces, uncles, aunts and cousins, let alone include all the respective spouses of their spouse's relatives amongst their own relatives. For most Greek-speakers there is similarly no doubt that the husband or wife of a (consanguineous) uncle (*thios*) or aunt (*thia*) is an aunt or uncle. So far as I can gauge, however, most Greek-speakers appear to be rather more ready than English-speakers to effect a series of terminological collapses between consanguineous and affinal relatives, so that it is not uncommon for Greeks to refer to their nephew's wife as their niece, or to their spouse's cousin as their cousin. Moreover, the assimilation of Ego's spouse's relatives with Ego's own relatives does have a basis in Orthodox canon law which interprets quite strictly the biblical injunction that a married couple becomes 'one flesh' (*Pidhalion* 1976: 743 n.1), and, as du Boulay has shown for the village of Ambeli, there is a parallel folk belief 'in the assimilation of the blood of a spouse into the person whom he or she marries'. Moreover, 'this blood absorbed on marriage is also thought to merge into a certain range of relatives surrounding that person' (du Boulay 1984: 546). It follows from such a merger (whether of flesh or of blood) that Ego's spouse's relatives must to some degree be considered Ego's own relatives, and, as we shall see, the rules of consanguinity and affinity set down by the Greek Orthodox church consequently forbid a pair of siblings to marry a pair of siblings (or a pair of first cousins), since as soon as a marriage has been contracted between two people and they have become 'one flesh', their respective siblings (or first cousins) are effectively each other's siblings (or first cousins). Similarly, marriage (necessarily a second marriage) is forbidden between a person and any of his or her deceased spouse's closer consanguineous kin (since they have already become via marriage that person's own kin). Nevertheless, for many urban Greeks the kinship status of, say, a cousin's spouse would be uncertain, and such descriptive phrases as 'my cousin's husband' or 'my cousin's wife' might seem more appropriate (as it does in English) than the designation 'cousin'. But any suspicion that we are here entering a grey area in bilateral kinship reckoning would not be unwarranted. The Spartokhoriots' systematic inclusion of all their affinally acquired relatives (both the relatives of their spouse, and the spouses of their own relatives and their spouses' relatives) to number amongst their own cousins, nephews, nieces, uncles, aunts, etc could be seen simply as an extreme example of a feature inherent in Greek kinship reckoning as a whole. But although I do not think that the Spartokhoriots' system of reckoning is a case of regional variation, I do think that their extension of kinship terms to include all the relatives of spouses and all the spouses of relatives points towards a variation in the role of kinship itself. An anecdote may clarify the situation.

One day an old Spartokhoriot referred to a certain Maria as his *kouniadha*. Since I knew the genealogy of the family, I was slightly surprised, for Maria was not the sister of the old man's wife (which is what I had understood to be the definition of a *kouniadha*, a spouse's sister) but rather his wife's brother's wife, the wife of his *kouniadhos*. It thus appeared from his usage that in Spartokhori there were two sorts of *kouniadha*: one who was a *kouniadha* in her own right, so to speak, and one who was the wife of a *kouniadhos*, and so a *kouniadha* by affinal assimilation. Anxious to ascertain that this was not some idiosyncratic usage, I went to the coffee-shop where I asked a group of elders what they called their wife's brother's wife. After certain computational difficulties (for the Spartokhoriots were quite as slow as anyone else at working out genealogical specifications when matters were put in this clumsy way), they unanimously pronounced that such a woman was without doubt a *kouniadha*. Suddenly, however, strenuous objections were made by the village's young rural policeman, who had been posted to Spartokhori from his hometown of Agrinion on the mainland. It was ridiculous, he said, to call such a woman a *kouniadha*. A *kouniadha* was your wife's sister. This woman, the wife of a *kouniadhos*, was merely a *simpethera*, a female affine (which, indeed, was what I thought to be the case). A heated argument then ensued, which ended with the young policeman storming out of the coffee-shop, but not without a parting shot: 'Well, how should *I* know? She could be a *kouniadha* here – it's a *village* isn't it?'

The policeman's remark was not constructively meant; nevertheless, I think he put his finger on the matter. Whether one calls one's *kouniadhos'* wife a *kouniadha* (or one's cousin's husband a cousin, or one's spouse's nephew a nephew) is not a question of 'regional variation' or even of the kinship system itself, but rather of the degree to which kinship is important in day-to-day life as a means of recognizing, classifying and ordering the individuals with whom one has constant dealings. It is, as Bloch argues, not a question of fixed denotations, but of the process of moral and tactical inclusion and exclusion (1971). For the urbanite whose kin may be scattered and seldom encountered, and for whom a range of other important relationships may be formed at work and in social life, a cousin's wife may be no more than a cousin's wife.[9] In the village, however (and even for those who are absent from it for substantial periods), the benefits and obligations of kinship are omnipresent realities, and the immediate effect of the system of reckoning I have described is exponentially to increase the number of kin whom any individual can claim. The very extensiveness of a system that regularly allows the incorporation of all one's spouse's relatives and all the spouses of one's own relatives and of one's spouse's relatives into the set of those whom one acknowledges as family enables kinship to embrace within its moral fold almost everyone whose actions (and existence) constitute the stuff of daily life. In short, the system allowed the near congruence of community and kinship, and placed most village interaction within kinship's covenant. In English the connection may now be a dead issue, but as Freeman reminds us, kin and kind are cognate terms (1968).

For the Spartokhoriots, this extension of kinship via affinity was not, then, really a matter of terminology pure and simple, but rather of the moral inclusion that use of the terminology implied, and I was repeatedly told that there was no difference between a person's own relatives and those of his or her spouse, or between such relatives and their respective spouses.[10] Thus, for example, when I once remarked on the fact that my old friend, Mikhalis, and a young sailor, Pavlos, were suddenly to be found keeping company, Mikhalis explained the matter by saying that he was drinking with his nephew. I foolishly protested that Pavlos was not Mikhalis's nephew, and was promptly reminded that Pavlos had married Mikhalis's brother's daughter a few months before. As Mikhalis said, 'I am very much an uncle', and they continued to drink together in their newfound kinship. It is also worth recalling once again the unhappy story of Andonis the builder. Andonis and his father-in-law were by no means the only immigrants to Spartokhori; so were many of the most prominent and respected figures within the community. The difference was that, unlike Andonis, most other immigrants had married women from Spartokhoriot families and thus, given Spartokhori's form of kinship reckoning, they had automatically acquired a whole host of relatives whom they regarded as their own. Marriage brought them immediate integration via the acquisition of kinship. Indeed, a number of the older men who continually boasted to me of the size of their kindred ('I am related to half the village') and who loudly proclaimed that they were *poli Spartokhoritis* (very much a Spartokhoriot) possessed, with the exception of their own children (and sometimes grandchildren), not one consanguineous relative in Spartokhori. They did, however, unhesitatingly count as their family all their wives' relatives, and all their children's affinal relatives, and then all the respective spouses and children of their wives' relatives, and this often did make up half the village. The whole of their enormous kindreds – and, be it noted, their identity as Spartokhoriots – depended on affinity.

[9] I have met young middle-class urban Greeks who have trouble distinguishing their *kouniadhos* from their *ghambros*, and who would be hard put to say who their *badzanakis* was (if they knew the term at all).

[10] This attitude did not, however, so readily extend to ascendants, but then neither did the terminology assimilate ascendants. Ego's spouse's parents did not become Ego's 'father' and 'mother', and Ego's spouse's grandparents (*papous* and *yiayia*) did not become Ego's grandparents.

Endogamy

The Spartokhoriots employed, then, a fairly standard bilateral kinship terminology, but it was bilateral to an extreme in that there was a systematic collapse of affinity into consanguinity, so that while as in any cognatic system relatives were counted through both male and female links, in Spartokhori they were also counted through affinal links. The Spartokhoriot kindred, the group of relatives at the centre of which each individual Spartokhoriot stood, thus consisted not only of cognates, but also of affines and of affines of affines. By definition, bilateral kindreds overlap, but given the Spartokhoriots' system of reckoning, the degree of overlap between each person's kindred tended to be very substantial, and in the end almost every Spartokhoriot could trace a relationship with almost every other Spartokhoriot, and importantly, often by multiple paths. This situation was not, however, the result solely of the Spartokhoriots' form of kinship reckoning, for it would not have occurred without their adherence to a fairly commonplace practice in rural Greece which, though not systematic, was strongly endorsed: namely, village endogamy (cf. Couroucli 1985: 68–9; Hart 1991: 57; Vernier 1991: 105, 151; Herzfeld 1983).

There was no rule that stated that a Spartokhoriot must marry a Spartokhoriot, but village endogamy was a practice that sustained village solidarity, and which in turn was largely justified by the prior fact of village solidarity, for the Spartokhoriots argued that a marriage in which both partners came from the village was the best marriage precisely because everyone involved already knew each other. Thus people married within the community, and the community in turn was defined by the interfamilial bonds created by marriage. It is worth examining this situation in a little detail.

If we take what I referred to in Chapter 3 as the core population (those whose normal place of residence was the village) of Spartokhori in 1980, then of the 169 married couples included, in 122 cases both partners were from the village. In thirty-two cases the husband was a Spartokhoriot but the wife had come from outside the village: in fifteen cases from the neighbouring village of Katomeri, in three from the small port hamlet of Vathi, in twelve from Lefkadha, in one from the mainland coastal village of Astakos, and in one from the island of Ithaki. In a further seven cases it was the wife who was a native Spartokhoriot, and her husband who was an immigrant from Lefkadha or the mainland. In most of these latter cases the men had been resident in Spartokhori for many years (in two cases for over fifty years) and their children and grandchildren had been born, and had married, in Spartokhori. These men considered themselves to be thoroughly Spartokhoriot and correctly likened their situation to that of the bulk of the Spartokhoriots' ancestors who similarly had come from various parts of Greece to marry and settle on Meganisi. Finally, there was a total of eight married couples (including Andonis the builder and his wife and her parents), where both partners were immigrants from Lefkadha or the mainland. In general these people were considered *kseni*, but in most cases they had become integrated into the village through the marriages of their children (or grandchildren) to Spartokhoriots whom they could then count as family along with all the relatives of their

Spartokhoriot affines. Andonis and his wife were exceptional, since although Andonis's wife was born in the village, she was the daughter of immigrants (none of whose other children had married in the village), and her husband was in turn an immigrant.

If these last eight couples are excluded on the grounds that their marriages cannot be said to indicate Spartokhoriot preferences, then it appears that nearly 76 per cent of the marriages of the present core population were village-endogamous, and a total of 87 per cent were island-endogamous, though it is a significant point that 'foreign' partners from Meganisi's other two villages, Katomeri and Vathi, were actually fewer than in-marrying partners from Lefkadha, the mainland and elsewhere in Greece, despite these villages' proximity. The Spartokhoriots' denigration of their neighbours was matched by their avoidance of marital alliances (and hence kinship) with them. Of course the above figures give only a crude picture of Spartokhoriot marriage preferences, since they exclude an uncertain number of women (and a smaller number of men) who had married out into villages in Lefkadha, other Ionian islands, or the mainland; they do, however, provide an accurate representation of the degree of endogamy actually to be found within the core population in 1980, and the marriages of Spartokhoriots who were not normally resident in the village at the time of my fieldwork appear also to have been largely endogamous. Given the degree of population dispersal (especially if overseas emigrants are taken into account), it was not possible exhaustively to account for all marriages, but a sample of 113 known marriages revealed that 65 per cent of Spartokhoriot males living outside the village (for the most part in Athens) were married to women from the village of Spartokhori, and 75 per cent had married women from Meganisi. There were, of course, extreme cases of out-marriage. One sailor was married to a Danish woman (who frequently visited the village with her husband to see his aged parents). Another young man, whose parents moved between the village and Athens, was engaged to a Korean woman from Seoul. A third man, frequently resident in the village, had a Romanian wife. Such marriages were the result of the Spartokhoriots' employment in international shipping, while overseas migration had also resulted in marriage with foreign partners, and although it seemed reasonably clear that even when Spartokhoriots were resident overseas, they preferred to marry at least fellow Greeks, exceptions were not rare and a number of village residents had foreign daughters-in-law or sons-in-law in Australia, the United States or Canada. When it come to the marriages of Spartokhori's overseas-born descendants, however, endogamy of any sort, whether national or village, approached its end – but then so too did anything that could meaningfully be called the Spartokhoriot community.

Nevertheless, overseas residence did not it itself necessarily diminish the importance of endogamous marriage, at least for relatives who remained in the village. When postwar emigration commenced in the late 1950s and 1960s, most emigrants were already married or engaged, and thus had Spartokhoriot spouses. Alternatively, male emigrants sent back for Spartokhoriot brides after they had established themselves in their new country. This latter pattern persisted up to the period of my stay, during which several Spartokhoriot brides were despatched overseas. But though in most cases emigrant bachelors had positively requested their families to find them a Spartokhoriot bride, or had themselves visited Spartokhori specifically to find a wife (a choice encouraged by the fact that many emigrants continued to see their overseas residence as temporary), in some cases it was clear that pressure had been brought on overseas migrants to comply with tradition to the social benefit of their village-based kin. In 1977 a young man returned to Spartokhori on holiday from Canada where he had been living for seven years (and where he worked for his uncle who had emigrated some twenty-five years earlier). He spoke excellent English, seemed thoroughly Canadian, and, at least in my company, was both embarrassed by, and critical of, village attitudes and behaviour. Yet on my return to Spartokhori after a year's absence I discovered that he had subsequently married a young woman from Spartokhori. The match had been arranged for him during his brief stay in the village, and shortly afterwards his parents had left for Toronto to deliver their future daughter-in-law to him and to witness their son's marriage before themselves returning to Spartokhori. No doubt the young man's marriage had been arranged in his own best interests, but it still brought his parents advantages within the village that were not negated by the fact that the young couple would be permanently resident overseas, for his parents' own kinship ties within Spartokhori had been considerably extended, just as they would have if the couple had remained in Spartokhori. Again, in 1979, another son of the village returned on holiday after twelve years' residence in California only to find himself engaged to be married. As he ruefully explained to me one evening over a drink, 'Shit, man, I'm not sure this is going to work out. I mean, she doesn't even speak English. I didn't want it to happen like this – but you know what they're like.'

The village family

If the sort of village endogamy that I have just described is considered in conjunction with the Spartokhoriots' form of kinship reckoning (whereby all of a person's spouse's relatives, together with all the spouses of his or her relatives and of his or her spouse's relatives, are counted as that person's own relatives), it is easy to see the basis on which kinship and community become virtually congruent. There were 384 genealogical specifications for various types of cousins, uncles, aunts, nephews and nieces, all of whom fell within the collateral bounds of second cousin, and who could thus without hesitation be considered members of a person's family: thirty-two specifications for first cousins; 128 specifications for second cousins; sixteen specifications for uncles and aunts; sixteen specifications for nephews and nieces; and sixty-four specifications for nephews, nieces, uncles and aunts who would be termed first cousins once removed in English. If great-uncles, great-aunts, grand-nephews and grand-nieces are also included, a further sixty-four specifications would be added, and to the genealogical array of an individual's family must definitely be added Ego's siblings, Ego's spouse's siblings, their respective spouses, Ego's direct ascendants, Ego's direct descendants and their spouses, and Ego's parents-in-law. Finally, there remains an uncertain number of specifications for other *simpetheri* (affines).

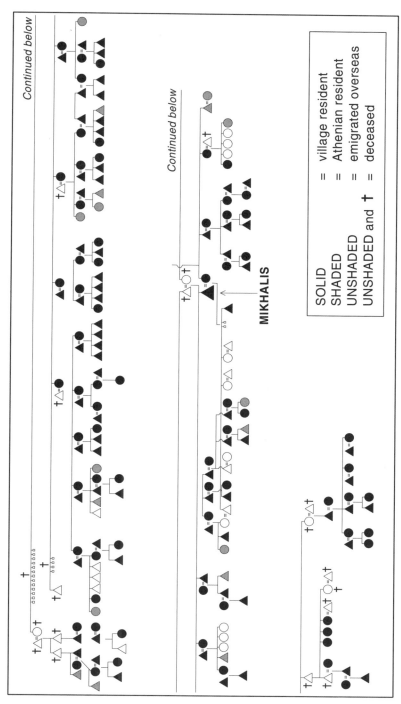

Figure 4.1 Mikhalis's family

The above computation is, of course, a purely theoretical one. It refers to the number of *genealogical specifications* for relatives who could be considered members of a person's family in Spartokhori, not to the number of actual relatives that any particular Spartokhoriot possessed. Nevertheless, the inclusive nature of this form of bilateral reckoning, coupled with the practice of village endogamy, did greatly increase the probability of any particular individual being able to count a very extensive array of kin within the village. It is also worth noting that although emigration reduced the absolute number of relatives whom most people had living in the village, it was unlikely to affect the relative proportion of their relatives to their non-relatives in the village, and it was, of course, this proportion which was the important factor for the degree to which kinship acted as a means of village integration. It is not feasible to display the full set of every Spartokhoriot's circle of village relatives in order to demonstrate the degree to which the theoretical possibilities I have just described resulted in the welding of the village population into a single, complex and internally inter-twined genealogical unit, but one simple way of proceeding is to take a single individual and to show the proportion of the total village population for which his family accounted. This at least provides an illustration of the situation (see Figure 4.1).

My old friend Mikhalis, a man in his mid-sixties, was one of the many older Spartokhoriots fond of remarking that he was related to half the village. This claim was not far from the truth, but it is important to note that Mikhalis's family does not appear to have been numerically exceptional. Since Mikhalis had four sisters and two brothers who survived to adulthood (and who were still alive and resident in the village in1980, their ages ranging from sixty-five to ninety) the number of his nephews and nieces (of various kinds) was high. But only one of Mikhalis's father's siblings, a sister, survived to adulthood, and Mikhalis's grand-father appears to have had no surviving siblings. The number of his patrilateral cousins was thus low. Indeed, in Figure 4.1 there are no second cousins displayed. Moreover, neither Mikhalis's mother nor his wife seems to have come from particularly prolific families. The number of his matrilateral and affinal relatives was therefore not out of the ordinary, although it may be that I failed to discover them all, since a person's relatives were not always pointed out to be relatives unless some specific occasion prompted the claim (a point of some significance to which I shall return in due course).

In Figure 4.1, then, I have marked in solid tint all of Mikhalis's relatives who were still alive and who were normally resident in the village in 1980, that is, they who were members of the core population. His collateral relatives – siblings, brothers-in-law and sisters-in-law, nephews, nieces and cousins – numbered 122. Added to these, Mikhalis had a further seventeen close *simpetheri* resident in the village whose relationship with him derived from the marriages of a son and a daughter (both of whom were resident in Australia). Including his wife and his remaining bachelor son, Mikhalis thus had a total of 141 relatives permanently in the village. But these were considerably less than the grand total of resident Spartokhoriots whom Mikhalis could count as family, for I have omitted (partly for reasons of space, and partly because of the inherent vagueness of the category) Mikhalis's many other *simpetheri* who were relatives of his siblings' spouses or relatives of his affinal nephews and nieces (for example, relatives of his brother's daughter's husband). Thus the *minimum* number of resident Sparto-khoriots whom Mikhalis could claim as family was 141, and if we take the core population as 551, then Mikhalis's kin accounted for at least 25 per cent of the village. If all *simpetheri* were taken into account, it would not be unreasonable to assume that he was related to half the village. It should also be pointed out that I have not included in this calculation many of Mikhalis's relatives who appear in Figure 4.1 but who were not year-round residents of Spartokhori, although Mikhalis himself would have counted them, for they included many of the most active members of the Spartokhoriot community.

As I have suggested, the size of Mikhalis's village family was not exceptional. What makes it account for so large a proportion of the village population is not particularly high fertility amongst his kin, but simply the method of reckoning kin. Two consequences of the size of village kindreds should be noted. First, it would be necessary to take only Mikhalis himself and, say, two or three of his cousins – especially cousins by marriage – for this group of closely related men to count between them virtually the entire population of the village as family. Second, not only would the individual families of these men overlap, they would also be found to contain a series of further interconnections resulting from marriages between their families. Overall, it was the extent of personal kindreds and their overlapping and intertwining nature that justified the assertion that 'we are all one family here'. It would even license us to talk not about Sparto-khoriot genealogies, but about a single Spartokhoriot genealogy. Despite Sparto-khori's history of continual immigration, village endogamy and the recognition of all types of affinal kin had welded the population into a single genealogical unit. Indeed, given the form of Spartokhoriot kin reckoning, an individual's own marriage was sufficient to equip him or her with a vast array of newfound kin and thereby to incorporate them into the Spartokhoriot village-family complex. Such genealogical isolates as Andonis and his family were rare and the result not of immigration itself, but of marriage between immigrant and immigrant. 'We are all *kseni* (foreigners) here' and 'We are all one family here' were not contradictory statements, but rather two aspects of Spartokhori's demography, the one his-torical, the other sociological.

The incest prohibition

In one sense, then, the Spartokhoriots were close marriers, and village endogamy was crucial to the maintenance and perpetuation of kinship connections within the village, even when those who married were no longer village residents. Nevertheless, the Spartokhoriots largely respected the marriage prohibitions of the Orthodox church, although Spartokhoriot practice, like that of many Greek communities, departed from church teaching in some respects.

The Greek Orthodox church's rules of consanguinity and affinity are set out in full in the *Pidhalion* (1976: 739–62), the church's guide book to canon law, and it is worth summarizing their major features, for inasmuch as the Spartokhoriots departed from them, they appear to have done so unwittingly. Certainly it was always the rules of the church that were invoked in all explanations of who might and who might not, marry, and given the degree of interrelatedness within the Spartokhoriot community, those rules were important, especially in relation to collateral kin and affines.

According to the church, marriage is never allowed between direct descendants and ascendants. More importantly, marriage is forbidden between collaterals down to and including the seventh degree, that is to say, down to and including a marriage between Ego and the child of his or her second cousin (a second cousin once removed, or in Greek, a variety of nephew or niece). Marriages between third cousins, being of the eighth degree, are permitted (*Pidhalion* 1976: 740–2). The *Pidhalion* further forbids marriages between affinally related kin down to and including the sixth degree (and in some cases the seventh), that is marriages in which an affinal link already exists between the respective kin of the two individuals involved (or, to put matters another way, where two marriages doubly unite two families). The *Pidhalion* particularly rejects such marriages when 'the names confuse', that is to say where the two marriages would result in a terminological confusion between kin such that, for example, someone would be simultaneously Ego's spouse's sibling (*kouniadhos* or *kouniadha*) via the one path, and Ego's sibling's spouse (*ghambros* or *nifi*) via the other. Thus, as I have already mentioned, a pair of siblings may not marry a pair of siblings, for once one marriage is celebrated, then the respective siblings of the married couple are already related. Similarly, a pair of siblings may not marry a pair of first cousins. A pair of siblings may, however, marry a pair of second cousins since the affinal relationship created by whichever was the first marriage would fall outside the prohibited degrees. Similarly a pair of first cousins may marry a pair of first cousins (*Pidhalion* 1976: 742–50).[11]

The *Pidhalion*, however, is only a guide for the clergy (du Boulay 1984), and in practice the restrictions on marriage it sets out need not be so extensive, for it is possible to obtain dispensations for such unions as do not greatly infringe the spirit of the law. Furthermore, in many areas of rural Greece, local conceptions of incest displace those of official church teaching. Thus in Athens and other urban centres, as well as overseas, and quite traditionally in some parts of rural Greece, it is not uncommon to find marriages between second cousins that have been celebrated by the church.[12] But though the Spartokhoriots were aware of such marriages, they neither approved of nor practised them (and in accordance with their generally anti-clerical outlook, would remark that if people paid a priest enough, no doubt they could do whatever they liked). Far from relaxing church law, the majority of Spartokhoriots interpreted it in a way that made the prohibitions on marriage between collaterals even more extensive than those officially set out. Thus the Spartokhoriots stated that marriage between third cousins was prohibited, and that the first permitted union was with the child of a third cousin. The basis of this village prohibition nevertheless remained a version

---

[11]Others of the extensive prohibitions included here relate to marriages that would necessarily be second marriages, that is, with the consanguineous or affinal relative of a deceased spouse, or between one pair of direct descendants (such as mother and daughter) and another pair of direct descendants (such as father and son).

[12]See especially Vernier (1991: 106) for very close marriages on Karpathos.

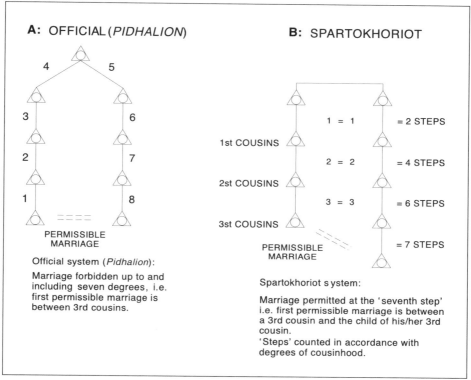

A: OFFICIAL (*PIDHALION***)**

B: SPARTOKHORIOT

Official system (*Pidhalion*):

Marriage forbidden up to and
including seven degrees, i.e.
first permissible marriage is
between 3rd cousins.

Spartokhoriot system:

Marriage permitted at the 'seventh step'
i.e. first permissible marriage is between
a 3rd cousin and the child of his/her 3rd
cousin.
'Steps' counted in accordance with
degrees of cousinhood.

Figure 4.2 Comparison of official and Spartokhoriot reckoning of degrees of
consanguinity

of the rules stated in the *Pidhalion*, that seven degrees set the limits of consanguinity. The divergence arose from the manner in which the degrees were
calculated.

In the *Pidhalion*, all degrees of relatedness are calculated from one of the
parties up to a common ascendant, and then down again to the other party like
a ladder (*Pidhalion* 1976: 740 n. 2). Thus siblings are two degrees removed from
each other: one degree from one of the siblings up to their father or mother, and
then one degree down again to the other sibling. By this method of calculation,
third cousins are eight degrees removed from each other and so may marry. (It
should be noted that in all such calculations a married couple counts as a single
person, being of 'one flesh'.) Village reckoning of the degrees, however, appeared
to be based not on this system, but on the everyday reckoning of cousins (see
Figure 4.2). Thus I was frequently told, 'You have two siblings (*adherfia*); their
children are [reciprocally] first cousins (*prota ksadherfia*); their children are
[reciprocally] second cousins (*dheftera ksadherfia*); their children are [reciprocally]
third cousins (*trita ksadherfia*), and so on.' In short, this system of reckoning does
not count from one party up to a common ascendant and then down to the other
party, but counts down from a pair of siblings. If it is used to calculate not

degrees of cousinhood but degrees of consanguinity, each step downwards has to be doubled to account for the two lines of descent, but instead of there being two degrees of consanguinity between a sibling pair, siblings are taken as a unity with no genealogical distance between them, and third cousins will end up being only six degrees removed from each other. Their relationship will thus fall within the incest prohibition of seven degrees. As if to compensate for the extensiveness of the prohibition created, however, seven degrees was then taken by the Spartokhoriots to be the first permissible degree for marriage rather than as the last prohibited degree, and so, according to the Spartokhoriots, a person might marry the child of his or her third cousin.

This rather commonsensical method of reckoning degrees of consanguinity by following the degrees of cousinhood finds a close parallel in the village of Ambeli, in Evia, where a sibling pair was similarly taken to be a unity, that is, to be 'one blood' and of the same '*zinari*' (literally a type of long belt) (du Boulay 1984: 537–8). First, second and third cousins and so on were then respectively one, two and three, etc *zinaria* (pl.) distant from each other. Given the basic similarity in the method of reckoning, du Boulay's analysis of Ambeliot descent, marriage and incest prohibitions may throw some light on the Spartokhoriot situation, for as du Boulay observes, in the Ambeliot system of reckoning 'the *zinari* cannot mean "one (canonical) degree of kinship", for siblings belong to the same *zinari*. Neither can one *zinari* mean "one generation", since any set of siblings are, although on an identical generational level with their cousins, distanced from them by one or more *zinaria*' (1984: 538). Rather, '[t]he concept of the *zinari* ... appears to be a way of understanding differentiation between one member of the kindred and another, not solely in terms of generation nor of degrees of kinship, but in terms of an integral vision of both the transmission and renewal of the blood' (1984: 539). Put simply, a sibling pair are thought to share a single common blood derived from the union of their parents. Each exogamous marriage of the siblings and their descendants (reciprocally first cousins, second cousins, third cousins and so on) is likened to the 'crossing' or turns of a belt (the *zinari*), an outward and cyclical movement that is seen to entail a progressive dilution of the original 'one blood' shared by the siblings up to the point where their descendants are considered to possess sufficiently different blood to allow their intermarriage. Traditionally, this point was set after three *zinaria*, a prohibition preserved in the proverbial statement, 'For three *zinaria* marriage is not allowed'. As du Boulay points out, however:

> it is clear that the crossing of blood which the *zinari* represents, refers not to individual marriages, but to the whole set of marriages contracted at each generational level of the kindred. It is the common stock, and not the several individual stocks, which is thought of as being renewed by the crossing, thus bringing it about that the children of siblings are separated not by two *zinaria* (the marriages of the two siblings) but by one (the common task on which both siblings have entered, of bringing about the birth of a new generation). (1984: 539)

To the best of my knowledge, the Spartokhoriots employed no concept (or metaphor) precisely analogous to the Ambeliots' *zinari* or turning of a belt, but the notions of siblings sharing a common blood, of that blood's progressive dilution through exogamous marriage, and of those exogamous marriages constituting

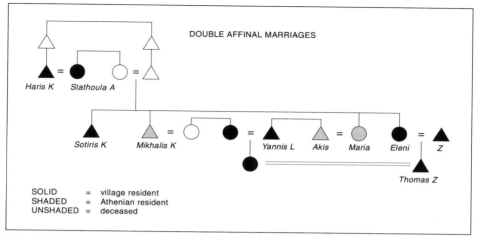

DOUBLE AFFINAL MARRIAGES

Haris K   Stathoula A

Sotiris K   Mikhalis K   Yannis L   Akis   Maria   Eleni   Z

Thomas Z

SOLID   =   village resident
SHADED   =   Athenian resident
UNSHADED   =   deceased

Figure 4.3 Affinal marriages

an outward or cyclical movement, all appear to have formed part of the Spartokhoriots' understanding of the marriage prohibitions, for the Spartokhoriot prohibition on marriage between third cousins (like the Ambeliots' proverbial statement 'For three *zinaria* marriage is not allowed') assumes a form of reckoning in which siblings constitute the original unity from which further degrees of kinship are calculated (rather than siblings being, as in the canonical system, two degrees apart). More specifically, however, the Spartokhoriots explained that marriage was allowed between a person and the child of his or her third cousin precisely because at the point 'the blood changes (*allazi to ema*)', and that when such a marriage occurred, 'the circle closes (*klini o kiklos*)'.

Marriages between affines

Scrupulous (not to say over-scrupulous) though the Spartokhoriots were with regard to the prohibitions on marriage between consanguineous kin, when it came to affinal relatives they in fact married closer than strict church law permits. According to the *Pidhalion*, marriage with an affine is forbidden up to and including the sixth, or even the seventh degree, especially if 'the names confuse'.[13] The Spartokhoriots regularly broke this rule, and there were numerous instances of a pair of siblings married to a pair of first cousins. It is through such affinal unions that village genealogies (or perhaps one should say *the* village genealogy) become most entwined. Not only was everyone related to everyone else, but in many cases the relationships were multi-stranded. A single complex example will serve as illustration.

Seven marriages are represented in Figure 4.3, six of which are affinal marriages. In the first generation shown, Haris K married Stathoula A, and Haris's

[13]Degrees of relatedness between affines are calculated in the same manner as for consanguineous relatives (described above), but each married couple is reckoned as a single entity.

patrilateral parallel cousin married Stathoula's sister. According to strict church law the marriages (or rather, whichever was the later marriage) were improper, since Haris K and Stathoula A were affinally related in the sixth degree as a result of the marriage between Haris's first cousin and Stathoula's sister. Moreover the 'names' confused, since as a result of the two marriages Haris's first cousin (his father's brother's son) was simultaneously his *badzanakis*, his wife's sister's husband. So far as the village was concerned, however, no shadow of impropriety hung over their marriage. The members of the next generation, of course, found themselves doubly related to their parents' collateral relatives. Long before my fieldwork Haris and Stathoula's children had immigrated to America (where they married foreigners) and Haris's first cousin cum brother-in-law (*badzanakis*) and his wife had died, but the latter couple left seven children, four of whom are shown in Figure 4.3. Haris was their 'uncle', but, as the Spartokhoriots put it, he was their uncle 'from both sides (*ap'tis dhio meries*)', that is to say, patrilaterally he was their father's father's brother's son (FFBS) and matrilaterally he was their mother's sister's husband (MZH). Here, however, there was no confusion of 'names', for however their relationship was viewed, in Greek terminology Haris ended up being their 'uncle'. Likewise they and their spouses were all unambiguously his nephews and nieces (*anepsia*), but again 'from both sides'.

But further doubling-up of kinship was created by the marriages of this generation, too. Sotiros K, like his uncle Haris, was a permanent resident of Spartokhori, and Sotiros's brother, Mikhalis, was a sailor resident in Athens. However, Mikhalis's wife, Evangelia, had a sister who was married to a village resident, Yannis L. Yannis also had a brother in Athens, and this brother, Akis, was married to Maria, the sister of Sotiros and Mikhalis K. The first three marriages shown in a line in Figure 4.3 thus produce a matrimonial circle that united three families (each with a different family name). Such marriages uniting three families in a closed circle are specifically mentioned in the *Pidhalion,* and some prohibitions apply (although the present edition admits that the earlier canons failed to specify them). The prohibitions are not, however, extensive, and in fact all three marriages shown in Figure 4.3 are legitimate in the eyes of the church. Indeed, the exact situation represented by Figure 4.3 is given in the *Pidhalion* as the example of a permitted series of marriages (1976: 752). A fourth marriage, however, is shown on the same level in Figure 4.3, since another sister of Sotiros and Mikhalis K, Eleni, married into the Z family. Her son, Thomas, a young sailor resident in the village, then married the daughter of Yannis L. Thus a further marriage in the third generation again bound the families together, and Thomas's wife was both his mother's sister's husband's brother's daughter (MZBHD) and his mother's brother's wife's sister's daughter (MBWZD). Again, this marriage was legitimate in the eyes of the church, but again it resulted in a doubling-up of kin, and in a series of relationships that can be traced from both sides. For example, Thomas Z was Mikhalis K's nephew, being his sister's son, and so Thomas Z's wife was reckoned to be Mikhalis K's niece by virtue of her marriage. But she was also Mikhalis K's niece because she was the daughter of his wife's sister. Actually she was yet further related to Mikhalis K by a third route, since as well as being his wife's sister, she was the child of his sister's husband's brother.

Such double (or triple) connections from both sides were often cited with pride by Spartokhoriots, at least when connections with a particular family or individual could be considered advantageous. Thus while spouses who happened to have been born with the same family name would hastily point out that they nevertheless came from 'different families' (lest any suspicion of incest be aroused), it would also be pointed out that a particularly favoured cousin or nephew was in fact a cousin or nephew 'from both sides', and whole families would also point out that they were 'very much related (*poli singhenis*)' with another family from both sides. Moreover, the doubling-up of affinal connections via two (or more) marriages was also extolled on the grounds that the desire for a second marriage between the same two families demonstrated how successful to all concerned the first one had been. Despite the impossibility of truly systematic marriages, there was thus a sense in which double affinal matches represented the reforging of successful alliances (though it might be suspected that the declared moral advantage of particular double alliances was as much a *post factum* interpretation placed on them as a real determinant of their formation). It must be stressed, however, that in the end systematic or repeated marriages between Spartokhoriot families remained an impossibility, and not simply because of the restrictions resulting from the church's rules of consanguinity and affinity (or the Spartokhoriots' interpretation of those rules). The real impediment to systematic marriage alliances was the absence of clearcut and bounded kinship groups between which marriages could repeatedly occur. The family as household or domestic unit extended out to become the family as kindred, which had no precise limit; moreover, since the family was bilaterally defined from the viewpoint of each individual person, each person's family was different from, but substantially overlapped with, the families of any number of his or her relatives. People were thus always simultaneously members of any number of different families. Spartokhoriot double affinal marriages would thus be seen rather as a thickening of the web of kinship relations between individuals, than as a form of repeated marriage between kinship groups.

Patriliny and the *soi*

I have emphasized the bilateral nature of Spartokhoriot kinship, and in so doing the extensiveness of Spartokhoriot kinship reckoning and the imprecision of the Spartokhoriot concept of family. I have also suggested that as a result kinship in Spartokhori did not create corporate groups within the village, but rather united the village as a whole into a single unit. This is a fairly standard consequence of bilateral kindreds, which by definition overlap, but it must be admitted that in principle nothing stands in the way of a bilateral form of kinship reckoning being coupled with any number of unilineal practices, or with the existence of corporate groups recruited on some other type of kinship basis (Needham 1971: lxxxvi). In this regard two aspects of Spartokhoriot kinship deserve attention: first, the composition of the *soi*, which in Spartokhori (and in contrast with some other areas of Greece) was agnatically defined; second, the Spartokhoriot system of hereditary godparenthood, which to an extent created corporate groups, and which will be discussed in detail in Chapter 5.

As we have seen, the Spartokhoriots referred to the bilateral kindred (replete in their case with affines and the affines of affines) simply as the *ikoyenia* or family. However, in both Campbell's account of the Sarakatsani (1963, 1964) and du Boulay's account of the village of Ambeli on the island of Evia (1974), the bilateral kindred is denoted by the term *soi*. This same term, *soi*, was also used in Spartokhori, but referred there to those who shared (or in the case of women, had shared before marriage) a common family surname (*eponimo*) or family nickname (*paratsoukli*); in short, it referred to an agnatically defined group of relatives who contrasted with the bilaterally defined kindred or *ikoyenia*.

Although the Spartokhoriot definition of the *soi* departed from what was reported in Campbell's and du Boulay's ethnographies, it was by no means peculiar, and as Herzfeld has pointed out, 'Increasing ethnographic evidence ... shows that the range of kin included in the *soi* is not the same everywhere in Greece, and that, indeed, there are some communities ... where the term is accorded an exclusively agnatic meaning' (1983: 157). I think it could now be suggested that an agnatic definition of the *soi* is quite common in Greece, but whatever the case, the real question (as Herzfeld makes clear) is not one of local terminology, but of the nature of local concepts and social institutions, and thus of whether or not an agnatic usage of the term *soi* in Spartokhori actually points towards anything that might substantially modify or depart from what I have described as a bilateral kinship system. I would argue that it does not, for the *soi* in Spartokhori had no corporate existence. Just as Herzfeld (1983) reports for the village of Pefko in Rhodes (where the term *soi* is similarly used in an agnatic sense to designate those who share a single surname) the members of a Spartokhoriot *soi* did not own any property in common or unite for any political purposes. Nor did they constitute an exogamous group or, for that matter, an endogamous one, although marriage partners who shared the same natal surname would sometimes point out that they came from different *soya* (pl.) if only to dispel any suspicion that their marriage might have been incestuous. On the whole, the *soi* seemed to exist in Spartokhori only in name, or rather, by virtue of names, and in all practical contexts it was the bilateral *ikoyenia*, not the agnatic *soi*, that was important. If people considered themselves relatives (whether agnatic or cognatic), they referred to each other as *ikoyenia*. If they were not so closely related as to count themselves family (that is to say, their relationship was beyond that of third cousins) but they still shared a common surname, they might remark, in recognition of their common agnatic ancestry, that they were nevertheless *soi*.

This situation would seem to be in clear contrast with the strong agnatic ties described by Herzfeld (1983; 1985) for the Cretan village of Glendi, where the *soi* again refers to an agnatic surname group, and to subdivisions of that group 'known by a collective form of the apical ancestor's nickname (*paratsoukli* or *paranomi*) or baptismal name' (Herzfeld 1983: 157). These patrigroups, as Herzfeld calls them, do not own property in common, but they are '*conceptually* and *ideologically* corporate, as is shown by the naming of whole neighbourhoods after such groups and by the fact that the groups ideally vote in solidary blocs in local (and sometimes also in national) elections' (Herzfeld 1985: 283, emphasis in the original). Moreover, 'any insult to the patriline becomes an insult to the person as well. Character traits are assumed to be transmitted, in the main, through the male line' (ibid. 53), while uterine kinship is considered a weaker bond, and there is even 'a preference for agnatic endogamy, provided that it does not conflict with the incest restrictions' (ibid. 54). Finally, '[p]atrigroup endogamy ... is theoretically justified on the grounds that this keeps the various family properties within at least the nominal possession of the *soi*' (ibid. 56).

Even in Glendi it would probably be risky to talk baldly of agnatic 'clans' or 'lineages' (hence Herzfeld's cautious formulation of the term 'patrigroups'), but on a sliding scale of agnation, the Glendiots are clearly at the top end, and the bilateral Spartokhoriots near the bottom. No neighbourhoods were named after surname groups in Spartokhori, and the *soi* was never mobilized as a political grouping (indeed, as we shall see in Chapter 6, the Spartokhoriots' bilateral system made kinship itself an ineffective basis for political action). Also there was no notion that character traits were transmitted through the male line rather than the female line, or any indication that insults to a person's patriline (as opposed to his or her relatives in general) were especially taken as insults to the person. Finally, the only form of endogamy that met with approval (other than village endogamy itself) were the double affinal marriages already discussed, and these did not relate to the *soi*. Yet despite these apparent differences between Spartokhori and Glendi, it should be stressed that the question of agnation or patriliny in Greece is a matter of degree, and that the characterization of a kinship system as bilateral or cognatic rather than agnatic remains to some extent a matter of interpretation (Leach 1961: 10–11). Let us reconsider the Spartokhoriot case.

The commonest definition of the *soi* proffered by the Spartokhoriots was simply that people who shared a common surname (*eponimo*) were *soi*. There seemed to be little more to it than that, and when, for example, one young man was explaining to me that his *soi* had no great historical depth on Meganisi (they had come from the mainland at the turn of the century), he pointed out that no one of his surname on Meganisi had *as yet* married anyone else of that same surname, clear evidence that the *soi* was not conceived of as having any corporate identity by virtue of being an exogamous group, for the young man's implicit point was that in the fullness of time someone with his surname would inevitably end up marrying someone else of the same surname (a common enough occurrence in Spartokhori) once his *soi* had been long enough on Meganisi for relationships between its members to have gone beyond that of third cousins, that is, the limits of the *bilateral* incest prohibition. But although this is evidence that the *soi* was not a corporate group for the purposes of marriage, it could equally be argued that it was still evidence for some form of identification with the *soi* and with a patriline that exceeded identification with other (cognatic) relatives and with other (cognatic) ancestors, if only because they were distinguishable by name. Such an agnatic bias is common in bilateral systems, but it should not be dismissed as inconsequential. Genealogical memory was shallow in Spartokhori (as it tends to be in most societies with a bilateral kinship system) because of the inevitable proliferation of ancestors. Everyone knew who their four grandparents were, but they often had little knowledge of all their eight great-grandparents or sixteen great-great-grandparents, let alone all their thirty-two great-great-great-grandparents. They could not, therefore, historically identify with them. They could, however, identify with a name. Thus when people said that they came from Lefkadha to Meganisi a hundred years ago, they were not referring to all the members of their bilateral kindred, but a surname-group, their agnatically defined *soi*.

Admittedly, such an identification is little different from, say, an English person's tendency to talk of 'we the Smiths' or 'we the Joneses', where once again the family starts to become thought of agnatically (particularly in historical contexts), in spite of the fact that most people would be unlikely to construe contemporary English kinship in terms of lineages or clans.[14] But although Spartokhoriot identification with a *soi* might be similarly seen to operate more in the realms of ideology than of practice, this does not make it fundamentally different from the Glendiot *soi*. Herzfeld supplies clear instances of agnatically based practices in Glendi, but his major claim is that the Glendiot *soi* is '*ideologically* and *conceptually* corporate', a matter of sentiment, feeling and self-identification (albeit translated into political action) rather than of unambiguous material, jural or categorical cohesion. Ethnographic differences between Sparto-khori and Glendi remain, but on the grounds of such ideological identification, it would be possible to talk of patrigroups in Spartokhori too, if one so chose.

That possibility is increased if the Spartokhoriot naming system is considered. Spartokhoriots had three, and sometimes four, different types of name: a baptismal or Christian name (*onoma*); a surname or family name (*eponimo*); a family nickname (*paratsoukli* or *ikoyeniako paratsoukli*); and sometimes an individual nickname (*paratsoukli* or *prosopiko paratsoukli*). Surnames or family names (an official requirement in Greece, as in most European countries) were inherited agnatically (as again they are in most European countries).[15] But although such surnames or family names were official (and, for example, entered on the identity cards that all Greek citizens are required to carry), they were not commonly used in the village, and if one needed to distinguish one Yorghos or Maria from another Yorghos or Maria, this was done not by referring to their official family names (which in Spartokhori were in relatively short supply),[16] but to their *ikoyeniako paratsoukli*, their family nickname. These family nicknames were again inherited agnatically, just like official surnames; and indeed most official surnames had once been family nicknames, fossilized, as it were, by the requirements of the state. But family nicknames were themselves fossilized individual nicknames, for although individual men acquired individual nicknames as a result of some particular personal characteristic or quirk, or some particular event in which they had been personally involved, they also transmitted them patrilineally to their descendants. Family nicknames could thus be seen to distinguish branches of the same agnatic *soi* or surname group. Indeed, when people were trying to give me a definition of the *soi*, some objected that it did not consist

---

[14]Some might wish to do so in the case of the Scots, but in practice contemporary Scots kinship is as bilateral as the English is.

[15]This is no longer officially the case in Greece, since as part of a radical overhaul of family law in 1983, children may now take the family name of their father, or of their mother, or of some combination of both. What a child's family name will be must be specified by a couple at the time of their marriage.

[16]There were 28 surnames in Spartokhori, but of these three were unique to individual families, and over half of the village's households were accounted for by five family names (see Just 1988a).

of everyone who bore the same surname, but rather of everyone who bore the same family nickname, since in some cases the (agnatic) relationship between two family nickname groups who bore the same surname was unknown, or perhaps did not exist. Others objected to this definition on the grounds that in most cases the different family nickname groups of the same surname group were only two or three generations old, so that clearly they belonged to the same *soi*. Nevertheless, new named subdivisions of the *soi* seem to have occurred every generation or so, for although not every man acquired his own personal nickname, if he did acquire one, and if he was in some way notable, then the chances were that his personal nickname would become his descendants' family nickname, and a new branch of the *soi* formed. At the same time, older family nickname branches of the *soi* would disappear.

All this starts to look remarkably like a classic agnatic segmentary structure, which is just how Herzfeld treats it for Glendi, where it forms an integral part of his description of a strongly agnatic society organized into patrigroups:

> Each patrigroup ... is defined by possession of a group name, derived from the baptismal name or *paratsoukli* of an apical ancestor; each *soi*, at whatever level of segmentation, is bound by ties of corporate solidarity, revealed with particular clarity in the conduct of local elections; and each patrigroup is liable to segment into subsidiary units in each generation. No currently existing Glendiot patrigroup exceeds a nominal depth of five generations, each one marked by segmentation of this kind. There seems, however, to have been some telescoping of generations, so that the oldest patrigroups cannot always specify the genealogical relationship between outlying branches. (1985: 284)[17]

Moreover, the same pattern of fission appears in the Corfiot village of Episkepsi, where it again forms a major part of Couroucli's argument for the existence of agnatic lineages:

> The lineage, or *genia*, is defined as a group of individual males descended from a common ancestor, who share not only the same family name, but also a second family name which takes the form of a nickname. This second name, inherited from father to son, remains the same for the members of the same lineage over three generations.
>
> At the end of three generations, one encounters a process of fission comparable to the African examples: the agnatic lineage which is characterized by a common name and nickname divides into small segments. These replace the nickname of the original lineage by new lineal names. Memory of descent from a common ancestor is then preserved only by the oldest people and is lost each time that a segment becomes in its turn a lineage. At the same time, the common family name is an indication of membership of the same large family (*ratsa*) without that necessarily implying a kinship link. (Couroucli, 1985: 55; my translation)

In Episkepsi, the terms *yenia* (*genia* in Couroucli's transliteration) and *fara* or *ratsa* (literally 'birth' or 'race') denote the agnatic groupings that in both Sparto-khori and Glendi are referred to by *soi*, but whereas in Spartokhori and Glendi *soi* can refer to both the surname group and nickname divisions of it, in Episkepsi *yenia* is reserved for the nickname group (which Couroucli calls a *lignage*), and

---

[17]See Herzfeld 1983: 'In Western Crete, the *soi* is invested with segmentary properties. In the village of Glendi, the same term is used for subdivisions of the surname group (the largest agnatic group so designated), each known by a collective form of the apical ancestor's nickname (*paratsoukli* or *paranomi*) or baptismal name. The fission which generates these subsidiary groupings occurs in each generation, although it appears that after about five generations the names of earlier ancestors are progressively forgotten.'

fara or *ratsa* denote all people who bear the same official surname or written name (*eponymo* or *onoma grameno*), and who are thus considered to be descendants of the same, but usually unknown, ancestor (Couroucli 1985: 59). But apart from these terminological shifts, the structure of the agnatic groupings and their process of fission appear to be very similar in all three villages. In fact any claim that Spartokhoriot kinship contrasts with Glendiot patrigroups or Episkepsiot lineages in being thoroughly cognatic has to appeal not to the way in which the *soi* is structured, but to the way agnation functions (or fails to function) in daily life.[18] Even here, however, the contrast is perhaps not so great. Consider the questions of property ownership and of agnatic neighbourhoods, referred to by both Herzfeld and Couroucli.

In Spartokhori, as in many areas of Greece, houses were inherited by sons to the exclusion of daughters, who married out and took their share of family wealth in the form of dowry. This in itself could be seen as a significant patrilineal bias within the kinship system, and certainly it contrasts with the matrilineal tendencies of the island communities of the northeast Aegean, where houses are inherited by and through women (Couroucli 1987; Papataxiarchis 1998). But it also meant that if a widow or widower grandparent, or a grandparental couple, was resident in a multi-generational household, then it was regularly in the household of one of their sons and his family, and not of one of their daughters and her family. Multi-generational households could thus be seen to constitute agnatic units, even if we are talking only about individual households that might consist of three (and in rare cases four) generations of men and their wives. But patrilineal inheritance of the family house, of the *patriko spiti* or paternal house as it was quite significantly called, had further consequences. Since married brothers did not share a common household, when property was passed on to the next generation either the *patriko spiti* was divided between brothers, or, if it was too small for physical division, one brother took the *patriko spiti* and the others built houses adjoining it on family-owned land. The result of these divisions (and expansions) over several generations was that the village of Spartokhori comprised what could be termed (but which, importantly, were *not* termed) agnatic neighbourhoods; that is to say, it was possible to walk down a street in Spartokhori and to note that neighbouring houses or divisions of an original house were all occupied by families that bore the same surname and whose male heads were all related to each other as brothers, or as patrilateral first cousins, patrilateral second cousins or patrilateral third cousins and so on, depending on when the divisions had been made or the houses built. Finally, what applied to houses applied to other major items of real estate: farming land, shops, an olive-oil mill. As result of the inheritance system, brothers, or patrilateral first, second, or third cousins, or simply men who were *soi*, would end up working land adjacent to each other, or owning adjoining shops, or jointly operating an olive-oil mill.

As we shall see in Chapter 7, the pattern of inheritance as I have briefly described it here is a simplification; basically, however, Spartokhoriot inheritance

---

[18]As Herzfeld rightly points out, the question of whether such agnatically constituted groups '"are" lineages or not can all too easily degenerate into mere nominalism' (1985: 283), hence his use of the neologism patrigroup.

resulted in a physical consolidation (but not incorporation) of property within the village that reflected the agnatic links between its owners. I would see this, however, as simply the consequence of a strongly androcentric bias in the transmission of property, rather than as the manifestation of a principle of agnation, or as evidence for the corporate existence of the *soi*. The agnatic consolidation of property-ownership within the village was, so to speak, merely the by-product of a system of inheritance that favoured men. But it must be admitted that this is a delicate issue, for the very concept of agnation has conventionally included the transmission of rights, notably property rights, and exactly the same form of inheritance system that existed in Spartokhori is partly what allows Couroucli to talk of 'lines' and 'lineages' in Episkepsi: 'plots of land like houses form collections of property belonging individually to the members of the same line (*lignée*) or the same lineage (*lignage*). The inhabitation of the village, spatially laid out in the form of a spiral, reflects, on the ground, the history of the successive installation of successive lineage groups in the region.' (Couroucli 1985: 51; my translation)

But the assumption that *individual* inheritance and ownership of land and houses by agnatically related men is constitutive of a lineage structure may well be an example of what Herzfeld has nicely described as an ironical reversal of the old error of confusing patriarchy with patriliny, so that 'it is now patriliny that is perceived where patriarchy would be a better – if by no means ideal – descriptive term' (1983). In fact the whole question of the existence or non-existence of agnatic lineages in Greece actually reduplicates an argument that I think was satisfactorily resolved by Leach in 1961 in relation to Sri Lanka. It is worth quoting Leach at some length.

> There are a large number of societies which possess some of the superficial attributes of unilineal systems yet lack clearly defined unilineal descent groups. The English with their patrilineally inherited surnames provide one example; Sinhalese society is another. The precise nature of the 'unilinearity' present in these marginal cases calls for close investigation, but it would be prejudging the whole issue to assume that the presence or absence of lineages was a diacritically significant factor.
>
> Other writers have suggested that patrilineal lineages occur in Sinhalese society .... In my view that is fallacious, yet it is perfectly true that the Sinhalese do possess, in certain respects, a patrilineal ideology. Is this patrilineality of the Sinhalese an enduring characteristic of Sinhalese culture or is it a reflection of the way the Sinhalese order their economic lives? (1961: 10)

But in the end I would argue that the difference between Episkepsi with its lineages and Spartokhori with its cognatic kindreds depends no more on the system of inheritance and property ownership than it does on the composition of the *soi* (or the *fara* or *ratsa*). Ultimately it depends on the way people think. It depends on the fact that '[i]n Episkepsi, the family is not in opposition to the totality of the community as with the Sarakatsani or the inhabitants of Ambeli in continental Greece (Campbell 1964: 184 ff. and du Boulay 1974: 142 ff.). Rather it is the patrilineage as a whole that confronts the totality of the community.' (Couroucli 1985: 55; my translation)

And here Couroucli is in close accord with Herzfeld, for although the inheritance of property in Glendi resulted in the same sort of agnatic neighbourhoods that exist in both Episkepsi and Spartokhori, Herzfeld is at pains to point out that the 'alienation' of patrigroup territory in Glendi through the sale of land to uterine and affinal kinsmen is so advanced that '[t]he physical layout of the village certainly does not suggest corporate patrigroup activity' (1985: 58). Yet he nevertheless states that land remains 'eternally the *conceptual* property of the patrigroup to which it historically belonged' (1985: 56, my emphasis), and thus (as in Episkepsi) neighbourhoods were named after patrigroups. The real difference between the agnatic neighbourhoods of Glendi and Episkepsi and those of Spartokhori is one of a local emphasis (or its lack) on what is objectively a common set of facts. In Spartokhori agnatic neighbourhoods were a *de facto* by-product of the male inheritance system. So they might have been in Glendi and Episkepsi too, but in Glendi and Episkepsi that *de facto* by-product received recognition and endorsement through its naming as part of an encompassing agnatic ideology that was entirely lacking in Spartokhori. Indeed, what Herzfeld emphasizes throughout his account of agnation in Glendi is not so much the formal characteristics or definitional features of Glendiot patrigroups as their role as *moral communities* in orientating action (1985: 283). Conversely, what I would point to is that although most of the formal characteristics and definitional features of agnatic groupings that exist in Glendi and Episkepsi were also present in Spartokhori, ties of agnation held no particular moral suasion there. The moral community in terms of which loyalties were recognized (or refused) remained the bilateral (and affinal) family, the *ikoyenia* in its various manifestations.

5
Godparenthood

Shortly after Christmas 1979 I was awoken late one night by music and shouting from down the street. I got up to investigate, for although men drank in the various shops until well after midnight in summer, in winter they retired early and usually few people were out after 9 pm. The noise was coming from Yannis's butcher's shop. The *pikup*, the record player, was blaring, and about half a dozen men were dancing while an equal number looked on. Most were very drunk. The dancers staggered rather than stepped, and were holding each other up as much as forming a circle, although the lead dancer could still manage some impressive twists and twirls, acknowledged by shouts of appreciation from the audience which was busy hurling bottles of beer on to the floor. Roaring with laughter, Yannis and his wife would rush forward broom in hand to clear up the mess, but another shower of glass and beer would soon follow as one of the dancers 'accidentally' swept clear a loaded table with his arm, or an onlooker lobbed another bottle to explode on the tiles. The lead dancer, Babis, was bleeding freely from several cuts on his hands and arms. 'It doesn't matter,' he shouted, 'It doesn't matter. I want to dance!' And more beer would be brought out, and more bottles would be broken, as Babis, weeping with emotion. staggered on through the glass, half-dancing, half-carried by his comrades. Eventually fears were expressed that neighbours would complain. It was time to go home. Babis did not want to leave. 'I want my *koumbaros*,' he cried. 'I want to dance with my *koumbaros*.'

A man called Nonios stepped forward.

'Go home. Do as your *koumbaros* tells you,' he laughed. 'You must always do what your *koumbaros* tells you.' And supporting Babis under the arms, Nonios shoved back into Babis's pocket the 1,000 drachma note that he was trying to slap down on the counter to continue the night and to pay for the damage. In the end, still sobbing and still embracing those who held him, Babis was persuaded to leave and the party broke up, though not before Yannis had accepted a rather large sum from Babis, who insisted that he was an honourable man who paid his debts.

Such emotional displays were not unusual in Spartokhori, and for men they were often assisted by drink. Sometimes they were also quite revealing. When I had previously met Babis he was a very different sort of person, and, like his brother, Savvas, he was considered a *poli sovaros anthropos*, 'a very serious man'. But while both brothers were held in near universal esteem within the village, their individual circumstances were rather different. Both had been sailors, but Savvas, the elder brother by nearly ten years, had gone to sea only in order to get his family through the critical years while his children were growing up, and he had remained a deckhand and had taken his pension at the age of fifty-five to resume what was effectively a peasant farmer's life. He was a self-conscious social conservative, and he and his family clung to village ways. His wife was one of the women who still wore traditional village dress, and it was expected that his daughters' lives would follow her model: a protected adolescence, early and arranged marriage, motherhood shortly to follow. By contrast, Babis had risen to the rank of second captain and was permanently employed on one of the ferries running between Italy and Greece. He and his family lived in Athens, and although Babis was not wealthy, his family's style of life certainly differed from his brother's. Babis's wife looked like any smart middle-class matron to be found in the capital, and it was intended that their only child, a daughter who was attending high school, should go on to university. Babis himself was always well dressed (usually in a blue suit and white shirt), and he was quiet-spoken, urbane and well informed if not particularly well educated – in short, a member of the new bourgeoisie. And yet, like his brother, he too was a villager. His emotional attachment to the village, his feeling of identity with it, were quite as strong as Savvas's, who lived there permanently and looked the part – unshaven, shabbily dressed, and off every morning with his donkey to work his plots of land. And what Babis was expressing that night, his clothes torn, his hands bleeding, sobbing as he danced, was precisely his comradeship with the village, for he had returned that day for a few weeks' 'holiday' to help his brother harvest the olive trees they still held in common. He was celebrating – and he explicitly made the point – being back amongst his own.

The relative whom Babis singled out that night, and who bore the brunt of his affection, was, however, neither a blood relative nor a relative by marriage. Nonios was Babis's *koumbaros*, his godparent, and for the Spartokhoriots godparenthood was a serious matter, quite as serious as any other form of kinship. But although godparenthood was a form of kinship, it also had a special significance, for it was in the theological sense of the word a mystical relationship, and the connections it forged were *pnevmatika* (spiritual). In what follows I shall, in keeping with the previous chapter, be concentrating on the structural aspects of godparenthood (its terminology, the rules by which it was governed, the nature of the groups that it conjoined), but it should be remembered that for the Spartokhoriots it was the spiritual aspects of the relationship that elevated it, so that while the obligations of kinship as a whole often tended to crumble in the face of life's exigencies, those of godparenthood or spiritual kinship remained always sacrosanct.

As elsewhere in Greece and the Orthodox Christian world, ties of spiritual kinship in Spartokhori could be instigated on either of two ritual occasions, baptism or marriage, both of which by church law require the participation of a sponsor (Aschenbrenner 1986: 62-3). As in many other Greek communities, baptismal sponsorship and marriage sponsorship were also closely linked (Peristiany 1963: 90; Campbell 1964: 218–19; du Boulay 1984: 544–5; Aschenbrenner 1986: 62–3). In discussing godparenthood, however, the

Spartokhoriots always placed the emphasis on baptism, which was universally held to be a *poli sovaro prama*, 'a very serious matter', and it was the intrinsic significance of the mystery of baptism and its contribution to the formation of a fully-fledged human being that gave the resultant ties of spiritual kinship their special status (cf. du Boulay 1974: 162–3; Aschenbrenner 1986: 122 n. 3; Stewart 1991: 196). Most Spartokhoriots were not regular church-goers and, as socialists or communists, most were markedly anti-clerical in their views,[1] but to be baptized, to be Christian, to be a Greek, and to be a full human being entitled to the respect and consideration that human beings owed each other were ideas whose concordance persisted, despite a frequently expressed form of liberal humanism whereby all people were naturally equal. A family of itinerant gypsies arrived one summer and camped on the beach below the village. They spent several days in Spartokhori mending wicker chairs, pots and pans, and sharpening knives and scissors. One of my friends, a middle-aged man of professed liberal views and a staunch communist, asked me if I knew about gypsies, and then whispered to me that they were a *vromikos laos*, a 'dirty people'. Perhaps noticing my unease, he quickly added, '*Vaftizoune, omos* (They baptize, nevertheless).' and went on to rehearse one of Spartokhori's most quoted adages, '*Imaste oli anthropi* (We're all people).' But it seemed that admission to the universal brotherhood of man was still more easily effected through channels that were religious (and thereby national).[2]

The importance of baptism for the recognition of a social persona was also evident in the Spartokhoriots' scrupulous withholding of all reference to a child's name until it had been baptized, on the quite logical grounds that, until it had been baptized and given a name by its godparent, it did not have a name. An unbaptized infant was referred to (and addressed) as simply *to bebe* or *to moro*, 'the baby,' 'the kid'. This was in spite of the fact that first-born sons were regularly named after their paternal grandfather, and first-born daughters after their paternal grandmother, so that what was bound to be the child's name was often common knowledge.[3] But even that knowledge had to be suppressed out of respect for both the right of the godparent to name the child and the sanctity of the ceremony of baptism itself. I once asked a young friend of mine in the coffee-shop what his recently born son's name was. He gruffly replied, '*Then ehi onoma* [He doesn't have a name].' Feeling rebuffed, and anxious to show my command of village custom, I persisted that surely the child would be called Mitsos after his grandfather. Obviously embarrassed by this public solecism, my friend shrugged and muttered, '*Mallon* (Probably).' Three months later the child was indeed baptized Mitsos, or rather, Dhimitrios, for which Mitsos is the diminutive. The following night I then overheard two old men conversing in the coffee-shop, one of whom asked the other what name the child had been baptized. 'Mitsos,' was

---

[1] Communism, socialism and anti-clericism in Spartokhori (and in much of Greece) should not be confused with a rejection of Orthodox Christianity. Most Spartokhoriots were strongly opposed to the church as an institution, and the local priest was openly derided. No one, however, would declare himself an atheist. See Just (1988b).

[2] For the conflation of religious and national identity in Greece, see Ware (1983).

[3] This is a fairly common naming pattern in Greece, though it is not rigorous, and there are also regional variations. For discussion of Greek baptismal names, see Herzfeld (1982b), Just (1988a) Stewart (1988), Sutton (1998: 173–201).

the reply. 'Ah, Mitsos!' exclaimed the first old man, as if surprised by the originality of the choice. 'Ah, yes, Mitsos. A very fine name.'

It was this giving of a name that was always singled out by the Spartokhoriots as defining the role, or the importance, of the baptismal sponsor. To pay the priest, to provide the child's baptismal robes, to provide the cross that henceforth the child would always wear, were seen as the sponsor's necessary and costly duties (cf. Aschenbrenner 1986: 64);[4] but in the end explanations of sponsorship always reverted to the essential feature of naming. The Spartokhoriots' repeated reference to naming was, however, a cultural shorthand, a variety of metonymy that summarized matters more difficult to express and which, in no departure from church teachings, united within the domain of kinship both spiritual and social considerations, for the godfather or godmother was considered a third parent of the child. Some Spartokhoriots went so far as to state that the godparent was not the third parent, but indeed the first parent, since he or she was the child's spiritual creator (*Pidhalion* 1976: 752; cf. du Boulay 1984: 547). The act of naming, which it should be noted is the act of supplying a 'Christian' name, the name of a saint,[5] was the manifest aspect of the godparent's otherwise mystical contribution to a child's creation, whereby what was made in the flesh by its father and mother was spiritually supplemented so as to be able to take its place as a fully formed and socially recognized human being within the Christian fold. By contrast, marriage sponsorship was considered a relatively frivolous matter, and despite the centrality of the *koumbaros*'s role in wedding ritual, no reference was ever made to any contribution to the mystery of marriage. It was considered simply a *filiko prama*, a 'friendly matter'. But in fact marriage sponsorship and baptismal sponsorship were closely connected, and here we approach the systematic nature of Spartokhoriot godparenthood.

Terminology

As noted, ties of godparenthood in Spartokhori were formally entered into on either of two ritual occasions, baptism and marriage, for by church law both ceremonies require the formal participation of a sponsor. In the case of baptism, the sponsor, the godparent, may be either male or female (regardless of the sex of the child being baptized). In the case of marriage, the sponsor, the rough equivalent of a best man, is required to be male.[6] In Spartokhori, as elsewhere in Greece (Campbell 1964: 217–24; Kenna 1971: 228; du Boulay 1984: 546; Aschenbrenner 1986: 64–5), both forms of sponsorship created not only a relationship between the individual sponsor and sponsored, but a matrix of

---

[4] Aschenbrenner calculates that in Karpofora the expenses incurred by a baptismal sponsor were equivalent to ten to twelve days' wages (1986: 64).

[5] Greek baptismal names are supposed to be the names of Orthodox saints. Since the late eighteenth century, however, names from Greece's classical past have been popular, and nowadays there is a tendency to import foreign or European names, such as Viki or Natali. At various stages the Greek clergy has refused to baptize children with 'non-Christian' Christian names (see for example Clogg 1976: 88).

[6] The role of the groom's best man was to some extent matched in Spartokhori at the wedding ceremony by the bride's *paranifi*, 'maid of honour'.

relationships between their respective families. For the most part, however, no terminological distinctions marked the various strands of godparenthood. The person who acted as a child's sponsor at the ceremony of baptism became that child's *koumbaros*[7] (masc.) or *koumbara* (fem.). Similarly, the man who acted as a couple's sponsor in the wedding ceremony was known as their *koumbaros*. Finally, as a result of either baptism or marriage an extensive set of the relatives of the sponsor and of the sponsored also recognized reciprocal relationships of godparenthood and could refer to and address each other as *koumbari* (pl.). The additional terms *nonos* and *nona* (fem.) could be employed to distinguish a person's baptismal sponsor from his or her marriage sponsor, or to distinguish a person's individual baptismal sponsor from all those other people who had collectively become his or her *koumbari* as a result of their familial relationship with that sponsor, but in Spartokhori routine usage of the terms *koumbaros, koumbara* and *koumbari* regularly conflated the relationships instigated by baptismal sponsorship with the relationships instigated by marriage sponsorship, and the individual relationship of godparent and godchild with the collective relationship of godparenthood between families. Moreover, since the term *koumbari* was reciprocally used, normally no verbal distinction was made to indicate the direction of the relationship between sponsor and sponsored, or between the members of their respective families. All became each other's *koumbari* (cf. Aschenbrenner 1986: 64–5).[8]

On the whole, this terminological conflation accurately reflected the system of godparenthood itself. Although the Spartokhoriots did sometimes distinguish godparenthood deriving from baptismal sponsorship from godparenthood deriving from marriage sponsorship, since baptismal sponsorship and marriage sponsorship were systematically linked, in most contexts the distinction was irrelevant. Similarly, while there were specific occasions when it was crucial to distinguish an individual sponsor or godparent (the *nonos* or *nona*) from all those other people collectively considered to be spiritual kin (*koumbari*), in the normal course of events little distinction was made between the role of the individual sponsor and those collectively designated sponsors. Only in failing to distinguish between sponsors and sponsored did the day-to-day terminology of godparenthood conceal an important distinction. In short, marriage sponsorship and baptismal sponsorship, and individual sponsorship and collective sponsorship, were all collapsed, for they operated within a system of hereditary and collective godparenthood, a system to which I shall now turn.

Spiritual kinship as a system

In 1968 Eugene Hammel published a short but brilliant monograph entitled *Alternative Social Structure and Ritual Relations in the Balkans*, which described and

---

[7] The term *koumbaros* is an early Latinate loan-word, cognate with the Spanish word '*compadre*', co-father.
[8] Official church terminology is rather more technical and distinguishes between baptizer and baptized. Nor is day-to-day terminology standard throughout Greece: see Hammel (1968: 67), Friedl (1964a: 72), Clark (1988: 243), Herzfeld (1985) for variants.

analysed the institution of *kumstvo* (godparenthood) in part of the former Republic of Yuglsolavia. As Davis later commented, Hammel's monograph 'reconstructs and analyses the most elaborately systematic godparenthood yet recorded [for the Mediterranean]' (1977: 224), for what Hammel discovered was essentially a form of 'asymmetric prescriptive alliance', or, as Lévi-Strauss termed it, 'generalized exchange',[9] in which 'godparenthood relationships ... were usually inherited in the male line and tended to be unilateral, so that members of one line were godparents to those of a second, who were godparents to those of a third, and so on' (Hammel 1968: 1). As Hammel emphasizes, in terms of this system of unilateral baptism, godparenthood was also conceived of as a collective relationship between groups, not a dyadic relationship between individuals: 'The roles of baptismal sponsor and marriage sponsor are played without internal differentiation by living members of groups A *vis-à-vis* the members of group B ... It is thus group A which is *kum* [godparent] to group B and not individuals from A who are *kum* to individuals of B.' (Hammel 1968: 45)

Moreover, not only was the Yugoslavian godparenthood system collective and unilateral, with group A sponsoring group B, and group B sponsoring group C, and so forth, but godparenthood, affinity and agnation were mutually exclusive structural alternatives (Davis 1977: 224) – hence the title of the monograph. Thus, broadly speaking, marriage and godparenthood could not be instigated between individuals who were agnatically related (who belonged, that is, to the same agnatic group of whatever order), but could only be instigated between groups, so that if godparenthood is viewed as a form of alliance analogous to marriage (cf. Friedl 1964a: 72; Davis 1977: 223; du Boulay 1984: 546; Aschenbrenner 1986: 62), then the Yugoslav kinship groups were both exogamous as well as, so to speak, spiritually exogamous. At the same time, ties of godparenthood constituted an impediment to marriage, so that groups that were related through godparenthood could not become affines. Affinity and godparenthood constituted mutually exclusive forms of alliance, and people could not marry those whom they had (collectively) baptized.

The system described by Hammel remains the most elaborately systematic on record, but it could now be argued that its main features (the unilateral direction of baptism, the inherited and therefore collective nature of sponsorship, and the impediments to marriage created by spiritual kinship) are all quite commonplace in southern Europe. Certainly Hammel's claim that '[g]odparenthood institutions in other parts of Europe do not have this collective character but are more easily described as a system of individual dyadic contracts in which other group members may become involved by extension' (1968: 45) now appears to be something of an overstatement. Even the brief overview of Mediterranean godparenthood provided by Davis in 1977 (227–32) was able conclusively to show that it often possesses a collective character, and that collective relationships of godparenthood regularly result in some impediments to marriage,[10] and du

[9] Hammel specifically relates his study to both Lévi-Strauss's (1949) and Leach's (1951) work on marriage alliance (Hammel 1968: 1).

[10]Davis overstates the case in suggesting that 'whatever the prohibited degrees of kinship may be in a local community, the same degrees are applied to godparents' (1977: 230), and that 'local prohibitions on marriage between spiritual kin are *coterminous* with the prohibitions between kin' (ibid. 231, my emphasis). In Greece, at least, the impediments to marriage between *koumbari* are

Boulay (1984) and Aschenbrenner (1986: 64) have shown that in some areas of Greece reciprocal baptism between families is forbidden (or at least avoided) and that godparenthood is contracted unilaterally or asymmetrically between groups. It might be argued, following Hammel, that in contrast to the Yugoslavian system these are all merely instances of extension from an essentially dyadic relationship, but like Davis (1977: 231) I think the term extension is misleading. In southern Europe as a whole godparenthood (like marriage) has always both an individual and a collective aspect. Local practice then varies in the extent to which it emphasizes the one or the other. In this respect the Yugoslavian system is not a unique case, but simply an extreme one.

This tension between individual and collective relationships is apparent even in church regulations, from which folk practice often departs, but to which it also appeals. On the one hand, the church (both Catholic and Orthodox) stresses the spiritual nature of the relationship between sponsor and sponsored, thus presenting it as an essentially dyadic one between individuals (as, for less elevated reasons, does folk practice when it comes to the expedient choice of a godparent who may act as a child's political or economic patron in later years) and its official consequences for the respective kin of the sponsor and the sponsored are minimal. On the other hand, simply by designating the sponsor a spiritual parent the church also opens the way for an understanding of godparenthood as a form of kinship whose ramifications, by analogy, would incorporate a large number of people other than the individual sponsor and sponsored.[11] As we shall see, the church itself does not follow far down this path, but the more folk practice assimilates spiritual kinship to profane kinship, the more baptism becomes a collective phenomenon relating not only individuals, but (like marriage) familial groups. Equally, the more the godparental relationship becomes one between groups, the more the individual members of those groups find the instigation of further relationships between them (whether of godparenthood or of affinity) subject to regulation.

It is, however, precisely the assimilation between profane kinship (or just kinship) and spiritual kinship that, in a subtle and influential essay, Pitt-Rivers (1976) sought to deny. For him the essence of godparenthood lies always in the spiritual relationship created between two individuals in which the godparent is 'to be the guardian of the child as an individual person rather than as an offspring', and in which he or she is charged with 'only the religious duty of ensuring the salvation of his *individual* soul' (1976: 320). Concerned exclusively with the personal destiny of the child (as opposed to his or her membership of a social unit), the godparent is, in Pitt-Rivers's terms, not a parent but an 'anti-parent' (ibid. 320–1) and (extended folk usages of godparental terms notwithstanding) spiritual kinship is not an analogue of profane kinship, but its antithesis.

Pitt-Rivers draws his data largely from Spain and from Latin America, but claims that his argument applies equally to Greece. According to him, it is only

---

[10](cont.) usually considerably less. See, for example, du Boulay (1984: 546).

[11]Even the understanding of the relationship between sponsor and sponsored as one of spiritual parenthood is a historical development. As Gudeman explains, 'In earliest times, it is usually held, spiritual paternity was recognized between the minister of the sacrament and the baptized; however a spiritual relationship did not obtain between the sponsor and the baptized' (1975: 231).

'when we turn to the material from rural Serbia, presented by Hammel, [that] everything changes: the institution of *kumstvo* appears quite anomalous' (ibid. 327). I think it is not. In Spartokhori, as in Serbia, godparenthood was hereditary, collective, contracted unilaterally, and to some considerable degree incompatible with affinity, and although these features were perhaps more pronounced in Spartokhori than in some other Greek communities, they do not appear to be uncommon in Greece. In one important respect, however, I would agree with Pitt-Rivers, for if Hammel's material is at all exceptional, it is not because in the Yugoslavian case baptism sets up a relationship between groups rather than between individuals, or because that relationship is asymmetrical, or because it results in impediments to marriage. What distinguishes the Yugoslavian system of godparenthood from the Spartokhoriot system (and generally from godparenthood in Greece) and what allows it to appear so much more elaborately systematic is not the nature of the relationships that baptism establishes between groups, but the nature of those groups themselves (Pitt-Rivers 1976: 329–33). For although in the Yugoslavian case the *zadruge*, the extended agnatic households, are well-defined corporate groups with discrete and non-overlapping memberships, generally in Greece (even given Herzfeld's and Couroucli's accounts of patrigroups and agnatic lineages), and certainly in Spartokhori, the bilateral and overlapping nature of the community's constituent kinship groups, its families, means that the godparental ties established between them are also more fluid. To this important qualification must be added another difference (though more one of degree than of kind): namely, that in Spartokhori the systematic determination of godparenthood coexisted with a considerable degree of free choice.[12] Where I would disagree with Pitt-Rivers is in the assumption that outside Yugoslavia the bilateral kinship structures of the rest of southern Europe (including Greece) amount to *no more* than nuclear families (Pitt-Rivers 1976: 330),[13] so that it is impossible for godparenthood to take on *any* form of a structured relationship between groups and thus for it to become analogous to (or equatable with) a form of kinship in its own right. In short, I think that both Hammel and Pitt-Rivers make much the same mistake: both take Yugoslavia to be the exceptional case, but whereas Hammel argues that Yugoslavian godparenthood is exceptional because it is collective, Pitt-Rivers argues that it is collective *only* because of the existence of well-defined corporate kinship groups. Neither of these related contentions is true.

The Spartokhoriot system

At first sight the Spartokhoriot system of godparenthood appears elegantly simple. If a man acted as a boy's baptismal sponsor (that is, became his *nonos*), he

[12]The difference here is perhaps not so great. As Hammel explains, for a variety of reasons godparental relations in Yugoslavia may lapse, and either the sponsor himself may suggest that he be replaced, or the father of a child may petition his sponsor for permission to choose a new godparent. But the godparent's permission is mandatory (1968: 42–3).

[13]Pitt-Rivers is firm on the point: 'The extension of the basic collectivity ... determines the field within which relations are structurally defined. The ambilateral nuclear family of the Mediterranean knows no extension; it *is* the basic collectivity. The lineage system of the rural Serbs extends the basic collectivity to the level of the clan' (1976: 330; original emphasis).

had the right later to act as sponsor at that boy's marriage. Further, the man who acted as sponsor at a man's marriage had the right later to baptize *at least* that man's first-born child, a quite commonplace sequence in Greece (cf. Campbell 1964: 222; du Boulay 1984: 544–5; Aschenbrenner 1986: 63).[14] Baptismal sponsorship and marriage sponsorship were thus linked, the one following from the other, and this was the manner in which the Spartokhoriots regularly explained their system. This description is, however, obviously a simplification, for it would be impossible for any single individual to continue to act as baptismal sponsor, then as marriage sponsor, then as baptismal sponsor and so forth for a man and his first-born descendants down the generations, and on the grounds of age it might be inappropriate for a man's baptismal sponsor later to act as his marriage sponsor. The second essential feature of Spartokhoriot godparenthood was thus that rights of sponsorship were transmissible. For example, as an adult A baptizes B, but since it is generally preferred that a marriage sponsor should be roughly the same age as the man whose marriage he is sponsoring, twenty-five or thirty years later it may not be A, but A's son, who acts as B's marriage sponsor, and consequently A's son who later baptizes B's first-born child. Alternatively, if A has acted as B's marriage sponsor, he may wish one of his children (in this case either a son or a daughter) to baptize B's child, and, in contrast with practice in Karpofora (Aschenbrenner 1986: 63), it was not uncommon in Spartokhori for baptismal sponsors to be themselves quite young children (which, if they were male, facilitated the possibility of their later acting in person as marriage sponsors for any male children they had baptized). The third and final feature of Sparto-khoriot godparenthood was that the relationship between sponsors and spon-sored over the generations was perpetuated asymmetrically. If A and his descendants acted as baptismal (and thus marriage) sponsors for B and his descendants, B and his descendants were prohibited from acting as sponsors for A's descendants, a prohibition which the Spartokhoriots explained in the same way as the villagers of Ambeli: '*Na mi yirizi to ladhi* (Let the oil not return)' (du Boulay 1984: 545). Thus two families could not reciprocally baptize each other's children, nor could the direction of baptism between them be reversed in succeeding generations. Already we have the main features of the system described by Hammel. In terms of this system, however, A and his descendants would be perpetually locked into spiritual kinship with B and his descendants as hereditary sponsors to hereditary sponsored, but in fact actual practice was both more complicated and less systematic, and for several reasons.

---

[14]In Ambeli the sequence of sponsorships from marriage to baptism of the first-born and so on by a *koumbaros* or his close relative was required to continue only so long as the original *koumbaros* was alive. On his death, new relationships could be inaugurated (du Boulay 1984: 544–5). Practice in Karpofora also appears to be a much weaker version of the Spartokhoriot system. According to Aschenbrenner, there was an 'operative rule' that a wedding sponsor ought to baptize the first child of the marriage he had sponsored. This was rarely violated before 1945, and at the time of Aschenbrenner's fieldwork, infractions amounted to scarcely 30 per cent of the total. However, although some people in Karpofora stated that a groom was supposed to ask his own godfather to be his wedding sponsor, this rarely happened because of the age difference. In the Mani, such rules were even weaker, and Allen states that there were only several cases of people choosing their marriage sponsor as baptismal sponsor for their first-born, and none for choosing the baptismal sponsor to act as the wedding sponsor (Allen 1973: 118–19, cited Aschenbrenner 1986: 122).

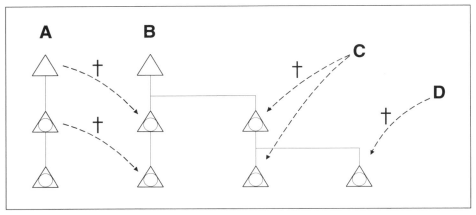

Figure 5.1 Simplified diagram of hereditary baptism showing possibilities of further baptismal sponsorships for non-first-born

Free choice

First, it was never claimed in Spartokhori that the system determined the sponsorship of all baptisms and marriages. First, even the most conservative Spartokhoriots conceded that the rights of A (or his children) to baptize the children of B (for whom A had previously acted as baptismal sponsor and/or marriage sponsor) applied rigorously only to B's first-born child, and that, for his part, if B requested A to baptize his first-born child, then he had fulfilled his obligations to his hereditary sponsor. After that, B was free to choose whomever he wished as baptismal sponsors for his subsequent children. Thus while A and his descendants might, as sponsors, be locked into a permanent relationship of godparenthood with B and his line of *first-born* descendants, it was still possible for B's godparental connections to ramify as he (and his first-born descendants at each generation) chose further godparents for their second or third children (see Figure 5.1).

This, however, was a delicate issue. In some contrast to what Aschenbrenner reports for Karpofora, where villagers protested that to contract further ties of spiritual kinship with an existing sponsor was senseless since it carried no advantage (1986: 63–4; cf. Friedl 1964a: 72), I was proudly told by many Spartokhoriots that they had baptized and 'crowned' (acted as marriage sponsor for) *all* of the so-and-sos – that is to say, an entire sibling group (cf. Hammel 1968: 62). Such a claim was usually made in the context of an account of the general importance of godparenthood, but clearly it was also an assertion on the speaker's part of his own social and moral standing, for if a godparent relationship was a happy one, then it was likely to be extended from the sponsorship of the first-born child to the sponsorship of all subsequent children. This, indeed, was the Spartokhoriot ideal, for such reiteration of the relationship served as public acknowledgement of the sponsor's worth. At the very least the sponsored family was making it clear that there was no one else whom they would prefer to baptize their children than the godparent bequeathed to them by the decisions of the preceding generation. They were not only accepting their hereditary sponsor by having him baptize their first-born child, but, as it were, embracing him by extending, on their own initiative, the invitation to baptize their subsequent children. Conversely, from the sponsor's point of view, the honour that in the first instance had been his hereditary right established by the role of his ascendants was now shown, by its repeated and voluntary bestowal, to be one that he personally warranted. Free choice and the system happily overlaid each other.

Many younger Spartokhoriots, however, were inclined to view the baptism even of their first-born child by a hereditary godparent as a concession to village tradition, and argued forcefully that people were, or ought to be, free to choose whomever they wanted as godparents for their children, since the relationship between the child's parents and its godparents, that is, between *koumbari*, was founded on individual friendship and respect (cf. Aschenbrenner 1986: 63; Pitt-Rivers 1976: 323-4). But if there was generational disagreement over the matter, it should be noted that even if the inclination was to create new spiritual ties, the sacrosanct nature of the godparental relationship meant that no one would readily admit to having fallen out with an established godparent. Both parties were usually at pains to explain that any failure to reiterate godparental ties had been entirely amicable, and face-saving devices for the established godparent were readily at hand. Thus an older man I knew was approached by his godson, a young sailor, who very much wished his own child to be baptized by his shipmate and close friend. The older man, having been kissed on the hand and having had his permission and blessing formally sought – in short, having had all due deference paid to him – generously ceded his rights. His godson had demonstrated his respect; he in turn had demonstrated his good will. Similarly, when another old man was requested to take up his right of sponsorship, but knew that the request was half-hearted, he gracefully declined on the grounds of poverty (for the expense involved was considerable) and suggested that, with his blessing, a younger and wealthier man might be sought (cf. Hammel 1968: 42). Again, credit reflected on both sides. The sponsored family had shown their respect by making the request; their hereditary sponsor had shown his sensitivity by declining it. Moreover, the very relationship of godparenthood that tied them together had been validated, for, categorically, *koumbari* may not quarrel, and it is important to note that whatever was decided, the two parties were still *koumbari*. There was no cessation of their own relationship. It was merely the case that the relationship was not to be reforged by further baptisms in the next generation, which would then extend the lines of sponsors and sponsored into the future. Indeed it could be argued that the ideology of godparenthood – of religiously sanctioned respect and good will – always allowed for its own amicable discontinuation. Godparents could not deny their godchildren their wishes, and those wishes might include the seeking of new godparents for their children, and the transformation of their own friends into spiritual kin.

Such discontinuations of a line of sponsorship (and creations of new lines) often occurred at the time of marriage rather than baptism, since acting as a wedding sponsor was a less serious matter than acting as a baptismal sponsor, and the hereditary sponsor was thus foregoing a lesser honour, although of course it would eventually result in the transference of the greater honour if the system reasserted itself, and the new marriage sponsor was later called on to baptize the child of the marriage at which he had officiated. Moreover, the festive role of the marriage sponsor in wedding celebrations meant that it was preferable for him to be roughly the same age as, or only a little older than, the groom. Given that in Spartokhori, as in Yugoslavia (cf. Hammel 1968: 46), young children could act as baptismal sponsors, it was always possible that the hereditary sponsor might be reasonably close in age to the man at whose wedding he should officiate, but more frequently he was not. As we have seen, in terms of the system the problem could be resolved by the transfer of the right of sponsorship from the established sponsor to his own son, but the celebration of a marriage provided an occasion on which the claims of friendship were readily recognized, and thus the idea of fresh sponsorship more easily entertained (cf. Hammel 1968: 44).

It would be a mistake, then, to think that the reality of godparental relationships in Spartokhori could be represented by two lines of descendants, the one baptizing and 'crowning' the other in perpetuity. Even in theory the system operated rigorously only for first-born children, so that there was a continual fission of spiritual kinship down the generations, while in practice even lines of first-born baptisms and marriages tended to break off as a result of pragmatic considerations (see Figure 5.1). In fact I could find no case where hereditary ties of godparenthood (from father to son) had endured for more than three generations. Nevertheless, what was continually asserted was that an established baptismal sponsor or his children had the *right* to continue to sponsor their *koumbari*, and that new sponsors could be sought only with his express permission (cf. Hammel 1968: 42). Nor was this right lightly dismissed. The permission of hereditary sponsors was generally sought for the instigation of any new godparental relationship, and the continuity of godparental relationships between families was in itself highly valued. Emigration, for example, obviously disrupted the continuity of godparenthood, but it was not uncommon to delay the baptism (and thus the naming) of a child for several years if it was known that an established godparent was about to return on holiday from Australia or Canada or the United States. Similarly, while I was in the village an old man in his seventies gamely made off on a three days' journey alone by bus to Larissa in order to act as the marriage sponsor for a young Spartokhoriot whom he had baptized some twenty-five years before. For both parties it was important that the relationship between them should not only be maintained, but remade.

Collective godparenthood

The genealogical depth of hereditary sponsorship in Spartokhori was shallow. Nor could the lines of sponsors and sponsored be likened to a pair of lineages or patrigroups corporate with respect to baptism, since it was not necessarily the case that even siblings shared the same baptismal sponsors. Godparenthood did, however, remain very much an *ikoyeniako prama*, a 'family matter', and creative of more than simply dyadic relationships between individuals. As already mentioned, the term *koumbari* (pl.) was used reciprocally by all members of both the families that had entered into spiritual kinship as a result of a baptism, a usage that very much resembled that of the term *simpetheri*, which refers to all those brought into an affinal relationship as the result of a marriage (Aschen-brenner 1986: 62), and it is perhaps worth noting that the kinship term used fictively to greet a stranger was either *simpethere mou* (my affine) or *koumbare mou* (my godrelative), the common denominator of both being that they were contractual relationships, and the polite implication being that the stranger was the sort of person whom one might like to make into an affine or a godrelative. But the specific term *nonos* (or *nona*), which referred to the individual baptismal sponsor, was rarely used in Spartokhori, since in most circumstances it was not important to distinguish the individual sponsor or sponsored from his or her close relatives. What was important for the Spartokhoriots was the relationship created between two *families*, who were reciprocally each other's *koumbari* (though it should be remembered that the term *koumbari* does not distinguish baptizers from baptized). This notion of collective sponsorship was, of course, in part the result of the hereditary system whereby rights of sponsorship could be transferred from parent to child; but in fact the term *koumbari* also extended both collaterally and affinally. When people mentioned to me that they were someone's *koumbaros*, and I asked them for clarification (in order to discover the direction of the relationship), they would often proudly say 'I baptized him (*Egho to vaftisa*)'. Despite the unambiguous usage of the first person singular, I would then discover that they were not the *nonos* or *nona* of the child, and that they had not personally officiated at the church ceremony. Sometimes the actual sponsor had been their son or daughter; that is to say, they had passed on their right to act as baptismal sponsor to one of their children (but still considered themselves to be godparent). In other cases, however, the actual sponsor turned out to be their brother or sister or (a special case, to which I shall return) their spouse. If I protested about the inaccuracy of their information, I was told, 'It's all the same'. The question of the individual sponsor was relatively unimportant. Godparent-hood was an *ikoyeniako prama*, a 'family matter' (cf. Hammel 1968: 46).[15]

Here, however, we strike something that, at least analytically, is separate from the issue of the transmission of baptismal rights, for if it was a person's brother or sister who had acted in the church ceremony as baptismal sponsor, then in time that brother or sister might transfer his or her rights of further sponsorship to one of his or her children (necessarily a son, if it was a case of marriage sponsorship). Siblings did not, however, transfer rights of sponsorship between each other, and yet siblings still considered themselves to be the *koumbari* of whomever their brother or sister had baptized (and of the whole family of whomever their brother or sister had baptized). In short, rights of hereditary sponsorship were transmitted *lineally*. Spiritual kinship itself, however, was conceived of *cognatically* – as a collective relationship that incorporated all the reasonably close relatives of both the individual sponsor and the individual sponsored and their affines (see Figure 5.2). There was, of course, an obvious juncture between the lineal and lateral aspects of Spartokhoriot godparenthood in terms of common points of origin, for

[15]Hammel's experience in southern Serbia seems identical. As he states, '*officiation* at a ceremony seems not to be the important point. Informants often became quite annoyed when I asked repeatedly who officiated at particular crisis rites, saying, *Ja sam ti vec rekao, nema veze, to je ista prodica* (I already told thee, it doesn't matter, it's the same family)' (1968: 46).

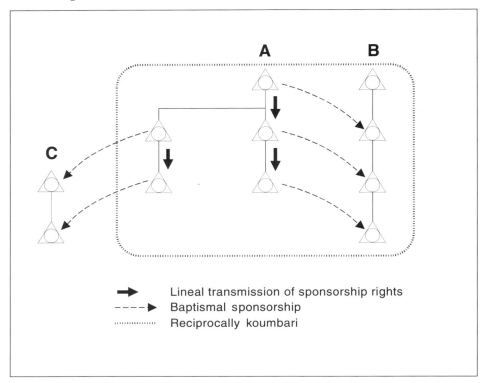

Figure 5.2 Lineal transmission of sponsorship rights coupled with cognatic claims to familial godparenthood

a sponsor might transfer his rights of sponsorship of one family to one child, and of another family to another child. In short, actual officiation at the ceremonies of baptism of various sponsored families might be divided up amongst siblings, who, together with their parents, were still all considered to be the godparents of whomever any one of them had baptized. Only in the next generation would collective sponsorship start clearly to divide as each of those siblings passed down rights of sponsorship to their own respective descendants. Nevertheless, claims to spiritual kinship were not limited by rights of succession, and if a person's brother or sister, uncle or aunt, nephew or niece, or even first cousin had acted as sponsor, then that person, along with the rest of the sponsor's family, was in a godparental relationship to the sponsored and the rest of his or her family. The set of relationships created by a godparental alliance was an analogue of the set of relationships created by a marriage alliance, and two bilateral kinship groups, two kindreds or families, became reciprocally *koumbari*, just as through marriage they became reciprocally *simpetheri*.

It is, however, precisely because spiritual kinship was contracted between bilateral families, between *ikoyenies*, cognatic kindreds rather than agnatic lineages, and cognatic kindreds that also included affinal relatives, that god-

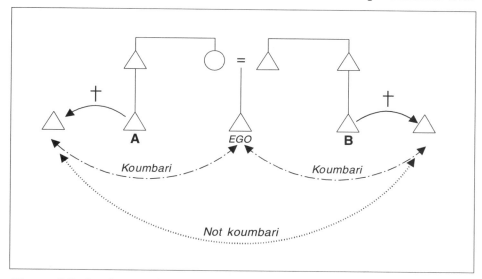

Figure 5.3 Overlapping *koumbaria* in cognatic kinship structure

parenthood in Spartokhori failed to achieve the fully systematic character of Yugoslavian *kumstvo*, despite its similarity to Hammel's material in almost every other respect. This was because in the Spartokhoriot case the groups between which ties of collective godparenthood existed were themselves fuzzy-edged, and their memberships overlapping. Thus, for example, Ego could claim to be the *koumbaros* of the person whom his patrilateral first cousin had baptized (together with his or her family), and the person whom his matrilateral first cousin had baptized (together with his or her family), but Ego's patrilateral first cousin could not claim (or would be extremely unlikely to claim) spiritual kinship with the person whom Ego's matrilateral first cousin had baptized, and vice versa (see Figure 5.3). In short, the ties of spiritual kinship of the three first cousins shown in Figure 5.3 (A, Ego, and B) are, like those of kinship, overlapping but not identical. In the case of the Yugoslavian agnatic groups, however, Ego and his patrilateral first cousin (and all other members of Ego's group) would share an identical set of spiritual kin, while Ego and his matrilateral cousin would have no spiritual kin in common. In the end, the clearcut and systematic perpetuation of Yugoslavian godparenthood is a function of the corporate nature of the agnatic groups involved, rather than of the rules of godparenthood itself. Conversely what for Spartokhori most thwarts the notion of two lines of descendants permanently locked into a relationship of sponsors and sponsored was not the latitude of the Spartokhoriot system in allowing a degree of free choice, nor even its fragility after two or three generations, but once again the bilateral nature of Spartokhoriot kinship. This, indeed, is in general accord with Pitt-Rivers's argument: godparenthood is different in rural Yugoslavia from the rest of Mediterranean Europe, but it is different because the social structure of rural Yugoslavia is different from the rest of Mediterranean Europe in being agnatic as opposed to bilateral (1976: 330–3).[16] But it is Pitt-Rivers's insistence that the bilaterality of the rest of the Mediterranean is reducible to *no more than* the nuclear or elementary family (and, indeed, his assumption that a clearcut and radical distinction exists between agnatic and cognatic kinship) that allows his further contention that godparenthood in the rest of the Mediterranean can never be collective, and hence analogous to kinship, but (since there exist no groups between which collective relationships can be created) must remain a dyadic relationship between individuals. And having thus isolated the essence of godparenthood as a form of anti-parenthood concerned only with spiritual welfare of an individual, Pitt-Rivers can go on to argue (*contra* Hammel) that even in Yugoslavia godparenthood is not '*by its nature* collective' but merely 'put to use by the collectivities of which the social structure is composed' (1976: 332; original emphasis).[17]

If, however, one dismisses Pitt-Rivers's axiom that bilateral kinship systems in the Mediterranean are incapable of giving rise to any forms of collectivity greater than the nuclear family (and I think there is ethnographically little to warrant its maintenance),[18] then the difference between the operations of godparenthood within an agnatic system and within a bilateral system start to appear not so great. Indeed it is perfectly possible for godparenthood in a bilateral system still to be contracted asymmetrically between *groups*. It merely needs to be pointed out that such groups are not corporate with respect to all aspects of social life, and that they are fuzzy-edged, that they emerge out of the overlapping network of bilateral relations with respect to particular purposes, obligations or prohibitions in just the same way as does the household, or the set of kin that falls within the incest prohibition. Consider again the matter of hereditary sponsorship. I introduced the Spartokhoriot system as if baptismal sponsors were male, and as if rights of sponsorship passed down a male line, since this was the clearest way of showing the connection between baptismal sponsorship and marriage sponsorship, and because it was also the way the system was explained to me. As we have seen, however, women in Spartokhori could act as baptismal sponsors, and frequently did so, often when they were still little girls, and on behalf of both males and females.[19] It was merely the case that when it came to marriage the groom required a male *koumbaros*. This presented no real problem, for a woman who had acted as the baptismal sponsor for a little boy could simply transfer her right to act as his wedding sponsor to her husband or her son. Importantly, this

---

[16]Hammel himself twice makes this same point: 'The general Jugoslav pattern differs from the Italian-Spanish-Greek one because of the enormous importance of agnatic groups in Jugoslav peasant society' (1968: 69), and again, 'It is the depth and continuity of agnatic relationship ... which lends stability to *kumstvo* relationships between descent groups' (1968: 90).

[17]I confess to being unhappy with the distinction between what a social institution is by nature and what it is in practice. Pitt-Rivers seems to come perilously close to reading theology as sociology.

[18]As Pina-Cabral protests, 'I must ... take issue with the supposed "atomistic and isolated" nature of Mediterranean families .... What is "isolated" about Sicilian families and their complex systems of association with kin? How would one find a way of describing a single "type of family organisation" that includes the matrifocal sibling-vicinalities that Davis describes, the divided households of the small mountain hamlets of Algarve, the kindreds of Aragon, the Corsican families, the stem-family households of the Pyranean region [which, incidentally, are found right in the middle of the Mediterranean Sea in Formentera (Bestard-Camps 1985)], the various types of Italian families and, finally, the *zadruga*?' (1989: 402).

[19]So they could in Yugoslavia, but there sponsorship was overwhelmingly male: between 78–100 per cent for recorded baptisms, and 91–100 per cent for recorded marriages (Hammel 1968: 46).

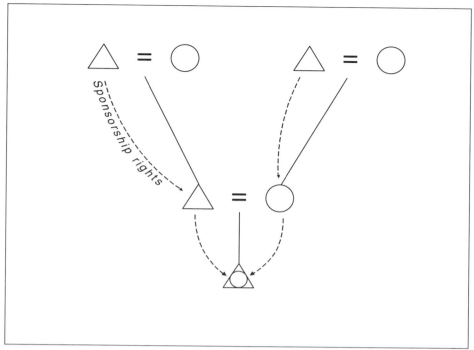

Figure 5.4 Bilateral inheritance of sponsorship

kept intact her *own* family's line of sponsorship. But since women could act as baptismal sponsors, and since rights of hereditary sponsorship could be conveyed to their children (whether male or female), while sponsorship rights certainly followed down a line of descendants, that line was not necessarily agnatic. Rather, it could wander through the network of Spartokhori's overlapping bilateral kindreds. Thus, for example, a man who had acted as a marriage sponsor (and who had perhaps previously acted as the groom's baptismal sponsor) decides, when a child is born of the marriage, to transfer his rights of baptismal sponsorship to his own young daughter. If the child whom she baptized was male, then twenty-five or thirty years later his female baptismal sponsor, upon being requested to exercise her rights, might have her husband officiate as *koumbaros* at her godchild's wedding ceremony. On the birth of child from that marriage, the right to baptize that child might then pass to either a son or a daughter of the female baptismal sponsor (the father's *nona*) and her husband, the father's wedding sponsor (*koumbaros*). To put the matter another way, both men and women could find themselves inheritors to lines of sponsorship that could as easily have commenced with their maternal grandfather as with their paternal grandfather (see Figure 5.4). Importantly, however, the lack of discrete kinship groupings clearly defined by some unilineal principle and between which ties of spiritual kinship could systematically be contracted does not negate the collective nature of Spartokhoriot spiritual kinship, or even the unilateral nature of the alliances formed. This becomes clearer if we also consider the prohibitions generated by godparenthood.

Prohibitions

As in Yugoslavia, godparenthood in Spartokhori was in various ways incompatible with both affinal and cognatic relations.[20] The prohibitions which I detail below (some few of which are also codified by the church) can be divided into two broad classes: first, prohibitions on godparenthood as a result of existing relationships of consanguinity or affinity; second, prohibitions on affinity as a result of existing relationships of godparenthood. A third class of prohibitions has already been touched on in the context of the hereditary and unidirectional nature of Spartokhoriot sponsorship, and it is convenient to review them here: namely, prohibitions on sponsorship as a result of existing ties of godparenthood. All three types of prohibition could perhaps be placed under the general rubric of spiritual incest, for all three relate to the confusion of kinship categories that would occur were the prohibitions not in place, and infractions of all three types of prohibition aroused expressions of unease and distaste amongst the older generation of Spartokhoriots. I use the label 'spiritual incest' hesitantly, however, for I was never given any explicitly metaphysical justification for the prohibitions (but see du Boulay 1984). Rather, older Spartokhoriots (including the village priest) expressed them by saying that certain forms of sponsorship between kin, or marriage between spiritual kin, 'didn't do (*dhen kani*)', or were 'ugly/unseemly' (*askhimo*)', or were simply 'not good'. It must also be admitted that in some instances the repugnance towards sponsorship of kin, or towards marriage between spiritual kin, also coincided with practical objections that have been widely noted in the ethnography of Greece, and which provide alternative explanations. In the end I would suggest that the prohibitions were overdetermined, and that it is not possible neatly to separate practical objections from moral (and metaphysical) ones. Moreover, for individuals, conformity at the level of practice does not necessarily entail a similar conformity of ideas motivating that practice. But at the very least, a notion of spiritual incest seems consistent with Spartokhoriot prohibitions.

Prohibitions on baptism as a result of existing ties of godparenthood

As noted, it was fundamental to the Spartokhoriot godparenthood system that baptismal sponsorship between two families should be repeated down the generations. *Koumbari* did, and should, baptize their *koumbari*. But despite the lack of any verbal distinction between baptizers and baptized, the enduring relationship between families was asymmetrical, and it was forbidden for 'the oil to return (*na*

---

[20]Put this way, the comparison may not seem accurate. Yugoslavian godparenthood is best described as being incompatible with affinity and agnation; but if one may not baptize agnates (members of one's own group) and equally members of those groups with which one has formed a marital alliance (affines), then the effect (as in Spartokhori) is to exclude cognatic relatives as candidates for baptism.

mi yirizi to ladhi)'. In short, one could not baptize one's baptizers. There is no church ruling on this matter (except perhaps implicitly, in that no individual could baptize his or her individual baptizer, since an essential qualification for sponsors is that they be members of the Orthodox church, which requires them to have already been baptized). The Spartokhoriot prohibition, however, followed logically from the collective nature of Spartokhoriot godparenthood. Since godparenthood entailed the virtual assimilation of the individual sponsor with his or her family, a reversal of the direction of baptism would result in a person becoming sponsor to his or her own sponsors, and two families would simultaneously be each other's spiritual parents and spiritual children. This is precisely the sort of category confusion to which, in the context of profane kinship and the rules of consanguinity and affinity, the church takes particular exception (though admittedly in the case of sponsorship the categories are not linguistically marked). Quite how far the resultant prohibitions extended was unclear (for once again it is necessary to take into account the overlapping nature of Spartokhori's bilateral kindreds), but it was certainly the case that people would not baptize any of the children of the person who had baptized them, or of the person who had baptized either of their own parents, or of the person who had baptized their spouse or their siblings, or of the person who had baptized their own children.

More than a confusion of categories may, however, be involved, for the same prohibitions occur in the village of Ambeli studied by du Boulay, where, at least within the period that godparental relations are thought to endure, baptisms must remain unidirectional from the group of the baptizer to the group of the baptized lest 'the oil turns back *(yirizi to ladhi)*' (du Boulay 1984: 545). Du Boulay argues that in Ambeli there is a precise parallel between the ideas that underlie this prohibition and those which underlie the incest prohibition, for just as a type of physical incest is seen in return marriages between certain categories of kin which would result in a reversal of the unidirectional flow of blood, the 'vehicle of natural life' (ibid. 550), so 'the spiritual parallel of incest is found in "returning" the oil, the symbol of spiritual life, to where it originated' (ibid. 545). This interpretation is greatly strengthened by the fact that in Ambeli villagers also conceived of baptism as creating a quite physical link between baptizer and baptized, and remarked, 'When a person baptizes a child, the child takes one vein (of blood) from him' (ibid. 546–7). No such quasi-biological account of baptism was offered me in Spartokhori, but given the striking similarities between the indigenous methods of reckoning consanguinity in Ambeli and in Spartokhori, and between the two communities' representations of the incest prohibition, it may well be that in Spartokhori too the prohibition on returning the oil of spiritual kinship was connected with notions of returning blood through incestuous marriages.

A prohibition on (or at least an avoidance of) reciprocal baptism between families has, however, been widely noted for Greece, and Gudeman claims that it is 'nearly a universal folk injunction' in the Christian world (1975: 233). Anything so particular as a notion of spiritual incest may not be the only idea that underlies them. In church terms and in popular conception, the relationship between sponsor and sponsored is a hierarchical one, for the sponsor is by definition superior to the sponsored, since it is the sponsor who has introduced the sponsored into the Christian church, a hierarchy made clear by the very terminology of spiritual parenthood (du Boulay 1984: 547; Gudeman 1975: 234). Moreover, it has been widespread practice in Greece (Friedl 1964a: 72; Campbell 1964: 246; Kenna 1971: 257; Aschenbrenner 1986: 74–6; Herzfeld 1985: 98; Vernier 1991: 74–7), as elsewhere in southern Europe and Latin America (Mintz and Wolf 1950; Foster 1963), to employ this doctrinal inequality as the basis for a relationship of material inequality, in that godparents (baptizers) were often sought amongst the socially, economically or politically privileged, thus turning godparenthood into a form of patron/client relationship. This occurred in Spartokhori too, although it was limited by the requirements of the hereditary system, and also rendered largely unnecessary for a younger generation of wealthy sailors who, when it came to the free choice of a godparent, could afford to put personal friendship before the advantages of patronage.

The situation may well have been different in the past. One old lady who had fallen on hard times after the premature death of her husband (a merchant and mill-owner) and the emigration of her children made a point of telling me that she was still very much 'respected' by the village, since she (and her husband) had baptized so many children. When I asked how they had come to baptize so many children, she looked at me as if I were an idiot and replied, 'Because we were *rich*. They cried for us.' But even if no material or social inequality overlaid the relationship (and with Spartokhori's rapidly changing economy, hereditary sponsors were often poorer than the families they sponsored) the intrinsically hierarchical nature of the relationship between baptizers and baptized may, as Gudeman argues (1975: 234), have been sufficient to make any reversal of the direction of baptism seem unseemly, to make it something that 'didn't do'. One point is clear, however. Whether the prohibition on reciprocal baptism stems from a notion of hierarchy, or from some belief related to a spiritual incest, it still makes sense only if godparenthood is understood in collective terms. For the church, the hierarchical relationship between baptizer and baptized is essentially dyadic and thus results in no strictures on subsequent baptisms. In folk practice, the assimilation of godparenthood to kinship makes it a collective relationship, so that the direction of baptism is constrained by existing godparental relations. In fact, the prohibition on the reversal of the direction of sponsorship between kinship groups starts quite markedly to resemble prohibitions on the reversal of the direction in which women may move between kinship groups in societies that are hierarchically organized by marriage. Just as wife-givers are superior to wife-takers, so that the direction of marriage cannot be reversed, so baptizers are superior to baptized, so that the direction of sponsorship cannot be reversed.[21]

Prohibitions on baptism as a result of kinship

The second set of Spartokhoriot folk prohibitions, those concerning the baptism of close relatives, similarly suggests a notion of spiritual incest, but they too find an

---

[21] Again, such an analogy is specifically denied by Pitt-Rivers on the grounds that 'in the rest of the Christian world' (that is, outside Yugoslavia) 'there is *no* notion of a collective relationship and, therefore, no possibility of a system of generalized exchange' (1976: 329; original emphasis).

alternative pragmatic explanation. According to the church, the only Orthodox Christians not eligible to act as godparents for a child are that child's own natural parents. The prohibition, which exists equally in the Western church, is usually explained as following from the inherent body/soul dualism of Christianity, augmented by the notion of original sin. Thus a child's carnal parents contribute to its physical birth, while its spiritual parents contribute to its spiritual rebirth and purification, and as different forms of parenthood, the carnal and spiritual cannot be vested in the same person (Pitt-Rivers 1976: 318, 323; but see Gudeman 1975). But while the church separates carnal and spiritual parenthood, it goes no further in maintaining a separation between profane and spiritual kinship, and according to church law it remains quite permissible for people to baptize even their own siblings (*Pidhalion* 1976: 753), thus becoming spiritually parents to those who by birth are their brothers and sisters.

Most Spartokhoriots, however, strongly disapproved of such practices and avoided baptizing close relatives. Nevertheless, in the neighbouring village of Katomeri a number of children had been baptized by uncles, aunts, first cousins and, in one case, by a sibling (cf. Aschenbrenner 1986: 63),[22] and although older Spartokhoriots were pleased to view these baptisms as a further example of Katomeriot degeneracy, even in Spartokhori one man had baptized his own nephew and a few children had been baptized by first cousins. Again, older Spartokhoriots (including the priest) claimed that such baptisms were a new departure, and viewed them unfavourably. Again, their disapproval is consistent with an overall assimilation of godparenthood with kinship, so that baptism of a close relative, like marriage with a close relative, becomes incestuous.[23]

Nevertheless, all that the Spartokhoriots would state was that such baptisms were 'not good' and that they 'didn't do', and given the vagueness of these formulations, it is once again possible that the Spartokhoriots' general avoidance of intra-familial baptism was, like their prohibition on reciprocal baptism, motivated by practical considerations. After all, even discounting the possibility of transforming ties of spiritual kinship into channels of patronage, relatives – and especially godrelatives – are people whom one should be able to trust and from whom favours and assistance may be sought. The overlaying of spiritual kinship on profane kinship might therefore have simply seemed profligate, as it did to the villagers of Karpofora (Aschenbrenner 1986: 64–5), and not to be done for that reason. Interestingly, older Spartokhoriots put forward a further practical consideration for the avoidance, which points to the seriousness with which spiritual kinship was taken. Despite the ideals of family, it was generally recognized (for reasons to be discussed in the following chapter) that it was amongst close

---

[22] Aschenbrenner notes that in Karpofora the child's grandparents are excluded as baptismal sponsors, and that aunts and uncles of the child's parents are ineligible. But for the rest, 'a baptismal sponsor may be anyone of approximately the parents' generation, including their brothers, sisters and cousins' (1986: 63). It seems that the folk prohibitions in Karpofora relate to age, not to the degree of relatedness.

[23] Here the data from western Europe are markedly different. In summarizing the rules for choosing a godparent in rural Spain, Pitt-Rivers states that '[G]odparents must be chosen from among the closest kin outside the nuclear family: preferably the parents and siblings of the child's parents,' and that the choice of the child's grandparents is the commonest feature of Spanish godparenthood (1976: 325).

relatives that quarrels were most likely to occur. Since it was imperative that *koumbari* should not quarrel, it was held that relatives should not baptize each other. Nevertheless the existence of some unarticulated notion of spiritual incest continues to be suggested if we consider the third class of Spartokhoriot folk prohibitions, those concerning marriage with spiritual kin.

Prohibitions on marriage as a result of spiritual kinship

Since the church sees godparenthood as a form of parenthood, baptismal sponsorship precludes marriage between the baptizer and the baptized. This prohibition is extended by the church to include the direct ascendants and descendants of the sponsor and sponsored. Thus people may not marry the mother, father, son or daughter of any person they have baptized; they may not marry the father, mother, son or daughter of the person who has baptized them; and they may not marry the children of the person who baptized either of their parents (*Pidhalion* 1976: 753). Despite this extension of the prohibition to the direct ascendants and descendants of the sponsor and the sponsored, the church still appears to see godparenthood as an essentially dyadic relationship, and it is expressly stated in the *Pidhalion* that the siblings of the baptized may marry the baptizer and vice versa (*Pidhalion* 1976: 753). Only one form of collateral prohibition is set down by the church, and it is of a rather special kind: two people who share a common godfather (*nonos*) or godmother (*nona*) may not marry, since they have become *pnevmatika adherfia*, 'spiritual siblings' (*Pidhalion* 1976: 753).[24]

Spiritual siblingship was often singled out by the Spartokhoriots when sponsorship was discussed, for given the preference for village endogamy, the prohibition could seriously limit the number of available marriage partners. Worse, it could result in a genuine crisis should a boy and girl who shared a common godparent fall in love. This was one context in which a clear and important distinction was made between the individual baptismal sponsor (the *nonos* or *nona*) and those who were collectively considered to be *koumbari*, for a simple expedient solved the potential problem. Once an individual had acted as baptismal sponsor for a child, from then on any further children he or she might baptize would be of the same sex. Thus no one would have a spiritual sibling of the opposite sex to whom he or she might in later years be attracted. But although in this context the individual identity of the baptismal sponsor was of importance (a baptizer of boys as opposed to a baptizer of girls), the system of collective and hereditary sponsorship was not challenged. In a sense, it came to the rescue, for if a man, for example, had baptized a little girl, and then in his role of hereditary sponsor was called on to baptize a little boy, that man's son or daughter or wife (who had previously baptized no one, or who had previously baptized only boys) could fill the role of *nonos* or *nona* in his place, since godparenthood was in any case a family matter.

Some inconsistency in the system does, of course, remain, since although in other contexts godparenthood was considered to be collective, the church

---

[24]Some further prohibitions do result, however, from husband and wife being considered 'one flesh': for instance, a man cannot marry the wife of his (deceased) spiritual brother.

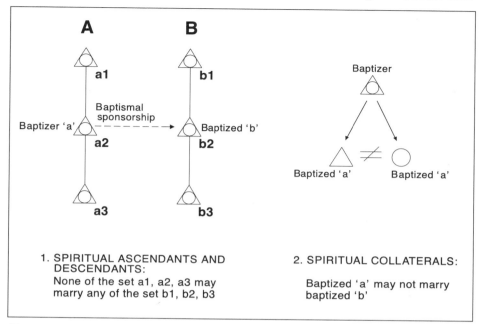

Figure 5.5 Prohibitions resulting from baptism

prohibition on marriage between spiritual siblings was circumvented by making sure that no opposite sex children shared the same *individual* sponsor. Yet if it seems inconsistent to stress the collective nature of godparenthood and then pragmatically to retreat to viewing it as an individual relationship as soon as practical problems arise, it is worth noting that although a man and a woman who had a common set of *koumbari* (the joint relatives of their respective *nonos* or *nona* who were husband and wife or father and daughter, etc), in Spartokhori it was still unlikely that their own respective families would be each other's *koumbari* (see Figure 5.5). At this point the familial nature of godparenthood was reasserted, for there appeared to be a considerable reluctance to overlay a godparental relationship between families with an affinal relationship. In short, as in Hammel's Yugoslavian study, godparenthood and affinity in Spartokhori tended to be mutually exclusive forms of alliance. Marriages between the baptized and the close collateral relatives (certainly the siblings) of the baptizer, or between the baptizer and the close collateral relatives of the baptized, or, indeed, between the respective siblings of the baptizer and the baptized, were viewed as inappropriate, despite the licence that the *Pidhalion* specifically grants such unions. In fact, a reluctance to marry people categorized as *koumbari* appears quite commonplace in rural Greek society (Campbell 1964a: 221; Friedl 1964a: 72; Kenna 1971: 228; du Boulay 1984: 555 n. 11; Aschenbrenner 1986: 62, 64), and certainly in terms of the Spartokhoriot system of collective godparenthood marriage between them would be tantamount to a marriage between the actual baptismal sponsor and sponsored. Moreover, there would be a confusion of

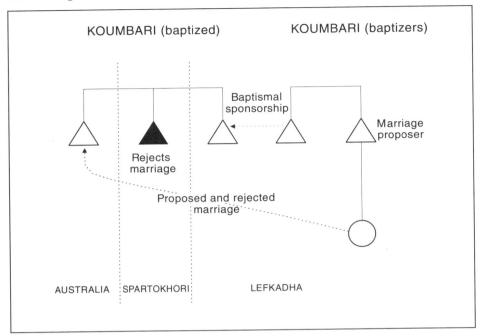

Figure 5.6 Marriage rejected on the grounds of spiritual kinship

names, for people's *koumbari* would become their *simpetheri,* and their *simpetheri* would become their *koumbari.* Significantly, I could find no case of such a marriage occurring, and when I questioned people about the possibility, general opinion was overwhelmingly that 'it didn't do'. According to some Spartokhoriots, however, the prohibition on marriage between *koumbari* was extended slightly further and into the next generation, as the following case illustrates.

Lakis, a Spartokhoriot in his late fifties, came from a large family. One of his numerous brothers had been baptized by a *nonos* from a village in Lefkadha (where that brother later settled). Another of Lakis's brothers later emigrated to Australia. In due course it became known that Lakis's Australian brother was seeking a wife. The brother of the *nonos* who had baptized Lakis's brother in Lefkadha thus approached Lakis with the request that he should act as a go-between in arranging a marriage between his daughter and Lakis's Australian brother (see Figure 5.6). Lakis, however, refused, and he explained to me that he had refused on the grounds that this would make his *koumbari* (godparents) into *simpetheri* (affines), and his *simpetheri* into *koumbari,* and everything would be mixed up. In short, Lakis forbade a marriage between his brother and the daughter of the brother of the baptismal sponsor of another of his brothers. This was a quite extensive collateral prohibition which grouped together as reciprocally and collectively *koumbari* Lakis and all of his siblings on the one side, and his brother's sponsor and his brother's sponsor's siblings and their direct descendants on the other. Lakis also made it clear that his unwillingness to sanction the marriage had nothing to do with practical considerations, but with a notion of category confusions – again, of something approaching spiritual incest. He was, however, well aware that the marriage he had forbidden was quite legitimate in the eyes of the church, and he ended his account with the comment that nowadays it was only the 'old(-fashioned)' men like himself who worried about such matters, and who were anxious that everything should be *sosto* (correct) and *katharo* (clean), a point with which Spartokhori's priest, who had been present throughout the conversation, ruefully concurred.

The village family: reprise

Despite a degree of uncertainty about the rules of Spartokhoriot godparenthood, certain general features emerge. First, baptism and marriage sponsorship were seen to be hereditary and collective, with the aim (amongst others) of establishing and perpetuating relationships between families rather than between individuals. Second, spiritual kinship was seldom overlaid on consanguinity or affinity. But a third feature that parallels the Spartokhoriots' preference for village endogamy should also be noted: the existence of a hereditary system of sponsorship not only limited the opportunities for the free choice of a sponsor, but tended to keep the ties of spiritual kinship internal to the community.

Baptismal records made available to me by Spartokhori's priest covered only the period from 1963 to 1976, and in many instances the entries were incomplete. Nevertheless a discernible pattern emerged, for of the total of 143 entries for 1963–76, in seventy-six cases the sponsors were entered as 'from Spartokhori'. A further twenty-nine entries failed to record the provenance of the sponsor. Some of these baptisms took place in Athens, and it was impossible to know with certainty whether the sponsors were or were not Spartokhoriots. A further seventeen entries recorded the sponsor as being resident in Athens, but to judge by the family names, ten of these were almost certainly Spartokhoriots. Interestingly there was only one baptismal sponsor recorded from Katomeri and only one from Vathi. As in marriage, so in godparenthood, the Spartokhoriots appear to have shunned their neighbours. Eighteen sponsors were recorded as living elsewhere in Greece (Lefkadha, Patras and as far afield as Ioannina). Again, seven of these were certainly Spartokhoriots, or of Spartokhoriot origin. But in sum, out of the total of 143 baptisms, ninety-three were almost certainly sponsored by Spartokhoriots, and the origins of the remaining fifty sponsors remain uncertain. Intra-communal sponsorship thus stood at a minimum of 65 per cent, and could well have been higher. Rather than acting as a means whereby links were created with the outside world (see Aschenbrenner 1986: 65–8), godparenthood, like affinity, thus reinforced and complemented relationships internal to and constitutive of the Spartokhoriot community. The net result of a system of godparenthood that was corporate, that did not reduplicate the ties of consanguinity and affinity and that was largely internal to the community, was to bind the Spartokhoriots yet more tightly and intricately into the one family of which they spoke. Indeed, spiritual kinship could be seen to fill in the few gaps left in the web of Spartokhori's internal relationships.

One last and important consequence of Spartokhoriot kinship reckoning must now be stressed. Ties of consanguinity, affinity and godparenthood bound the community together, and provided the empirical basis on which the very claim to community ('we are all one family') could be made, and on which Spartokhoriot identity ('I'm very much a Spartokhoriot – I'm related to half the village') were predicated. Ties of kinship were what distinguished *ta pedhia mas* (our people) from *kseni* (outsiders). The barrier thus erected was, as I have tried to show, a quite porous one, for the community readily absorbed people through marriage, and the effective collapse of affinity into consanguinity immediately equipped in-marriers with a host of relatives whom they could claim as their own, and through whom they could assert a Spartokhoriot identity. Nevertheless, what distinguished us from them remained kinship. Paradoxically, however, it was the very extensiveness and ubiquity of Spartokhori's internal kinship ties (whether of consanguinity, affinity or godparenthood) that for individuals *within* the community substantially prevented kinship from being the practical determinant of daily action. For if the morality of kinship had been properly maintained, then no one would ever have been able to quarrel with anyone, faction would have been impossible and the village would have been united in continual harmony – and that, as we shall see in the following chapters, most certainly was not the case.

6
The Back-to-Back Community

I have attempted to describe the rules and structures of consanguinity, affinity and godparenthood in Spartokhori: the forms of relationship that were recognized, the terms by which they were specified, the manner in which they were generated – but these are not, in the end, what Spartokhoriot kinship was about. They constitute instead the foundation upon which was constructed a morality, a set of consciously held values and ideas which maintained that those who fell within the ambit of family were bound together by ties of mutual trust, affection, loyalty, respect and cooperation (Bloch 1971). Such ideas were translated into action. They formed the grounds on which claims were made and services rendered. But as I have suggested, this morality was also manipulated and limited – not with respect to the values it entailed, but with respect to those whom, at any particular time, it could manage to embrace. Family became, perforce, a negotiable category (Bourdieu, 1990: 16).

At one extreme, family could incorporate the entire village. Here ideas of trust, affection, loyalty, respect and cooperation had to remain largely rhetorical and sentimental. They were nonetheless important, for it was to the notion of family and to the values it ideally entailed that villagers routinely appealed in expressing to themselves and to others that complex sense of belonging that made the village a community. But precisely because the notion of family was so extensive, congruent with the community itself, it could not act to suppress or to obviate those quarrels and animosities integral to village life or even to specify the individuals with whom people would cooperate – except to assert, ideally, that it was with everyone. At the other extreme family could be identified with the household, the basic social unit of village life (Peristiany 1965). Here no discrepancy between the ideals and practice could be tolerated. Whatever conflict was internal to the household remained swathed in secrecy and the *spiti* presented itself to the world as a unit whose solidarity was unquestionable (cf. du Boulay, 1976). Family in this sense specified those with whom one *had* to cooperate. But between these two extremes the values of kinship and family still operated, and operated in quite practical ways; although their operation was necessarily selective, their invocation a matter of strategic choice, their success always open to doubt.

Public virtue and private vice

The experience of daily life is not something easily conveyed; nor, by the villagers,

155

was it something clearly articulated. For nearly six months I was told little other than '*Ine kalos kosmos edho* (They're good people here)'. This remark tagged every Spartokhoriot's enquiry about how I saw the village and was regularly enlarged on by accounts of how the village was all one family: 'When someone laughs, we all laugh; when someone cries we all cry; we're ... all one family here.' And those who were not permanently resident in the village were perhaps all the more insistent that Spartokhori's *kosmos* (people) was *kalos* (good). But little by little a change took place. 'How do you see the village?' I would be asked.

'Very nice. They're good people here,' I would reply in sage imitation.

'Yes,' my companion of the moment would say, 'They're a *kalos kosmos*, only ... there are five or six *pedhia* (people/ 'boys') here who are, excuse me, shit.'

After nearly two years in the village I was still being asked for confirmation that the village was a good village, and certainly the only acceptable response from myself was that it was. But by then my friends' comments had swung to the other extreme. 'Yes, they're good to you because you're a *ksenos*. But if you're a Spartokhoriot they 'eat' you. They rip out your eyes. That's what people are like here. You don't know them.'

Needless to say, what I was witnessing was not some decline in community relationships but a change in the Spartokhoriots' assessment of my own relationship to the village. What was required to be presented to an unknown foreigner was a vision of the village as a cohesive and mutually supportive community – all one family and a *kalos kosmos*. What by the end of my stay could more candidly be conveyed was an altogether different picture, a Hobbesian society in which the pursuit of self-interest was leavened only by gratuitous malice. It would, nevertheless, be a mistake to think that what I was seeing was the gradual removal of some camouflage of deception which, when finally thrown off, would reveal the Spartokhoriots' naked estimation of each other. As Herzfeld (1985, 1987a, 1987b, 1992, 1997) has shown, there is a constant tension between the outward- and inward-looking aspects of Greek self-presentation. It was important that, as an outsider, I should appreciate the village in terms of its first characterization. It was inevitable that, as insiders, the Spartokhoriots should live their lives mindful of its second characterization. But both views of the village were genuinely held. And I do not think that a notion of self-deception should replace that of deception. The contradiction was not between rhetoric and reality, but between two sorts of rhetoric and two sorts of reality. It was a question of context.

Talking to a stranger was a situation that demanded an account of the village in terms of amity, concord, cooperation and affection. And it was believed in by those who related it. That the village was a good village, that its people were a good people, was a matter of conviction. Moreover, any challenge to this judgement by someone such as myself would have been deeply resented and quickly countered. On the other hand, day to day and amongst themselves it was the village's animosities, quarrels and factions that bore most immediately on the lives of its inhabitants. This is what generated the Hobbesian view, but it was a view no more real to the Spartokhoriots than that informed by the ideal values of concord and amity. It was merely the view derived from an internal perspective which it was their privilege alone to enunciate (cf. Herzfeld 1997: 48). What allowed both judgements to coexist with some logical consistency was that both occurred in a form of moral discourse that was relative to social position and social context. They were judgements about the speaker's own moral worth relative to society at large, and they were judgements about the group with which the speaker was identifying himself or herself relative to society at large. What constituted society at large and what constitutes the group identified with were the variables. When a Spartokhoriot talked to an outsider or when the Spartokhoriots were considering themselves in relation to the outside world, then Spartokhori was the genuine locus of their affections and was seen as a morally superior realm. Within the village and in relation to their fellow villagers, allegiances were to smaller groups, minimally to the household, so that the village itself became the hostile and degenerate world against which one defined oneself. In both cases, however, the appropriation of virtue was to one's own.

Public and private

In such a situation the village could be both the family to which one belonged and the world from which one sought refuge in the family. And it is perhaps one of the paradoxes of Greek (or even Mediterranean) rural society that a people so committed to the privacy of domestic life[1] nevertheless choose to live in a form of settlement so compact that one house is literally on top of another, and the avoidance of one's neighbours is achieved only by the exercise of considerable skill and the scrupulous observance of social boundaries in defiance of topography. Much of the tension of village life could be seen in terms of the incompatibility between the village's physical space, where to step outside the front door was to enter the arena of public life, and the closed nature of the household, which was determined to keep its secrets to itself (cf. Hart 1991: 179).[2] Both, however, received ideological endorsement, and as du Boulay (1976) so beautifully illustrates for Ambeli, village life was simultaneously intensely public and intensely private, a series of open forums and tightly closed doors. The effort was to maintain the division for oneself and to break it down for others. '*Pou pas?* (Where are you going?)' was the standard question whenever one walked down the street. '*Pouthena* (Nowhere)', was the equally standard reply.

But if public discourse was deliberately unrevealing, such questions had still to be asked, and an answer had to be given. Evasion was expected, but indifference was unpardonable. No person simply walked past another, and a quite rigid etiquette pervaded village life. This was not always evident, for it was not a matter of obvious pomp and circumstance, much less of ritual, but simply of the constant requirement for mutual recognition. '*Pos ise?* (How are you?)', '*Ti nea?* (What news?)', '*Pos pai?* (How's it going?)', '*Ti yinese?* (How have you been?)' or

---

[1] I have often heard said in Greece, and by way of a joke, that there is no term in Greek for 'privacy'. This is not quite true, but if Greek does lack a single word that exactly translates 'privacy', there is no doubt that the concept of privacy is deeply embedded in rural Greek society.

[2] Hart recounts that when she was negotiating to rent a house in the village of Richia (Peloponnese), 'I was told many times that it was [a] desirable [house] because it had two exits, and it would be difficult for anyone to keep track of one's comings and goings' (1991: 179).

most simply '*Yia sou* (Good-day/Cheers)' were the obligatory greetings between people who had seen each other day in, day out, for ten, twenty or fifty years, and who had been exchanging these greetings day in, day out, for ten, twenty or fifty years. The content of such exchanges may have been minimal, but their performance was certainly meaningful, for it constituted the touchstone of endorsed morality. '*Imaste oli anthropi* (We are all human beings)' was the most frequently repeated village moral maxim, and human beings had to greet each other as part of the constant affirmation of their common humanity. Only those who were acknowledged enemies failed to do so, withholding from each other this basic recognition, while inadvertent neglect of the convention caused certain offence, for the communal ethos was egalitarian and strongly so.

Yet equality remained something that had continually to be asserted, its recognition demanded rather than assumed. '*Anthropos, dhen ime?* (I'm a human being, aren't I?)' was the outraged cry of someone who felt slighted, and no one would say him nay, for the appeal was to a morality no one could dispute. But the appeal itself betrayed the delicacy of the situation: people who failed to assert their equality would find it no longer existed, for equality, just like honour (for which it was a necessary precondition), though granted as part of the human condition was nevertheless always at risk (Campbell 1964: 316–20; Peristiany 1965; Pitt-Rivers 1965). The assumption of equality was not that everybody was one's equal, but that no one was one's better. Such formalities as greetings, then, were markers of the community's mutual recognition and mutual respect (*sevasmos*), of its solidarity as a community of equals; but they were also counters in a continual competition to maintain that recognition and respect. The constitution of a *parea* (a group of male friends drinking together) is a case in point.

There were some seven places in the Spartokhori where people drank, referred to simply as *ta magazia*, 'the shops'. And in a village where, to be frank, there was often not a lot to do, sitting in the shops could approach a full-time occupation. Men casually drifted from one to the other throughout the day. But not *so* casually. In fact when a man entered a shop only one of three things could happen: if there was an empty table, he could sit down; if other men were already seated at a table, one might cry '*Katse na pyoume*' (Sit down [with us] and have a drink); but if all tables were occupied (even by men sitting on their own), and no invitation was extended, he could only leave. The silence may have been a condemnation, but to have forced the issue would have risked mortification.

I do not mean to suggest that this last situation created a continual series of social impasses. Since people were always wandering in, wandering out, standing in doorways, rocking on their heels, or walking in small circles as the day slowly passed, no obvious crisis of social embarrassment was caused. But what was certainly the case was that on no account could a man simply sit down with others uninvited. Moreover, the degree to which men were invited or not invited, greeted or not greeted, immediately entered into the never-ending collective computation of individual social worth. In a village in which there were only about 200 adult males permanently resident, all of whom had known each other from birth, some for seventy years or more, the invitation had still to be extended, and extended on every occasion. And as one old fellow leaves after loitering in the doorway for a few minutes during which no one asks him to join them, my companion nudges me and whispers, '*Bah, dhen ehi aksia, aftos* (He has no worth, that one).'

For men, then, the coffee-shops and drinking places constituted a public world where conspicuous attendance was obligatory, for a man who kept himself to himself or who remained at home was seen either to be failing in his social duties towards others or to be admitting to his own inadequacy. Public life was the arena in which individuals demonstrated their respect for their fellows, their commitment to the community, their solidarity with their equals; but it was also the testing ground for the respect in which the community held them, for the measure of their worth, for their claim to equality (cf. Pitt-Rivers 1965).[3]

'To sit together, to have good company (*parea*), a chat, a few drinks and a few jokes – that's what life's about, isn't it?' And 'the rich' or, given Spartokhori's rapid social mobility, those who had achieved by emigration, education or sheer hard work a degree of social standing in the wider world were always open to the accusation of turning their backs on their fellow villagers and of remaining (and drinking) at home. A man passes down the street, nods to the 'boys', but refuses their invitation to join their company. When he has passed but is still within earshot, the indignant comment comes in penetrating *sotto voce*, 'Where's he off to? We're men (*anthropi*) aren't we – or are we animals (*zoa*)?' Conversely, the very old, the sick, the genuinely impoverished, or simply those who by common repute were held to be tight (to have 'crabs in their pockets'), betrayed by their lack of participation their disabilities either of circumstance or of character – and for the Spartokhoriots the difference was often not great. 'Where is old so-and-so whom I've only heard about?' I would sometimes ask. 'At home. He doesn't come out, that one,' and an element of contempt is implicit in the statement of fact.

The public world was the arena where village solidarity was pledged and village reputation gauged, but that public world was literally flanked by the doors through which men escaped into the guarded, mysterious world of their private and domestic lives into which few but their closest relatives could follow. Here one was with one's 'own' in the strongest and most restricted sense. And though relationships within the household were often less than harmonious (cf. du Boulay 1974: 18–19; Clark 1988: 382–413), the members of a single *spiti* would not and could not 'talk' of each other outside the home (cf. Friedl 1964a: 87–8; du Boulay 1974: 21–2 and 1976). And they could not reveal outside the house what their intimates had said about others within it.

To a degree the covenant of the household's external closure, and therefore of its internal openness, applied even to those who were its temporary guests. What I was told within a household often contrasted greatly with what I heard expressed outside it. What I had taken to be perfectly amicable relationships between individuals and families were there often revealed to be fraught with resentment, jealousy and even hatred. A small tale of petty meanness or of doubtful honesty or of foolishness would be related about someone with whom, in public, daily intercourse was friendly, even jovial, and the remark would

---

[3] In Pitt-Rivers's famous definition, 'Honour is the value of a person in his own eyes, but also in the eyes of his society. It his estimation of his own worth, his *claim* to pride, but it is also the acknowledgment of that claim, his excellence recognized by society, his *right* to pride' (1965: 21; original emphases).

follow: 'That's the sort of person he is – and so was his father. *Mia fatsa, mia ratsa, i idhia pasta* (One face, one race, the same paste).' This could be said to me within the house, for I too was bound to silence. After all, anything I disclosed would confirm what everyone in any case suspected, that we had been 'talking', so that the disclosure itself would invite condemnation. The privacy of the household was thus both sanctuary and sanction.

There is a word for 'gossip' in Greek, *koutsombolio*, but what was usually said in Spartokhori was simply that someone 'talked', for the assumption was that to talk about someone was to talk to their detriment. It was wise to make it clear when this was not the case. In the coffee-shop conversation would turn to some person or persons and immediately the phrase '*Dhen milao kaka, katalavenis* (I'm not speaking ill, you understand)' would be introduced. Indeed, casual mention of anyone's name was likely to be prefaced with '*Ine kalo pedhi*' ('He/she is a good 'child'), lest what followed be construed as criticism. These, of course, were the tactics of caution, so ingrained that at times they appeared no more than linguistic reflexes. On the other hand the possibility should not be discounted that the person spoken about was genuinely considered a *kalo pedhi*. A world of faction implied a world of alliances, and friendships, even love, were not lacking between individuals. Nevertheless the assumption was that to talk was to talk ill, and it was not without foundation. The situation fed on itself. Suspicion generated gossip. Gossip justified suspicion. 'So-and-so is a *kalo pedhi*' was a sounding out, a declaration of strategic neutrality that awaited the slight hesitation in agreement that signified the allowance of some possible qualification that would be amplified with mutual satisfaction once both parties had avoided the trap of committing themselves to criticism before the other was committed. Then all was safe, for the ensuing conversation could not be repeated without self-compromise.

Private vice

In this context severe constraints were placed on public conversation. What could openly be said was only that which could safely be said. Accusations of a generic sort were made: that people were uncooperative, that the Spartokhoriots are a *kakos kosmos* (a bad people), that the villagers 'ate' each other, for on this, all would agree. Each person's private resentments contributed to public acceptance of the generalizations. But specific examples were seldom adduced. Public life had to be lived publicly, and the semblance of harmony was essential. Agreement was reached on a general condemnation of the village precisely because the fiction maintained was that one was always speaking to the judges and never to the judged. *Ex hypothesi* the sinners were absent. But of course each person knew that since the Spartokhoriots were a *kakos kosmos*, then, in the privacy of some household or other, his or her own actions and character would be taken and unjustly judged even by those with whom they were now talking – further illustration of the truth all deplored. This, indeed, was what made the Spartokhoriots a 'bad people' in their own eyes: that they continually watched each other and condemned their neighbours. Public life was always a matter of dissimulation, private life always an area of suspicion.

Women were supposed to be at home (Hirschon 1978). Their entertainment was confined to the house. But the man who kept himself to himself and was known to entertain at home was liable not only to accusations of social pretension or social inadequacy but also of using his home as a base from which to deride the community. A set of brothers who had become ship-owners in Piraeus together with their *ghambri*, their sisters' husbands, was a case in point. Whenever they were in Spartokhori (which was frequently) they were careful to express their solidarity with their fellow villagers by going the rounds of all the shops. But they often congregated for an evening together in one or other of their village houses. Their absence would be noted, and the comment made, 'Hah, they drink at home, those rich.' Such a comment was expressive of slightly more than offended egalitarianism, for the reference to drink was as telling as the one to wealth. In fact most Spartokhoriot males were heavy drinkers. Drinking remained, however, a nominal vice, and to say 'he drinks' was a commonplace condemnation of character. Drinking itself was licensed and justified precisely because it was integral to the male gatherings of *public* life, but men who would each day drink a litre of wine and half a bottle of ouzo could still accuse those who were absent of engaging in secret vice. 'He drinks at home', knowingly said of anyone (like the priest or the schoolmaster) who did not drink in public was always a deflation of apparent virtue. But although drinking, when transferred from public to private, automatically underwent a moral alchemy whereby it changed from the licensed indulgence of good-fellowship to the illicit activity of the fallen, what was yet more important in the case of the ship-owners was that they conducted their gatherings at home; that they formed an unseen *parea* that could create nothing but suspicion, and suspicion of which the ship-owners themselves (still villagers, after all) were well aware. I was once invited to such a gathering. Perhaps mistaking my slight hesitation for disapproval, my prospective host quickly added that the purpose of the evening was *not* 'to talk', but to have some 'good conversation (*kales kouvendes*)' and to tell a few jokes. 'We never "talk" in the house,' he stressed. But of course they did.

At this stage it might reasonably be asked what so much gossip was about, or what could have inspired such suspicion. In substantive terms the answer was often little at all. The areas in which conflicts of interest between villagers could occur were limited. Disputes over property, land and trespass arose, but they were not frequent. Theft was almost non-existent, though it was always feared and constantly discussed. In general the decline of agriculture and the growth of an economic base removed from the village meant that the villagers had little opportunity materially to vex each other. Nor were there effective positions of power and authority within the village that could provide a means of hampering enemies.[4] Finally, real scandals touching on the chastity of women and the honour of their families seemed rare indeed, for the social controls exercised by the village appeared sufficient to ensure that they seldom occurred.

This is not to say that a host of minor trespasses did not take place, or that from time to time real causes of conflict did not arise. During the period of my

---

[4] The positions of village president (*proedhros*) and membership of the village council (*simvoulio*) were contested, but they carried little power, since all decisions involving expenditure of public monies were in the hands of the nomarch of Lefkadha, appointed by the central government.

stay disputes over property, usually between neighbours, and therefore often between close kin, did sometimes end in court proceedings. The owner of one of the village's coffee-shops, for example, was taken to court and fined on three occasions over one summer for disturbing the peace with the loud music that came from his premises after 11.00 pm while he was entertaining parties of tourists off the yachts. The prosecutions resulted from anonymous depositions made to the long-suffering gendarmerie who were reluctantly forced to act on them.[5] The coffee-shop owner, of course, was certain that he knew who had laid the depositions, and why: his rival coffee-shop owners out of *zilia* (jealousy). Any suggestion that sleepless nights might have been a genuine motivation was dismissed as absurd. And perhaps he was right, for my own employment as a fisherman was brought to a halt as a result of a similar anonymous deposition, or at least the threat of one. In fact I was not employed since I received no payment for my work; but I did not possess a work permit, and as the young gendarme explained to me with a deal of embarrassment, though he himself was well aware of my amateur status, if someone did lay a deposition, then either I was going to be in some sort of trouble and have to prove that I was not working illegally in Greece, or else he was going to be in trouble for not following up a complaint. I assume that he had already been informally approached, and that whoever approached him was an enemy of Alkis, the man for whom I was fishing, since the only effect of my forced retirement was to leave Alkis short-handed.

Nevertheless, the capacity that villagers had to inflict serious material suffering on each other was out of all proportion to the universal assumption among villagers that neighbours were the source of all their ills. Vasso sat on her doorstep spinning wool in a melancholy mood.

'Ah,' she sighed, as I stopped to chat, 'You don't know our pains here, Rogeri.'

'No,' I said hopefully, 'What are they?'

'Hah,' she replied mysteriously, 'people!'

And it was to the malevolence of people (*anthropi*), the world (*o kosmos*), outsiders (*kseni*) that suspicion automatically turned, people, the world, outsiders who were now construed not as those outside and beyond the village, but as those outside and beyond the sheltered, private, ultimately cohesive domain of the household; construed, indeed, as the village community itself. Take, for example, the reactions of Maria, the wife of another coffee-shop owner. Her husband went to Lefkadha for a few days to secure provisions, leaving her to run the *kafenio*. Maria seized on such occasions to wash, scrub and polish the few square yards of the establishment otherwise denied her: the area behind the bar where, amongst other things, cooking facilities were located. The *kafenio* always looked the better for her work on such days, though in fact its custom fell off, since few men could stand to listen to the dual lament about the coffee-shop's filth and the unfortunate fate of women that accompanied Maria's labours. By midday Maria was exhausted, but also extremely agitated. The top of one of the gas rings was missing. Had I seen it? I had not, and we spent the next hour looking for it. Maria became more and more distressed. Her husband was going

---

[5] The village policemen (*khorofilakes*) posted to Spartokhori were by law non-locals. Their position was a difficult one, for on the one hand they were reluctant to become caught up in village faction; on the other, they could not afford to ignore official complaints.

to 'kill' her on his return. It was quite clear, she said, that someone had stolen it. I tried to argue that this was absurd. Why would anyone steal the top of a gas ring, in itself a useless item?

Exasperated by my naivety, Maria told me why someone would steal it. Because the gas ring would not *function* without its top. And, casting significant looks in the direction of one of the other coffee-shops, she went on to relate that the Spartokhoriots were a *kakos kosmos* (a bad people), that they were all *kakouryi* (criminals), and that they were eaten up with *zilia* (jealousy). Furthermore, if someone had sabotaged her husband's coffee-shop in this way, it stood to reason that this same person must have come behind the bar where the cash was kept. No doubt that had been pilfered too. Did I know how much money there should have been there? But importantly, the whole of this exchange and our frantic search had to take place during the odd periods when no one else was in the shop. No mention of the 'theft' was made to any villager, while I, a foreigner and neutral party, was sworn to silence, for if news of the missing gas-ring top got round, people (*o kosmos*) would laugh (cf. du Boulay 1976). Maria's rage was thus the rage of the impotent, for even to admit the crime's existence would have been to fulfil the aims of its perpetrators. I was actually on the point of making a secret voyage to Lefkadha to buy another gas-ring top in order to preserve family peace when the missing article was located on top of a tin on one of the shelves where Maria had put it while cleaning.

But suspicion did not always require even so slight a material cause. In large part it was self-generating, for since everyone assumed that everyone else was watching and waiting not only to commit some mischief but to glean some compromising information about what was really going on inside the households to which they had no access, the only defence was to watch and wait and gather information in turn. The suspicion that neighbours were continually prying was founded on the knowledge that one was prying oneself. Turn quickly down a side lane, for example, and one would often enough spy an old grandmother pressed flat against the wall, her head peeping round the corner, observing what was taking place in a neighbour's yard. And my own privileged position within the village (privileged not only because I was treated as a guest, but because I was presumed innocuous) was deftly exploited. I would return from a meal in some household, and the casual interrogation would start.

'Did you eat well?'

'Yes, very well.'

'Yes, they're a good family, the so-and-sos. And what did you eat? Meat? Beans?'

Thus another snippet about a neighbour's economic conditions was filed away.

Ideally, of course, people ought to have minded their own business and have had nothing to hide. In practice, everyone minded their neighbours' business and hid their own. The mutual hostility that resulted was what everyone publicly deplored, and in the end what was most gossiped about was the fact that other people gossiped. Secrecy became a self-generating obsession. People guarded the slightest details of their private lives in the conviction that any knowledge of them would be turned against them. The question posed was not what the intrinsic importance of the information might be, but why someone should have gone to the trouble of getting it. I once mentioned to a middle-aged woman that

I had been chatting to her elderly father, who lived at the other end of the village. With eyes narrowed and hands on hips she angrily asked me who her father might be. When I correctly identified him, she asked how I had known who her father was since she had never told me. Rather lamely I replied that after so many months in the village I knew who was who, while she, suddenly realizing that the whole situation was rather silly, burst into laughter. But the example illustrates the trivialities that could be taken seriously. If I knew her family history, who had been discussing it?

One final example may help convey the atmosphere created by the twin obsession with others' activities and one's own privacy. And if again I introduce myself into the narrative, this is because it was only when I was directly involved in events that I appreciated their full complexity.

Oil for the anthropologist

Like most Greeks, the Spartokhoriots prided themselves on their *filoksenia* (hospitality/generosity) and, as a foreigner, I was the recipient throughout my stay of a great deal of very genuine kindness. Shortly after my arrival in Spartokhori, I found it necessary to procure some olive oil for cooking. Innocently, I went to one of the village's general stores and bought two litres. The cost was little more than the wholesale price. Within the day, however, old Mikhalis, later to become my friend and protector, upbraided me. Oil, he explained, was not something anyone *bought* in Spartokhori. The Spartokhoriots were producers of oil. Why had I not simply come to him and asked for oil? I apologized for my mistake, but Mikhalis went on to inquire how much I had paid for the oil at Stathis's shop. I told him the price per litre. He was outraged. And it did not do any good to point out that what I had been charged was no more than he himself would have received when selling oil to a merchant – a price, moreover, about which Spartokhori's oil-producers bitterly complained. Mikhalis remained unmoved. Stathis (in whose shop Mikhalis regularly drank, with whom he was on friendly terms, and to whom he was related) was a 'thief'. It was a disgrace, but '*Etsi ine o kosmos edho* (That's what people are like here).'

Several days later I was in the coffee-shop when Mikhalis appeared at the door. '*N'as po?* (Can I have a word with you?)' he said. I excused myself and stepped outside. Carefully wrapped in newspaper, and secreted inside the flap of his jacket, Mikhalis was carrying what could only be a large bottle of oil. He suggested we go up to my room. Once inside, Mikhalis unwrapped the bottle of oil and presented it to me. I began to thank him. My thanks were dismissed as unnecessary. Instead I was instructed to make no mention of the matter to anyone, but to inform him immediately I was again in need of oil. I considered this would not be for some time, since I now possessed nearly a gallon of it. I returned to the coffee-shop. Mikhalis carefully took a different route home.

A few days later one of the old men who had been present in the coffee-shop when Mikhalis had called (and who doubtless had overheard or guessed something) asked if perchance I needed oil. I thanked him, but replied that I had plenty. Oh? From where had I got this oil, then? I replied that ... that someone had kindly given it me. Very well, said the old man, but when I ran out, I was to come to him, and to nobody else, and he would give me oil. And on absolutely no account was I to *pay* anyone for oil. And by the way, I hadn't paid that someone who had 'given' me oil, had I? I assured him that I had not.

A few weeks passed when a third old man, Haris, a close friend of Mikhalis, knocked discreetly at my door. He was carrying a plastic bag in which a bottle of oil was again carefully wrapped up in newspaper. He unwrapped it and placed it on my table. Again I began to thank him. 'Shh!' he said, 'don't say anything to anyone. Just tell *me* when you need oil.' He also took the opportunity to survey my room.

'How much do you pay for this room?'

I told him. He exclaimed that it was a very great deal of money. I said I thought it reasonable. No, no – it was a great deal of money, he insisted, far too much. But *'Etsi ine o kosmos edho* (That's what people are like here).' And with that, he took his leave.

In due course Mikhalis asked me why I had not come to him for oil, since surely I could have none left. I explained that I did still have some because his friend, Haris, had kindly given me another bottle. This news was remarked on in silence. A few minutes later, Mikhalis asked me how much I paid for my room. I told him. This news too was silently received. Then, after a deal of reflection, and with due solemnity, Mikhalis informed me that not everyone in Spartokhori was a good man, illustrating, by reference to the unequal lengths of the fingers of his hand, the innate inequalities of humanity (a commonly employed analogy, as I was later to find).

At length my supplies of oil did run out. I now realized that it would be impossible for me to purchase oil at any of the shops without news of the purchase reaching all three of my actual or potential donors. I therefore decided that since Mikhalis was the person I knew best, and since he had been the first to offer, I should resort to him. I too now carefully wrapped my empty bottle in newspaper and made my way to Mikhalis's house. Unfortunately it was on the main street and directly faced one of the coffee shops. Inevitably I encountered someone in the street. 'Where are you going?' asked the man, looking at my wrapped-up oil bottle (for an oil bottle wrapped in newspaper still looks remarkably like an oil bottle).

'Nowhere,' I replied in the village manner.

But when I arrived at Mikhalis's house, everyone in the coffee-shop opposite could see me. I was invited in, and placed my oil bottle on the table. Mikhalis served an ouzo, and we chatted about a number of matters. No mention was made of oil. As it came time to leave, I began to wonder if perhaps Mikhalis did not have all the oil he claimed, and whether I was causing him embarrassment. Hesitantly I mentioned oil. I was cut short with the word, 'Tomorrow', and for the benefit of the coffee-shop I thus left Mikhalis's house empty-handed. The next day, as good as his word, Mikhalis arrived at my room with a bottle of oil, once again swathed in newspaper.

Over the following weeks further enquiries were made about the state of my oil supply, and further offers made by various people. Since I thought it wrong continually to trade on Mikhalis's generosity, when I did eventually run out once more, I accepted a bottle from one of my many other potential suppliers. I met Mikhalis the next day. He was in a black mood. I asked what was wrong. 'Nothing,' he said, but, after a prolonged silence, finally exploded, 'Why didn't you come to me if you needed oil?' I apologized and explained that I had accepted the oil on the spur of the moment. But Mikhalis was offended with me for several days, while I, over the next two years, spent sleepless nights planning routes and manoeuvres by which I could accept oil from one person without another knowing, learnt to lie on reflex, and wished dearly that I could pay double the commercial price at a shop to avoid what was becoming a time-consuming and, in the closed world of the village, obsessive problem. It was ridiculous, I kept reminding myself, to be creeping down side streets with oily newspaper-wrapped bottles concealed under my coat, and to be continually involved in petty dissimulation. How could anything so simple have become so complicated? But then, I reflected with some venom, '*Etsi ine o kosmos edho.*'

Public virtue

Suspicion, gossip, malice and the presumption of others' suspicion, gossip and malice all informed the Spartokhoriots' attitudes towards each other and their collective judgement of themselves. The picture is an unflattering one, but inasmuch as such attitudes determined judgements and oriented actions they can be classed as partaking of Spartokhoriot values. At the least, they were routine grounds for Spartokhoriot evaluations. But it must be stressed that they were also the very antitheses of what was explicitly upheld, which was to be open (*aniktos*), upright (*orthios*), honest (*timios*), honourable (*filotimos*), hospitable (*filoksenos*), gentlemanly (*kirios*) and a good fellow (*chiftis*).[6] It was in contrast to these ideals that the Spartokhoriots' dire estimation of each other was formed, but it was also by their collective appropriation of these same ideals that the Spartokhoriots lauded themselves. Nor was it the case that such values existed only as part of self-conscious moral discourse. Public life required their implementation or risked its dissolution. It was adherence to such ideals that, after all, made the ship-owners go the rounds of all the shops instead of only gathering in their homes. Equally, it was adherence to such values that made Mikhalis and his peers so keen, genuinely keen, to demonstrate their generosity towards me (even if this also entailed their disparagement of each other). And though it was impossible ever to win everyone's whole-hearted approval in terms of these ideals, in public life such approval nevertheless acted as both a fundamental constraint and a fundamental motivation.

Hypocrisy here would be too strong a word to use (though the Spartokhoriots were wont to use it). In fact it was only the proximity of public and private within the village that brought into such sharp relief the values and attitudes that sustained each. As I have suggested, private life could be maintained only by the scrupulous defence of boundaries in defiance of topography; but the proposition

---

[6] *Chiftis* was a common term of praise and self-praise on Meganisi. Zakhos glosses is as 'someone of rare character and spirit. From the Turkish 'çift' = double. In other words, a person who counts for two'. (1981: 502)

could easily be reversed. It was only by a commitment to the values of village solidarity, to the notion of finally being all one family, that the community did not fracture into its component households locked together only by mutual antagonism and the contingencies of architecture. Private life was based on the assumption that everything outside the immediate confines of the household was potentially hostile; public life was made possible by the belief that this ought not to be the case. The 'good man', the *kalos anthropos*, was still the man who could, and would, go everywhere; who greeted all and who was greeted by all; who did not gossip and who acted generously; who, in short, demonstrated his possession of the virtues that created public harmony. And since deviation from these virtues was exactly what, in an ungenerous world, everyone knew people would pounce on, a presumption of secret hostility became a motivation for public amity.

Ideally, of course, the very division between public and private ought not to have existed. Family as the closed world of the household and family as the village itself ought to have blended harmoniously. The household ought to have extended its welcome to the world, and at times, during weddings, baptisms and funerals, it did so. The *spiti* was opened to become a font of public *filoksenia*, of hospitality and generosity to all. And though demonstration of such household *filoksenia* was in practice limited to these ritual occasions, the adage still went that one should always set a place for the unknown guest. In practice this did not occur, but the pretence that the house was always open to all had still to be played out, as the slightly anomalous arrangements suffered by those who ran shops or coffee-shops demonstrates.

Katerina and Babis, who owned one of Spartokhori's coffee-shops, would take their midday meal in the bar itself, which would simply be closed down for an hour or two while the rest of the village slept. But insomniacs or late diners occasionally called round on the off-chance that the coffee-shop might still be open (as it always was if Katerina was away in Lefkadha and Babis was on his own). On seeing the family at table, however, they would quickly apologize and take their leave. Katerina, and to a lesser extent Babis, used to grumble about these interruptions. Dinner was their one time to sit together and to talk. And yet without fail Katerina would cry '*Katse na fame* (sit down and eat)' to whoever appeared at the doorway. Indeed, the invitation would be extended to anyone walking past who could see the family through the shop's glass front. And it was an invitation proffered with some force. Fortunately it was always declined, for I hesitate to imagine the annoyance that would have been created had it ever been accepted. In fact the strenuous invitation was a charade, and known to be so; but it was a necessary charade, and in strict accordance with an accepted obligation to extend hospitality and good will to all in the outside world.

Much more frequently, however, the public world had to accept the minor intrusions of the private, for not all negotiations between men could take place in the seclusion of the *spiti*. Indeed, since men who were not closely related did not normally enter each other's homes, the bulk of their negotiations did not enjoy the protection of its sanctuary. A group of men would be sitting together in a coffee-shop when someone would appear at the door and say to one of them, '*Yanni, n'as po?* (Yannis, can I have a word with you?)' Without apology or explanation, Yannis would then rise and together the two men would set off through the village for a *volta*, a stroll, locked in some private conversation. Ten minutes later, business concluded, Yannis would return to his seat and resume his conversation as if absolutely nothing had happened. Nor would any questions ever be asked. This little scene was repeated a dozen times a day. But a tacit understanding protected such *lacunae* in the flow of public life. After all, since nothing but generalities, or people and events outside the village could safely be discussed in the coffee-shop, these peripatetic *tête-à-têtes* provided the only opportunity for unrelated men to discuss their private affairs. And if suspicion was sometimes aroused by what might have been being discussed, the fact that the men had been *publicly* seen during their *private* talk offered at least some assurance that what had passed between them would not be to anyone's immediate detriment.

Kinship and cooperation

The atmosphere of mistrust and veiled animosity that hung over village life was not, I should stress, an oppressive one, nor was it a constant one. It did not deny genuine friendships and real generosities, nor, importantly, did it deny the sense of corporate identity that the Spartokhoriots had as co-villagers. It emanated from the competitive relationship between the village's constituent households (cf. Campbell 1964: 39; Friedl 1964a: 76; du Boulay 1976), but it was internal to a community which nevertheless still saw itself as a community. Nevertheless, it formed the background against which kinship provided the basis of extra-domestic cooperation, for in a hostile or latently hostile world, whom does one trust? The village might have been all one family, but it was within (and against) this village family that each household had to compete and struggle and live out its day-to-day life. The solidarity of the household itself was not called into question. But the household was not always sufficient unto itself, and when help, assistance and cooperation was required from beyond its bounds, then once more it was the morality of family that was invoked – a morality that, after all, was in theory never limited to the household.

Between late September and early November was the winemaking season. By the late 1970s no one in Spartokhori grew grapes in quantity, but a number of people (not least some of those who lived most of the year in Athens) continued to make wine, buying and transporting grapes from southern Lefkadha. I happened to be in one of the village's olive-oil mills when about 2,500 kilos of grapes (which would have produced about 1,500 litres of wine) were receiving their second pressing in the mill's hydraulic press. It seemed that five men were directly involved in the enterprise, but I asked the son of one of the mill's joint-owners for whom so much wine was being made. Irritated by what he thought a silly question, the young man replied that 'naturally' the wine was for 'all the brothers, and all their *ghambri* (sisters' husbands) and *kouniadhi* (wives' brothers), and their *petheri* (fathers-in-law), and all the rest'. If my informant's answer was not quite precise (he did not name names), this was because he was stating what he took to be the obvious, that the wine was for its makers and all their *family*.

   In fact three brothers, one of their fathers-in-law and the husband of one of their sisters were actually involved in the making of the wine; then, as silent partners, some of the husbands of their other sisters, some of the brothers of their wives and, of course, their own father were also to take a share of the wine. Finally, the caique used to transport the grapes from Lefkadha was owned by their patrilateral first cousin, although this particular cousin was not a member of the wine-making group, but employed by them (a point to which I shall return). All in all the grouping represented a good example of one of the commonplaces of Mediterranean anthropology: cooperation amongst members of the bilateral kindred, amongst relatives. And further examples of this commonplace were not difficult to find. Fishing provides a convenient one. As already mentioned, fishing in Spartokhori ranged from a pastime that might supplement the household food supply to a profession which, though seldom anyone's exclusive occupation, might provide the major part of their income. But whatever the case, the *parea*, the 'company' that fished together, was almost always recruited from kin. Thus while many of Spartokhori's older residents would fish for a couple of hours a day in summer in the immediate coastal waters with light nets (*ta psila*) or hook and line, whenever their sailor sons were home, and especially if the shoals of *palamidhia* (horse-mackerel) were running, they would be joined by the younger generation and small crews consisting of some combination of fathers, sons, fathers-in-law, sons-in-law, brothers and brothers-in-law would be formed. Amongst those who fished for a living more formal financial partnerships sometimes occurred, for the cost of professional equipment was high. Thus one man might own a caique, another its engine and another the nets (with the division of the catch being based on a combination of capital contribution and labour).[7] But even though each partner owned outright his particular item of equipment and could thus withdraw from the partnership if it soured, such partnerships were still formed almost exclusively from kin – brothers, brothers-in-law and cousins.

   It could, of course, be argued that such economic cooperation amounted to no more than the good-natured sharing of time and resources between people who had always lived together in easy intimacy, and who were likely to have been at some stage members of the same household. And so perhaps it did. But the specific importance granted to kinship was highlighted by the part it played in actually instigating (and limiting) cooperation in an almost automatic way. I noticed one day that two brothers who regularly fished together in a rather old caique were fishing in a new and well equipped one, and in the company of a young man, Lakis, whom I had never seen fishing before. The next day the brothers were again fishing in the new caique, but this time with Lakis's father, who to the best of my knowledge had also never been a fisherman. The events behind the formation of this new *parea* were as follows.

   The two brothers had a sister whose husband, a fisherman, had recently and unexpectedly died, leaving his widow with an only child, a daughter of about

---

[7] The division of the catch was clearly set out by convention, and notably egalitarian: one share for boats, one for the nets, one for the engine and one for each member of the crew. If the catch was too small to distribute properly, then those men who did not own any part of the capital equipment, but were simply workers (*ergates*), took the first shares (see Just 1995).

sixteen years of age. In order to provide a man for the house, a marriage had been quickly arranged between this daughter and Lakis, himself only twenty years old. Since Lakis's bride-to-be was an only child and thus an 'heiress', her dowry was to be the entirety of her father's estate, including his caique. Lakis, however, knew little about fishing, and so in practice the caique reverted to his two newly acquired 'uncles' (WMBs), who were in need of better equipment, and who could at the same time instruct Lakis in the use of his new acquisition. But since Lakis still had his military service to perform, and since his new family would need an income during his absence, the uncles were going to go into partnership with Lakis's father. The familial rearrangements caused by death and marriage thus immediately resulted not only in the creation of a new configuration of kin, but also in a new fishing *parea* and a new financial partnership.

In general, however, it should be noted that the ties of affection and intimacy that made it seem natural for a couple of brothers to go fishing together were of substantially the same order as those which might result in a family-owned shipping company. Indeed, to revert to the wine-makers, their joint village holiday activities were parallelled by their joint business enterprise in the Piraeus, and as ship-owners they had also been in partnership with their matrilateral first cousins, another set of brothers. Moreover, the *badzanakis, ghambri* and *kouniadhi* who were sharing the wine with them were all officers or captains on their ships. A continuity existed between casual familial cooperation and a formally constituted business enterprise, because no threshold was perceived through which one passed into an impersonal world of commerce where the affections of family and kinship were to be subordinated to some presumption of impersonal constraints as the guarantee of trust and fair dealing.

This attitude was nicely revealed when it was rumoured that a company in Lefkadha was considering establishing a ferry-boat link to Meganisi, which would probably run the local ferry caiques out of business. It was loudly proclaimed in the coffee-shops of Spartokhori that the Spartokhoriots were fools and that those who owned (or who had owned) large caiques ought to have pooled their resources years ago, established a company and purchased a ferry boat of their own. 'Ah, forget it,' laughed Christos, who had once owned a ferry caique, 'It wouldn't have worked anyway. How many times have I quarrelled with Yannis? We could never run a company together.' This, of course, was part of the discourse of collective self-denigration: we are a *kakos kosmos*, a 'bad people'; we cannot cooperate; we are always at odds with each other. But it was immediately pointed out by the listeners (partly in a spirit of self-defence) that Christos himself now owned his new fishing caique in partnership with his wife's brother, Pavlos, and that that partnership was working well enough. 'Certainly,' replied Christos, 'But Pavlos and I are *family*.'

In fact Christos and Pavlos's relationship provides an interesting example of the sort of kinship-based economic cooperation to be found amongst those who might be classified as professional fishermen, for in this case they were joint-owners of very expensive capital equipment (precisely the situation that Christos had laughed out of court if it involved non-kin). Christos and his wife's brother, Pavlos (who also owned one of the village's coffee-shops), had bought their new caique after Christos had returned from a period of six years' emigration to the

United States, and they started their fishing in the spring of 1979. They were shortly joined by Lefteris, Pavlos's only son, an amiable lad who had just finished his military service but who preferred to remain in the village to inherit his father's *kafenio*, rather than to seek his fortune in Athens or at sea. But although they owned the best equipped caique in Spartokhori, as fishermen all three were comparative novices, and they were thus joined in their expeditions by Manolis, arguably the most experienced fisherman in Spartokhori despite the fact that he did not own his own boat.

Manolis was not, except in the most distant way, related to either Christos or Pavlos, but his position as an apparent exception to the rule that it was kin who cooperated can be explained very simply on the grounds that Christos and Pavlos needed his skill and experience. And here we broach an important point, for in fact there was no real rule that required explanation for its exception. Neither the obligations of kinship nor the preference for kin resulted in any explicit proscription of non-kin. The Spartokhoriots found it natural to cooperate with someone on the grounds that they were family, but they would have found it unnecessary to adduce extenuating circumstances to explain why they were cooperating with someone who was not family. The norms of behaviour did not present themselves as a series of codified prescriptions, and the Spartokhoriots often blithely claimed friendship to be as viable a basis for cooperation as kinship. Morality asserted that trust, honesty and fair dealing were the attributes of kinship; but they remained its attributes, not its definition. Moreover, the realization of such attributes through kinship was more a moral expectation than an experiential certainty. Partners were chosen in the hope that they would prove honest, trustworthy and fair, and so people chose kin, but they did not take on relatives whom they distrusted or who were useless. And, to refer to the case in point, people did not exclude non-relatives whom they did trust, or who were useful. The strength of kinship lay merely in its ability to arouse the expectancy of those virtues which, ideally, ought to have been universal.

Manolis's position was not, then, extraordinary. He was a friend and he was an asset. Nevertheless it should be noted that although he fished with the family team of Christos, Pavlos and Lefteris, he was not their financial partner. He received his share of the catch, but he had no stake in their capital outlay. That would have been to subject friendship to too grave a test, for the other strength of kinship was to create the expectancy that those virtues which ought to be universal are seldom to be found outside its embrace. Manolis did, however, have a financial stake in the equipment of another fishing team, for although he did not own a boat, he owned nets, and he had paid for the new engine that had been installed in a boat jointly owned by his two *kouniadhi* (wife's brothers). In fact Manolis's cooperation with Christos and Pavlos was part of a larger compact. The idea had been that they, together with Manolis, should fish in their larger boat for *palamidhia*, and Manolis's two brothers-in-law, using Manolis's drag-nets (*trata*), should fish in their smaller boat for whitebait and sardines. The combined catch of both boats was then to be shared by all. As it happened, local fishing that year was so bad that the plan was abandoned and Manolis eventually went to Patras to work as crew in the fishing fleet that operated from there.

But this was not the first time an interfamilial cooperative venture had been attempted by Manolis. Two years earlier he and his two brothers-in-law had come to a similar arrangement with Alkis, the fisherman for whom I worked, who possessed the largest caique and *palamidhia* nets in Spartokhori. Again, Alkis was not their relative, and the fact that this venture too was short-lived is a further reminder that the fund of good will existing between non-kin was limited. No accusations of malpractice were ever made, and Alkis appeared to be on friendly terms with Manolis and his brothers-in-law even after the dissolution of their agreement. But although Alkis did not claim to have been cheated, he certainly felt that he had been outwitted, for, as he frequently complained to me, although the catches of the two boats were equally shared, his boat was larger and consumed more fuel. Alkis saw his contract out, but when the agreed period of time elapsed the arrangement was not renewed. In fact I doubt that the arrangement had been as unfavourable as Alkis made out, but the experience of having to hand over half of the occasional good catch to outsiders (*kseni*) when fishing was generally poor and his own family and relatives were clamouring for fish probably went too much against the grain. Regardless of its long-term equity, Alkis found himself bound by a contract that involved the continual short-term denial of obligations to his own relatives and immediate family.[8]

By contrast, in the height of the season when there was easy money to be made, Alkis regularly took on his father-in-law, Massos, as crew, and when Massos's son, Babis, was home from his voyages on super-tankers, he too joined them, taking my place. As it happened, Alkis and Massos were temperamentally an extraordinarily ill-matched couple and fishing expeditions with them were marked by a series of explosive confrontations which often ended with Massos swearing that he would never set foot again on Alkis's boat, which, as he reminded everyone, he and his son Babis had laboured many days to repair. But after a few days' absence, Massos always reappeared, as Alkis knew he would. In short, blood was thicker than water, and if that particular cliché seems mis-applied for the relationship between father- and son-in-law, it should be remembered that Alkis's children were Massos's grandchildren. Despite his arguments with his son-in-law, Massos was even to be seen cultivating the land that he had given Alkis as dowry (since Alkis was too busy with his boat and his truck), muttering that he did this 'so that *my grandchildren* will have something to eat'. And in the same spirit he also handed over half his catch to his son-in-law's household whenever he went fishing on his own with a hook and line.

Migration

Fishing is merely a convenient context within which to observe the fact that at such times as cooperation between individuals or between individual households was required, it routinely followed along kinship lines, for with the real source of Spartokhori's wealth removed from the village, there were few other activities

---

[8] Fish was most people's preferred food, and since fish were scarce, fishermen found themselves making promises to relatives to reserve some part of the catch for them, and were thus subject to recriminations when those promises were not fulfilled.

that required the recruitment of extra-domestic labour. Nevertheless, the preferential extension of favours and assistance between kin was a constant feature of village life, and its workings were often both complex and subtle.

As I have mentioned, the two brothers-in-law, Christos and Pavlos, were willing jointly to invest in the acquisition of an extremely expensive piece of capital equipment and to operate it together as a family, but inter-household, venture. This, however, was only one part of a history of cooperation that had locked their kin together over the years. Christos had invested in the new caique with Pavlos after his return from the United States where he had worked for six years as a barman in order to support his son, who was studying for an American degree in business management. Indeed Christos had emigrated to America in advance of his son in order to fulfil the residence requirement that in turn would qualify his son for entry into a state college. But in order for this scheme to be put into operation, Christos's emigration had to be sponsored by an American citizen. That citizen was none other than Pavlos's brother (or, to put it another way, the other brother of Christos's own wife), who had settled permanently in the United States many years before. One *kouniadhos* (wife's brother) was thus Christos's fishing and business partner in the village; his other *kouniadhos* had been his sponsor, and indeed employer (for he owned a hotel) in the United States.

By the 1970s overseas emigration had become one of the most important areas of familial cooperation, and the same men who fished together on Meganisi might be found running restaurants together in Ohio or North Carolina. Takis, for example, a man in his late fifties, had six children, three sons and three daughters. All three sons emigrated to the United States where together they owned and ran two steak houses. They were soon joined by two of their sisters and their respective husbands, also from the village, thus establishing a Spartokhoriot family-based business of three brothers and their two brothers-in-law (which incidentally supported Takis, who frequently visited his *pedhia* in America, in some style). Nor were such overseas enterprises confined to the cooperation of siblings and their spouses. The overseas kinship links utilized in emigration were often considerably more removed and extended over generations. Thus Yannis emigrated to Montreal in the 1950s where he worked for five years in a knitting-mill. He did not prosper overseas and returned to the village in the 1960s on the grounds of ill-health. All was not lost, however, for in the late 1960s his son was able to return to America where he went to work for his father's *kouniadhos* (wife's brother), who had emigrated to Montreal at about the same time as Yannis and who had opened a successful restaurant. By 1980 Yannis's son was in partnership with his maternal uncle in building a new restaurant in Montreal with residential apartments above.

Beyond such commercial ventures there was also the more general business of helping relatives settle in a new country and, importantly, of sponsoring their immigration. Thus Andhreas had two sons who owned and ran a restaurant together in North Carolina. It was the elder son who first emigrated, working a variety of jobs in order to accumulate sufficient capital to start the restaurant. Once it was established he was joined by his younger brother whose immigration he sponsored. But their father, Andhreas, had also spent nearly four years in the

United States at various intervals, and it was Andhreas's *ghambros* (sister's husband) who, having gone to America five years before Andhreas, sponsored his immigration, which subsequently led to Andhreas's sons going to America. Shortly before I left the village Andhreas himself once more left for the United States, partly to visit his sons and partly because he needed only a few more years' residence and employment there in order to qualify for a pension, at which stage he intended to return once more to Spartokhori.

But emigration sometimes required the assistance not only of overseas relatives, but also of relatives who remained in the village. Thus Vasilis, who spent twelve years in Canada, had handed over his land on Meganisi at a nominal rent to his 'nephew', his wife's brother's son, for safekeeping while he was away. Other emigrants (including many who had moved to Athens) had simply given the use of their land free to close relatives, receiving perhaps a supply of oil for domestic use. And to revert to the case of Takis and his children, although his three sons appeared to have decided to remain permanently in Ohio, his two daughters and their husbands were anxious to resettle in Greece. For financial reasons this resettlement had to be a gradual process, and Takis and his wife were called on to assist. Thus Takis's wife went to America for a year to look after her grandchildren, leaving Takis to live a bachelor life in the village. She then returned to the village with her daughters, sons-in-law and grandchildren, but after a few months, the two young couples returned to America to economize further, leaving their children in Greece: two in the village with their grandparents, Takis and his wife, and one with their aunt, Takis's third daughter, who lived in Preveza.

Patronage

Cooperation between relatives was not limited to such major questions as family companies, capital investment or overseas emigration. The groups of women who took turns lighting their brush-fired ovens for the weekly bread-baking were almost invariably sisters or sisters-in-law, or perhaps first cousins. The domestic cooperation that was for many of them mandatory when they were members of the same household continued later in life when marriage had separated them and they were established as *nikokires* (mistresses) of their own house. Similarly, the groups of men who regularly drank together, though by no means exclusively composed of kin, had a solid core of related members, and patronage of a particular coffee-shop, or indeed of any shop, was itself connected to kinship.

I frequently sat in the general store of one of my friends, chatting with him and his customers. They were overwhelmingly his relatives: brothers, sisters, uncles, aunts, cousins, nephews, nieces, brothers-in-law, sisters-in-law and a variety of other affinal relatives and godrelatives. The store's transactions were commercial (though by no means impersonal), that is to say, the shop was most certainly not a kin-group cooperative, and it was run by my friend and his wife on strict profit-making lines, the degree of that profit being loudly complained about by the store's customers, and equally loudly defended by its owners, as all fought their private battles with inflation. Credit was given, but as in all

Spartokhori's shops (and in contrast to the prewar period) it was short-term, and amounted to no more than a convenience when women happened to find themselves without their purse, or when small children were dispatched on an errand. Moreover, should any other shop be offering an outstanding bargain, then provided no outright quarrel was being pursued, customers went where prices dictated. But all things being equal (and generally they were), it was clear that relatives patronized the establishments of their relatives. And though no particular economic advantage accrued to either side – that is to say, neither more nor less than the commercial price was given or received – such patronage still amounted to a form of kinship cooperation, and was consciously construed as such. Part of accepted and expected morality ordained that if one's brother-in-law or nephew ran a shop, then one should shop there. And that this morality involved no reduction of kinship to pragmatic self-interest was clear from the fact that no economic favours were granted or received. Indeed economic self-interest or the chance to exercise it occasionally overrode considerations of kinship.

The coffee- and wine-shops also had their own clientele, of which the owners' relatives constituted an important section. Here, however, a certain ideological contradiction occurred. On the one hand, a man was expected to patronize the establishments of his relatives; on the other hand the coffee- and wine-shops were the centres of male sociability, and a man was required to affirm his recognition of the community at large by being seen in all the village's gathering places. Conversely, going the rounds of all the shops constituted a public demonstration of his own standing, that he was indeed welcome and respected wherever he went. The commitment to a public personality thus both modified and concealed the obligations of kinship, and although individuals clearly had their particular haunts where they were amongst family, often this would be explicitly denied on the grounds that they were 'good men' and could go 'wherever they liked', and such assertions frequently led back to the rhetoric of Spartokhoriot communal life as all one family.

The clientele of Nikos's *kafenio* provides a particular example. Nikos was devoted to his wife's brother, Savvas. As he often told me, no better man existed in the village than his *kouniadhos*. Savvas was loved and respected by all, and would certainly be voted president (*proedhros*) in the next election. And in listing his *kouniadhos*'s virtues Nikos had little hesitation in introducing the fact that Savvas always 'helped' him. For the most part, Savvas's 'help' consisted of patronizing Nikos's coffee-shop, for, according to Nikos, wherever Savvas drank the best men in the village followed, thus increasing not only the quantity but, importantly, the quality of Nikos's trade. But Savvas's maintenance of the very virtues that Nikos continually lauded – that he quarrelled with no one, that he was liked by everyone, that he was the first to buy a drink for all and the first to be bought one – necessarily precluded Savvas's exclusive patronage of Nikos's shop. Ideally Savvas had to be everywhere, but mostly at Nikos's.

Nikos's coffee-shop was similarly patronized by a set of ship-owning brothers (first cousins to the wine-makers), who lived in Athens but who spent nearly half the year in the village. The company (*parea*) they and their friends formed was of considerable worth to Nikos, for they drank whisky and tipped generously. Again, Nikos drew attention to the fact that their father, old Captain Fotis, had been his own marriage sponsor (*koumbaros*) and by rights would have baptized Nikos's son, had Nikos and his family not been in South Africa at the time. The ship-owners 'helped', Nikos explained, because they were friends and because they were family – because, indeed, they were all his *koumbari*. They were also, of course, rich, which is why their help took the quasi-economic form it did; but again it should be noted that such economic assistance was only the appropriate manifestation of a relationship whose real nature lay in the generalized obligations of kin.

For his part, Nikos was required to reciprocate in a rather difficult way, for the brothers' father, old Fotis, had been told in no uncertain terms by his doctor that he was not to drink, and he had been a great drinker. Nikos, out of respect for his *koumbari*, was required to refuse their father ouzo, but to do so in such a way as not to offend his dignity, by placing a lemonade or a coffee in front of him before the old man could cause embarrassment by demanding a drink. Had Nikos failed in his obligation and allowed the old man to get drunk, he would probably have forfeited the patronage of his ship-owning *koumbari*; but again, the relationship was never construed in terms of a specific *quid pro quo*. Rather, each side was pleased to see the other as simply acting in the way that family should. And if ideology here seems to mask the inequalities of wealth and power, it should be remembered that this particular godparenthood relationship could not have been established by Nikos with any clear idea of future economic benefits in mind, for the ship-owning brothers were all self-made men from what had been a very poor family in their father's day.

The real economic patronage Nikos received came from outside the village and from his 'aunt' (his second cousin once removed), who had settled and prospered in South Africa. She had later sponsored Nikos's emigration, given him a job in the hotel she owned, and eventually (and contrary to custom) baptized his son. She regularly sent Nikos $1,000 a year towards the education of her godson, and as Nikos very simply explained it, she was rich, he was poor, she loved his son and she was his son's *nona*. Considerations of economic inequality, personal affection and the obligations of (spiritual) kinship flowed together. But again, although it was the fact that this aunt was godmother to Nikos's son that most readily accounted for her generosity, it was still no automatic part of a godparent's definition to shoulder so great a financial burden. It was rather that this burden having been taken on, reference to godparenthood satisfactorily and concisely encapsulated the sum of virtue and solicitude it represented. It took something of a village cynic to remark that baptism was sometimes a commercial matter (*emboriko prama*), although, as I have suggested, in the past the connection between godparenthood and patronage may have been more explicit. At the time of my fieldwork what was stressed, however, was the affection and respect godparenthood entailed. But there is perhaps not so much difference between the two views. What the Spartokhoriots denied was that the relationship was instituted with a view to material advantage; what they asserted was that its importance lay in the sentiments, attitudes and dispositions that it engendered (and which, it should be noted, were those that ideally characterized all relationships between close kin). But if the circumstances were appropriate, such sentiments, attitudes and dispositions could be expected to manifest themselves in tangible form, or else their existence would be doubted. A godparent was not defined as a material benefactor; but if the need arose and the ability was there, from whom else might benefaction more properly flow? If a change had occurred in the function of godparenthood from the prewar period, it stemmed, I suspect, from a change in the relative abilities and needs of individuals within the community, from the end of inequalities between land-owning and landless peasants as a result of employment in the merchant marine. In short, there was no longer any overwhelming need to exploit the potentialities of patronage that lie embedded in the institution. Meanwhile, favours continued to flow between godrelatives as manifestations of affection and respect. For example an old shepherd, Theodhoros, had a *koumbaros* (I do not know who baptized whom) who lived in Athens and who annually supplied Theodhoros with clothes: shoes, trousers, a jacket, whatever he most needed. Theodhoros in turn supplied his *koumbaros*'s Athenian household with cheese (just as he supplied his son's and his daughter's households in the village). Who profited most from the arrangement would be hard to calculate; but it was not conceived of as an exchange. Rather, both Theodhoros and his *koumbaros* were demonstrating their mutual concern and respect by independently making each other gifts. In the best Maussian tradition, reciprocity was the by-product of the relationship, but the degree to which spiritual kinship could confer economic advantage and be clearly recognized as doing so, whilst at the same time being considered as something other than a mechanism for gaining advantage, was nicely illustrated by the dilemma in which old Christos found himself. Christos was in his late sixties and was becoming markedly long-sighted. He complained to me frequently of the difficulty he had in reading, and I suggested that he should go to Lefkadha to get a pair of spectacles. This he refused to do, first on the grounds that he was a healthy man; but subsequently, on the grounds that he had baptized the ophthalmologist in Lefkadha (or rather, that his son, then in Australia, had baptized the ophthalmologist, which amounted to the same thing). Since the ophthalmologist was a 'wonderful boy', and since they were *koumbari*, Christos claimed that inevitably he would be prescribed his spectacles free of charge. It was thus *dropi* (shame) that prevented him from going, since the relationship would be demeaned by the very economic advantage it would confer. But on the other hand, neither could he go to any other ophthalmologist in Lefkadha, since if his *koumbaros* heard of it (as he would), he would be mortified.

The idiom of kinship

The above examples are sufficient, I hope, to demonstrate that cooperation between kin in Spartokhori was a reality. The ideals of kinship – of trust, good will, fair-dealing and the preferential extension of favours – were continually translated into practice. Those ideals, however, confronted another reality: the very extensiveness of kinship itself within a small-scale but largely endogamous community. That confrontation substantially modifies any too easy understanding of the consequences of kinship.

As we have seen, one way or another almost everyone in Spartokhori was related to almost everyone else. Moreover, genealogical connections between people were frequently multi-stranded, a folding-in of the community's links such that people were related to each other *ap'tis dhio meries* (from both sides). Kinship virtually exhausted the space of the Spartokhoriot community. But if this elevated kinship to a principle of Spartokhoriot social cohesion and communal identity, paradoxically it also severely limited its determinant role in day-to-day social interaction. Let me start with a simple example. It was conventional for all relatives up to and including second cousins to be invited to any major celebration, like a wedding party, and one might state without further ado that major celebrations involved the participation of all members of the bilateral kindred. In Spartokhori, however, the bride's family and the groom's family held a quite separate series of celebrations, each inviting their own kin. Not infrequently an individual would be closely related to both bride and groom, as uncle or aunt to one, for example, and cousin to the other. No real problem was created. That person attended the celebrations of the party to whom he or she was most closely related, or attended some of the celebrations of both, or – a point of some significance – attended the celebrations of whichever of the two families he or she was on most friendly terms with. But although no social impasse was created, such a situation demonstrates that even when kinship was the explicit criterion of selection and inclusion, it could not be counted on to settle matters. Further considerations had to be taken into account, for what kinship failed to do was to divide people into discrete and definable familial groups with categorical obligations. Individual choice had almost always to be exercised. This can be shown in the more complex context of village politics.

Most Spartokhoriots had strong political views. They assiduously read newspapers (and those who could not read had newspapers read to them). National and international politics were debated in the coffee-shops, and political disputes were very much a matter of party ideologies and divergent political philosophies. Nevertheless, it was freely admitted that politics, and particularly village politics, could also be a family matter (*ikoyeniako prama*), that votes could be, and were, mobilized along kinship lines. In 1980 village elections for the position of *proedhros* (president) and for positions on the village council (*simvoulio*) were held, for which two teams (*sindhiasmi*) competed, each led by their candidate for the position of *proedhros*. In theory village elections at that time were supposed to be non-political, unrelated to national party politics. The left, however, and especially the students studying in Athens and the new Athenian-dwelling class of professionals and business men, were strong supporters of the socialist party PASOK, and rallied round one of the candidates, Petros, himself a communist from civil-war days. The rival team centred on a shopkeeper, Yerasimos. They too were quite left wing, but also strongly anti-communist. They also tended to be anti-PASOK, perhaps because they represented the more traditionalist villagers rather than the emergent bourgeoisie. In the end, Petros and the left won handsomely, an accurate enough reflection of the political climate in Greece at the time, but parallel to party politics ran questions of kinship.

A friend of mine, Pavlos, had a *kouniadhos* (wife's brother), Kostas, whom he immensely admired. Kostas stood for a place on the village council as a member of Yerasimos's losing team. The problem was that Kostas's younger brother,

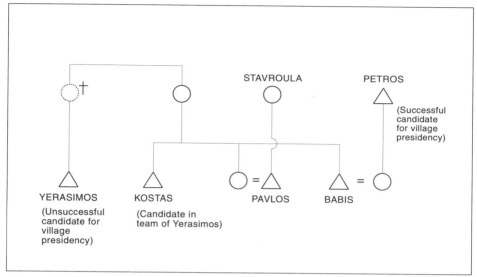

Figure 6.1 Politics and kinship

Babis, was also the son-in-law of the winning candidate, Petros. If politics had been simply politics, perhaps everyone could have voted according to their ideals and with a clear conscience; but since kinship could not be discounted, Pavlos and his family were placed in a genealogical double-bind, although the person in the most invidious position was Babis, for he had to choose between his brother and his father-in-law. I do not know the grounds of Babis's choice, though I suspect they were ones of political conviction. At all events, he opted for his father-in-law, and quite decisively. But if Babis decided his position on the basis of political convictions, this certainly did not stop him trying to further his father-in-law's cause through family connections. In fact Babis went the rounds of all his and Kostas's relatives and advised them not to vote for his brother. In this he must have been quite successful, for as Pavlos later explained to me, though Kostas put up a respectable showing and secured a place on the council, the votes he received were all *filika psefismata* (friendly votes) and not *ikoyeniaka psefismata* (family votes). As Pavlos put it, the family had 'brought Kostas down (*to riksane*)'.

Needless to say Pavlos was also caught up in the affair, and, with the rest of the family, voted against his *kouniadhos*, Kostas, and for his much more distant relative, Petros. The exception was Pavlos's wife, who did vote for her brother. As Pavlos explained, she could scarcely have done anything else, although, as he admitted, it did result in the embarrassing oddity of a husband and wife voting differently. As for Pavlos's aged mother, Stavroula, she voted for whom she was told to, for Petros (see Figure 6.1).

Kostas himself was outraged by this family betrayal and went so far as to boycott Pavlos's coffee-shop for several months. Pavlos thus paid a price for his part in the family/anti-family pact, and it should be noted that this price was itself exacted in terms of the values of kinship: the loss of the patronage of his beloved *kouniadhos*. But the real interest of the episode lies in the fact that although it was clearly recognized that votes could be mobilized along family lines – hence Babis's visiting of all his relatives and Pavlos's contrast between friendly votes and family votes, in the final analysis kinship was incapable of controlling the vote, and not because the appeal to kinship lacked persuasion or because everyone had their own political views, but because the ties of *kinship itself* split the vote. Instead of providing the basis for corporate action, the very multiplicity of kinship connections meant that, politics aside, people's loyalties were divided. Kinship could be appealed to; its weight could be thrown on to the scales; but nothing resulted from it automatically. One might be expected to vote for a relative, but in the end one could only vote for the relative with whom one most agreed.

At this stage it is convenient to revert once more to the wine-makers. It is perfectly true that their cooperation in the village was based on kinship, just as their business enterprise was in Piraeus. But again the constitution of this kin-based group was scarcely automatic. Between them the bilateral and affinal kindreds of the three brothers would have accounted for well over half the village, but half the village was not in partnership with them. Those of their wives' brothers and sisters' husbands who were involved in the wine-making were also those who, as high-ranking ship's officers, were involved in their shipping company, and they were all wealthy men. By contrast, their first cousin who transported the grapes from Lefkadha was not wealthy. He was a humble fisherman and storekeeper. Nor was he a member of the wine-making group. He was employed by it. That in itself might be construed as an example of the preferential extension of favours towards kin, but what gave the wine-makers their identity, what made them a recognizable group, what bound them together even in such holiday activities as wine-making (and what excluded their cousin), was not kinship itself, but the fact they shared a common life-style and a common financial (and cultural) ascendancy. They were known (along with a number of others) as 'the rich', 'the Athenians'. Not all of even their quite close relatives fell into that group. Indeed, the brother of one of the wine-makers' *ghambri* was amongst the poorest men in the village. His house adjoined his brother's, being an equal share of their father's dwelling, but it remained a tumbledown near-ruin (which he inhabited year-round), while his brother's half was a substantially renovated and extended edifice (used only seasonally or when the pleasures of village life called). In this case architecture bore witness to both what united them and what separated them: kinship on the one hand, economic disparity on the other. And when it came to being a member of the wine-making group, it seemed it was economics not kinship that prevailed. Indeed, just as in the village elections kinship could not determine who would vote for whom (since it failed to create discrete kinship groups), so with the wine-makers kinship was so extensive that some other basis had to be sought to explain their solidarity: call it class, or perhaps a common life-style and shared expectations, or, to use that least structural of concepts, just friendship.

It may be objected, however, that in querying the determinant role of kinship I am neglecting an obvious point, for the examples of cooperation I have adduced are between close relatives – brothers, sisters, brothers-in-law, etc – whereas my argument about the ineffectuality of kinship as a determinant of social relations has been illustrated by reference to the more distant ties of cousinhood and the like. To a degree this objection is valid. People were more likely to maintain that there *ought* to be cooperation between close kin than they were for more distant relatives, and obviously the further one moves from Ego, the greater the proliferation of kin and the greater, therefore, the necessity of choice (cf. Campbell 1964: 107–9; du Boulay 1974: 150–2). In the case of the village elections, however, the choice for Babis was between a brother and a father-in-law. But even amongst the closest of kin, genealogical proximity was no guarantee of good relations. If anything, the opposite was true. In Spartokhori (as elsewhere in Greece) brothers were idealized as the very paradigm of disinterested affection, amity and loyalty, and while they were unmarried and members of the same household, this was often true. But if one considers the serious rifts within the village – those people who were not on speaking terms, who had been cold towards each other for twenty years – then, for the classic reasons of property, inheritance and its division, they were more likely to be brothers than anyone else (Davis 1977: 176-97). In fact the chances of brothers being best of friends or worst of enemies was about equal. But it is the existence of such chances that must be stressed, for whatever form those chances took, it was they, not the morality of kinship, that supplied the real determinants of cooperation. And inasmuch as the prognosis for close kin relations was bad, and recognized to be so despite the high ideals, it is worth recalling the priest's comment that one reason for not baptizing a close relative was that close relatives were likely to fall out.

Relatives, then, might be friends, but just as easily (and with rather more consequence) they might be enemies, and the interplay and contradictions of friendship and kinship formed part of common consciousness. Alongside the constant appeal to kinship as the basis for cohesion ran a series of counter-statements to the effect that friends were better than relatives were because, after all, one could *choose* one's friends. My old protector, Mikhalis, had an inseparable companion, Thomas. The two old men had been friends from childhood and were always to be found together in one coffee-shop or another. I eventually discovered that they were related, for Thomas's son-in-law, Alkis, was Mikhalis's nephew, his sister's son. Moreover, I think they had a further kinship connection via Mikhalis's mother, although I could never determine the precise relationship. But despite these connections, I never heard them refer to or address each other as *simpetheri* (affines), nor, after nearly two years, had they ever indicated to me that they were related. When I reproached them for this omission, their blithe response was, 'Ah, forget kinship (*singhenia*); we're friends (*fili*), that's what's important.' But then, if only to disconcert the literal minded, they added, 'Why, we're not just friends, we're brothers (*adherfia*).'

It is, I believe, such metaphorical reassertions of the value of kinship that point to its true importance in Spartokhori: not as the determinant of interfamilial affection and cooperation, but as the ever-present idiom in which affection and cooperation could be couched. The very pervasiveness of kinship as an objective reality within the community simultaneously rendered it experientially compelling, rhetorically powerful, but also, as it were, sociologically impotent. As

Loizos observes for the Cypriot village of 'Kalo' (Argaki), 'Kin and affines are not dispersed, but concentrated within the village, so they are less a scarce resource to be cherished, than a fact of life, to be judged on merits and usefulness' (1975a: 63; cf. Campbell 1964: 106–9; du Boulay 1974: 150–5; Friedl 1964a: 73–4).[9] Kinship and family could be (and were) used to explain almost everything, but in fact they determined relatively little. Instead, they provided a set of values on the basis of which people's actions could be judged and, importantly, social relationships entered into. They could not, however, predict what the quality of those relationships would be, nor could they even specify with which individuals they would be formed. Cooperation was sought with and from relatives in ways that it would not be sought from outsiders, but the question still remained: with and from *which* relatives. Outside the household the real bases for cooperation, loyalty, amity and trust lay elsewhere. Kinship was their cover.

So what is left of kinship? Could it all be taken away to leave everything just as it was before? In objective terms the answer might almost be yes. In ideological terms the answer is definitely no. It all depends on whether one is concerned with reasoning or result, with motive or effect. As I have said family were those to whom loyalty was owed and family were those who owed one loyalty. Ideologically this was not open to doubt. If, on occasion, the Spartokhoriots argued that friendship was more important than kinship, a closure was still created and the morality of kinship preserved by figuratively recategorizing friends as kin: 'We're not just friends; we're brothers.' And though it would have been frankly presumptuous to greet strangers as 'brother' or 'sister', it was still commonplace to address them as '*simpethere* (affine)' or '*koumbare* (godparent)'. And of course such closures were not always fictive. Marriage and baptism, affinity and godparenthood, were ways of transforming friendship into kinship. Let me take up again the story of Christos and Pavlos.

As well as being part owner of the fishing caique, Christos's brother-in-law, Pavlos, owned a coffee-shop which he had inherited from his father, who had died young shortly after his return from a period of temporary migration to the United States in the 1940s. Pavlos and his siblings had thus been left 'orphans'. As it happened, it was Christos's father, Thomas, who looked after the orphans, and who for fifteen years (1949–64) ran the coffee-shop on Pavlos's behalf, perhaps because, a generation earlier, he too had been left an 'orphan' after his own father died in the United States, or perhaps just because he and Pavlos's father had been friends. At all events, it was out of this kindness that Christos's and Pavlos's relationship was born. Pavlos and his orphan siblings had been cared for by Christos's father. But this interfamilial connection was both cemented and transformed when Christos married one of Pavlos's sisters. Pavlos and Christos could explain their cooperation and mutual affection in terms of being family, but their kinship was itself the result of a history of familial friendship. Similarly, when Spartokhori's younger sailors protested about the restrictions placed on their choice of a godparent because of the hereditary system and claimed that baptismal sponsorship should be a personal matter based on friendship rather than on rights of succession, in a sense they were not

[9] A similar argument is put forward in relation to British kinship in Firth, Hubert and Forge (1969: 87–118).

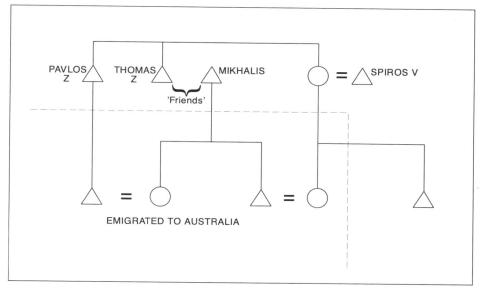

Figure 6.2 Double affinal ties of Mikhalis

arguing that individual friendship should displace the ties of kinship. What irked them was the fact that the system limited their freedom to turn their friends into their kin and to use godparenthood as a means of transforming an arbitrary relationship based on the contingencies of affection into an enduring one underwritten by the morality of kinship. Friendship could always become kinship. The moral covenant of the latter could be made to embrace and justify the arbitrary relationships of the former. Thus the idiom of kinship survived.

But in a village such as Spartokhori where existing links of kinship were so numerous, the idiom of kinship was also maintained not only by transforming friends into kin, but by strategically tracing lines of kinship back to friends. Mikhalis used continually to remark on what a fine family the Zs were. Integral to his explanation of their virtues was his own double affinity with them, for one of his daughters had married the son of a certain Pavlos Z, while one of his sons had married the daughter of Pavlos Z's sister. In short, Mikhalis's son and daughter had married a pair of first cousins (see Figure 6.2). It also happened, however, that Mikhalis was a great personal friend of Pavlos Z's brother, Thomas. Thus, in praising his friend Thomas, Mikhalis would praise the whole Z family; and in praising the whole Z family, Mikhalis would point out his double connection with them. They were a fine family (*kali ikoyenia*), and he, Mikhalis, was very much related to them (*poli singhenis m'aftous*). But who were the Zs? Here the whole ambiguity of family comes into play, for although Mikhalis's daughter had certainly married a Z, Mikhalis's son had not – or rather, he had not married anyone by that name. He had married the daughter of Pavlos and Thomas Z's *sister*, and this sister was married to a certain Spiros V. Mikhalis's son had thus married a member of the V family, not the Z family – at least if one gives any definitional value to family names. Spiros V was not, however, any particular friend of Mikhalis, and in Mikhalis's *ad hoc* genealogical construction, Spiros V's existence was simply passed over. So far as Mikhalis was concerned, his connections were with the Zs. Indeed, when Mikhalis referred to this sister, he referred to her as a Z, not as the *wife* of Spiros V, but as the *sister* of Nikos and Thomas Z. And, so far as I could see, Mikhalis's reasons for construing his affinal relationships exclusively with the Zs rather than with the Zs and the Vs hinged simply on his friendship with Thomas Z.

In short, given the plethora of kinship relations within the community, the value of kinship could be added where and when it was advantageous and politely ignored when it was not. And this could be a matter of occasion as much as of individual connection. It was notable that kinship terms were used with particular frequency during the period leading up to and immediately following a marriage. People who normally addressed each other as Yannis or Maria or Spiros or Eleni would take to calling each other *ksadherfe mou* (my cousin) or *thia mou* (my aunt) or *anepsie mou* (my nephew) or *simpethere mou* (my affine) in celebration, as it were, either of the new-found kinship into which they had been or were about to be drawn, or of their longstanding interconnections as the relatives of one or the other of the parties thrust momentarily into prominence. Kinship connections which otherwise appeared dormant (or which normally passed unremarked) were suddenly asserted, for they were the pathways that linked individuals to each other and to an important event. 'My niece, Maria, is getting married next week – she's a wonderful girl.'

'Your who?'

'My niece – her grandmother and my mother were cousins.'

And thus it was that entire blocks of genealogy were suddenly revealed.

Fame, then, was the trigger; familial connection the claim. One day I paid a formal visit to Spartokhori's newly elected president, who I hoped would finally allow me to study the village records. Like most things in Spartokhori, my visit did not go unnoticed, and on my return to the coffee-shop one of my friends greeted me with the words, 'Ah, you've been seeing my uncle, the president?'

'Your uncle?' I said, since at that stage I was entirely unaware of any kinship connection between them. Moreover, I had thought that they were not on particularly good terms. But I was not the only one a little surprised, for one of the older men drinking in the shop indignantly echoed, 'What uncle? The president is your uncle?!'

'Of course he's my uncle,' my friend smoothly replied, 'He's my wife's brother's wife's father. That's an uncle (*thios*), isn't it?'

Perhaps even by Spartokhoriot standards he was stretching a point, but the claim was reluctantly allowed. 'The *proedhros* and I, we are family,' my friend smugly concluded.

The real point, of course, is that kinship in Spartokhori was not so much a determinant of social relations as a moral system whose authority was largely independent of empirical falsification. But it should not be imagined that because kinship was everywhere, because it was strategically invoked, and because the values it entailed could not be arrived at by simple induction from observable behaviour, kinship was a mere gloss on other interests. To construe social interaction in terms of kinship might have been to give that interaction a *post factum* significance which obscured its immediate motivations; but the significance thus attributed was real enough, and if I might hazard a generalization, *post factum* constructions are often the more significant counters with which people play out their lives. In a society which placed high value on the obligations of kinship, betrayal by a brother was so much the worse because it was a brother who betrayed. Assistance from an uncle was so much the sweeter because it was an uncle who assisted. The statistical probability of the betrayal or the assistance did not affect those evaluations. Nor did they affect the morality on which the evaluations were based. As Davis comments:

> Kinship carries with it some extra value which makes association with kinsmen more desirable than with others ... Obligations are often ignored. Trust may be betrayed, the relation itself denied, but it is nevertheless true that men who wish to attract the support and cooperation of others will do so in the name of prescriptive obligation – and will express an even greater sense of betrayal than if they are let down by an acquaintance or friend. (Davis 1977: 222)

The fisherman waiting at dawn for the arrival of his cousin to make up our crew was met instead by his cousin's little boy who came with the message that his father was not well (that is, he wanted to stay in bed). Furious, the fisherman appealed to me. 'You see! That's the sort of wanker (*malakas*) he is. He does this to me, his cousin.' Conversely, I am done a favour by someone in the village and remark on it to a friend. 'Ah yes, of course, he's a wonderful boy. He's my nephew, you know. A good family.'

In short, the morality of kinship and the set of expectations that derived from it were not subject to empirical confirmation or falsification, because kinship was a value in itself. I should now reveal that when Pavlos voted against his *kouniadhos* in the village elections he did have a personal axe to grind. As I have mentioned, Kostas's team was headed by a shop-keeper, Yerasimos, and Pavlos and Yerasimos were arch-enemies. Since I was on good terms with both, both were somewhat circumspect in their criticism of each other to me, but Pavlos would not set foot in Yerasimos's shop and even had to buy his cigarettes by proxy (usually me) since Yerasimos had the tobacco concession. But they were first cousins, or rather, Pavlos's wife and Yerasimos were first cousins (which incidentally meant that Pavlos's wife's two brothers, Kostas and Babis, were also Yerasimos's first cousins: see Figure 6.1). Quite truthfully, then, Pavlos explained to me one night when we were both attending a wedding feast and alcohol had got the better part of caution, that his real reason for not having voted for his beloved *kouniadhos* Kostas was because a vote for Kostas would have been tantamount to a vote for Yerasimos, the leader of Kostas's team. Pulling himself up, however, he then stated that the reason he had not wished to cast a vote in Yerasimos's direction was because Yerasimos had been village president once before and had not proved particularly energetic. Somewhat weary of this obfuscation, I broke with niceties and suggested that the real reason that he had not wanted to vote for any team headed by Yerasimos was that he and Yerasimos detested each other. But we were in public and could be overheard. Pavlos contrived to look shocked. 'No, no,' he cried. 'Yerasimos is a very good man. I love Yerasimos. Yerasimos and I are cousins. We're family.'

7
Household & Inheritance

The place of households

I was sitting one afternoon in the house of Andhreas and Lopi where I had been invited for lunch. This was a rare event, because the Spartokhoriots did not normally entertain at home. They were, nevertheless, a hospitable people. I could not walk into any of the village's coffee-shops without being bought a drink, and it took well over six months before I was allowed, even then grudgingly, to buy one for anyone else (Allen 1973: 12). That, of course, related to my special status as a *ksenos*, as a foreigner and a guest. I had to remain a receiver, not a giver. The inequality defined my place, and in a sense it kept me in my place (cf. Herzfeld 1987b). But the Spartokhoriots were generous enough towards each other as well. Spartokhoriot men were forever buying each other drinks and inviting their fellows to share whatever little treat they had purchased for consumption in the *kafenio*: some pickled octopus, a tin of sardines, slices of *kokoretsi* (offal bound in gut and roasted on a spit). A plate of tidbits and glasses of ouzo would arrive at a table for the *parea*, the company, that sat around it, despatched by someone at another table through the intermediary of the shop's proprietor who would whisper '*Ap' to Vasili* (From Vasilis)'. The moment the food and drink were touched, but never before the food and drink were touched, the recipients would raise their glasses with the toast '*Stin iyia sou* (To your health)' and briefly turn towards their donor who would acknowledge their good wishes with a dignified inclination of his head and a sip of his own wine before resuming his conversation. This was all part of male camaraderie. Up to a point, it was also all part of male competition, a delicate game of giving and receiving (the one as important as the other) through which men acknowledged their peers and reckoned their own acknowledgment by them (and which, of course, had its strategic omissions and oversights). On the whole, however, it was a hospitable game. But it was a decidedly public game. That, indeed, was its whole point: men entertained each other in public to demonstrate their place in the public world. They came out of the house to be part of the village. They did not invite the village back to be part of their house.

The fact that I had been eating with Andhreas and Lopi as part of their family was thus something of a social oddity, and it was an oddity that again followed from my status as a *ksenos* (for despite my best efforts I was not a member of the village, and I never could have been save by marrying into it, about which there

186

were occasional jokes, but no serious offers). In general men rarely entered each other's houses, except on those special occasions – engagements, baptisms, weddings and funerals – when the house was officially open (and even then, not to the whole village), or unless perhaps the men were father and son, brothers or brothers-in-law. Men were punctilious in their observation of this social propriety, and even those who were close friends and constant companions would shout for each other in front of an open door rather than step over the threshold of their neighbour's house. And they would not be invited to do so. Their friend would appear at the door, exit the house, and together they would walk down the street to discuss whatever bit of business they had. And even though my own status was exceptional so that from time to time I was invited home for a family meal, still, in nearly two-and-a-half years of fieldwork I went inside not more than twenty houses, usually those of elderly couples whose own children had emigrated and for whom I supplied some younger companionship. Significantly, however, I always ate with a family whenever I had done a day's work for them: when I had helped repair their house, press their olives, transport their grapes. Over two summers I thus ate quite regularly with Alkis the fisher-man and his family whenever he decided that we should not spend the night out at sea but come home after laying the nets and go out again at dawn to pull them in. I intuited that this was some form of recompense, or at least some form of thanks for my assistance – and so it was,[1] for it was not simply sociability (and did not happen if I was not working with the family). But it was not offered as any sort of explicit payment. Rather, inasmuch as I was working for the household – but only for so long as I was working for the household – I was deemed to be part of the household. And members of a household not only worked together, they ate together.

For women the situation was a little different. The equation of 'public' and 'private' with 'male' and 'female' has recently come under some criticism in the anthropology of Greece (Herzfeld 1986) and in feminist anthropology as a whole (Moore 1988: 21–4). Certainly the two oppositions cannot neatly be caulked on to each other. In Spartokhori women did participate in public life. Rather more noticeably, men had their private lives. Nevertheless, if women's influence extended beyond the household, and if men constantly retreated to the household, the association of women with the house (Hirschon 1978; Dimen 1986; du Boulay 1986) did mean that women visited each other at home with rather more freedom than did their husbands or brothers or sons. This was forcefully brought home to me when a young English woman found herself stranded in Spartokhori owing to the vagaries of the weather and the ferry-caique. She did not speak Greek. She did not much like Greece. And she was very upset about having to spend a week in Spartokhori, where she was obliged to rent the room next to mine. Nevertheless, within a matter of days she had entered every second house in the village (while I silently fumed), for she had only to walk down a street for one woman or another to signal her across for a coffee and an attempt at conversation. In short, she was extended the sort of hospitality deemed appropriate for her (anomalous) position as a single woman,

---

[1] In the days when people had been hired as workers (*erghates*) by the larger landowners they normally received meals as well as their day's wage.

just as I was extended in the coffee-shops the hospitality deemed appropriate to mine. Nevertheless, women did not have free run of each other's houses any more than did men. Instead, denied access to the coffee-shops, they had their public gatherings, their 'companies', on each other's doorsteps. The house was not really a female place; it was more a family place. It was not a shelter for women; it was a shelter from the public world. And as I sat that afternoon with Andhreas and Lopi and their family after lunch, we did what people so often did within the house, and what people could do only inside the house: we discussed other people. We 'talked'. Encouraged by the frankness of the conversation and relieved at for once not having to watch my every word, I too aired my own small grievance about some trivial matter, some irritating encounter. Suddenly, thinking better of my remark, I added that absolutely nothing should be said to the person in question, at which point everyone clicked their tongues and raised their hands in that most reassuring Greek negative of negatives (that seems to proclaim even contemplation of the deed an impossibility), and Andhreas solemnly declared, 'Don't worry. We're in the house.'

The phrase was telling. The house was separate from the village. It was sealed off from the village. And for all that the idiom of kinship allowed the Spartokhoriots to construe their solidarity in the affective terms of all one family, experientially the prime locus of solidarity and intimacy remained the family in its minimal sense, the household or *spiti*. The world of the village-as-family existed side by side with the world of the household-as-family, and by contrast, that latter world was private and guarded. Despite the rhetoric of community, from one point of view the village could be seen as an aggregate of so many individual households each aspiring to a form of moral self-containment, each holding itself aloof. As we have seen, cooperation between households existed, sometimes out of necessity, sometimes out of friendship, most often flowing along the lines of kinship and family. But in the final analysis the *spiti* was the only social grouping that was by definition a unity, for only the *spiti* had a corporate identity founded not only in sentiment or convenience, but in its members' strict ties of mutual dependence such that their cooperation was not contingent, but definitional, and their reputations not competitive but collective (cf. Campbell 1964: 190–3; Peristiany 1965). As mentioned in Chapter 3, when I first questioned the villagers about the size of the Spartokhori's population, their natural inclination was to enumerate its constituent households; this was a mnemonic device perhaps, but also a habit of mind that took households, not people, as the obvious starting point. People, after all, were always members of households (even if, as in the case of elderly widows, they were reduced to being members of households of one, survivors of social units still known by their husbands' names).

Households and families

Such an account of the household requires, however, careful qualification, for it is open to misinterpretation. First, to talk of the moral unity of the household and of its enclosed and self-contained nature is not necessarily to assert that this unity is tantamount to a state of uniform and permanent harmony between the household's individual members. Second, it is not necessarily to make any simple equation between family and household. Third, it is not to imply that the composition of the household can be taken as a natural and ahistorical given. These points require emphasis, for in what is probably the most detailed study of rural Greek households yet undertaken, Clark criticizes many earlier accounts on the grounds that they have done all these three things (1988: 26-37). Let me comment briefly on each.

'In their emphasis,' writes Clark, 'on the solidarity of the family household and the opposition between family households, most scholars de-emphasized or ignored the conflict of individual interests within the family household and cooperation outside of it.' (1988: 30) In fact, households in Spartokhori were often riven by internal disputes, quarrels, animosities, competing ambitions and generational antagonisms, just as Clark found to be the case for Methana. If one is privileged to gain an internal perspective on the household's internal relations, then (not surprisingly) they show a considerable (though variable) degree of friction. The picture given by Friedl (1964a: 87), du Boulay (1974: 17; 1986: 146), Dimen (1986: 30) and others of the household as a refuge from conflict and competition, and as a nurturing, united and totally cohesive group, was to some extent an idealized one. But its idealization was very much the point, for it is precisely an ideal that Greek villagers themselves entertain, and which, as du Boulay has so eloquently conveyed, they are constrained to present to the outside world lest '*yelai o kosmos*', lest 'people mock [us]' (1976). Far from challenging the moral unity of the household, the reality of its internal conflict actually necessitates the united front that it displays. '*Ta en iko, mi en dhimo* (The affairs of the house must not be public)' is a proverb that every Greek knows, and which certainly the Spartokhoriots knew (cf. du Boulay 1986: 146). But more importantly, the solidarity of the household was not simply a fiction maintained in the face of public scrutiny. The covenant of the household's closure genuinely moulded its internal relationships if only by creating an area of intimacy in which people could frankly express their private feelings towards each other, including, importantly, feelings of frustration and anger. It was the licence granted personal relationships between members of a household (rather than their harmony) that distinguished the quality of life within the co-residential group from that of all other forms of association. That licence was born of an intimate (too intimate) knowledge of each other. In turn, it was that knowledge of each other (of *ta mistika mas*, 'our secrets', as the Spartokhoriots said) that made the household an irreducible unity; not necessarily shared ambitions or a singular purpose, not necessarily unwavering mutual devotion, but simply the fact that to reveal what went on inside the house was to reveal oneself. Note that the phrase was *ta mistika mas*, 'our' secrets. To that extent, household members were each other's hostage, and their unitary reputation was not always something willingly invited from each other, but something inevitably imposed on each other.

Clark is right to remind us, however, that household and family are not analytically interchangeable concepts (despite their frequent conflations in Greece and elsewhere). The point is a well-established one (Bender 1967; Bestard-Camps

1991: 75). As stressed in Chapter 4, however, what the Spartokhoriots referred to as *ikoyenia* (family) was not reducible to the domestic unit. *Ikoyenia* was used to embrace all those people with whom one could claim a kinship relation, and although it was also used as a synonym for household, the *definition* of the household as a social unit lay in co-residence, not in a particular genealogical configuration. After all, the basic meaning of '*spiti*' is 'house', a piece of property, a piece of architecture, not a piece of kinship. Nevertheless, some form of an equation between household and family is still warranted in Greece – to which the very interchangeability of *spiti* and *ikoyenia* in common speech should alert us.[2] For all the cross-cultural and historical evidence that justifies a distinction between household as a residential unit and family as a kinship unit on the grounds that households may incorporate people who are not kin, or who are only distantly or fictively related, there was only one household in Spartokhori that included a non-family member. But if this is so, the question remains (as Clark insists) of which family members normatively constitute a household at any given historical period.

As we have seen in Chapter 3, the composition of the household in Spartokhori ranged from single widows or widowers through to four generations of family members; however, with very few exceptions Spartokhoriot households still conformed to a single underlying pattern. Their core was a married couple and their children, that is, a nuclear family. What distinguished the composition of one household from another was the stage it had reached in the developmental cycle (Goody 1958). As children married, property (including the family's house) was divided to form new and separate households, but the original couple, or the surviving widow or widower, was normally incorporated into the household of one of the married sons. Most nuclear family households thus temporarily became stem family households, and, depending on the accidents of mortality, might reach a lineal extension of four generations. Alternatively (and again depending on the accidents of mortality, but more often on the opportunities of migration), nuclear family households might in time reduce to elderly married couples or widows or widowers living alone. But what were not found in Spartokhori (and what appears to be rare in Greece) were laterally extended households with two or more married siblings cohabiting (let alone households containing cousins or other more distant collateral relatives).

The tragic paradox

The limits of the household's expansion in Spartokhori – the fact that in rare instances it might extend lineally to include four generations, but never laterally to include married siblings or other collateral relatives – was, as I have already intimated, a consequence of the rules of inheritance and the division of property. What held a household together, what ultimately defined a household (and what, it should be noted, distinguished the household from any particular configuration of kin despite its substantial congruence with the extensions and contractions of

---

[2] And as du Boulay points out, *ikoyenia* (family) is itself a compound of the classical and puristic Greek word for a house, *oikos*, and the term for a 'stock' (1974: 18).

a nuclear family) was its members' dependence on shared material resources: a house and agricultural land.

Local rules and customary law governing the inheritance and devolution of property vary considerably within Greece and the Greek-speaking world. In the so-called 'matrilineal' societies of the northeast Aegean, in parts of Cyprus and in areas of Athens, houses and property are inherited through women (Papataxiarchis 1998; Loizos 1975b; Hirschon 1989). Vernier documents in detail the singular case of Karpathos where two separate, gendered and restricted lines of inheritance existed, with first-born sons inheriting their fathers' property and first-born daughters their mothers' property to the exclusion of their younger siblings (1991: 11, 53–9). The rules that governed the devolution of property in Spartokhori, however (and which resulted in the fluctuation of households from nuclear families to stem families), conformed to a much more common pattern in Greece: the equal division between sons of land and of the family house (significantly referred to as the *patriko spiti*, the 'paternal house') on the death of their father (or at such stage as he was willing effectively to retire), with daughters receiving their share of family wealth in the form of dowry, usually monetary, at the time of their marriage. Only if they had no brothers, and were consequently 'heiresses' (*klironomi*), did women stand to inherit. This rule of equal division of house and land between sons was absolute, and upheld even in those numerous cases where a son or sons had emigrated. Any attempt by one son to abrogate the rights of another on the grounds of the latter's absence from the village was resisted as a scandalous transgression of natural rights. Equally strongly resisted was any attempt by a daughter (or her husband) to lay claim to a share of the paternal house or fields on an equal footing with her brothers.

Actual practice was of course more complicated. Brothers, especially if some of their number were no longer permanently resident in the village, often came to an arrangement amongst themselves whereby some bought out the shares of others. Alternatively, brothers might arrive at an agreement whereby property was effectively ceded to whichever brother(s) remained in the village in return for a share of produce (if those absent were resident in Athens or Patras) or simply for safekeeping (if they had emigrated overseas). Such mutually acceptable arrangements had always been part of village practice even before the advent of postwar overseas and urban emigration. Local emigration to nearby islands and villages (often coupled with strategic marriages to 'heiresses') along with the accidents of fertility and infertility also conspired to modify the neatness of a system of equal inheritance between sons, and served as traditional mechanisms for the redistribution of paternal estates. But whatever the complexities, the *spiti*, the house, divided from generation to generation. It divided as a piece of property, with a single structure being turned into two, three or four houses by the construction of a second storey, or of new internal walls and external doors, or of new adjoining buildings on either side or at the rear, until a practical limit was reached and the construction of further houses by brothers had to take place on family-owned land at a distance from the original dwelling.[3] But, concomitantly, the *spiti* also divided as a social unit. The rules of inheritance, the division of

---

[3] See Hirschon (1983) for details of a similar process in urban Greece, but in which daughters, not sons, inherit houses via dowry.

house (and land), resulted in a repeated redistribution of family members within new households rather than the perpetuation over time of a single household. And herein lies the tragedy of the *spiti*, for it was doomed to disintegration as the developmental cycle progressed. For all that it constituted the basic social unit of village life, the *spiti* was fundamentally unstable, subject to continual fission as sons established their own *spitia* (pl.) and daughters transferred on marriage to the *spitia* of others. Every household created the seeds of its own destruction, and the moral force and suasion that bound it so tightly together was matched only by that which in the end pulled it apart to create successors in its own image.

Given this continual division of the household (characteristic not only of Spartokhori but of many European peasant societies), it is perhaps one of the minor oddities of anthropological history that much of the renewed interest in households arises not only from the recent work of European social historians, but also from the somewhat scattered writings of Lévi-Strauss on what he terms '*sociétés à maison*' (1983a, 1983b, 1984, 1987, 1991; Carsten and Hugh-Jones 1995: 6–9).

> Lévi-Strauss stresses that in complete contrast to the temporal instability and fragmentation of the household, *the house as a grouping endures through time*, continuity being assured not simply through succession and replacement of its human resources but also through holding on to fixed or movable property and through transmission of the names, titles and prerogatives which are integral to its existence and identity (Carsten and Hugh-Jones 1995: 7; my emphasis).

Ironically, Lévi-Strauss's notion of the house (modelled on the noble houses of medieval Europe) seems singularly inapplicable to the peasant household that has for so long been a central concern of Mediterranean and European anthropology.[4] Yet ideationally and emotionally this may not be quite the case, for if the Spartokhoriot *spiti* as both a material entity and a social unit was doomed to disintegration and multiple recreation, if it had to rip itself apart in order to spawn it own likenesses, the dreams and aspirations of its members – at least of its older members – were often of its perpetuation and continuity. Sons (as opposed to daughters) were frequently complained of because of their desire to hasten the division of the *spiti* and to become the heads of independent households, but sons (again as opposed to daughters) were also considered a boon since they preserved the house and the name, as if (contrary to what everybody knew) the house together with the family name could endure through time as the sort of unity that Lévi-Strauss describes. But even if the division of the *spiti* was seen as inevitable, it did not take place without severe emotional strain, for the ideals of solidarity and of independence were pitted against each other. For the older generation, the unity of their household was something they sought to preserve as long as possible, for all their efforts had been invested in its support, growth and maintenance. Its dissolution spelled not only their own marginality (and impending mortality), but also the demise of the collective entity to which they had been for so long committed. Their house, their *spiti*, would not endure. Anger, frustration, self-pity, sorrow, at best a weary resignation and a vicarious

---

[4] Ott's study of French Basques (1981) provides a notable exception. Houses remain undivided and, ideologically, endure through time.

pleasure in the successes of the new households their own had created were standard responses. So too was a romanticization of the past when, they claimed, large extended families were the norm and sons married and brought their brides back to live under the roof of the paternal *spiti* with no divisions occurring – an account, as we shall see, of considerable historical dubiety. For the younger generation, the desire for independence from their parents' *spiti* outweighed their solidarity with it. But again this was at a price, for however fraught familial relations might become, however strong the yearning to control their own destinies and to command their own resources, the morality of familial solidarity within the *spiti*, and perhaps more importantly the experience of familial solidarity within the *spiti*, could not lightly be thrown off. Moreover, their desire to escape the *patriko spiti* was not a desire (at least in the long term) for a life of unfettered individual freedom. The commitment of the younger generation to the values of family – to marriage, the raising of children and the worldly success of their own household – was quite as strong as that of their parents. Ironically, it was their very recapitulation, their very re-embodiment, of their parents' ambitions that set the younger generation against the older. And not only against the older generation, for as the separate inheritors of their parents' estate, brothers too found themselves placed in an at least potentially conflict-ridden situation. They too, therefore, looked back to a romanticized past in which division had not occurred, and brothers had continued to cohabit even after marriage and to work their land in concert. Alternatively, they claimed that the necessity of dividing the paternal house and its land arose not from their own desire to separate from each other, but from the inability of their respective wives (not members of their natal *spiti*, after all) peacefully to cohabit.

The quality of personal relationships existing between members (and erstwhile members) of a household could be viewed as a direct consequence of the rules of residence and inheritance (Davis 1977: 168), but it must be stressed that the sentiments that informed Spartokhoriot family life were not uniform. Individuals coped in individual ways. There is, however, no need to enter the realms of individual psychology, or of character or personality, to comprehend something of the resultant diversity, for the range of people's affective states still related to values that were culturally embedded. In fact the rules of division and inheritance were themselves often modified by other socially engendered concerns and sentiments (cf. Vernier 1991: 15–16). Here Lévi-Strauss's insights do apply, for, as Carsten and Hugh-Jones summarize (1995: 8–9),[5] he suggests that the house combines within itself principles or social forms normally treated as opposed (amongst them filiation/residence, patri-/matri-lineal descent, descent/affinity), and that whilst apparently being founded in kinship, the primacy of the house as a social unit means that economic and political considerations (rather than kinship *per se*) steer marriage choices, inheritance and succession (Lévi-Strauss 1983a: 187; 1987: 155). This can be seen if we turn to the history of one particular Spartokhoriot house and the various households to which it gave rise (see Figure 7.1).

[5] Since Lévi-Strauss's writings on the house are dispersed throughout a number of works, I refer to Carsten and Hugh-Jones's excellent summary, which brings Lévi-Strauss's views together into a coherent whole.

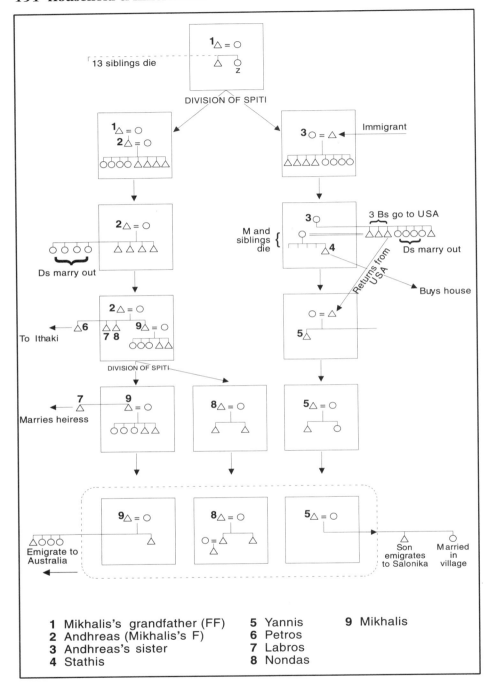

Figure 7.1 The history of Mikhalis's grandfather's house

The history of Mikhalis's grandfather's house

Mikhalis was in his sixties. His family's original house (of which Mikhalis's share in 1980 constituted something less than one-third) was built by his grandfather in the latter half of the nineteenth century. Mikhalis was a relatively poor man, but his grandfather must have been prosperous, for the house (whose original outlines could still be traced despite its subsequent modifications and extensions) was a large one. Mikhalis's share, however, consisted of only three small rooms: a *saloni* (living room), a bedroom adjoining it and a kitchen/eating room that had been built as an extension. Mikhalis's house was nevertheless entirely self-contained, and had its own front door.

Mikhalis's grandfather had had fifteen children, but only two survived to adulthood (or rather to married life): Mikhalis's own father, Andhreas, and an older sister. This sister (Mikhalis's aunt) married an immigrant from Lefkadha who had come as a labourer, an *erghatis*, to work on the estate of one of Meganisi's then wealthy landowners. Being landless and houseless himself, this labourer received a portion of Mikhalis's grandfather's house as dowry, or at least as a result of his marriage, since whether he first lived as an *esoghambros*, a resident son-in-law, within his father-in-law's household, or whether a separate portion of the house was made over to him as dowry immediately on his marriage, I do not know. At all events, during my fieldwork this portion of the original house was owned and occupied by his grandson, Yannis, who was thus Mikhalis's 'nephew' (his FZSS, or, in English terms, his first cousin once removed), and it should be noted that inheritance via marriage of this portion of the original house had been effected despite the existence of a male heir, that is, Mikhalis's father, Andhreas. The rules of inheritance seem never to have been so rigid that they could not be modified by particular circumstance or need, and clearly a daughter's marriage to a houseless immigrant constituted just such a circumstance. One consequence of this breaking of the rules of patrilineal inheritance in favour of a daughter and her husband was, of course, to set up a new and differently named line of descendants and inheritors within what otherwise was to become a complex of agnatically related households whose members all bore the same family name, for the continual subdivision and extension of a single house over time (as brothers inherited to the exclusion of their sisters) normally resulted in neighbouring households, and sometimes entire sections of the village, being inhabited by agnatically related kin (cf. Herzfeld 1985; Couroucli 1985). The inheritance at some time of a house (or portion of a house) by a daughter, however, resulted in the intrusion into an agnatic neighbourhood of a household (or households) whose members bore different family names. Such was the case with the descendants of Andhreas's sisters and her husband, whose history I shall also briefly follow, since cognatically they were part of the same family as Mikhalis.

The sister of Andhreas and her immigrant worker husband had eight children, four girls and four boys. The daughters all married within the village and moved into the households of their respective husbands. During the early part of the century three of the sons emigrated to the United States in search of work. One of these sons was the father of Yannis, the owner and occupier in 1980 of a portion of the original house built by Mikhalis's grandfather. Another was the father of a certain Stathis (Yannis's first cousin), a man in his mid-seventies who, like Yannis, was also Mikhalis's 'nephew', though somewhat older than him (see Figure 7.1). Shortly after the departure of Stathis's father for the United States, however, Stathis's mother (who had been left behind) and all of Stathis's siblings died in an influenza epidemic. Stathis was thus effectively left an orphan in the village, and was looked after by his paternal grandmother, the sister of Andhreas, in her share of Mikhalis's grandfather's house.

Stathis's father never returned from the United States, but he regularly sent money for Stathis's support. In 1939 he died there, and Stathis became the beneficiary of his father's overseas savings. With this money Stathis bought a house and land, for he was still without either, although technically he should have inherited his share of his paternal grandfather's house, that is, a portion of the portion of the original house that had been acquired by marriage by his grandfather, the immigrant worker from Lefkadha. As it happened, the whole of his grandfather's share of the house was inherited by Stathis's uncle, the father of Yannis, who was the only one of the four brothers to return from the United States. At about the same time, Stathis married one of three sisters who had no brothers and whose father had died, thus leaving them to inherit their father's house by equal division. In short, Stathis married an 'heiress'. Stathis did not, however, take his wife's share of her paternal house on marriage. Instead, both he and the husband of another of the sisters sold their shares of their wives' house (which they received as dowry) to the husband of the third sister on the grounds that they each already possessed a house. (Stathis had recently purchased a house with his inherited money, and the husband of the other sister had inherited by the normal process his share of his own *patriko spiti*.) According to his own account, Stathis never received full payment for the share of his wife's house, but let the matter drop since he was financially secure, and also a close friend of his *badzanakis*, his wife's sister's husband. A similar situation may explain why Stathis had also taken no share of his paternal grandfather's house (in which he had been brought up by his grandmother): either he received monetary compensation from his uncle (his father's brother) or he waived his rights on the grounds that he was in a position to purchase a house with his father's American savings. Stathis's wife died having borne only one son. Stathis then remarried when he was in his early fifties, making the very unusual step of taking a childless widow somewhat older than himself. She too brought a house as dowry. This house, however, remained closed at the time of my fieldwork, and Stathis continued to live in the house he had purchased in 1939 with his second wife, his son (in his forties), his daughter-in-law and his granddaughter.

The breaking of the rules of patrilineal inheritance whereby the sister of Andhreas and her immigrant husband received a portion of the house built by Mikhalis's grandfather thus resulted, three generations later, in there still being a division of the original house built by Mikhalis's grandfather that was owned not by one of Mikhalis's agnatic relatives, but by a cognate, Mikhalis's father's sister's son's son, Yannis (see Figure 7.1). On the other hand, overseas emigration (and mortality), the acquisition of a house through money earned overseas and a fortuitous marriage with an heiress meant that there were no further divisions of that section of the original house, or expansion of the number of households in that location, that belonged to Mikhalis's cognates. Meantime, however, division (and extension) of the original house between Mikhalis's agnatic relatives progressed.

Mikhalis's father, Andhreas, inherited the major portion of his father's *patriko spiti*. He and his wife had twelve children, of whom four died in infancy. Of the remaining eight, four boys and four girls, Mikhalis was the youngest. All four daughters married into other households within the village. The oldest brother, Petros, married and settled on the island of Ithaki. His descendants on Ithaki still own some land on Meganisi; but when Petros married out of the village he sold most of his share of his father's land together with his share of the paternal house to his three brothers, Nondas, Labros and Mikhalis himself. The middle brother, Labros, then acquired a separate house in the village when he, too, married an heiress. Presumably he sold his share of his *patriko spiti* to his brothers Mikhalis and Nondas, but this was far from clear, for no one would discuss the matter with me, and Labros has not been on speaking terms with Mikhalis and Nondas for many years. It was whispered that this had something to do with a dispute over the inheritance of the house. At the time of my fieldwork there were thus three separate *spitia* on the site of the original house: that of Mikhalis; that of Mikhalis's older brother, Nondas, and that of their (cognatic) 'nephew', Yannis.

Mikhalis himself had seven children, two of whom died in infancy. Of the remaining five, four (a son and three daughters) emigrated to Australia in the 1960s. Only Mikhalis's youngest son, Stavros (who was in his early thirties, and still unmarried), remained in the village in his parents' house. He stood to inherit Mikhalis's house by equal division with his brother in Australia. Mikhalis's older brother, Nondas, did not marry until he was well into his forties, whereupon he had two sons, Andhreas (named after his paternal grandfather) and Haris. Both were ship's cooks. Haris, then in his early twenties and still unmarried, also worked occasionally in restaurants in Athens and, preferring the excitement of the city to life in the village, visited Spartokhori only during the summer months. Nevertheless he considered Spartokhori his home, and claimed that he would eventually settle there. He stood to inherit half of Nondas's *spiti*. Nondas's elder son, Andhreas, married young in 1977 (under pressure from his ageing father, who wished to see grandchildren born). Andhreas brought his village bride to reside with his parents in the family's *spiti*, and she gave birth to a son during my stay. Nondas's household, a stem family, thus contained two generations of married couples plus, nominally, his unmarried son, Haris, as well as a third generation, his baby grandson (named Nondas after his grandfather).

At this stage, however, something of an ambiguity arises in the definition of the *spiti* depending on whether one puts the emphasis on the kin-based group (the household) or on questions of architecture (the house). There was no doubt that Nondas and his wife and unmarried son Haris, together with Andhreas and his wife and baby son, were all classified by the village as constituting a single *spiti* in the sense of a household (or family). Indeed, with the possible anomaly of Haris's urban adventurings, the composition of the household conformed nicely to the standard pattern of a stem family. But in fact the house had been modified and extended, and young Andhreas and his (nuclear) family had their own quarters within it, including a separate *saloni* (sitting room) and entrance, as a well as a separate bedroom. Significantly, however, both generations of married couples ate together and used a common kitchen, and as Hirschon has emphasized for Yerania, conceptually separate kitchens and separate eating arrangements are diacritical of separate households (Hirschon 1989: 64–6). Nevertheless, in effect the house had already been divided, and it was intended that on Nondas's death, Andhreas and his family would retain the section of the *spiti* they already occupied, and Haris would take the part occupied by his parents (their mother, Nondas's widow, living with one or the other son), thus formalizing the division. Indeed, that the senior couple (Nondas and his wife) and the junior couple (Andhreas and his wife) together with Nondas's unmarried son (Haris), were all considered to live in one and the same *spiti* was more a matter of ideology than of architecture.

The history of Mikhalis's grandfather's house spans a quite lengthy period (from the end of the nineteenth century to 1980) and illustrates both the principles that governed the devolution of property in Spartokhori and the modifications to those principles that had often to be made. Several points should be emphasized. The first is that despite a high birth rate (Mikhalis's grandparents had fifteen children, his parents twelve, and Mikhalis and his wife seven), for most of the time the various households mentioned did not constitute large extended families. Admittedly, only two of Mikhalis'ss grandparents' children survived, but even in the next generation when eight children survived, a large extended family was not produced – or at least not for any length of time. Mikhalis's father's sister's household had already split off to become a separate *spiti*, probably soon after her marriage to the immigrant worker from Lefkadha. This would have left the household in which Mikhalis grew up to consist of two generations of married couples, Mikhalis's parents and paternal grandparents, plus Mikhalis and his siblings – in short, a stem family rather than a laterally extended family (albeit one consisting of twelve individuals, four adults and eight children). Two further interrelated factors must now be considered, for they also contributed in preventing the household's expansion into a large extended family: a late age of marriage for men, and a rule whereby all daughters had to be married before sons were free to marry (cf. Campbell 1964: 82; Clark 1988: 362 n.33).

In Mikhalis's family this rule was adhered to, and all four of Mikhalis's sisters married and left the household before any of their brothers married. This would have meant that, with the death of the grandparents, Mikhalis's natal household was soon reduced to Mikhalis's parents and their four sons. Mikhalis, the youngest son, then married early by village standards (at the age of twenty-six, and while his parents were still alive), but Nondas, his senior by ten years, did not marry until he was in his forties, and after the death of his father, when the property was divided. At no stage were married brothers co-resident within a single household. The requirement that daughters should marry out of the household before any of their brothers could marry, and the resultant late age of marriage for men, effectively limited the number of married couples within the household, for the developmental cycle of the household was slowed down, and mortality given a head start on fertility. By the time brothers were married, the point was approaching when the *spiti* would in any case divide on the death of the father, whose presence (and ownership of its resources) held it together.

Second, the equal (and continual) division between male heirs of a single patrimony was substantially modified by local emigration and strategic marriages. Households that produced a large number of sons obviously faced difficulties, but emigration or marriages with brotherless daughters (or frequently a combination of both) limited the subdivision of both houses and land. On the death of their father, Mikhalis and his brother Nondas divided their *patriko spiti* into two (each becoming head of a separate nuclear household), but their older brother Petros had already emigrated to Lefkadha where he married, while their other brother, Labros, acquired a house in Spartokhori via marriage to an heiress. It is worth noting that Petros's departure from the household (and from Meganisi) matched the arrival and incorporation into the household in the preceding generation of the landless migrant from Lefkadha who married Mikhalis's aunt (see Figure 7.1). At that stage, with only two surviving offspring (Mikhalis's father and Mikhalis's aunt), the household could afford to take in an extra male via marriage, while in the next generation, with four potential male heirs (and having lost a portion of the house to the migrant from Lefkadha) the oldest son was forced to find his fortune (and residence) on Ithaki, and another son acquired a house within the village as a result of marriage with a brotherless daughter. Similarly, of the three sons of Mikhalis's aunt who emigrated to the United States, only one returned to inherit her portion of the house. By the rights of patrilineal succession his nephew, Stathis (who had been left behind as a baby and whose mother and siblings perished in the influenza epidemic), also stood to inherit a share of that same house, but instead Stathis purchased one when his father died in the United States. And although Stathis bought his own house with his father's American savings, it is notable that coming from a landless family he too married one of three brotherless daughters. Admittedly, he waived his rights to his share of his wife's house, but fifteen of the thirty *stremmata* of land he owned were acquired as dowry. Marriage and migration thus appear to have worked over several generations as compensatory mechanisms to adjust the inequalities of fertility, or rather, of surviving sons. To put the matter another way, despite the rules of patrilineal succession (which could be construed as a strongly agnatic feature of Spartokhoriot kinship – see Chapter 4), in practice the inheritance and division of a *spiti* followed along broadly cognatic lines, and although the house did not endure through time as a unity, its regeneration (rather than its perpetuation) allowed, as Lévi-Strauss suggests, alliance and affinity to substitute for descent.

The past ideal

Changes in household composition cannot, however, be seen solely in terms of the rules of inheritance and division. If the *spiti* must, by its very nature, be considered temporally – as part of a process rather than as a fixed structure – it is also the case that the process itself must be viewed historically, for developmental cycles are themselves affected by wider economic and social changes that bear on the household's normative composition. As shown in Chapter 4, households in Spartokhori in 1980 were quite small. The 186 houses that were occupied on a year-round basis yielded an average of less than three persons per household. Moreover, though it was common to find two generations of married couples within a single household, I have stressed that in no case did married siblings share a common household. This situation contrasts sharply with the oldest generation's nostalgic accounts of their youth when, they claimed, every house was full, containing ten, a dozen or fifteen individuals, and certainly in the postwar years three developments occurred that affected the composition of Spartokhoriot households. The first was a greatly reduced birth rate. Spartokhoriots in their sixties and seventies at the time of my fieldwork regularly came from families of five, six and not infrequently ten or twelve children. By the1960s, however, very few Spartokhoriot families were having more than two children, and three was a maximum. The effect of this change on Spartokhoriot household compositions was, of course, purely numerical. More important were the forms of overseas and urban migration discussed in Chapter 3, which meant that a large number of elderly married couples, widows and widowers who might have expected to end their days in the household of one of their sons found themselves living alone in the village for at least the major part of each year (and often for years on end). In short, emigration had in many cases arrested the development of a stem family out of a nuclear family, and instead reduced it to an aged couple or a single person. Finally, even amongst the younger generation who remained within the village, a strongly expressed preference for neolocal residence on marriage had arisen, rather than for the formation of a household that included the husband's parents, widowed mother or widower father. This shift had economic roots, for it was enabled by the prosperity of the younger generation of men employed as sailors who could afford to build a new house for themselves rather than wait to inherit a portion of their *patriko spiti*, a prosperity which, as we shall see in the following chapter, also affected such related matters as dowry and the age of marriage.

The reduction of the household to a nuclear family or stem family was something that most of the older generation of Spartokhoriots rued, but they looked back to a time not only when each household was full, but when, they claimed, each son had married and in turn brought back his bride to live under the roof of a single and undivided *patriko spiti*. In short, they asserted not only that households had been larger in their youth, but also that they had contained numbers of married brothers and their wives and children all living under the authority of their father and all working the family's land together: laterally extended families rather than simply stem families. The older Spartokhoriots were insistent on this point, and yet, as we have seen, it is not borne out by the history of Mikhalis's grandfather's house, nor is it borne out by the remarkably detailed census of 1870, which throws considerable light on household compositions of the past.

Although the Greek government census of 1870 does not provide data on the individual villages of Spartokhori, Katomeri and Vathi, it does record the deme of Taphos, that is, the island of Meganisi, as having an 'actual' population of 928 (of which 17 persons were from other demes) and a 'registered' population of

951.[6] Importantly, it further states that the island had a total of 148 *oikoyeneiai*, the classical and puristic Greek term for families.[7] If we take the 'actual' population of 928, the average size of a family on Meganisi in 1870 was 6.3 persons. Alternatively, if we take the 'registered' population of 951, the average family size was 6.4 persons. In either case, the average family size was over double what I recorded for 1980, but it still does not square with the Sparto-khoriots' own account that families in the old days regularly consisted of a dozen or more people. Happily, the census also breaks down the 'actual' population of 928 by sex and marital status, recording four widowers, thirty widows, 325 unmarried men, 243 unmarried women, and 163 married men and 163 married women (which might or might not represent 163 married couples).[8] A difficulty arises, however, in trying to distribute these individuals to households. On the face of it one might assume that the *oikoyeneiai* to which the census refers were in fact households. However, the census also states that there were 180 *oikoi* in the deme of Taphos (as well as seven 'other constructions', *eterai oikodomai*), and the word *oikos* in classical and puristic Greek means a house, what in demotic or vernacular Greek is now referred to as a *spiti*. Thus if the 148 families (*oikoyeneiai*) accounted for the entire population, then thirty-two houses (*oikoi*) must have been uninhabited. This is not impossible, but it does seem unlikely. I can only surmise that: (a) the census reserved the term *oikoyeneia* (family) to refer to a household containing at least one married couple; and that (b) most of the four widowers and thirty widows listed in the census occupied houses (*oikoi*) on their own and therefore did not constitute families (*oikoyeneiai*). Alternatively (but much less likely), it might have been that some of the 325 unmarried men and 243 unmarried women were occupying houses on their own and similarly were not classified as constituting families (*oikoyeneiai*).[9] Either hypothesis or some combination of the two would reconcile the number of houses (*oikoi*) with the number of families (*oikoyeneiai*), but while it remains impossible accurately to reconstruct household compositions for 1870, two things are clear. First, the average household size was not particularly large: at most a little over six persons (and if all the widows and widowers were living on their own, the average household size would reduce to just over five persons). Second, and more significant, it simply cannot have been the case that many households contained more than a single married couple. If there were 163 married men, 163 married women, 148 families and 180 houses, then however one manipulates the figures or however a family was defined, the great majority of households must have contained only one married couple. Indeed, with the exception of the number of unmarried persons (which merely reflects a greater number of children), household composition in 1870 appears to have been much as it is was in 1980.

---

[6] The 'actual' population refers to persons present in a locality at the time of the census; the 'registered' population to those officially registered as members of a local administrative unit.

[7] I transliterate the puristic (*katharevousa*) Greek terms used in the census according to the classical system, in order to preserve their distinctiveness.

[8] I have no explanation for the remarkable imbalance between unmarried men and unmarried women, unless the excess of unmarried men represent shepherds from villages in Lefkadha (see Chapter 2).

[9] It is possible that some widows and widowers were living on their own, but unlikely that any young man or woman would have set up house before marriage.

Such a finding accords well with other historical and demographic studies both of Greece and of European peasant communities in general: the large extended family was not the norm (Panayotopoulos 1985; Laslett 1972; Bestard-Camps 1991: 71). But it is difficult to believe that the older Spartokhoriots' account of their youth could have been entirely a figment of collective self-deception. A number of factors may explain the discrepancy between what older Spartokhoriots recalled of the old days, that is from about the turn of the century to the Second World War, and what can be deduced from the 1870 census. First, it must be admitted that a tendency towards exaggeration pervaded most Spartokhoriots' historical accounts, especially when the topic allowed a contrast between present conditions and the hardships of the past. Despite their nostalgia, enormous families crowded into a single house were part of a rhetoric of poverty, hunger, back-breaking labour and unsanitary conditions in a time 'when we lived like animals, not like humans' which the old readily rehearsed. Second, and allied to such exaggeration, there may have been a tendency to generalize from individual cases: if a particular household had contained fifteen people, then this was licence to state that in the old days houses contained fifteen people. Third, the Spartokhoriots' recollections of the past, and data from the 1870 census, are not strictly comparable. Even the oldest Spartokhoriots were referring to conditions this century, and what later (though less detailed) census data do show is a population explosion on the island that commenced from about the time of the 1870 census.[10] As we saw in Chapter 2, within a period of roughly thirty years the population of Meganisi doubled from 778 in 1865 to 1,460 in 1896. By 1907 it had risen to 1,663. This rapid growth was more likely to have been the result of immigration than of the birth rate, but, as Couroucli has suggested for Corfu (1985: 66), population growth after 1870 might have placed a strain on accommodation so that household sizes in, say, 1920 were genuinely larger than they were at an earlier period, and household composition substantially different. I would argue, however, that the real explanation for the discrepancy between the size and structure of the Spartokhoriot household as it appears for 1870 and what the older Spartokhoriots claimed to have been the case in their youth lies neither in the exaggerations of memory nor in genuine change, but again in the nature of the household's continual division and reconstitution. It is the timing of this process that allows a reconciliation between the older generation's claims and historical records, for even if in the past sons did all introduce their wives into their father's household, given the late age of male marriage, the point at which any particular household became a large laterally extended family would not greatly have preceded the point at which it divided on the death of the father. It is possible that many households did pass through the stage of becoming large laterally extended families, but the duration of that stage was short, and the number of extended households at any particular time few. What the old remembered in 1980 was not the overall pattern of village household compositions, but the 'peak' period of their own household.

[10]Unfortunately later census reports do not contain the details provided by the 1870 census. It is not therefore possible to trace changes in household composition from 1870 onwards – if, indeed, such changes occurred.

The unity of the household

Size and (possibly) structure were not the only features of the Spartokhoriot household that had changed within living memory. So too had its function. Many older Spartokhoriots still prided themselves on maintaining a household that was self-sufficient in bread, oil, wine, cheese, vegetables and even, in some rare cases, meat. '*Oti thelis, ekho* (Whatever you want, I have),' I would be told. '*Ta panda* (The lot).' Other people looked back to the days when their house had also been a storehouse of *oula t'aghatha* (all the good things), not only comestibles, but lacework, carpets, rugs and blankets which the women had crocheted, spun and woven for their trousseaux, and of which older women still keep a great store piled high in an alcove or cupboard to be admired by a foreign guest such as myself while I was being given wine *ap'to spiti* ('from the house'), cheese *ap'to spiti*, almonds *ap'to spiti*, raisins *ap'to spiti*, fruit *ap'to spiti* and even bread *ap'to spiti* (cf. du Boulay 1974: 38, Hart 1991: 64). The provenance of the produce was as important as its quality, and conceptually the two were linked, for whatever was best was always 'from the house'. These ideals of economic self-sufficiency, and of the household as a storehouse, were still upheld at the time of my fieldwork. However, although most women continued to make lacework, and some still wove carpets (to be contributed to their own or their daughters' trousseaux), the decline of agriculture, the employment of men on the ships, and the continual movement of families between the village and urban centres meant that for most people the household was no longer a unit of production. Its wealth derived not from the combined agricultural activities of the whole family, but from the monetary incomes of the younger generation, and money could buy whatever was no longer produced. At the same time, the preference for neolocal residence by the village's younger married couples meant that even if children had not emigrated overseas or to the cities, the older generation, who clung to the ideal of household self-sufficiency, were deprived of the labour that could make that ideal possible.

But although the *spiti* had become primarily a unit of consumption rather than of production, the dominance of the household as a moral unity had not been challenged. The co-residential family was still at the centre of every Spartokhoriot's life, and there existed a local comparative anthropology in terms of which the family was held to be a uniquely Hellenic possession. Those who had lived overseas or travelled the world asserted with all the more confidence that only in Greece was the family important, and that only in Greece did members of the family care for each other. I was frequently told that the English, the Americans, the Canadians or the Australians didn't have family. If I protested that this was not quite the case, it was politely pointed out to me that in my *patridha* (fatherland) everyone got divorced, offspring left their parents as mere children and family members did not economically provide for each other. And (horror) were not the elderly placed in institutions? The Greeks, by contrast, were *poli demmeni* (very much tied together). After all, what was I doing on my own in Spartokhori? Why wasn't I married? (Did I not want children?) If, as I said, I was still studying, why weren't my parents regularly sending me money? Many

Spartokhoriot couples who had returned to the village or to Greece from overseas explained that they had done so precisely because there was no family life in America or Australia or Canada, and because they wished their children to grow up Greek in a country where the family was still respected.

In view of the degree of emigration from Spartokhori and of the number of elderly couples who lived in periodic or permanent separation from their children and children's children, this continual stress on the unity of the family and the enduring nature of its ties had its pathetic side. My every visit to any house of an elderly couple always involved a display of the prized photographs of their *pedhia* who were overseas or in Athens, and an account of their successes there. I sometimes asked such doting grandparents why they did not join their children and grandchildren. The answer was always the same. I was assured that their families had begged them to do so, but that it was not possible. Who would look after the house and the land in Spartokhori? And, if their children were overseas, how could they (who were old) learn to cope with a foreign language and foreign ways? As for Athens, it was too noisy and too crowded. In either case, '*Pou na pame?* (Where could we go?)' They would be shut up in the house, they said. They would be 'closed off' like sheep. They would be dependants.

It would be unjust to dismiss the validity of these explanations or to underestimate the practical difficulties alluded to, and most emigrant children did maintain contact with their parents and send back money back to assist them. Athenian-dwellers also returned regularly to the village, and the generations were then reunited. But the protestations made by the elderly about their children's desire to have them join them often masked, I suspect, a realization that if they actually were to go, they might find themselves not so welcome – if only, indeed, because of those practical difficulties which they cited. And for all the lauding of family ties, even within the village and between generations of the same family who had not been separated by migration, financial support tended to be very much in one direction. Parents would make immense sacrifices to ensure the material well-being of their children, but in old age most expected little more than a helping hand in return: pocket-money from their children to make life a little more pleasant; the occasional meal sent round to them if they were ill or indisposed (cf. Hart 1991: 73). No parents expected to be fully supported by their children in old age. Moreover, since it was universally recognized that people's primary loyalties were owed to the *spiti* in which they lived, to the other members of their household, the increasing reduction of households to nuclear families placed the older generation outside the bounds of those for whom full responsibility had automatically to be accepted.

In fact the younger generation's preference for neolocal residence on marriage was itself indicative of a relationship between the generations that, despite an ideology of respect for one's father and devotion to one's mother, often entailed a degree of friction – as, indeed, it always had done. The shift towards neolocal residence represented less a change in social attitude than simply a change in economic feasibilities. Young couples could now do what they had always wanted to do, for the primary source of conflict between the generations had lain in the distribution of power and authority within the extended family. When Spartokhori was an agricultural community, married sons might find themselves still economically dependent on and under the authority of their fathers well into the time when, as adults, they wished to be subject to no one. As subordinates within the *spiti*, they were required to show the traditional attitude of respect (*sevasmos*) towards their fathers. But the actual consequences of that inequality and of the frustrations it engendered were as likely to result in hostility. By 1980, with the relationship of economic dependence broken by the younger generation's new-found wealth, in some cases respect had simply given way to indifference. In contrast to an earlier time, economically the old had little to promise and little to withhold.

But to refer to friction between older and younger generations rooted in the distribution (and redistribution) of economic power is not to assert its inevitability. It is merely to point to the specifically social causes of animosity in those cases where animosity arose, and to the potential lines of stress and tension created both by the structure of the traditional extended household, and by its dissolution in changed and changing times. Many fathers and their married sons successfully negotiated the problems either of co-residence in the paternal *spiti*, or of the younger generation's shift to neolocal residence, and still enjoyed a close relationship. And certainly the ideal of respect for fathers still held sway. My old protector, Mikhalis, was inclined to indulge in something close to ancestor worship when it came to mention of his father Andhreas, though he was, of course, long since dead. His refrain was '*O Khristos protos; o pateras mou dhefteros. Then iparhi allos,*' ('Christ first; my father second. No other exists [*sc.* who is his equal].') It was this form of respect, born of admiration as much as subordination, that formed the ideal. If the two could go together, it was because one should admire one's superiors because one superiors were admirable. But respect in a sentimental sense was certainly not the automatic consequence of paternal authority. Respect in Spartokhori was a decidedly moral rather than a psychological formulation of the relationship, and as such it existed as a cultural value that could be at some odds with individuals' feelings. As a moral value it is worth tracing in some detail, for it supplied a cultural idiom often manipulated to obscure or to mitigate the *Realpolitik* of family life.

Fathers and sons

Few fathers in Spartokhori would speak ill of their sons. Most recited with manifest pride the virtues and achievements of their boys. Yet curiously fathers and sons were seldom seen together in public. Some old man would tell me that his son would shortly be returning from the ships. The event was anticipated with obvious pleasure, and I would be instructed at all costs to make this son's acquaintance, for I should find him an incomparable *pedhi*. Time would pass, and I would spot the old man in one of the coffee-shops still with his same old crowd of cronies, and still with no sign of his cherished son. I would ask if perhaps his son had returned. 'Yes indeed, some days ago.' And then, very discreetly indicating a young man at the other side of the coffee shop, my old friend would whisper, 'That's him there. Go across and talk to him. He's a fine boy.' Yet the father himself would make no move, offer no introduction, and had he not pointed out his son to me, nothing would have indicated their relationship. Father and son were never to be found in the same *parea* even if they happened to be in the same coffee-shop. A careful but casual avoidance was practised, perhaps all the more noticeable after a while because it was so studiously casual. The *parea* of which the father was a member and the *parea* of which the son was a member might fall into conversation, but father and son would never actually seat themselves together. In short, they never publicly presented themselves as father and son.

As background to this avoidance, it is worth noting that in general the members of a single household were seldom to be seen together publicly (cf. Hart 1991: 74). Only on the occasion of a village festival, a *panayiri* or *festa*, when everyone was dressed in their best and on display, would people exhibit themselves as family groups. In large part this family dispersal can be explained in terms of gender segregation. Husbands and wives were not seen together unless they were working in the fields because their respective public obligations were separate. And, for the same reasons, fathers and daughters, mothers and sons, and brothers and sisters were not public companions.[11] But sisters constantly kept each other company, and so did brothers if they were still unmarried. Mothers and daughters, too, were close companions. In short, it was the relationship between fathers and sons that was exceptional. They moved in the same circles. Their avoidance was therefore deliberate. But whenever I asked my old friends why they did not make company with their sons, they always at first denied that this was the case. If I persisted and produced sufficient evidence to provoke some more elaborate response, I was usually told two things: that inasmuch as they did not publicly associate with their sons, this was: a) because fathers and sons saw quite enough of each other at home anyway; and/or b) because their sons preferred to form a *parea* with young men of their own age. Both responses seem perfectly reasonable, but they will not stand scrutiny. If sons were unmarried and/or still living in their father's household, then doubtless father and son did see a lot of each other at home. But the majority of married sons did not share their father's *spiti*, and in that case (so far I could observe) saw relatively little of each other even in the privacy of their respective houses. In any case, private association does not explain public avoidance. Unmarried co-resident brothers drank together in the coffee-shops. As for the claim that younger men preferred each other's company to the exclusion of their fathers', while it was of course true that younger men had their younger friends and older men their older friends, in Spartokhori there was little separation of the generations. Men in their twenties and thirties would happily sit and drink with men in their sixties and seventies.

When I asked younger married men why they avoided their fathers in public, their answers too were vague or dismissive. They didn't really avoid their fathers, they said, or if they did, it was only because *i yerondes*, 'the old blokes', had their own interests which they did not share. But significantly, they often added that it 'didn't do' to sit with your father in a coffee-shop, a point elaborated by the responses of younger *unmarried* men, students and sailors still part of their

---

[11]Not so, however, in Athens, where young Spartokhoriot men regularly escorted their sisters.

fathers' households, from whom a clear admission of avoidance was forthcoming. And the explanation given was respect. It was not possible, said such young men, to sit with your father in the shops and drink with him and smoke in front of him and laugh and tell jokes in his presence, since this would be construed by him as a lack of respect. Exactly why this should be so, my companions were unsure. As one remarked, 'How do I know what goes on in the old man's head? But he would think that I didn't respect him.' Such feelings were, nevertheless, mutual. One group of young men I was talking to had just been dancing to a bouzouki record and admitted that had any of their fathers been present they would have been 'ashamed' (*drepomaste*) to dance. And the same applied to card-playing. If their fathers were present in the same coffee-shop, 'shame' (*dropi*) would prevent them playing cards. For the same reason most claimed that they did not smoke in front of their fathers even inside the house, although interestingly some said that they did, adding that since their father knew they respected him, he did not take offence.

But it is not so difficult to intuit why the sort of behaviour they mentioned (smoking, drinking, playing cards, the range of coffee-shop pastimes) was avoided in their fathers' presence. All the young men were in their late teens or early twenties, and none was married. They were not, therefore, properly adults. As students, most were financially supported by their fathers, and all, whether students or sailors, were members of their fathers' households. The respect they were required to show was thus founded on – or at least in accordance with – their status as juniors and dependants. Smoking, drinking, playing cards, however, were all the activities of adult males, and therefore indicative of the status of autonomous individuals (and financially autonomous adult males, at that). Their *public* performance in a father's presence would thus amount to a precocious assertion of independence, and thereby a *public* denial of paternal authority. But it should be noted that they did not amount to a series of codified or ritual prohibitions. They were merely the sort of thing that could be taken as indicating a lack of respect. If, as I have suggested, it is easy to intuit why, it is also the case that intuition, not explicit rules, lay at the heart of the matter for the young men and their fathers too. It was the likely interpretation of the activity, not the activity itself, that counted, hence the fact that some young men *did* smoke at home in their father's presence, confident in his knowledge of their respect. It is all the more necessary to appreciate the subjective and intuitive nature of judgements about what did and did not imply respect when it comes to attempting to understand the behaviour of fathers and older married sons, between whom no clearcut difference of economic or domestic status obtained (or between whom economic status had in fact been reversed). Fathers at first denied that they did not keep company with their sons, and I do not believe that this was intended as deception, for there was no rule that fathers and sons must not associate. Indeed, there was no explicit formulation of the avoidance at all. Rather, both fathers and their adult sons simply felt a certain unease in each other's presence, which was born of the contradiction in which they would be placed by being seen together in public where they would simultaneously be in both a hierarchical and an equal relationship: hierarchical in that they remained father and son, equal in that they were both adult males. The one status could not help but compromise the other, and a sensitivity to the situation drove them to adopt a mutual stance which was, after all, sanctioned by the history of daily practice: public avoidance. But my own bald assertion, 'You never make company with your sons,' could be denied because there was no explicit formulation to match my observation. If what I presented to them as an account of their behaviour could, on reflection, result in qualified assent, it still had to be qualified, for otherwise it would challenge an ideal that, by contrast, was quite explicit: that fathers and sons should enjoy a close and enduring relationship (of which respect was an integral part).

To an extent, this ambiguous distance maintained between fathers and sons (which can variously be seen to stem from a son's respect for his father, and from a son's respect for himself) allowed the tenets of accepted morality to persist immune from the realities of economic power. Children were supposed always to respect their parents, but as I have remarked, despite the vaunting of family loyalties, the direction of material support between the generations tended to be one way. But old men, anxious to assert their honour and their position within the community despite their manifest poverty, would point out that their daughters had all married well and that their sons were first mates, captains, doctors or lawyers. At the same time they would explain that they themselves no longer worked very much, and were not concerned with money, since the *pedhia* were all married. In having seen their children through to marriage and the establishment of their own households, their life's work was complete. 'Now we just sit.' No such overwhelming responsibility fell on the younger generation to provide for the older. Morality asserted, of course, that it was the duty of children to care for parents in old age, and many children were extremely dutiful in this regard. But in other cases the attention given the elderly was perfunctory, and the traditionally distanced relationship between father and son played some part in obscuring what might otherwise have appeared as an obvious dereliction of duty. Since fathers and sons habitually avoided each other in public, sons were in a position to ignore their fathers without incurring the charge of neglect. Parents were never left to starve or suffer severe deprivation, but it was difficult not to be struck by the fact that old farmers who subsisted largely on their pensions, who could scarcely afford to buy their cigarettes, and who nursed their two-drachma glasses of ouzo in the coffee-shop, had middle-aged sons, high-ranking ship's officers, who could regularly be found in another coffee-shop drinking Scotch whisky. And the process whereby respect was translated into avoidance which in turn could mask indifference was actually abetted by the old men themselves, for to accuse their sons of neglect would be to admit that as fathers they were no longer respected, a slight on themselves as much as their offspring. The tendency was to make much of such favours as were received, or to pass over their absence in silence, and old men who rationed their cigarettes and ouzo not only stressed how much their sons had prospered (for that was to their credit as fathers), but also pointed out that '*Mou dhinoune* ('They give to me')' – pocket money of 1,000 drachmes a month, and meals sent round to the house. '*Me sevonde*,' they insisted, 'They respect me.' Given its symbolic value, whatever they received was sufficient for the older generation to make the claim of being respected, especially since their children's virtue was a register of their own. Old Harilaos complained to me that age had made him incapable of bringing in his olive harvest. '*Drepome* (I'm ashamed),' he gloomily pronounced. 'Why don't you ask your son Stathis [a middle-aged sailor, and his only son] to help you?' I asked. 'Stathis! Hah!' snorted Harilaos. But then, quickly changing his tone, he went on to explain that Stathis was very busy because he was an honourable man (*filotimos*) who spent all his spare time helping his son-in-law, his *ghambros*. The direction of responsibility was clear.

The ideological maintenance of the extended family

The eventual division of the *spiti* had always been an inevitability. What the elderly resented were its premature dissolution and their exclusion from a stem family as a result of neolocal residence by the young. Some old men fought back. Thomas and his father Mitsos provide a good example of the animosity between father and son that could arise. Thomas was an only son (though he had two married sisters), and therefore stood to inherit the entirety of his father's *spiti* into which, being an only son, he should have brought his wife to form a stem family. But Thomas and his family did not live with Mitsos and his wife. They built a new house. Though well into his seventies, Mitsos, in retaliation, retained the entirety of his landholdings which Thomas also stood to inherit, but which he might have expected to be made over to him in his father's old age (and which he certainly would effectively have controlled had he and his father been part of the same household). In fact Thomas did not engage in agriculture, but made a living by fishing and by running a small store. He did, however, own seven *stremmata* of land, one which he had obtained through his wife as dowry, and six which he had acquired by purchase with money he had saved during his fifteen years at sea, including, notably, the land on which he had built his new house. As Thomas angrily related, he had received absolutely nothing from his father. In fact, I was not in a position to know whether the animosity between Thomas and Mitsos preceded Mitsos's refusal to make over any property. All Thomas would say was that his father was old, ignorant (*aghrammatos*), and closed (*klistos*), and that he, Thomas, possessed one mentality (*mialo*) and his father another. But inheritance (or its lack) was certainly involved in their dispute. Once again, there was a quite traditional element in this: the younger generation's impatience to obtain from their fathers the resources that would guarantee their economic independence; the older generation's reluctance to part with that on which, in the final analysis, their authority had always rested. But within this traditional area of potential conflict, new factors had come into play. Like the majority of Spartokhoriots in early middle age, Thomas was not really dependent for his livelihood on a patrimony. Fifteen years on the ships had left him with considerable capital, and it was this that had allowed him to build a large new house despite his father's refusal to make over any land, and equally despite the fact that the *patriko spiti* could not be considered crowded. Mitsos and his wife were its only occupants, and in this case neolocal residence could not be construed as a necessity, and was revealed for what it was: the result of a desire to escape the authority of the older generation. That desire did not escape the notice of such old men as Mitsos who complained that they were left alone and uncared for and muttered that children were like birds who eat everything, and then fly from the nest. They fought back by intensifying their hold on what, under changed circumstances, was no longer sufficient to stop the resented dissolution of their household, for their grip on land and property – on the once indispensable resources of a peasant economy – merely aggravated a situation it could not prevent. Some even threatened to bequeath their property, or some substantial portion of it, not to their sons, but to their *ghambri*, their sons-in-law, if in the end it was their daughters (on whom no traditional responsibility to remain within the *patriko spiti* had ever rested) who cared for them. Although in accord with the possibilities of Greek testamentary law, the threat posed a momentous transgression of the locally sacrosanct rules of inheritance (hence its ideological weight). In their economically, and hence socially, disadvantaged position, however, it was at least a threat that old men were willing to make.

But the case of Thomas and his father was extreme. On the whole the desire of the young to establish separate residence was accepted with good grace by the older generation. Some parents felt neglected. Some were neglected. To eat alone was cited as the nadir of human existence. But generally speaking most of the older generation admitted neolocal residence on marriage to be a good thing, or rather they admitted cheerfully enough that nowadays it was to be expected. Sadness or resentment at the break-up of the extended family was, after all, compensated for by the manifest evidence of their children's worldly success, their fine new houses. And given the competitive nature of interfamilial relationships, it was a moot point for the older generation whether living in an extended family with their married children was better than having their children prematurely establish their own households. Cohabitation could always be cited with pride by the elderly as evidence for the closeness of familial bonds and the respect in which their children held them, but it was also always possible for cohabitation to be construed by neighbours as a sign of poverty, and an admission that sons had not done so well that they could afford to construct a new house. Besides, the reasons for neolocal residence were well understood by the older generation. They were the same as those that had always been responsible for the eventual break-up of the extended family once the father died. Just as the blame for the eventual fragmentation of the *spiti* when brothers went their separate ways after their father's death was conventionally attributed to the supposed inability of their wives to cohabit, so in changed circumstances it was the *nifes*, the 'brides' or daughters-in-law, who had to shoulder the responsibility for a son's immediate neolocal residence on marriage. Few young women, parents explained to me, were nowadays willing to live under the domestic authority of their mother-in-law. Equally, few young women were willing to tolerate the habits of old men. 'We're old fellows (*yerondes*),' said my coffee-shop companions, 'and perhaps we cough a bit in the night, and so the *nifi* doesn't want us', whereupon followed such a spirited demonstration of hacking and gargling that the argument was substantially validated on the spot. But although neolocal residence on marriage was usually accepted, and its desirability for the younger generation generally conceded, the stress on the solidarity between the generations was all the more important lest a *spiti* prematurely divided be thought a family riven by strife. As might be expected, the assertion of solidarity was of more concern to the senior generation than to the junior, and old men and women who proudly pointed out the new dwellings constructed by their sons quickly added that they themselves were also respected by their children who never failed to give to them. In this context, the question of undivided land (as opposed to an undivided *spiti*) took on a separate moral significance.

In recounting the situation of Thomas and Mitsos, I have already introduced a distinction between the inheritance of land and the inheritance of a house: Thomas knew that he would not inherit his father's house until Mitsos was dead, but he had expected that his father would make over some land to him while he was still alive. The stated rules of Spartokhoriot inheritance spoke only of the equal division of both between sons, but for several reasons some distinction had always to be made between land and houses. First, on purely practical grounds, land could be divided to a degree that houses could not. Second, although in principle both land and houses were reserved for sons to the exclusion of daughters, the *patriko spiti* was more rigorously the male inheritance, and a small amount of land was often transferred to daughters by way of dowry. Finally, it was not necessarily the case that the division of land occurred simultaneously with the division of the house. By the time of my fieldwork a disjunction between co-residence within a single household and common ownership of land was an established feature of Spartokhoriot inheritance. What was difficult to determine was the extent to which the disjuncture was a result of recent economic and demographic changes. At all events, sometimes land was still held in common between a father and sons despite the fact that one or more sons had already left the *patriko spiti* and set up a separate household; sometimes land was still held in common between brothers after their father had died and after they had already divided the *patriko spiti* between them and set up separate households; sometimes a division of land was already made between father and son(s) while both generations were still co-resident within the same household.

To take the last possibility first, Yorghos and his wife, and Yorghos's son Takis and his wife and children, all lived together in the one *spiti*. Moreover, Yorghos and Takis worked their land together. When I asked about ownership of the land both were adamant that the land was theirs together – they were, after all, father and son, and what belonged to the one belonged to the other. However, according to forms filled in for the Agricultural Bank, as early as 1963 Takis owned six *stremmata* of land in his own name which he had acquired by gift (or *inter vivos* inheritance) from his father (and a further three *stremmata* had come to him as part of his wife's dowry). For his part, Yorghos had thirty *stremmata* separately registered in his name. It should be stressed that when it comes to inheritance (and dowry) in rural Greece, legal title is not necessarily the issue (Clark 1988: 335–5), and it is possible that for the purpose of acquiring loans from the Agricultural Bank there had been some advantage for Yorghos and Takis to present themselves as independent landowners. But most likely what Yorghos was doing in making over land to Takis *inter vivos* followed along the lines of established practice. Since Takis was an only son, in due course he would in any case inherit the entirety of his father's estate (as would Thomas, Mitsos's threats notwithstanding); but in the meantime Yorghos was granting Takis a modicum of independence as an expression of good will and as part of a gradual transition of authority from one generation to the next. It should be noted that the personal relationship between Yorghos and Takis was an extremely close one.

The nature of actual legal title notwithstanding, fathers and sons who lived separately also often claimed to hold and to work their land together, and the phrase *'Then khorisame'* ('We haven't divided') was pronounced with pride, for it suggested the maintenance of the *patriko spiti*'s unity despite divided residence. The further implication was that those who had divided had thereby demonstrated their lack of familial cohesion. But whatever the moral advantage that could be wrung from the situation, the paradox was that precisely the same set of changed economic circumstances that allowed the early dissolution of the *patriko spiti* were also often responsible for the non-division of land between the generations. The wealth that had come to the younger generation allowed them to set up their own households before their father's death and the full receipt of their patrimony, but equally, employment in shipping meant that the younger generation were not seriously interested in agriculture. For the most part, not dividing land meant simply leaving in the hands of the older generation an asset that the young had no particular urgency to realize.

A similar situation obtained between brothers. Brothers who had divided their land were adamant that joint ownership and joint management of their paternally inherited estate were impossible. One brother would always want to do one thing, another would want to do another (so they said), and thus conflict would inevitably ensue. Better to divide the land and let everyone go their own way. But those who lived more or less permanently in Athens were often content to leave their land in the care of a brother or brothers resident in the village in return for a modest share of the produce, and once again this could be construed as the maintenance of an undivided estate and described with a strong element of moral self-congratulation. 'No, we haven't divided. We are brothers – why should we?' Here convenience was in new and happy accord with an old ideal – new, because what had previously made the ideal impossible (competition for those economic resources on which social autonomy was predicated) no longer applied.

Brothers

As mentioned in Chapter 6, the relationship between brothers was upheld as the model of loyalty, amity, equality, disinterested affection and cooperation. Brothers supplied the paradigm for friendship, and close friends often referred to each other as brothers. The phrases *'ena filiko prama'* and *'ena adherfiko prama'*, 'a friendly matter' and 'a brotherly matter', were used interchangeably, and though it may seem strange that friendship should express the nature of kinship, it should be remembered that the essence of friendship lies in the fact that it is a relationship between equals, and brothers in Spartokhori were supposed to be precisely that, for in terms of kinship only age distinguished them. In all other respects, and unlike parent and child or brother and sister, they were equals within the family. It was, however, from their very equality that difficulties arose, for, unlike friends, they had not come together as equals but been cast as equals, and their equality derived not only from their genealogical identity, but from their shared dependence on a single patrimony. Whereas friends might assert their equality by calling themselves brothers (thereby turning a blind eye to any actual differences of circumstance), brothers had to maintain their equality in order to remain friends. In their youth brothers were indeed friends and equals because nothing distinguished them (not sex, age or parentage), and because everything united them (their common economic contribution to their *spiti*, their common responsibility for the welfare of their sisters, their shared reputation as sons of the house). But once the *spiti* divided and brothers married, the pursuit of equality became the cause of their friction, for now it could be maintained only in the face of competing claims to those same resources that were once shared. This development did not occur, it should be noted, between sisters, since they did not normally inherit, nor therefore between brothers-in-law, whose relationship was assimilated to that of brothers, but which did not have to encounter the tensions created by a house destined to divide.

This ambivalence of the relationship between brothers was well recognized by the Spartokhoriots. Indeed it could hardly escape their notice, and while the commonplace metaphors of daily life continued to assert brothers as the paradigm for friends, everyone waited for them to fall out. The village was disturbed one day by a screaming match that echoed from one end of Spartokhori to the other, and all the more clearly since it was past midday when everyone was supposed to be asleep. The elderly protagonists were neighbours. They were also brothers, and their houses, exact divisions of a paternal *spiti*, adjoined. The immediate cause of the confrontation was a newly erected drainpipe that trespassed a matter of inches from one property into the other. The old men were amply supported by their wives. A crowd quickly gathered, and the argument spread. Some people took sides, but most intervened in an attempt to quell the dispute (never a very successful undertaking in Spartokhori), since so public a display of animosity was considered unseemly, and all those who were related to the brothers felt their own standing undermined. Furious shouts of '*Dropi! Dropi!* (Shame! Shame!)' were exchanged. However, one old grandmother who had wandered out to see what all the fuss was about, and who stood on the outskirts of the crowd next to me, simply commented to herself, 'Bah! Brothers again!'

Naturally the dispute had not remained fixed on the question of the drainpipe. A whole history of minor irritations, transgressions and crimes was raked over. But whatever the accumulated causes for the outburst, it was clear that the basis for the brothers' animosity lay in the rules of inheritance which specified an equal division of property, but which did not specify how that division was to be made. Practice appeared to be quite various. Most Spartokhoriots were firmly of the belief that it was a good father's business to make it clear to his sons exactly what each was to inherit (cf. Clark 1988: 333). This could entail some calculation of the value of a share of the *patriko spiti* set against, for example, any paternal land already made over for the building of a new house by a brother or brothers who had already married and left the family home. But the stress laid on a good father's obligation to make such matters clear was based on the Spartokhoriots' acute awareness of the conflicts that had resulted over the years between brothers when division of the patrimony had been left entirely to the heirs. One old man pointed out to me his *spiti* which was an exact half of his father's two-storey house, and which he and his brother had split straight down the middle. He then showed me another freestanding double-storeyed building on the other side of the street, which had also belonged to his father. It had once been a shop, but it had been shut up and unused for years. He asked me whether I did not think it would make a perfectly good house, and whether I did not think it a shame that it was closed and unoccupied. I hesitantly agreed that, yes, it was a shame. This, he triumphantly affirmed, was his opinion too. He had wanted to take that building and turn it into a home, leaving the *patriko spiti* in its entirety to his brother, or *vice versa*. It was, he pointed out, only logical. But his brother was not, alas, a logical man. He was a closed and stupid man. And so his brother had insisted that an equal division be an equal division, with both buildings shared half-and-half, with the result that both he and his brother now had houses that were only half as big as they could have been, while the other building remained vacant. The division against which my companion railed had been made some thirty years before. The brothers had not been on speaking terms since.

Finally, just as no procedure existed for determining what an equal share of a house (and land) was, so, in the past, no procedure had existed to decide which son was to form a stem household with his parents (or widowed mother or widower father) within the *patriko spiti*, and which were to move out (if the *patriko spiti* was too small for division) to find or construct new residences.[12] Perhaps too many contingencies had always borne on the matter to allow it to become systematic, although in almost all cases it was the youngest son who looked after his aged parent(s) and remained in the *patriko spiti* or their share of it (cf. Clark 1988: 215). He received, however, no extra or larger share for performing this duty, and ultimogeniture certainly played no part in the Sparto-khoriots' own construction of the situation.[13] They stressed that both house and land were always divided equally between sons, regardless of birth order, and regardless of where sons might happen to be living at the time of their father's retirement or death. The only concession was that brothers were free to sell their portion of a house (or land) to each other. What numerically looked like a convention of the youngest son remaining with his parents was explained away as being no more than the natural result of age differences: older brothers tended to marry before younger brothers and (despite statements to the effect that in the old days everybody used to live together) married brothers tended to move out of the paternal household leaving younger unmarried brothers at home. Moreover, men who were not living in a share of their *patriko spiti* but who had acquired a house either by marriage or purchase, or who had built on family land near their natal *spiti*, invariably explained that they had moved out on the quite pragmatic grounds that the *patriko spiti* was too full.

[12]By contrast, see, for example, the elaborate systems reported by Friedl (1964a: 60–4) and Saulnier-Thiercelin (1985).

[13]But see, for example, du Boulay (1974: 20). In Ambeli (as in other parts of Greece) it had been standard practice for youngest sons to inherit the house.

The contradictions of agnation

Sons were set against fathers, brothers against brothers. These were at least the fault lines of potential conflict in a patrilineal system of inheritance that reserved the means of production and reproduction of an agricultural society for those in whom, ideologically, its continuity was vested: men. The interrelated social and economic changes that occurred in the postwar years – overseas and urban migration, the demise of agriculture, employment on the ships, the shift to a wage-based economy, the substantial enrichment of the younger generation – did not change the inheritance system itself. What had changed were some of the consequences, both material and immaterial, of the system to household composition and domestic relationships. Sons still stood to inherit their share of a *patriko spiti* and their share of land, but with the shift in the mode of production sons were no longer dependent on their patrimony in order to take their place in society as economically independent and autonomous adults. The rupture of the peasant economy thus spelled the rupture of its constituent social unit, the household, for sons were able to construct their own neolocal residences on marriage. Except in the long term, the inheritance of agricultural land was not an economically important issue for the younger generation. The resultant changes in household composition were not, as we have seen, wholesale. In 1980 20 per cent of Spartokhori's households still constituted stem families, and conversely the large extended family household of the past appears to have been in some respects a myth. Nevertheless, by 1980 there was no doubt that for the younger generation neolocal residence even in the village was the new ideal (and an ideal that, of course, matched the domestic arrangements of those who had emigrated to the city). Whether this change made the traditionally somewhat vexed relationship between fathers and sons worse is, of course, difficult to know and impossible to quantify, but certainly it added a new dimension to it. Some fathers, at least, felt betrayed and accused their sons of deserting them. Some few went so far as to withhold while they were alive any property from their sons, even a building-block for a new house, and threatened to bequeath on their death their property to their daughters (or rather, to their sons-in-law). Sons, for their part, often complained that the old men were difficult, closed, ignorant, and there was no doubt that such charges related to their fathers' attempts to interfere with their domestic plans and arrangements. Other fathers and sons negotiated changing conditions and changed aspirations without difficulty.

Between brothers, however, the same social and economic changes had probably ameliorated relationships. Brothers who were not on speaking terms, who were quarrelling with each other (*malomeni*) or cold towards each other (*krii*), were always old men whose inheritance disputes dated back to a time when a house and land were a family's only and indispensable economic resources. By 1980 no married man even contemplated a joint household with a married brother (if, indeed, that had ever been the case), but joint management (as opposed to joint ownership) of land had become *de facto* part of the system of inheritance, if only because men who were employed at sea or who lived in Athens profited from any brother who happened to remain in the village and who was willing to take care of their land. More importantly, however, with the village's economy effectively removed from the village itself, brothers were no longer in competition with each other for their share of paternally inherited resources in order to make a living, and although ownership of houses and land remained an issue (for its potential value was well understood), none of the friction and tension involved in deciding whether to work their land together, or how to work their land together, applied.

But whether one considers the circumstances of 1980, or what can be inferred for an earlier period, Spartokhori's system of patrilineal inheritance involves something of a contradiction between what once would have been labelled its social structure and the nature of personal and affective relationships that accompanied that structure. I argued in Chapter 4 that Spartokhori's kinship structure was bilateral. At the same time I suggested that, on strictly empirical grounds, Spartokhori showed most of the features that have led some anthropologists, in particular Couroucli (1985) and (more cautiously) Herzfeld (1983; 1985), to talk of agnatic relations as dominant. Spartokhori's system of inheritance is one of the features that could be considered as strongly agnatic. Property (like names, both official surnames and nicknames, and like member-ship of a particular *soi*) was transmitted from father to sons. As Herzfeld rightly cautions, however, such a system of property transmission might better be under-stood in terms of 'patriarchy' than 'patriliny' (Herzfeld 1983), a strong preference for male inheritance and control that results in an agnation as a by-product. Nevertheless the system resulted in the creation of agnatic (though in Sparto-khori's case unnamed) neighbourhoods, with fathers, sons, brothers and patri-lateral first, second and third cousins living in close proximity (as well as owning adjoining farmland, and in some cases jointly owning, for example, an olive-oil mill). And yet these very features of the inheritance system that could be construed as indicative of an agnatic social structure were also those that tended to create not solidarity, but conflict. Overwhelmingly close relationships between men were not those between agnates, but those between matrilateral relatives or affines. This contradiction between structure and sentiment – and it appears to be cross-culturally a common contradiction within agnatic systems[14] – becomes clearer if we now turn to the complementary aspect of Spartokhoriot male inheritance and its social consequences: namely, to dowry and to the personal relations created through women and via affinity.

[14] See, for example, Peters (1976). The contradiction appears even in Evans-Pritchard's classic account of an agnatic society, *The Nuer* (1940: 210).

8
Romance & Dowry

In 1979 Roula's brother, Kostas, got married. Roula herself had married in about 1965 with what was considered to be a good dowry of 100,000 drachmes (approximately £1,600 at the time), sufficient, at all events, to set up the general store which she and her husband, a farmer and fisherman, ran together, and which provided them with the better part of their annual income. But when her younger brother Kostas married in 1979, he received no dowry from his wife. In fact the young woman he married was an orphan (that is to say, her father had died), and she had been brought up in the household of her brother, already a married man with children of his own. This brother had most certainly offered Kostas a dowry, for the full responsibility of arranging a sister's marriage and of providing her with a dowry had always fallen on brothers if their father was dead. And so when Kostas proposed marriage, the young woman's brother (being a generous man, and solicitous of his sister's welfare) asked Kostas what he wanted to take. Kostas declined to take anything. His reasons were twofold. First, he was a ship's officer earning in excess of 50,000 drachmes a month, while the young woman's brother (older than Kostas) made a precarious living as an olive farmer. Under the circumstances Kostas considered that it would have been a matter of shame (*dropi*) to demand a dowry when he was so much wealthier than was the man who was offering to provide one. But second, Kostas had professed (quite truthfully, it would seem) that he was deeply in love, and that dowry was therefore irrelevant.

A number of old men were standing around in the general store when Kostas's sister, Roula, related this story of her brother's recent marriage. All chimed in to agree vociferously that this was now the way things were: '*Ta pedhia dhen zitane prika simera* (The boys don't seek dowry nowadays).' But in a story related to me precisely to demonstrate the unimportance of dowry, there was an odd inconsistency. In the course of her account, Roula also mentioned that Kostas had declined to take dowry not only on the grounds that he was in love with his future bride, and that he was a relatively rich sailor while his prospective brother-in-law was a relatively poor farmer, but also because his prospective brother-in-law had two daughters of his own to consider. The implication was that in due course this brother-in-law would need whatever financial resources he had in order to dower them. But by 1980 such inconsistencies and contradictions were not uncommon. Dowry had become a complex issue, and strange things were happening. Three different but interrelated developments were involved: first, urban migration;

second, the greatly increased wealth of the younger generation of seamen; and finally, what can best be described as a general attitudinal change in the relative weightings of personal attraction and material considerations in the formation of a match. The results were not entirely predictable. Some young men, like Kostas, were marrying young women with only a nominal dowry, or without any dowry at all. However, in many instances what was being given vastly exceeded the value of dowries twenty years before, and dowry was undergoing the same sort of inflation widely reported for other areas of rural Greece in the 1960s and 1970s (Friedl 1964a: 66; Allen 1979; du Boulay 1983). Because of the change in attitude towards dowry, however, where it was given and such inflation took place, it was accompanied by a recategorization. What was given to women on marriage was no longer *prika* (dowry), but *voithia* (help), so that in general what the old men said (and what everybody else in Spartokhori said) could still be claimed as true: 'the boys don't seek dowry nowadays'. In short, while the pattern of male inheritance (equal division of the *patriko spiti* and of land between sons) remained stable despite changed circumstances, when it came to the provision of a dowry towards the establishment of the new household that on marriage a woman would form with her husband, the system appeared to be undergoing a series of quite radical changes.

The radical nature of these changes cannot be doubted. The proportion of a family's wealth taken by women on marriage had in some cases increased more than tenfold; in others it had diminished to nothing. Ideationally, dowry, once viewed as a basic consideration in the choice of a marriage partner, was now being seen to compromise the true nature of marriage's bond. Dowry was being pulled two ways, caught in a nexus of economic and ideological shifts. Yet there were continuities. The Spartokhoriots said of the past, 'We gave whatever we could.' That, in 1980, was what they continued to do. And although 'help' had replaced 'dowry' when it came to assisting a daughter (or sister) to create a new household, for the most part dowry had always been just that, a form of help. What people could give in 1980, however, was extremely various depending on where they were situated in Spartokhori's changed economy, while the denial of 'dowry' and the stress on 'help' followed from a more general ideological shift in which personal attraction, the sway of emotions, in short love, rather than economic security, was seen as the proper basis for marriage, a form of modernity rendered all the more persuasive since for most young people economic security had already been achieved. Thus while romance and dowry might seem a strange coupling for the title of a chapter, since the two are often seen as mutually antithetical (and were so seen by most Spartokhoriots), by 1980 they were also subtly intertwined.

Dowry in the agricultural economy

As elsewhere in rural Greece, dowry had been important in Spartokhori not only for the receiver, but also for the giver. A family's ability to marry its daughters well was a measure – indeed an outstanding measure – of its social and moral worth. The size of a woman's dowry was clear indication both of the concern her parents had to establish her in the best possible position, and of their ability to do so (cf. Friedl 1964a: 69). Nevertheless, as inheritors of their families' wealth, daughters took second place to sons. Older Spartokhoriots were insistent that in accordance with their general poverty, dowry in the past had been meagre. People simply gave what they could: some sheep or goats, a few trees, a small plot of land. But though livestock, trees and land all featured in accounts of the old days, Spartokhoriots made it clear that in the majority of cases the major portion of a dowry had been money; not agricultural land (much less a house) on which, in an agricultural economy, the reconstitution of the household depended, but rather that economy's hard-won surplus, its scarce reserves of cash (cf. du Boulay 1974: 272).

Files kept by the Agricultural Bank in Lefkadha which recorded the amounts of land owned by clients as well as its mode of acquisition (inherited, acquired by purchase, or given as dowry) roughly confirmed the Spartokhoriots' accounts. Out of a total 3,584 *stremmata* of land recorded, only 397 *stremmata*, or approximately 11 per cent, had been acquired by dowry. Just under a further 11 per cent had been acquired by purchase, and the remaining 78 per cent appears to have been patrilineally inherited. A more telling statistic is that out of the 101 (male) landowners accounted for by the files, only 36 stated that they had acquired any land via their wives' dowries. In short, 74 per cent of women had brought no land with them on marriage. Even these figures may overestimate the contribution of dowry to a family's landholdings, for the sample included certain exceptional cases. Two men had acquired the totality of their landholdings via dowry; one man had acquired nineteen of his twenty-five *stremmata* via dowry; and one man had acquired nineteen of his twenty-six *stremmata* via dowry. If these cases are discounted, then the proportion of land transferred via dowry was only 9.4 per cent. It is worth noting that three of these four men had been immigrants to Spartokhori, and all four had married 'heiresses'. In fact where men had acquired land via their wives' dowries, in over half the cases the amount of land they acquired was more than the amount of land they had inherited.

Receipt of land as dowry thus clearly correlated with an absence of inherited land, or with a disproportionately small amount of inherited land, and whatever role personal attraction had played, the available figures suggest that it was immigrants and poor men who were motivated to seek out the sort of bride who could mend their fortunes, or else that the parents of such brides felt compelled to supply their sons-in-law with land to support their daughters. But normally, and preferably, dowries had been money; only since money was scarce, some families gave what they could by offering olive trees, some livestock, or a small field. Some families, too, had sold land in order to acquire money for dowries. Only by depriving sons of part of their due and expected inheritance, however, could this be done. One example may show the gravity with which this expedient was viewed. Old Harilaos, a retired farmer, had seven children, four sons and three daughters. Two of his sons were prosperous sailors, but Harilaos himself was extremely poor. In the late 1960s one of Harilaos's daughters married an Athenian resident, and in order to provide an appropriate dowry Harilaos had begun to sell land. Alarmed by their father's actions, Harilaos's two sailor sons contributed fifty thousand drachmes between them towards their sister's dowry 'so that *kseni anthropi* ['foreign people', ie. non-family] should not have our land.' Harilaos himself contributed a further forty thousand drachmes, and a satisfactory dowry was raised. The interesting point is that in return for their monetary contribution towards their sister's dowry, Harilaos's two sons immediately received olive trees and land from their father. In effect they bought from their father a part of their own inheritance rather than see it lost to outsiders.

Dowry inflation

In most respects Harilaos and his sons had responded conventionally enough towards the prospect of a daughter's marriage, and towards the prospect of land not being transmitted to its rightful heirs, Harilaos doing his best to ensure that his daughter married well, and his sons intervening to ensure that they did not lose their patrimony. But by the 1960s the effects of changing economic circumstances were already evident. Harilaos was not marrying his daughter to a village farmer for whom a satisfactory dowry might have been a modest monetary settlement, or failing that a plot of land, or some trees, but to an Athenian-dweller. Similarly, what enabled Harilaos's two sons to rescue their patrimony was the fact that they, too, were not farmers. The money they could afford to expend came from their employment in the merchant marine. Monetary dowries, which had always been the commonest form of dowry because land was reserved for sons, were now becoming a requirement because agricultural land no longer provided an income for urban migrants. The real difference lay in the amount of money, which continued to increase from the 1960s onwards. Accurate figures were difficult to obtain (for the Spartokhoriots were understandably reluctant to reveal precisely what they had given or received), but Harilaos and his sons had given 90,000 drachmes between them, and it was generally agreed that in the late 1950s and early 1960s dowries ranged between 50,000 drachmas and 100,000 drachmes, with the latter being considered a very good dowry. By 1980, an amount of 500,000 drachmas rather than 50,000 drachmes was considered good, but not excessive.

In the simplest of terms, many Spartokhoriots were giving a great deal more to their daughters on marriage because many of them had a great deal more to give, certainly in terms of money, because the influx of wealth into the community from the 1960s onwards had been precisely monetary, consisting of money earned in wages and salaries aboard the ships, and money remitted from overseas emigration and employment. But not only were Spartokhoriot parents able to afford larger dowries; their daughters and sons-in-law also required larger dowries, for urban migration meant that the husband's *patriko spiti* no longer provided a young couple with their normal place of residence. It was left to dowry to provide them with their urban home. And since urban real estate was expensive, dowry had to increase (cf. Allen 1979; du Boulay 1983). A few examples will illustrate this combination of increased wealth and increased need. Christos dowered two of his daughters in the late 1960s. One married a resident of Katomeri, Spartokhori's neighbouring village. She received a dowry of 75,000 drachmes plus some land and trees. The other daughter married a Spartokhoriot sailor, and she and her husband were intent on moving to Athens. The result was that this daughter received a monetary dowry of 250,000 drachmes, a matter which Christos was not above complaining about. Similarly old Captain Panos married his daughter in the early 1970s to a sailor from Spartokhori. He gave the couple a house in Athens as dowry, and it was, as he stressed, a house, not an apartment, and had cost well over 1 million drachmes. Such a dowry would have been unheard of in the 1950s, though it was also unlikely that Panos supplied it himself. It was his wealthy sons, sailors and ship-owners in their own right, who were in the position to provide their sister with such a dowry, just as it was they who had built for their father the large village house in which he lived. Similarly Mitsos, an immigrant to Spartokhori who in the 1950s had secured his own house and land in the village by marrying an 'heiress', provided a dowry house in Preveza in the 1970s for one of his daughters who had married a ship's captain. Mitsos lived in some style in the village, but again his wealth derived from his four sons, who, in partnership with their brothers-in-law, owned two successful steak houses in the United States.

Where, however, dowry took the form of urban real estate, it was not only its value that increased, but the whole balance of its contribution towards the reproduction of the household. Within the agricultural economy, the family house had been provided by the husband's inheritance of his share of the *patriko spiti*. With urban migration, it was increasingly dowry that supplied a family's place of residence. Thus the pattern of Spartokhoriot inheritance was arguably undergoing a transformation whereby the economic contribution of the bride's and the groom's families were being inverted, the bride's family supplying a couple's major material asset. In a sense, uxorilocal residence was replacing patrilocal residence (cf. Allen 1973: 90–5, 1979; Loizos 1975; Clark 1988: 42). Nevertheless, men who had shifted to Athens still stood to inherit their share of their *patriko spiti* in the village, regardless of the contribution made by their wives' dowries towards their urban residence. And it was still the husband or the husband's family that provided a house when a newly married couple elected to remain in the village, though this usually involved the building of a new house, rather than sharing with the husband's parents. Indeed, with their new-found wealth, some young sailors were going so far as to construct and furnish new village houses merely in anticipation of marriage, something that looked very much like a form of male dowry. As one old woman approvingly remarked, 'No boy gets married these days without his own house.' By 1980, however, the cost of building even a quite modest village house stood at approximately 1.5 million drachmes, and if paternal land for a building-block was not available (or had not been made over), it too was expensive and difficult to come by, partly because of the increased amount of building taking place, partly because of the reluctance of villagers to sell land to their fellows. In these circumstances it was not uncommon for the bride's family also to make some contribution towards the cost of neolocal residence. There was only one case of a new village house actually being constructed as a dowry-house (and to an extent it was an ambiguous case, since the bride-to-be had no brothers and thus in any case stood to inherit her father's property), but in several marriages that took place between 1977 and 1980, the bride's parents' provided a building-block; given the traditional mode of property

222 Romance & Dowry

succession within the village, this was itself a significant innovation (though one for which urban migration had doubtless set a precedent).

In sum, then, by 1980 something like a system of dual inheritance was emerging in Spartokhori, a new tradition whereby women provided their family's place of residence in the city, and men continued to provide a house in the village (Allen 1979; Clark 1988). The former cannot be talked about in terms of matrilineal succession, nor does it quite match the seemingly traditional system of the northeast Aegean or even the system that developed this century in the Piraeus suburb of Yerania (Hirschon 1983, 1989: 106–33), for houses were not transmitted from mother to daughter(s). Instead, the provision of a family's urban place of residence was effected through a greatly augmented dowry that still represented the contribution of the bride's father (and/or brothers) towards her new household. In this respect it closely resembled the system in rural Cyprus whereby each daughter receives a new house on marriage, a system which Loizos has shown to have been an innovation of the 1920s resulting from male overseas emigration, and thus a shortage of men and an inflation of dowry (1975). At the same time, although male inheritance of the *patriko spiti* remained unchallenged, and although (as a result of the preference for neolocal residence) the ability of young men to provide houses in the village was given even greater emphasis to the extent that some were building them in the mere expectation of marriage, a contribution to the construction of a new village house by the bride's family was also becoming accepted.

The decline of dowry

In spite of the evidence presented above, the commonplace assertion in Spartokhori that dowry was no longer of any importance also had empirical justification, and paradoxically as a consequence of the same set of economic changes that had in other cases resulted in parents giving greatly increased dowries. The shift from peasant agriculture to wage labour resulted not only in an influx of wealth, but also in a reversal of the traditional distribution of economic resources between the generations. Generally speaking it was the older generation of farmers who were the poor, and the younger generation of sailors who were the rich. This new inequality played havoc with the dowry system, for the generation of men who, as prospective sons-in-law, ought to have been receiving dowry had in many instances become considerably wealthier than the generation of men who, as prospective fathers-in-law, ought to have been giving dowry, at least if wealth is measured in terms of disposable income and not the ownership of land. Thus both the tradition by which land was reserved for sons, and the shift in the village's economy to wage labour, meant that if the older generation of farmers were to give dowry, then they were required to give precisely what they did not have, money, and to give it those who already had plenty of it. After all, a young sailor could earn in a month what an old farmer might make in a year.

In this context the assertion that the boys do not seek dowry any more was open to a double interpretation. It reflected (as it was intended to) a certain change in attitude towards marriage in general, but it also derived from the Sparto-

Plate 8.1 Carrying the *roukha*

khoriots' own awareness of economic disparities. In the end what inhibited young men from seeking a dowry were in fact quite traditional sentiments, those of honour (*timi*) and shame (*dropi*). Just as in the past it had been a matter of honour to dower one's daughter well, so now it was also a shame to seek, or to be seen to seek, a good dowry from one's father-in-law. The reversed economic inequalities between potential dowry-givers and potential dowry-receivers had in many instances become too great for any young man who blatantly sought a large dowry not to appear positively rapacious. Some people pointed out that of course there was always the *roukha*,[1] the lacework, linen, carpets and rugs that every young bride still brought to her new house as trousseau, and which represented a considerable investment in both money and time, but the consideration was contemptuously dismissed by others (cf. Friedl 1964a: 56).[2] The *roukha* were costly, but they scarcely made up a dowry. In general, it was affirmed, dowries were no longer important. The boys no longer sought them, and happily married without them. It was merely a question of those who have, give; those who don't have, don't give.

Marriages between sailors and the daughters of farmers thus did take place without dowry. Still, there remained something of a difference between a young man not seeking dowry, and an older one not offering it. In 1977 a friend of mine who was earning nearly 50,000 drachmes a month at sea married the daughter of a farmer, one of the poorest men in the village. Yet he did receive a dowry. It amounted to 13,000 drachmes (about £215 UK at the time). As a contribution to setting up a new household, the amount was negligible, especially in the light of the groom's income. Nevertheless, it still represented a considerable sacrifice on the part of the bride's father, who thereby showed himself to be an honourable man. He had, after all, given what he could. At the same time, no one could say that the young sailor had married for money. His bride was beautiful, and at least from his point of view, the marriage was a love match. Credit reflected on all sides. Similarly, during my first year of fieldwork, Stathis, a retired sailor, was working night and day to build up a dowry for his elder daughter. Stathis was approaching sixty, and had been a sailor for twenty years, but he had started late and never risen in the ranks. He was by no means a wealthy man when he retired and reverted to the life of a farmer, but it was at this stage that his daughter became engaged to a ship's cook who, by contrast, was receiving a very high salary. No dowry was sought by this young man, but not only did Stathis give his daughter the better part of the lump sum he had received on retirement,[3] he also took on whatever labouring jobs were available in the village in order to supplement it. Any suggestion that a dowry was a requirement for his daughter's marriage was nevertheless strongly rejected, not only by Stathis but by everyone else who discussed the matter.

In all likelihood Stathis's attitude represented no great departure from the past.

---

[1] Literally *roukha* means clothes, but it was used in Spartokhori (and elsewhere) to refer to all the trousseau articles and soft furnishings (Salamone and Stanton, 1986).

[2] Salamone and Stanton report that in Amouliani, a village in Khalkidhiki, 'this part of the dowry may alone approximate or exceed the family's annual wage-earning power'(1986: 107). However, Amouliani seems to be exceptional in the emphasis put on *roukha*.

[3] Superannuation received by sailors consisted of two parts, a pension and an *efapaks*, which was a lump-sum payment.

Parents were solicitous of their daughters' welfare and concerned for their own good name. All the same, the continual stress on the fact that dowries were no longer important and played no part in determining a marriage did contrast with what I was told of the old days, when, said the elderly, marriage contracts were drawn up specifying in fine detail the amount of money and goods to be brought by a woman on her wedding day (cf. Vernier 1991: 55). According to my coffee-shop companions, the items were checked off against the contract before the actual ceremony, and should anything be missing, then the wedding was off. 'But,' laughed the old men, 'that's all gone now.' What appeared to have taken its place was something like competitive gift-giving where the motivation lay in a moral and sentimental concern to do well (and to be seen to do well) by a daughter and her husband, rather than in any necessity to supply a dowry in order to marry a daughter. It was the perceived removal of this necessity that made it possible for the Spartokhoriots to deny the importance of dowry despite its continued existence and frequent increase. But in fact the requirement of dowry had merely lost its rigidity, and been placed in a morally ambivalent area where it could be both a shame to ask for one, and a shame not to offer one. And such a situation could be exploited. One young sailor from Spartokhori was about to marry the daughter of a farmer from Katomeri. The girl's father had said, 'We're not selling a pig, you know – ask for whatever you want and it's yours.' In the face of a remark that so pointedly rejected any notion of an economic transaction, and substituted instead a boundless generosity inspired by paternal knowledge of the young woman's own worth, the sailor felt unable to demand anything, and consequently received nothing. I do not know if the story was true, but it was circulating amongst the old men in Spartokhori's coffee-shops, who found it extremely funny and pronounced the girl's father admirably 'cunning' (*poniros*).

The denial of dowry

Not all marriages, however, were between wealthy young sailors and the daughters of farmers. By the late 1970s many of Spartokhori's sailors already had marriageable daughters of their own, as did some of Spartokhori's professional elite who lived in Athens. As I have mentioned, there was already a tendency for the wealthier and better educated to marry the wealthier and better educated. Amongst this group there was no inversion of economic position between prospective dowry-givers and prospective dowry-receivers. Indeed, if the groom was a young professional, or training to become one, then in contrast to the young sailor it was likely that he would not be financially independent. Perhaps paradoxically it was amongst the more socially mobile and successful that the traditional inequality of financial resources between the generations was restored, with members of the younger generation being dependent on the older generation until they had established themselves in their chosen careers.

It was, however, precisely amongst the wealthier and better educated that the notion of dowry was most vehemently rejected. Here the rejection stemmed not so much from changed economic circumstances, as from what might be deemed their secondary and ideological consequences, from the fact that such people were educated and socially mobile, and therefore saw in dowry a potent symbol of backwardness from which they were anxious to disassociate themselves. Through newspapers, magazines, television and radio they had become extremely sensitive to the bad name that dowry had long had amongst Greek intellectuals and reformers, by whom it has been seen as one of the chief mechanisms of female subordination (Pandazi-Tzifa 1984; Yotopoulos-Marangopoulos 1986; Tzannatos 1986; Skouteri-Dhidhaskalou 1984), and they had become even more sensitive to the notion that as a Greek tradition (often thought to be an exclusively Greek tradition – see Kaklamanaki 1984) dowry was something that marked their nation off as non-European – a perception sometimes confirmed by the remarks of foreigners and tourists (happy to discover in Greece the exotic-as-primitive) as well as by their own experiences overseas where dowry was seen as a Mediterranean or a Hellenic atavism. In short dowry stood in the way of *to moderno*, 'the modern', which was somewhat vaguely understood as conformity with 'the West's' generic representations of itself. Indeed, their opinions closely matched those which, only three years later, Greece's newly elected socialist prime minister, Andreas Papandreou (whom most educated Spartokhoriots supported) was to pronounce on the occasion of dowry's so-called 'abolition':[4]

> [Dowry] was an anachronistic institution that humiliated women and adulterated the essence of marriage by turning it from a free choice of a profoundly human relationship into a coarse financial transaction symbolizing the woman's submission to the dominant male (Andreas Papandreou, quoted by Mario Modiano, *The Times*, 1 December 1982: 8).

Spartokhoriot rhetoric was not quite so bombastic (and it might not even have been so sincere), but it roughly followed suit, and if the educated class discussed dowry, then either it was carefully placed in the past where it could assume a certain folkloric charm (along with piracy, murder, wife-beating or simply unimaginable poverty, of which one might be almost proud provided it was clear that such things no longer existed), or else it was attributed to 'them', that is to say the unprogressive and uneducated amongst the villagers, as opposed to 'us', the discussants (and, of course, the anthropologist). For such people the exclusive motivation for marriage had to be love, and dowry was seen to compromise the purity of that sentiment, or to render it suspect. But it was also amongst this group that the material transactions attendant on marriage were so much in excess of what had earlier been the case. Daughters commonly received either an apartment in Athens or a substantial sum towards the purchase of one. This involved not hundreds of thousands of drachmes, but millions. Village grandparents (for whom the matter still presented itself in a simpler light) were inclined to boast about the amount of money their sons had expended in providing their grand-daughters with such magnificent dowries, but both the younger generation and their parents argued that such donations were not dowry at all,

---

[4] Dowry was not in fact abolished except in the sense that: a) it no longer existed as a specific form of legal conveyance (with associated restrictions on its disposal, and a reduced form of taxation), and b) it could no longer be demanded or required by a son-in-law. The settlement of property on a daughter at the time of her marriage remains perfectly legal, and the 1983 family law revisions specifically permit parents to make over to their children, whether daughters or sons, up to 5 million drachmes each at a taxation rate of 50% of the rate applied to gifts, exactly the rate that previously applied to dowries (*Simvoulio Isotitas ton Dhio Filon, Ikoyeniako Dhikeo*, n.d.: 21).

or at least not really dowry, because the property had not been settled on daughters *in order* to make them more marriageable. And the young men who married them did not seek it. The question of property was thus not relevant to the formation of a match, but subsequent and supplementary to it. Marriage itself was motivated by love and love alone; only parents were naturally anxious to do everything in their power to give their children (whether daughters or sons) the best start in the world. The gift of money or property at the time of marriage was therefore merely a form of assistance to make the young people's lives easier. And of course for the most part that is what dowry had always been about, a form of *inter vivos* inheritance designed to assist in the establishment of a new domestic unit at the moment of its inception; a form of female inheritance that represented within a bilateral kinship system the contribution of the woman's family to their daughter's household and, thereby, to their grandchildren.

If anything other than rhetoric had really changed here, then it was less dowry's intrinsic rationale than a consequence of its existence that could occasionally be exploited by those individuals willing or forced to do so: namely, the degree to which dowry could also make a woman marriageable, rather than being something she brought with her on marriage. As one older man said to me, once upon a time if a woman was a 'bit ugly' or a 'bit old', then her parents could always find her a husband by supplying a good dowry. Nowadays it did not matter how much parents were willing to give, no man would marry her. And it was with this shift from the recognition of dowry as an at least possible motive for marriage to the stricture that dowry should be merely a form of assistance on marriage that the recategorization had occurred. Since dowries were not sought as a condition of marriage, what parents gave their daughters was not dowry. And surely, people asked me, parents in Australia and England must love their children and attempt to assist them in a material way? I had to admit that in an irregular fashion this was often the case.

Love and marriage

The Spartokhoriots' ambivalence about dowry was symptomatic of more general ideological shifts in the late 1970s that surrounded the whole question of marriage and of the relationship between men and women, shifts that were part of the agenda of Greece's new socialist party, PASOK, but which found their reflection in village discourse;[5] shifts that also resulted from the villagers' exposure to the stereotypical Western notions of love and romance disseminated by radio, television and popular magazines. Almost all Spartokhoriots, whether young or old, educated or uneducated, semi-migrants or permanent village-dwellers, made two seemingly contradictory sets of remarks about marriage (although their emphases varied). First, they claimed that with rare exceptions individuals married, and always had married, for love (*aghapi*). Second, they claimed, with equal generality, that marriage was an *ikoyeniako prama*, a 'family matter', and pointed out that the majority of matches in the village (and between villagers

[5] PASOK instigated a major overhaul of those parts of the civil code related to family law, and, amongst other things, founded a Council for the Equality of the Two Sexes.

living in Athens) were contracted by *proksenia*, 'arrangement' through intermediaries. As we shall see, there was less of a contradiction between these two claims than might at first appear to be the case, for in practice what an arranged marriage determined was merely the constraints within which love might legitimately flourish. What was necessary was merely that a young man or woman fall in love with the right person, and not with any wrong one, but this did not rule out their desiring the partner whom others desired for them, and they were probably predisposed to do so. Conversely, given these constraints and the extremely limited opportunities for any social contact between young men and women in the village, exactly what love then referred to is not so easy to say (if it ever is). Let us allow, however, that the Spartokhoriots were at least talking about the psychological and affective states of two individuals, and when, for example, a young woman who had had virtually no contact since childhood with any young man other than her brother or a close (and therefore forbidden) cousin was suddenly told by her father, her mother, her brothers and a respected uncle or family friend who was acting as go-between that a certain young man whom she had regularly seen in the village, whom she knew to be popular, good-looking and successful, and whose virtues had been explained to her in detail, was madly in love with her, and when, furthermore, she had spent a considerable amount of time watching programmes and reading stories that extolled love and romance as both sublime and expected experiences, then it is perhaps not surprising that she too should have declared herself in love (cf. Loizos 1981: 33), nor, I think, would there be any legitimate grounds to gainsay her. Thus whether a marriage had been a love-match, or had resulted from a family arrangement, was to some degree a question of the interpretation placed on events by the parties involved, and so far as most Spartokhoriots were concerned, 'love' (*aghapi*) and 'arrangement' (*proksenia*) were not mutually exclusive.

Ethnographies of rural (and working-class) Greece have, nevertheless, repeatedly stressed that the role of love or romance was traditionally a limited one in the creation of marital unions, and even explicitly rejected as detrimental to their future success (Campbell 1964: 124; du Boulay 1974: 93–4; Hirschon 1983: 304, 1989: 116; Clark 1988: 340). Marriage was a weighty matter with consequences not only for the couple themselves, but for their respective families. As such it was unwise to leave its instigation to the accidents of individual infatuation. Both the economic standing and the moral reputation of the families from which the prospective bride and groom came had to be reciprocally considered and judged, as did the personal qualities and social prospects of the bride and groom themselves; they also had to be judged by all those who, as a result of the marriage, would thenceforth find themselves related. In Spartokhori, the process of *proksenia*, of arranged marriage, effectively dealt with those considerations, but in the light of what has been reported about rural Greek attitudes to marriage, it is interesting to note the continual emphasis placed on love.

I was never privy to the actual negotiation of a match, but both in accounts of the past and in describing contemporary practice people routinely explained *proksenia* in the following way. A boy decided that he wanted to get married. He 'saw' (*idhe*) a girl and 'fell in love with her' (*tin aghapise*). She gave him some sign that she welcomed his attention. He then spoke with his father, telling him that he wished to marry the girl. If his father was a good father, he would take note of his son's wishes and speak about the girl to other members of the family – brothers, uncles and cousins – as well as to friends who could be trusted to keep the matter confidential. Having assured himself that the girl was a 'good girl' (*kali kopella*), he would approach the girl's father who would similarly consult members of his family, and similarly ascertain whether the boy was a 'good boy' (*kalo pedhi*). Then he would ask his daughter whether she wished to marry the boy in question. If the answer was yes, further negotiations ensued, most notably those concerning dowry, or at least the future financial prospects of the couple. If those matters were satisfactorily concluded, an engagement would be announced, followed by marriage within roughly a year. If, however, matters appeared from the start to be uncertain or difficult, the boy's father might seek the services of an intermediary, a go-between, who in Spartokhori was always referred to as a *simpetheros*, the term normally used to denote an affine. This *simpetheros*, usually an older man, would be chosen on the grounds of his mutual friendship, or even mutual relatedness, to both families, and his reputation as a trustworthy and honourable man.[6] His task was to make discreet enquiries about the possibility of the match and of the likelihood of a proposal being accepted, and to 'talk' with the girl's father to explain what a 'good boy' her potential suitor was. No doubt the process of *proksenia* was in practice a more complex affair than my synthetic account suggests, and no doubt in many cases the arts of persuasion were exercised to their full, but two points were always stressed: first, that the young man and young woman married freely and without coercion; second, that they married for love.

Again, it was the wealthier and better educated Spartokhoriots who were keenest to stress that marriage was not something ever forced on anyone. For them, arranged marriage, like dowry, was something that generated a degree of embarrassment, especially when they were talking to a foreigner. It was not modern, it was not Western, it was not sophisticated, and so it was played down. No boy or girl was made to wed unwilling. Such a thing, they admitted, might have happened in the past, and even today some old men could still be difficult and attempt to impose their will on their children or to place obstacles in their way. But, they asserted, in general marriages were freely entered into, and nowadays instigated by the couple themselves. *Proksenia* was the proper form, simply because it was not possible in the village for a boy directly to approach a girl, or to be seen talking to her. In Athens, they explained, things were very different; but in the village, if a boy wanted to marry a girl, then he would have to approach his father, and his father would naturally make enquiries about the girl, and her father would make enquiries about the boy, and so forth. That was *proksenia* of a sort. And when they themselves had become engaged in the village some twenty years before, then of course everything had been done properly (*sosta*) and all negotiations had been made through their respective families or a go-between. Nevertheless, they too had wanted to get married; they too had been in love. For the older generation, and for those who had spent their lives within

---

[6] The standard term for a go-between is *proksenitis*. The term *simpetheros* may have been used in Spartokhori because the go-between was ideally an affine of both parties.

the confines of the village, the term *proksenia* created no such embarrassment. Older women would say without hesitation, 'My father [or my brother] *gave* me to so-and-so,' and older men would talk of having found, or indeed of still finding, a partner for someone by acting as a go-between. This was a position of trust, and therefore of honour. For them, *proksenia* was the manner in which marriages had to be contracted, the only alternatives being elopement or 'theft' (cf. Campbell 1964: 130; Kenna 1971; Handman 1983: 85; Hart 1991: 184–5). But even the older generation still injected an element of romance into their accounts (though a romanticism that took little account of anything except male infatuation): 'A boy sees a girl; *he falls in love with her* (*tin aghapai*); he talks with his father,' and so on. Virtually without exception, older men would claim that they had married because in their youth they had 'seen' their wives and fallen in love. It was only the old women who occasionally admitted that of course in the old days no girl would have dared reject a match approved by her father (cf. Handman 1983: 84), and it took a rather exceptional old woman, a widow for fifty years and notorious for her independence, to state flatly that marriage had been an *emboriko prama*, a 'commercial matter'. She had come from a coastal village on Lefkadha where her father had been a wealthy merchant. Since her father had needed a caique to transport his goods, and since the only sailors of renown came from Meganisi, he had married his daughter to a Spartokhoriot. She had not wanted to come to Spartokhori, nor had she wanted to marry the man who became her husband. But, as she said, 'What could I do? I was a woman.' Over fifty years later her opinion of Spartokhori and Spartokhoriots had not much improved.

In all likelihood, however, there was a substantial historical continuity in the way in which marriages were made in Spartokhori. What had changed, and changed with retrospective effect, was not so much practice as a form of discourse; but I say 'discourse' and not just language, because the change involved not only how things were described, but the insertion of a new concept into the description. Love had become the only acceptable motivation for marriage. Nor is there any need to question the sincerity of those who professed it, or to define what they meant by it, in order to register the change its elevation signified. Much the same social and economic criteria for marriage remained, but they had become for the Spartokhoriots (as they have generally become throughout the modern world) obscured and displaced by a belief in the moral primacy of a psychological and affective state whose determining role was not to be challenged.

Courtship

Just as by the late 1970s love had become the socially endorsed motivation for marriage; so too ideas of courtship were being accepted: hesitantly within the village, more openly amongst the Spartokhoriot community in Athens. The students who returned to the village on a seasonal basis moved between two worlds of propriety, and self-consciously so. Mixed gatherings of young Spartokhoriots in Athens were innocent enough, and usually there was some form of unobtrusive chaperonage, but at least they took place, while attendance at universities, polytechnics, trade schools and simply life in the city entailed a degree of casual social contact between the sexes. Organized social events also brought Meganisiot boys and girls into regular contact, and here the island association, *O Mendis*, played a major role.

O Mendis, a regional association formed in 1975, stressed that it was the association of all Meganisiots regardless of their village of origin and where they lived. The association's driving forces, however, its founders and executive, were almost exclusively Athenian professionals (doctors, lawyers, teachers and businessmen), and its active membership consisted predominantly of students studying in Athens together with a few of the younger sailors resident there.[7] Its activities included the production of a monthly newspaper, *Meganisiotiki Andilali* (*Meganisiot Echoes*) and, in summer, the presentation of theatrical performances and various exhibitions on the island itself. Students, both male and female, played a major role in the organization and execution of these activities. In Athens, clubrooms hired by the association also provided a venue for the young to play cards or *tavoli* (a form of backgammon) in the evening, or simply to sit and chat and listen to music. In complete contrast to village social life, such evening gatherings were always mixed. On a friendly basis, then, young Meganisiot women and men came to know each other well, and after meeting at the club rooms they frequently went off as a group to one or other of Athens' hundreds of small restaurants or cafeterias for a drink or a snack or a coffee. There were always one or two older men in attendance at the club, but their presence did not constitute obvious oversight (for the club was not officially a youth club). In any case the public nature of the club was hardly conducive to clandestine liaisons. Later, at restaurants and cafeterias, girls were always accompanied by their brothers. But despite these subtle forms of supervision, in Athens Meganisiot girls and boys enjoyed an easy familiarity.

Back in Spartokhori the students and younger sailors who returned for holidays had to comply with a very different social code. The young men congregated in the coffee-shops. The young women stayed at home, or promenaded through the village arm in arm. The very same young women and men who sat chatting and joking together over a coffee in Athens now passed each other in the street with little more than a nod or a smile. It was an acknowledged charade, a conscious and graceful submission to the demands of village propriety. 'What can we do?' the young men wryly commented. 'You know how it is here. If the old women see boys and girls talking together, they'll gossip and there'll be trouble.' For these students and sailors, however, the submission was a temporary one. For their homebound comrades – brothers, sisters, cousins, friends – the submission was permanent. Not that all young sailors were sexually inexperienced. For many, the prostitutes of Glasgow, London, Marseilles, Tokyo, Singapore and Rio de Janeiro were their regular recourse. This was talked about without embarrassment, but equally without bravado as an accepted fact of maritime life, classified simply as the satisfaction of a physical need (cf. Hirschon 1989: 149). But in the village their social contact with unrelated young women was minimal, and for those girls who were not attending high school or university in Athens, the constraints under which they lived were probably little different from

[7] For the importance and activities of regional associations in Greece, see Dubisch (1977), Sutton (1978) and Kenna (1983).

those that had been imposed on their mothers and grandmothers. Cotton dresses and blue jeans had taken the place of the traditional Lefkadhiot costume, but young women still lived within a segregated female world whose boundaries were strictest for those as yet unmarried. They made lace, sowed, spun, cooked and talked in the company of their mothers, grandmothers and aunts; they looked after younger siblings, nieces and nephews; and awaited the time when they too would marry and have children of their own. And although when they walked arm in arm in twos and threes around the village they would acknowledge the polite greetings of young men, if they were on their own they would always lower their heads and return little more than a shy nod to any youth who had been bold enough to address them. Indeed, young women were scarcely to be noticed in the village, and in many cases I was as unaware of the existence of someone's daughter or sister as I was of some bed-ridden grandfather or grandmother. Discreet enquiries were usually answered with, 'Oh yes, so-and-so has *dhio kopelles* (two girls) *sto spiti* (in the house).' The invariable phrase '*sto spiti*' (in the house) was not, I think, intended to make any particular point, but it still betrayed a natural and unthinking association of daughters with that private and protected realm of the household (cf. Hirschon 1978, 1981; du Boulay 1986: 141–5).

In such a situation courtship was necessarily oblique, and whatever falling in love meant, it did not entail a detailed personal knowledge of the loved one. I was shopping in Lefkadha town one day when I ran into Dhimitris, who owned a coffee-shop in Spartokhori. He showed me a new laminex table he had just bought, explaining that now the family was growing, he needed a bigger one. I expressed some surprise, since Dhimitris and his wife were both in their late forties and had only one child, a son, Takis.

'Well, Takis might be getting married soon,' explained Dhimitris.

'I didn't know he was engaged,' I said. 'No, he's not,' replied Dhimitris, 'But who knows? He's finished his military service, and he might fall in love in the next few months.'

In Dhimitris's view of the world, love, like marriage, was a question of ripe time.

Takis's courtship (if there was one) was not something I witnessed, but there were standard occasions and standard venues where it could have been displayed. Spartokhori's saint's day, the day of Ayios Yeoryios, of St George, falls on 23 April. By the late 1970s its celebration had sadly declined, but in 1980 one coffee-shop proprietor was persuaded to hold a sort of *panayiri*, a festival, in his establishment. There were no live musicians (as there ought to have been), but there were tapes and records, and part of the floor was cleared for dancing. *Panayiria* (pl.) were rather exceptional occasions in that the coffee-shops which sponsored them ceased for that night to be all-male preserves, and villagers attended in family groups, husband, wife and children all dressed in their best, and each family sitting at its own table. The dancing and the composition of the groups that took the floor were various. Sometimes the *parea*, the company of dancers who held the floor, was mixed, and consisted of an entire family or several related families. Sometimes it consisted of just the young girls (*kopelles*). But overall the dancing was dominated by groups of young men, and then it was an exhibition. Young men would affect to enter a near trance-like state, so much were their energies apparently concentrated on the music and on the expression of their feelings, but in the end there could be little doubt but that they were dancing for an audience. On that particular night the dance was at one stage being led by Dhimos, a young man of about twenty-six. He was dancing with energy and skill, which I remarked on to my old friend Mikhalis with whom I was seated. 'He dances well,' admitted Mikhalis, and then, chuckling, added, 'He's in love (*aghapai*).' I asked Mikhalis with whom Dhimos was in love, and he whispered to me that it was with the daughter of Nonios.

Nonios's daughter, a girl of about seventeen, was sitting with her mother and father at the far end of the coffee-shop. She seemed to be paying Dhimos no particular attention; but Mikhalis insisted that Dhimos was in love with her, and that he was dancing to impress her. Mikhalis went on to comment that she was a fine girl, and that since Nonios had two daughters but no sons, whoever married them would get *ta panda*, 'the lot'. I do not know to what piece of information Mikhalis was privy that made him so sure Dhimos was seeking to marry Nonios's daughter, for he would only say, 'I know,' though it should perhaps be noted that Mikhalis's own daughter had married Nonios's brother (with whom she lived in Australia) and Mikhalis's son (also resident in Australia) had married Nonios's first cousin. Mikhalis was thus 'family', and so perhaps he had been consulted on the matter. But whatever the case, it was clear that Dhimos's behaviour that night was the sort of behaviour deemed constitutive of courtship: not a direct approach, still less a serenade, and no direct social contact between the prospective couple. What was necessary prior to the opening of negotiations with the girl's father was simply for Dhimos to make himself noticed by her. Almost by definition this had to take place in public where the rules of decorum were most in force. The aim was to impress at a distance, and then to await some sign that an impression had been registered.

Dancing and festivals were not, however, the only occasions at which those desirous of marriage had to cut a good figure. For young women, attendance at church was an opportunity to dress up and to be noticed, and equally to take note of the young men. The Spartokhoriots were not regular churchgoers, but at Easter, Christmas, weddings and baptisms the young came under mutual regard. As one Athenian student muttered to me as we stood in the men's section towards the front of the church, 'You see all the girls up there [on the balcony at the back of the church]? They're all looking at the *ghambri* (grooms).' Indeed, on such occasions it was difficult not to be aware of the fact that one was being scrutinized, assessed and even singled out for comment, and the equation between appearing at one's best and seeking a wife was so embedded that the appearance of any male, whether young or old, married or unmarried, who happened to be unusually well-dressed that day would provoke the comment, 'Ah, you're a *ghambros* (groom)!' Display equalled courtship, and the line of old men, most of them grandfathers, who pulled up their chairs outside Nick's bar in the evening to watch the antics of the yacht-loads of tourists became known simply as the grooms, a longstanding joke.

Courtship in the sense of a couple keeping company together, seeing each other and being seen to see each other, had to await an official engagement, the *arravones*. The Spartokhoriots insisted that the engagement had no religious standing. It was nevertheless an important ceremony, and took place in the house of the groom-to-be, whose *koumbaros* (his best man and possibly baptismal sponsor) placed the gold wedding rings on the fingers of the couple, an act to be repeated in the church by the priest at the time of marriage, immediately before the crowning that marked the inception of the union. But few engagements were broken, so that from this point onwards couples were allowed some freedom to express their affections.[8] The period of engagement – usually between six months and a year – was a time when prospective fathers-in-law and sons-in-law made a point of keeping company, of drinking together in the shops, and of publicly demonstrating their close and amicable relationship. For a young woman, however, it marked her introduction into the public world. Her fiancé would visit and take meals at her parents' house. She, likewise, would visit his parents' home. During meals they would sit close together and even surreptitiously hold hands (cf. Loizos 1981: 33). Some couples would go so far as to walk through the village hand in hand, and by 1980 it was not uncommon for a young man to bring his fiancée into one of the coffee-shops for a soft drink or a beer, where she would also meet his male friends and, somewhat uncomfortably, be made part of the company there. But such public courtship was a recent departure, a compromise between the mores of village society and the styles of romance popularly disseminated by the media. The engagement created a liminal period in which the assurance of marriage made it possible for a couple openly to demonstrate their mutual attachment, while the role of wife and mother had not yet forced the young woman back into the domestic sphere. But if the liminality of the period had always existed (in that engagements had always been binding without being constitutive of marriage), the use to which this space was put was a new one. A woman's appearance in a coffee-shop was itself an index of changing conventions, but more specifically, the display of mutual affection during the period of engagement was a substantial departure from the past – and not one approved of by many old men, who remarked that nowadays people had no honour (*timi*). In their youth, engaged couples most certainly had not visited each other's houses, or promenaded together, and they themselves had never spoken to, or been in any way familiar with, their brides up to the day of their marriage. But today, '*Oti thelis, kani* (Whatever you want goes)'. But then, for such elderly critics, the social criteria of marriage still far outweighed notions of romance.

Endogamy and the age of marriage

Prominent amongst those social criteria was the provenance of the bride and groom. Marriage within the village was still considered *o kalliteros ghamos*, 'the best marriage', for as a familial alliance it was best made between those who were in a position to know and to judge each other, and also between those who could look forward to profiting from it in their daily lives. As we have seen, Spartokhoriots married Spartokhoriots, and in 1980 nearly 75 per cent of the

---

[8] It was noticeable that when I asked women for the dates of their marriage, they commonly gave me the date of their engagement.

village's married couples had married within the village. Familial considerations promoted village endogamy (even in the face of the community's dispersal to Athens and overseas), but for most Spartokhoriots marriage within the village was also considered a good in itself, for in the end it was what bound the community together and made of it all one family. A number of students even confided in me that in their opinion one of the effects of the establishment of *O Mendis* – if not an unspoken part of its agenda – was to encourage the continual intermarriage of young Meganisiots despite their move to Athens and the wider opportunities to strike up relationships that existed there. A degree of social engineering may thus have existed, but for those who lived in the village simple proximity played a part in encouraging village endogamy. People married those whom they were in a position to see and to desire. A marriage was to be celebrated one Sunday, and the old Spartokhoriot who was telling me of the event emphasized that the two families involved lived on opposite sides of the same street. 'The boy watched the girl through the window, and the girl watched the boy through the window. They were neighbours. That's how these things happen,' he explained with mildly salacious glee. Doubtless matters were in reality seldom so simple. Young women were not so cloistered that a couple's only opportunity 'to fall in love' was provided by their mutual gaze through an open window. But the old man seemed to have little doubt that such was the progress of romance, and a young sailor of twenty-seven (who had become engaged during my stay to a girl of sixteen) gave me a frank account of his own courtship that seemed not so different. His house, or rather his father's house, overlooked the village's primary school (which girls might attend until they were 13). He had watched his future bride in the playground for years, and had decided that he would 'have this one'. It was, he remarked, 'like a spider with a fly'.

Village endogamy thus appeared to be largely surviving the effects of urban migration and the Spartokhoriots' employment as sailors, but other changes in marriage patterns were occurring. The negotiations that led to a marriage were certainly not the direct concern of the whole village. Nevertheless, marriages were to be numbered amongst the major social events of village life, and most people, whether directly involved or not, had their opinions on any union, and on the individual merits and demerits of the couple involved and their respective families. These, with varying degrees of frankness, they discussed. Of course what could be said behind closed doors and what could be pronounced in the coffee-shops or on the doorstep varied radically. Public morality demanded the expression of public good will, and at no time more strongly so than before a wedding. But in 1979 and 1980 many people, particularly members of the oldest generation, were voicing their overt displeasure at what they saw as a new and disturbing trend exemplified by one after another village engagement or marriage: namely, the very young age of the bride.

Average marriage ages of Spartokhoriot men and women for the years 1932–80 are set out in Table 8.1 and Figure 8.1 (although unfortunately there is a lacuna for 1941–9).[9] As Figure 8.1 shows, the drop in women's marriage ages

---

[9] Figures for the years 1932–78 were taken from the Spartokhoriot village register. The relevant volume for the years 1941–9 (which corresponds with the period of Greece's involvement in the Second World War and the ensuing Greek civil war) could not be located.

Table 8.1 Annual average marriage ages, 1932–40 and 1950–80

Year	Men average age	Women average age	Number of marriages	Brides aged 20 yrs and under	Brides aged 30 yrs and over	Bride older than groom
1932	26.0	25.0	2	0	0	0
1933	30.3	24.0	6	0	0	0
1934	32.0	27.2	5	0	0	1
1935	28.0	25.4	7	2	1	1
1936	29.6	26.8	8	0	3	2
1937	31.4	25.2	5	0	1	0
1938	30.6	26.6	8	1	2	1
1939	24.8	26.1	6	0	1	2
1940	32.6	27.8	7	0	2	1
1950	31.0	28.3	13	1	4	1
1951	31.0	27.3	7	0	3	0
1952	28.0	24.3	7	0	0	0
1953	26.8	25.2	5	0	0	0
1954	28.7	24.8	7*	1	1	1
1955	27.1	27.6	6	0	1	3
1956	28.3	23.9	15	0	1	0
1957	28.0	21.5	2**	1	0	0
1958	30.3	25.2	6	0	0	0
1959	28.8	27.8	7	1	3	1
1960	30.5	28.7	8	1	4	3
1961	29.0	26.5	10	1	2	3
1962	34.2	26.7	4	0	1	0
1963	30.0	25.2	9	1	2	1
1964	36.6	29.0	5	0	2	0
1965	29.8	26.3	9	2	2	1
1966	34.5	24.6	9	4	1	0
1967	31.0	30.0	2	0	1	1
1968	30.3	26.6	3	0	1	1
1969	31.2	22.1	4	1	0	0
1970	27.6	23.1	8	2	0	1
1971	28.8	27.0	6	0	2	2
1972	33.0	23.8	5	0	0	1
1973	29.6	23.6	5	1	0	1
1974	34.2	28.2	5	0	3	1
1975	29.6	21.3	6	3	0	0
1976	31.0	27.0	3	1	1	0
1977	25.0	18.3	3	2	0	0
1978	26.4	22.0	5	2	0	0
1979	28.0	17.3	3	3	0	0
1980	28.5	17.7	6	6	0	0
Total			247	38	45	30

* One further marriage registered without age.

** Six further marriages registered without age.

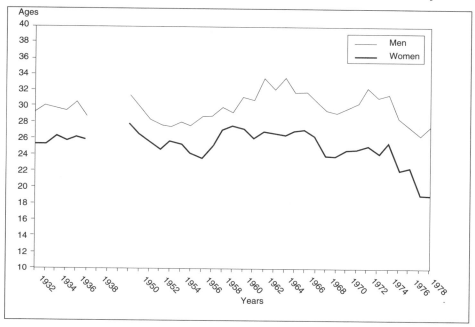

Figure 8.1 Marriage ages, 1932–80 (plotted in 3-year running averages)

after 1975 is quite pronounced. For the years 1932–74 (excluding the missing years 1941–9) the average age of women at marriage was nearly twenty-six, and for men it was just over thirty. Moreover, before 1975, in only twenty out of the total of 221 recorded marriages was the bride aged twenty years or less, and during this period the youngest brides in Spartokhori were never less than eighteen years old, and that too was rare: one case in 1938, the next not until 1963 and a further case in 1965. But forty-four (or nearly 20 per cent) of the brides before 1975 were thirty years of age or older, and despite its generally being held in Spartokhori that a husband ought to be five or so years older than his wife, in thirty cases (or 14 per cent of the total) the bride was older than the groom. The preference for village endogamy, the extensiveness of the laws of consanguinity and affinity, and thus the restricted number of available partners may explain this deviation from the stated ideal, but it seems that up to the mid-1970s there was nothing particularly abnormal about the marriage of, say, a thirty-two-year-old woman to a twenty-seven-year-old man.

The situation changed markedly after 1975. For marriages between 1975 and 1980 the average age of brides dropped to 20.6 years (and for men, too, there was some decrease to just over twenty-eight years). Moreover, out of the twenty-six marriages which took place in that period, seventeen involved women who were twenty years old or less; only one bride was thirty years old, and no bride was older than her husband. It is worth examining these twenty-six marriages in detail. Of the six women married in 1975, one was twenty-eight years old, but the other five were respectively twenty-one, twenty-one, twenty, twenty and eighteen years of age. Only three marriages occurred in 1976, and they upset the trend: one bride was nineteen, but the other two were respectively twenty-nine and thirty-three years old. In 1977, however, the drop in women's marriage ages continued. The three brides for those years were respectively twenty-one, eighteen and sixteen years old. In 1978 the trend was again upset by the marriage of one twenty-six-year-old bride, but of the other four brides two were twenty-three years old and the other two respectively twenty and eighteen years old. Finally, in 1979 and 1980 all nine brides were less than twenty years old, and six of them were only seventeen or eighteen years of age.[10] Admittedly the statistical picture is not conclusive, for the number of marriages in Spartokhori per year was small. But in the neighbouring villages of Katomeri and Vathi the same commentary and the same complaints were being made: that nowadays men were marrying children. Statistics aside, the drop in women's marriage ages was something that had deeply impressed itself on the consciousness of all Meganisiots.

The older generation's hostility towards the new fashion in marriage was generally couched in terms of a sentimental concern for the plight of young brides. 'How can it be good,' it was argued, 'to be a little girl one day, and a mother the next?' Those blamed for the situation were the young men for snatching child brides, and the parents of girls for allowing, and even encouraging, their early marriage. Correctly or incorrectly, old women looked back on the fairly lengthy period that they had spent between adolescence and marriage as one of freedom (however restricted) before the cares of marriage and motherhood were upon them, and as a time when, in the flower of their youth, they were at liberty to dance and (ever so discreetly) to be admired (cf. Campbell 1964: 158). In their opinion such pleasures were now being denied their grand-daughters. Old men, though they shared similar sentiments, sometimes added more practical (though rather spurious) objections. How could a girl who did not know how to make a cup of coffee be expected satisfactorily to perform the duties of a wife? The girls were as ignorant as they were young, complained the old men, and as everyone knew, running a household, looking after a husband and children, were serious occupations. But then, as one man resignedly put it to me, the whole business of the drop in women's marriage ages was simply 'a question of economics'. I think he was largely right, and here it should be noted that the child-bride marriages all involved sailors and the daughters of villagers rather than members of the Athenian-based elite.

In discussing dowry, I suggested that the wealth of Spartokhori's sailors and the switch in the dominant mode of production from peasant agriculture to wage labour substantially inverted the relations of economic authority between the generations. The consequences of this for the age of marriage were several. First, there was no longer any need for a young man to delay marriage until such time as his father might be expected soon to die, or was so old that he was willing to make over most of his holdings to his son(s). Young men were no longer dependent on their fathers either for their means of livelihood or for their place of residence. The age of marriage of men did not, however, substantially drop as a result, for it still took a young sailor some time to accumulate sufficient money to

---

[10]See Kalafati-Papagalani (1989) for a similar age drop in Ayios Petros, Lefkadha.

build a house and to feel economically secure enough to take on the responsibilities of marriage. If sons had become free to go their own way, the more noticeable result was not in terms of when they married, but rather in terms of their liberty to exercise an unhampered choice in whom they married, and those whom they chose were increasingly young girls. Old men and old women grumbled, but they lacked economic authority, and they knew well enough that if they stood too much in the way of their sons' preferences, they ran the risk of being dismissed as difficult. Individual choice thus triumphed over family counsel, and that, from a young man's point of view, was a licence to fall in love.

Two other results of the shift from agriculture to wage labour also bore on the age of Spartokhoriot brides: the redundancy of female labour and the changed role of dowry. In an agricultural economy, the acquisition of a wife was also the acquisition of an important source of labour. Olive-gathering was women's work, and so had been the bulk of the digging and hoeing of the terraces on which wheat and barley had once grown. A sturdy, skilled and experienced labourer was sought as a wife, not a seventeen-year-old girl. The old could complain that the young brides were useless and fit only to sit around the house, but, in comparison to their grandmothers' duties, that was all they were really required to do (cf. Buck Sutton 1986). As for dowry, it was, as we have seen, no longer a critical factor in the marriages of village-dwellers. If a sailor fell in love with a young and pretty girl, he was in a financial position to marry her regardless of what her family might contribute. The same factors seen from the point of view of the bride's family reciprocally pushed down women's marriage ages. Just as a young man no longer needed a wife who was an experienced agricultural labourer, with the decline of agriculture a young woman's father had little interest in delaying the marriage of a daughter who once would have contributed to his household's labour supply. From the bald perspective of economic rationality, the role of women in Spartokhori was increasingly being reduced to the procreative and the decorative. If a woman was not cherished as an attractive wife and the mother of children, then she was just one more mouth to feed. Moreover, it had not escaped the notice of parents that dowry was no longer a necessity if they had a young and beautiful daughter. Instead of delaying her marriage in order to provide her with an appropriate dowry, they could save themselves the expense by trading on her youth.

But the local appreciation of prevailing social conditions went one step further, and resulted in what, for want of a better term, might be called a feedback process. If the old and the conservative were troubled by the fashion for child-brides, those who had adolescent daughters were even more troubled by the thought that the fashion might endanger their daughters' prospects if they acted too slowly. People stressed to me that in the past it was a father-in-law who chose his son-in-law. The important relationship was between these two men, not between the bride and the groom. A girl's father was thus content to wait until an approach was made to him by a *ghambros* of whom he approved. But having witnessed the engagements and marriages of one seventeen-year-old girl after another, parents had been made uneasy, and were only too ready to accept the proposals of young sailors lest they found themselves encumbered with a daughter in her twenties whom no one would marry. And the situation could not be remedied, as in the past, by the provision of a larger dowry. Rather than resisting what they did not approve of, parents encouraged the early marriage of their daughters in a new race in which the iniquities of dowry had been replaced by those of nature.

To this reasoning must be added one final consideration, the true role of which is difficult to assess, for it flowed from the diffuse consequences of rapid social readjustment. Many matrons (notably those whose daughters were safely wed) whispered to me that the real reason for the drop in women's marriage ages was the fear that if a girl was not quickly married, then she might bring shame to her family. In the old days, it was pointed out, girls were always carefully watched. Now they went off to high school in Lefkadha, Athens or Patras. Some even went to university. All of them visited friends and relatives outside the village. How could they be supervised effectively? A degree of female emancipation had occurred, and it was making parents anxious (cf. Vernier 1991: 217). Better, then, that a girl should marry quickly before some catastrophe occurred, for though young sailors now sought a different sort of bride from their fathers, one thing had not changed. No sailor would marry a girl who had 'known' someone else. Virginity was still an absolute requirement. And, according to the matrons, since sailors still wanted to marry a virgin, choosing a sixteen-year-old was nowadays the best guarantee of finding one.

Fathers-in-law and sons-in-law

It may have been true that fathers-in-law were less scrupulous in their choice of sons-in-law, less able to control events, than once they had been, but in Sparto-khori the relationship between a man and his son-in-law remained a particularly close one, and, in public, almost the antithesis of the relationship between father and son. Drinking companies were composed of friends, but usually they also included men who were closely related to each other. A set of brothers often formed the core of a company of younger men, and frequently they were joined by their brothers-in-law, their sisters' husbands. But if an older man was with them, he would invariably turn out to be one of the company's father-in-law, a man who would drink with them, laugh with them, joke with them, and appear to be their intimate and equal. Fathers, if they were in the same coffee-shop, would at most look on from another table. The contrast between a man's relationship with his parent and his affine, with his father and his father-in-law, could hardly have been greater.[11] The public demonstration of amity between father-in-law and son-in-law was most intense during the period immediately before and after a young man's marriage, when they would become inseparable companions. But in most cases a close relationship between the two persisted throughout their lives, and a man and his father-in-law were normally good friends. That, perhaps, is in part the point, for the very instigation of the relationship between father-in-law and son-in-law was based on friendship, in

[11] A point of elementary logic: for a brother, a brother-in-law and a father-in-law to be in the one company without anyone's father being present, it is necessary that the company include a man and his wife's father and sister's husband (*ghambros*), but not his wife's brother (*kouniadhos*).

the sense of a relationship of choice entered into between equals. It thus differed not only in practice from the relationship between father and son (so often informed by antagonism and friction), but also in terms of its ideals, for however close father and son might be, their relationship was one based on respect.

In attempting to account for the difference between the father-in-law/son-in-law relationship and the father/son relationship it is worth recalling the composition of the household as an economic and a moral unity, for except in those slightly abnormal circumstances when a man married an 'heiress', men were neither economically dependent on, nor under the authority of, their fathers-in-law. Not only was a man independent of his father-in-law with respect to his long-term wealth, he was also his father-in-law's immediate beneficiary via his wife's dowry. Nevertheless, it would be a shaky sociological generalization that proposed inheritance from a father to engender a distanced relationship, while receipt of dowry from a father-in-law resulted in familiarity. In theory a man might feel beholden to his father-in-law for both dowry and daughter, that feeling being translated into a public attitude of respect.

Inasmuch as it is possible to account for normative personal relations between categories of kin such as fathers-in-law and sons-in-law, I would suggest that a more important factor was the competitive relationship between households. All of Spartokhori's wedding ritual, from the songs and the pattern of after-service feasting to the bride's reception at the door of her new house by her father-in-law and mother-in-law (a somewhat contrived procedure given the prevalence of neolocal residence), stressed the same thing: a woman's departure from the closely knit world of her parents' household and her entry into the new and strange household of her husband's family within which she would be referred to as a *kseni yineka*, a 'foreign woman' (cf. du Boulay 1989: Hart 1991: 173). Physically, the move might be no more than twenty-five yards down the road, and daughters continued to have a close relationship with their natal family (a point to which I shall return), but there can be no doubt that, for a woman, marriage was seen to involve her transfer from one autonomous household to another (du Boulay 1989). In this situation the public amity displayed between father-in-law and son-in-law formed, as it were, a bridge between their respective households. The latent antagonism that existed between households was ostentatiously suspended by the formation of a personal relationship which, though it overlaid one of kinship (for the members of the two households had become affines), was nevertheless required to take on the additional form of friendship. The logic of affinity, always a means of transforming friends into relatives, was reversible, and those who through marriage had become family were also required to show that they were friends. And it was not only fathers-in-law and sons-in-law who were thus drawn together. Brothers-in-law (*kouniadhi* and *ghambri*) and *badzanakia* (men married to a pair of sisters) also enjoyed a notably affectionate relationship (cf. Hirschon 1983: 315–19). In the Realpolitik of masculine life, it seemed that it was through women – through daughters, sisters and wives – that men could allow themselves to be brought close. Finally, however, it must be admitted that the competition between households aside, the very closeness of the ties that existed between parents and daughters probably encouraged the warm relationship that standardly obtained between father-in-law and son-in-law. In the light of what has often been reported for rural Greece, however, the closeness of the parental ties with daughters deserves comment.

Daughters

I was talking one afternoon to a young middle-aged woman outside her house. Two little boys, about eight and ten years old, were playing in the street. I asked if they were her sons. 'Yes,' she said, 'and better that they were girls!' Somewhat surprised by the force of her statement, I asked why. The answer was simple. Daughters cared for their parents; sons went off on their own.

'Look at my father,' she said (who at that moment appeared from his house a few yards down the road). 'Where are his sons? Hah! One's in Athens; one's in Canada. But I'm here. Isn't that so?' Her father (who had joined us) hastened to agree. In fact the claim that every father made that his sons respected him had not prevented the growth in Spartokhori of a carefully generalized set of maxims to the effect that daughters were better than sons, for daughters always cared for their parents while sons (alack) did not. The closeness of the mother/daughter relationship in rural Greece has been noted (Dubisch 1991: 36–8; Hart 1991: 175), but the openly stated preference for daughters by both men and women in Spartokhori was surprising given the generally biased evaluation of the sexes, and the premium placed on the procreation of sons, that has been reported in the ethnographic literature on rural Greece (Campbell 1964: 56; du Boulay 1983). That bias was fossilized in Spartokhoriot ritual, in which before the wedding ceremony a male child was bounced on the marriage bed, while throughout the ceremony the bride's godmother or godfather clasped an iron key, both acts signifying a desire that the *nifi* should bear a son. Moreover, most people, whether men or women, said it was natural that a father should want to have a son. But they also remained adamant that on the whole daughters were better than sons, and that although a father might wish to have a son to carry on his name, the absence of daughters was something truly to be regretted.

How long this attitude had existed, and how much it stemmed from Spartokhori's recent social and economic changes, is difficult to judge. One man, ruing the fact that he had four sons but no daughters, expressed what was probably a longstanding point of view: that although he too had wanted a daughter, the greater loss was to his wife, for a daughter would have provided her with a constant companion and a continual domestic helper. Indeed it was an often expressed and firmly held conviction in Spartokhori that mothers and daughters never fell out, and that theirs was an enduring relationship that survived the dissolution of the natal *spiti* and the daughter's marriage into another household (cf. Hart 1991:175; Dubisch 1991: 37). But the same man went on to state what had also become central to most people's opinions on the matter: that daughters were better than sons were because sons left, while daughters stayed and continued to care for their parents. One elderly couple who had five married children, four daughters and a son, pointed out that their family had always produced a preponderance of daughters. Their only son's two small children were also daughters. 'But,' they went on, 'what good is a son? Only for the house and the name.'

Such statements that bear on both the ideological perpetuation of the house-hold and its practical dissolution should be taken seriously, for as Dubisch warns, it is all too easy to see the sentimental ties between mother and daughter (and, in the Spartokhoriot case, between father and daughter) simply as the consequence of natural affections, whereas such sentimental ties are likely themselves to be culturally constructed and integrally related to social structure (1991: 38–40). On empirical grounds, the Spartokhoriots' remarks about sons leaving and daughters staying were extremely suspect. Admittedly sailors were often away at sea, while their wives remained in the village, but emigration involved both sexes, and there were as many daughters absent in Athens or overseas as there were sons. What underwrote the complaint that sons left while daughters stayed was rather the older generation's thwarted expectations, for under the traditional system of patrilocal residence and the creation of stem families, parents were supposed to be cared for in their old age by at least one of their sons (or rather, by one of their daughters-in-law, on whom in practice the burden fell). With the shift to neolocal residence, parents thus saw themselves abandoned by their sons. But no obligation to remain in the paternal household had ever rested on daughters. Quite the opposite: daughters married out, leaving the *patriko spiti* to be shared by their brothers. Ties with a daughter's (and son-in-law's) household had not, therefore, been affected by neolocal residence, thus making them seem the more stable and secure. Old men and women who should have been living with a married son and his family found themselves living on their own, and if they were offended by this, they turned to their daughters whose departure from their household was what tradition had always ordained. And here it should again be remembered that despite the patrilineal succession of the *spiti*, kinship in Spartokhori was essentially bilateral. Male inheritance related more to a general assumption of patriarchy than it did to any notion of agnatic groups. A daughter's children were just as much a person's grandchildren as a son's children. It was not, therefore, as if links with a daughter and her household were being created that had not existed before; merely that they were thrown into prominence by the shadow cast over the relationships with sons.

As in most of rural Greece, however, the most fraught family relationships had been between daughters-in-law and mothers-in-law (cf. Danforth 1991: du Boulay 1989), since in the traditional stem family, the daughter-in-law, the 'foreign woman', was placed under the direct authority of her husband's mother. The stereo-type of the tyrannical, interfering mother-in-law is as much a part of Greek popular culture as it is of Anglophone culture, though given different residence patterns, the relationship singled out in Greece has been between mother-in-law and daughter-in-law rather than between mother-in-law and son-in-law (du Boulay 1989). Moreover, the figure of the mother-in-law was much less a joke in rural Greece than a reality with which young women had to cope. Mothers who had brought up their sons became mothers-in-law who supervised their sons' wives. Thus while old men in Spartokhori might jocularly suggest that neolocal residence was preferred because today's brides did not cherish the prospect of looking after old blokes who coughed a bit in the night, it was common knowledge and no laughing matter that few young women would any more tolerate living under the authority of a *pethera*. Herein, said many people, lay the real reason for neolocal residence.

The strength of affinity

I have concentrated in both this chapter and the preceding one on the division and reconstitution of the household, and on the sentiments that these processes engendered in familial relations. We arrive at a paradox. Kinship in Spartokhori was bilateral. The ideology of kinship which asserted the binding obligations of family embraced both matrilateral and patrilateral kin, and both kin and affines. Nevertheless a strongly agnatic bias was given to kinship by the rules of residence and of inheritance, by the composition of the *spiti* and the transmission of its resources. Daughters married out, and, at least in theory, the traditional household consisted of parents, their sons and daughters-in-law, and their sons' children. Strong doubts must be expressed about the historical frequency of married brothers cohabiting, but it is nevertheless the case that both ideally, and during the periods of its maximum extension, the *spiti* was organized on patrilineal lines. Given the primacy of the *spiti* as the basic social unit, this agnatic bias ought to have been important, for the *spiti* circumscribed that group of kin between whom cooperation and mutual loyalty were not contingent, but obligatory. And yet if we examine the state of personal relationships between close kin, everything would seem to militate against agnatic solidarity. The relationship between father and son was reserved, sometimes hostile; the relationship between mother-in-law and daughter-in-law was notoriously embittered; the relationship between brothers, though close during their youth, tended towards friction and competition in later years. By contrast, relationships between close kin whom the rules of residence and inheritance did not unite – between fathers and daughters and sons-in-law, between mothers and daughters, between sisters, between brothers and sisters, and between brothers-in-law – remained for the most part close and amicable. It is almost as if the *spiti* united the most unlikely candidates for familial cohesion and excluded the most likely.

The paradox is, of course, a superficial one (nor is it an uncommon one). The animosities that existed between the members and erstwhile members of a *spiti* existed precisely because they were, or had been, the members of a single *spiti* whose resources they had to divide. Had the rules of inheritance and residence been differently framed, then so might be the conflicts to which they gave rise, for although neolocal residence on marriage and the premature dissolution of the *patriko spiti* had in some cases aggravated relationships between parents and sons (or at least changed the nature of their complaints), brothers were perhaps more inclined than before to remain good friends, for their employment and their wealth had diminished the importance of their patrimony. Nevertheless it is interesting to note that matrilateral and affinal ties were still the more demonstrably affectionate, and although there was no move within the village towards matrilocal residence, in many cases the location of matrilateral (or affinal) relatives had determined where a new house was built. Sons who had not inherited land from their fathers purchased land or a house from matrilateral kin, and as one prosperous middle-aged sailor explained to me, he had deliberately purchased his house from a maternal aunt in order to get away from the area of the village where his father and brothers lived, and where he had experienced continual *fasaria* (trouble). It was connections between and through women that survived. And here perhaps Lévi-Strauss's formulation deserves reconsideration. The Spartokhoriot household was doomed to disintegration, and along agnatic lines. By contrast, Lévi-Strauss's 'house' perpetuates itself through time, and by whatever necessary means (hence the reconciliation of the opposing principles of filiation and residence, patrilineal and matrilineal descent, descent and affinity). But the disintegration of the Spartokhoriot household also took place against a desire for continuity, a yearning for a form of immortality. And it was that yearning – the house and the name – as much as the actual rules of division, that made agnation so problematic.

9
A *Kalos Kosmos*

I have described the Spartokhoriots as all one family, for that is the way they described themselves. It is a description justified by the overarching morality of kinship to which they subscribed, and simultaneously by the manifold genealogical connections that existed between them. Ideologically and empirically kinship and community were congruent. But I have also described the Spartokhoriot community as one riven by jealousy and strife, a description which, though it did not equate with their public rhetoric, nevertheless informed their private self- estimations. The Spartokhoriots were, in their own words, a *kalos kosmos*, a 'good people', and prided themselves on so being. On the other hand, they also denigrated each other as *kakouryi* (criminals), *keroskopi* (opportunists) and, most trenchantly, *roufiani* (pimps/informers). Their positive evaluation of their community coincided with their perception of themselves as a single family. The animosity they bore each other derived usually from the highly competitive manner in which each family pursued its own ends. One last anecdote may serve to convey the sort of friction that pervaded village life, for it relates the outstanding example of real material hindrance that I witnessed during my two years in the village. Like any story it relies on a body of culturally specific assumptions for its full comprehension, that I have tried to lay bare in an analysis that necessarily transforms what was assumed by the Spartokhoriots into what may be dwelt on by the reader, and shifts what was dispersed throughout daily life into a focus of academic attention. What others take for granted is, after all, what ethnography takes to explore. I shall, however, seldom pause to indicate the connections between events and the cultural context in which they occurred. Let me simply state at the outset that my purpose in relating this anecdote is not only to convey the friction of village life, but also to demonstrate how that friction was contained and constrained. If the Spartokhoriots were, as they said, doers-of-evil, opportunists and informers, they also remained one family and a 'good people'. That contradiction is their own, and I make no apology for it.

The battle of the tourists

The first year I spent in Spartokhori was the year the yachts first arrived. Nikos pinned his hopes on them. All his overseas savings had been invested in his coffee-shop, but the coffee and the lemonades he served daily to the old men and the ouzo and the beer he served in the evening to the sailors scarcely provided him with a living. He needed the tourists.

Such tourists as came to Spartokhori came to Nikos's coffee-shop, for his was the only establishment that could provide them with a meal. They came sometimes a dozen at a time, sometimes in a party of thirty or more, as the flotillas of package-tour holiday-makers made their fortnightly cruises around the Ionian islands – but still, they came only occasionally. Nikos was intent on increasing his trade, and so he disappeared to Lefkadha on business. He made phone calls, he saw friends, he sent and received messages by caique, he gathered information from every possible source, and he could pinpoint on any particular night where the flotillas were and where they ought to be the next. He dispatched me and some of the village boys as scouts to sit on the cliff-top at the village's entrance to search for the white sails out to sea. We relayed our information back. It looked as if the yachts were coming. Risks had to be taken. Expensive meat had to be thawed. Chairs and tables had to be found. Nikos's wife, Maria, had to prepare to cook.

Nikos's labours proved fruitful. The yachts called more frequently. Nikos made friends with the captains, the tour-leaders, and came to a regular arrangement with them to bring their punters to Spartokhori. But Nikos still kept going across to Lefkadha. To Maria's considerable annoyance he was doing the rounds of the yachts' other ports of call, visiting other restaurant-owners whom he knew, drinking and chatting with the tourists there, and of course, proposing that they should visit Spartokhori. Nikos was a convivial man. He enjoyed these nights out. But he was whipping up trade, and as he daily explained to me, all his efforts to turn his coffee-shop into a profitable concern were being made not for his own benefit, nor for Maria's, but for the future of their only son, Loukas, who had been born in Canada and was therefore a Canadian citizen. It was hoped that Loukas might one day return to Canada to study to become a lawyer, an architect or a doctor. In the meantime, he had to complete his schooling in Greece, and complete it well. But Nikos could not afford to live in Athens. He was not a wealthy sailor. And so Loukas went to school in Lefkadha where Nikos rented a house for his wife and his son. Maria stayed there to cook for Loukas, clean for Loukas and make sure that Loukas pursued his studies. Nikos looked after himself in Spartokhori as best he could. But the house in Lefkadha was costing him 6,000 drachmes a month in rent alone, and then there was food, gas and electricity. There was also another 6,000 drachmes a month required for Loukas's lessons at one of the frontistiria, the private coaching-colleges which the majority of Greek students attended to supplement their schooling. Money was important.

In Spartokhori Nikos was helped by his friends. None of them (except myself) actually did much other than patronize Nikos's coffee-shop. The ouzo, beer and retsina they drank was not a great contribution to his income, but it helped a little. For the most part Nikos's friends came to make an appearance, to demonstrate their good will. They also came to watch the tourists, and with me as translator (when I was not cooking, serving, or washing up behind the bar), to chat with them. And whether Nikos's friends knew it or not (Nikos certainly did), the tourists came to watch them, as they made a pretty picaresque bunch, a _tableau vivant_ of the real Greece, straight out of the tourist brochures. Like Nikos, they were also gregarious, and their _filoksenia_ (hospitality/generosity) played a large part in getting the evenings going. The sailors (who could afford to) sent glasses and bottles of ouzo or retsina across to the tourists in the time-honoured manner: nothing said – just the presentation of the drink at the tourists' tables with Nikos indicating which parea, which company, had bought it. The tourists were generally overcome by both the hospitality and the ouzo. They reciprocated and invited Nikos's friends to join them. Some of the sailors, those who had a few words of English and the confidence to hold their own in any company, did so. Other men, the older and the poorer who could not afford to buy for the tourists, but whose honour prevented them from being bought for, politely refused, but they continued to look on, enjoying the scene from the sides, and if spirits were high, both they and the sailors would dance. Nikos had his floorshow ready-made, and he slipped readily into the compère's role. It was like a wedding every week in Nikos's coffee-shop.

My old protector, Mikhalis, elected himself Nikos's special patron. He was Nikos's senior by fifteen years or so, and he was also in a sense Nikos's uncle, for his father and Nikos' father had married women from the same family. Moreover, Mikhalis had a special place in his heart for foreigners. His elder son and his three daughters had all emigrated to Australia where they had become rich. They owned their own homes and several other houses which they rented to Australians. Mikhalis thus loved all foreigners, for it was amongst foreigners that his children dwelt, and amongst foreigners that they had prospered. Mikhalis was always at the coffee-shop whenever tourists arrived. This was his way of both helping Nikos and expressing his affection for foreigners. Most of the foreigners were from Loughton, Ealing, Slough or Didsbury, not Melbourne, Sydney or Geelong; but that didn't matter. _Kseni_ were _kseni_. With not a word of English, with me as intermediary and with his hand on his heart, Mikhalis would tell them his tale and talk of his overseas _pedhia_.

Mikhalis was a sentimental man. In his company the tourists became positively maudlin. 'Tell him,' they said to me, 'tell him the Greeks are the most wonderful people in the world.'

I told Mikhalis.

'_Ghamo to_ (fuck it),' he said, 'tell them the Greeks are the _worst_ people in the world. They're all thieves.'

The tourists looked slightly shaken. 'Well, tell him that everybody on _this_ island is absolutely wonderful. We went to Vathi, and ... what's the name of the other village a bit up the road? They were all so hospitable.'

'They say all the Meganisiots are good people, and very _filokseni_ in Vathi and Katomeri,' I translated back to Mikhalis.

'The Vathiots and the Katomeriots!' exploded Mikhalis. 'They're the worst of the lot. They're thieves _and_ drunks.'

'The people in Vathi and Katomeri are also not to be recommended,' I explained to the tourists. 'They're thieves too, and drunks.'

'Well, what about the people in this village, then?' enquired the tourists rather desperately.

'And the Spartokhoriots?' I asked, turning to Mikhalis.

Plate 9.1 Dancing

'The Spartokhoriots, ' said Mikhalis firmly, 'are a *kalos kosmos* (a good people)'.

Somewhat relieved to have arrived finally on safe ground, the tourists toasted the Spartokhoriots, the Spartokhoriots toasted the tourists, somebody remembered to buy me a drink and I toasted myself. Then Mikhalis felt compelled to dance and another party began.

As Nikos's business prospered, more flotillas of yachts began to make Spartokhori one of their regular stops. Then suddenly Nikos received a summons, presented himself at court in Lefkadha and was fined. Loud music was prohibited after midnight in a residential village, and Nikos's weekly festivities were disturbing the peace. Nikos was incensed, and his business prospects badly damaged. He had the option of applying for a special late licence, but it would eat deeply into his profits. But without a special licence he would be compelled to turn off the music by midnight or risk more fines, which would hurt both his trade and his pride. He needed to put on a good show for the tourists, and while the complaints might have been justified, Nikos was convinced (and I suspect rightly) that it was his enemies who were causing the trouble and that their motive was jealousy. Somebody had lodged a complaint with the police, and that somebody remained anonymous, which, as Nikos and his supporters pointed out, was typical of the Spartokhoriots. Had not *roufiani* (pimps/informers) denounced other Spartokhoriots to the Italians for hiding food during the war? Had not secret letters been written informing on people during the Junta? The Spartokhoriots were a *kakos kosmos* (bad people). Nikos would never openly state to me who his enemies were, perhaps because I was, after all, a foreigner; perhaps because he knew I was attempting the difficult task of being on good terms with everyone. But though I never knew who lodged the complaint with the police, I did know Nikos's enemies well enough.

One of them had recently returned to the village for six months' holiday after nearly twenty years in America. He and Nikos were roughly the same age and apparently had been childhood enemies, though why their enmity should have been re-established I do not know. Perhaps, on returning from America, this man felt the need to reassert himself in the village of his birth. Perhaps he did not like seeing foreign tourists in the village. Certainly he was very patriotic and somewhat xenophobic. But whatever the case, his complaints about Nikos and his tourist parties found a ready enough audience amongst a number of families within the village. The police officer who had charged Nikos was, however, a thoroughly decent man. He had a difficult job in Spartokhori, and he did it by sticking to the letter of the law, though the results were sometimes unfortunate even for him. After the summons, the police officer, who was not, of course, a Spartokhoriot, made a point of drinking in Nikos's coffee-shop towards the end of each evening, partly to show that he was not partisan in the affair and regarded Nikos's coffee-shop as a pleasant place to be, and partly to remind Nikos of closing time. And that was how the second catastrophe occurred.

Nikos sold two brands of retsina, one superior to the other. A large table of tourists had elected to drink the superior brand, and continued to do so all night. In fact, they paid for very little of it. Over half the bottles consumed were bought for them by a group of young sailors at another table. Nikos, whose grasp of the finer details of profit margins sometimes lapsed as the night wore on, had also supplied them with several bottles free of charge. But when they ordered a further bottle, Nikos found to his embarrassment that he had run out. Rather than admit to this, Nikos went behind the bar and filled an empty bottle with the inferior brand. The police officer saw him and, infuriated at having witnessed one of the oldest tricks in the world, threatened to charge Nikos the next morning and walked out. Nikos was crushed by the injustice of it all. The price difference between the two brands was less than ten drachmes, and in any case the tourists had received most of their drinks free. What about the bottles he himself had donated? Nikos was convinced that the police officer was in cahoots with his enemies, and that they were bent on ruining him. At this stage old Mikhalis, patron and protector extraordinary, went to work. It took him a couple of days to sort things out, but I found him one evening in Nikos's bar looking particularly smug. Nikos, too, seemed to have cheered up. I asked what was going on. After the usual prevarications, Mikhalis told me the story. Mikhalis affected to despise all police on principle, but face to face he got on very well with the officer. The police officer, too, valued Mikhalis's company, for being a policeman in Sparto-khori was a lonely job. At all events, the officer had encountered Mikhalis in one of the coffee-shops and (as happened all the time) offered him a drink. 'Thank you very much,' said Mikhalis, 'but I've just had one,' and left. That same afternoon Mikhalis and the officer again ran into each other in another coffee-shop. Again the officer offered Mikhalis a drink, and again Mikhalis politely declined. This situation repeated itself several times over the following day. '*Psikholoyia* (Psychology),' Mikhalis explained to me, tapping his head. In fact, Mikhalis had been engaged in a fairly subtle process of moral blackmail. The threat was his withdrawal of friendship, of his becoming cold towards the officer, but this was only part of a softening-up campaign. When Mikhalis finally accepted a drink, he put Nikos's case in the course of a long conversation, and the charge was with-drawn. Mikhalis considered the whole matter a personal triumph, explaining to me (out of Nikos's hearing) that he had to look after Nikos because, after all, Nikos was an only child and had no brothers.

The triumph was short-lived. A week or so later Nikos again overstepped the mark. A further complaint about noise was anonymously lodged with the police, and Nikos stood to be fined once more, this time double the previous amount. He was in despair. His behaviour, however, conformed to a pattern that I later came to recognize as fairly commonplace in Spartokhori: a period of withdrawal and silence followed by one of almost manic activity. I am no psychologist, and I offer no comment other than to remark that the pattern was common, and occurred when someone suffered a major reversal, whether to do with social relationships within the village (as in this case), or with some family tragedy (a death or injury). The reaction was recognized and categorized by the villagers, who would comment that so-and-so was for the moment a little sick (*arrostos*) due to his or her misfortune. Nikos's period of silence lasted about a week, then he suddenly erupted. He rang all the sheep bells that decorated the front of his shop. He shouted out his own name, both in Greek, 'O Nikos!', and in the form of his adopted English *nom de travail*, 'Nick the Greek!' He turned on the *pikup*, the stereo, full blast. And he proceeded to get exceedingly drunk. He still served all who came into his shop, but he did so weeping and in a state of near hysteria, regaling them with tales of the injustices he was suffering. And he stood outside

Plate 9.2 Psychology

his shop crying his virtues at the top of his voice, running through the gamut of Spartokhoriot ideals: '*Ime filotimos* (I am honourable/magnanimous), *filoksenos* (hospitable/generous), *kirios* (a gentleman), *chiftis* (a good fellow), *kalos* (good), *timios* (honourable/honest)!' The repetition of these words became almost incantatory. Many of his friends attempted to calm him. With their arms round his shoulders they agreed that he was *filotimos*, *kirios*, *chiftis* and all the rest, and they assured him that all would be well. Indeed, they were quite visibly moved by Nikos's distress, and with great affection rallied round to convince Nikos of their concern. But he shunned their consolation. '*Ghamo to Spartokhori* (Fuck Spartokhori)! Fuck *all* the Spartokhoriots!' was his constant refrain. The village was a *kakos kosmos* (bad people), and he would have nothing further to do with any of them. He made his money from foreigners, from tourists. From now on he would concern himself only with foreigners. He had spent years in Canada. He had lived amongst the *kseni*, he knew what they were like. They were a good people (*kalos kosmos*). He loved the *kseni* and they loved him. The village could go to hell.

Maria, his wife, was away in Lefkadha during this period of emotional overflow. Her widowed mother-in-law, old Vasso, who from her room above listened day and night to everything that went on below, emerged from her exile and entered the coffee-shop, a rare (and ominous) occurrence. She sat at a table beside her sobbing son, her eyes gleaming. Yes, Spartokhori was a bad people, a *kakos kosmos*. She had come to this village from Ithaki, and she had given the village a son, and what did they do to him? But it didn't matter. From now on it would be just the two of them, Nikos and Vasso against them all. I never saw her so happy. But Vasso's moment of glory was brief. I do not know what degree of calculation had been prompting Nikos's actions, but if he had been aiming to provoke a particular response he could not have set about it better. Two men came into Nikos's coffee-shop at about 1.00 am. They were Manolis, one of the village's rural guards, and '*O Ghatos*', 'the Cat', an old communist guerrilla leader from the civil war days. Both men commanded considerable respect throughout the village: Manolis, because he was an amiable and easy-going man; the Cat, because of his wartime exploits and because he was still tough enough always to speak his mind. Moreover, both had extensive family connections within the village, even though Manolis was himself an immigrant and had acquired his relatives through marriage. Apparently both were friends of Nikos, though I had never seen the Cat in Nikos's bar before. He had his own little general store, where many of the oldest men drank and where he held permanent court. Both were also said to be family with Nikos, though a quite careful check through my village genealogies did not reveal any close relationship. The Cat, however, had looked after Nikos when he was a little boy (and an orphan), for Nikos had wanted to follow him into the mountains during the war. The Cat refused to let him come because he was too small to carry a gun. As for Manolis, together with Nikos he had helped arrange the marriage of Nikos's 'niece' (his wife's brother's daughter) to old Mikhalis's nephew. Nikos and Manolis were perhaps family to that extent.

Both men, it turned out, had been going the rounds of the village from door to door 'talking' with people. What they effected seems to have been a general mobilization on Nikos's behalf, for over the next few days a quite peculiar thing happened. Villager after villager called in at Nikos's shop on one pretext or

254 A *Kalos Kosmos*

another to have a coffee, an ouzo or a lemonade. These were men (and occasionally women) who, while not Nikos's enemies, did not normally drink at his shop, and who were certainly not his close associates. Indeed, in many cases this was the first time that I had seen them in Nikos's shop, for they had their other haunts, their other companies based on kinship and friendship, and their other loyalties to other coffee-shop proprietors. Their arrival at Nikos's coffee-shop was not dramatic. They didn't say much to Nikos beyond the usual banalities of public greeting. They didn't do much except sit around and chat and pass the time of day for half an hour or so. To anyone who did not know the village, everything would have seemed quite normal. But I was astounded. This was – however unstated, however seemingly casual, however subtle – the expression of solidarity on a grand scale. I do not mean to suggest that all fences were mended. Nikos's particular enemies remained his particular enemies, and unfortunately the charge lodged with the police could not be dropped. As things turned out, Nikos's childhood enemy cut his holiday short and returned to the United States. It is possible this decision was influenced by the degree of support Nikos was receiving within the village. At any rate the man's sister, Nikos's next-door neighbour, who had always been on good terms with Nikos and taken his kitchen refuse to feed her goat, ostentatiously avoided Nikos's coffee-shop for several weeks afterwards. But on the whole, the village closed around Nikos and enveloped him in its fold.

This story's happy ending could be interpreted simply as demonstrating that the Spartokhoriots were a *kalos kosmos* (and this remains my overall judgement). Realizing that one of their number was being treated unfairly, they did, as they put it, care for or sorrow for him. But I think the story says something further. Although the Spartokhoriots' conception of their village as all one family was denied on a daily basis by their quarrels and animosities, that conception was still something they held dear. Nikos, beset by the realities of Spartokhori's internal jealousies and strife, had openly challenged that conception, and therefore necessitated its practical reaffirmation. What had hitherto been whispered amongst the Spartokhoriots was now shouted on the street; what had been accepted as a dark generalization was now turned into a clear case in point – the Spartokhoriots were a *kakos kosmos* ('bad people'). By refusing to accept the consolation even of his friends, and by lauding the *kseni*, the foreigners, and turning his back on the village, Nikos accused not just his enemies, but the community as a whole. He challenged the validity of the village's collective self-conception, and he challenged it in public and in relation to the outside world where it was imperative that it should hold sway. To be sure, there was no radical change of heart by those who had caused Nikos's difficulties, but those people who had been neutral, ambivalent or mildly critical – that is to say, the majority of the village – were shamed by their own self-estimation into rallying around. The Spartokhoriots were required to live up to their claims, to show, now that Nikos had resorted to bringing out his complaints from behind closed doors and into the public arena, that they were all one family whose rifts and quarrels were in the end subordinate to their solidarity. Nikos had called the bluff of public rhetoric, and so it had to be proven to be not mere rhetoric. If the Spartokhoriots could not believe that they were family, if they could not factually demonstrate their ideals to themselves, they would have lost a major plank of their identity.

Epilogue

I completed my fieldwork on 22 April 1980. I had spent a total of twenty-two months on Meganisi, twenty in Spartokhori, and a final two in Katomeri. Then, as much by accident as design, I found myself back in Greece living and working in Athens for another three years from February 1982 to December 1984, but during that period I visited Meganisi only once, and only for a few days. It was fourteen years after the end of my fieldwork, in October 1994, that I finally had the opportunity to spend some weeks on the island. Fourteen years is a long time. Not everything had changed, but a lot had – enough, at any rate, to warrant this brief epilogue, for I fear that any reader who visited Meganisi today might find it hard to reconcile even my physical description of the island with what they would now encounter.

The island and its surroundings were, of course, as beautiful as ever. But even in terms of the cautious account I have given of what could be considered in Greece remote, Meganisi no longer qualified. The changes, the opening-up of the island, started to become apparent on the journey there. The old pulley-bridge that in 1980 connected the northeast tip of Lefkadha to the mainland had been replaced by a highway that flew straight across the marshland to Lefkadha town, and Lefkadha town, a ramshackle collection of wood and corrugated-iron structures, mockingly (but quite accurately) referred to as a 'cowboy town' by its inhabitants at the time of my fieldwork, had been turned into a charming turn-of-the-century Italo-Greek settlement, carefully 'restored' by European Community funds to what in fact it had never been, for in the nineteenth century Lefkadha was, as one British traveller reported it, 'the third worst real town to be found in civilized countries' (though he did not say what the first two were) (Ansted 1863: 136). Nor was it any longer necessary to find out from some local source when, and from where, one or other of the two old caiques might be sailing to Meganisi. Two large well advertised drive-on car ferries provided a regular twice-daily service to the island, which was rapidly becoming a tourist resort.

On the little bay beneath Spartokhori, the *molo*, the quay, had been extended to cater for yachts. Four open-air restaurants (all owned and run by Spartokhoriot families), one grandly named the Meganisi Yachting Club, surrounded the bay, and all offered hot showers, for water had finally been piped across to the island under sea from Nidhri, and Spartokhori's women no longer had to pound their washing in the brackish water that seeped into the bay. The zigzag concrete path up the cliffs to the entrance to the village had been widened and resurfaced with bitumen, as had the village's entrance, the 'crown', but in any case no one any longer had to trudge up it, for a small bus, owned by Meganisi's newly constituted *dhimos* (municipality), drove the ferries' passengers to the village – if, that is, they did not drive themselves in cars they had brought across by ferry. The old coffee-shops that I had drunk in still existed, but two of them had been substantially refurbished as restaurants, and there were two new and very smart establishments flanking the entrance to the village, serving meals, snacks, coffee and drinks. One of the old general stores had also been transformed into a quite sophisticated cocktail bar. My truck-driver and fisherman friend, Alkis, had turned the houses he had built for his children into a large and well-stocked supermarket (where, indeed, his children worked), and he had plans to construct a hotel just outside the village. Another hotel was already in the process of construction, and many of the private houses were offering rooms for rent. There were also more private houses, and even more that had been renovated, though in a new style with wooden balconies and verandahs (now common in Greece) that pleasingly recreates some largely imagined tradition. From the inland side of the village, the road across the island connecting Spartokhori to Katomeri and Vathy had been surfaced, and a new road was being bulldozed around Meganisi's coast to give access to its inlets and beaches. There was even a bitumen road across to the coast of the Meganisi channel and the little chapel of Ayios Yannis where, on sleepy afternoons, I had escaped the village and gone swimming. A fish-restaurant now stood near the chapel. I couldn't help laughing when I remembered how many times I had become lost for hours among the olive trees as I had tried to follow the meandering goat-path that had led to this once secluded spot.

People, too, had changed. Many of my old friends had died, though not as many as I had feared. All of them remembered me, though not all of them recognized me. But beyond the inevitabilities of mortality, there were social changes. I was walking across the newly surfaced road to Katomeri when I was passed at high speed by a pick-up truck. It shot past me, screeched to a halt, 'chucked a U-ey' (as we say in Australia), returned at high speed and stopped beside me. It was driven by Poppi, the wife of a fisherman and store-keeper from Katomeri. One hand on the wheel, one hand dangling out the window, she cried 'Rogeri!'

'Poppi!' I exclaimed in surprise – for I was not used to seeing vehicles on Meganisi, let alone one driven by a local woman. 'You're driving,' I said, somewhat foolishly.

'Eh! Well, things have changed. Women drive now.'

I declined her offer of a lift back to Spartokhori, promised to visit her and her husband, and she roared off on her way. The example is, of course, entirely trivial, and Poppi had in any case always been an independent woman. But the picture of Poppi in her pick-up truck stuck in my mind, because (rightly or wrongly) it did seem indicative of what had occurred during my absence. The island had opened up. It was conforming more and more to the mores of the wider world. And it is important to stress that the ferries, the cars, the roads, the cafeterias, the restaurants and the cocktail bar, and even the hotel, were not just for the tourist trade. Admittedly they would not have been built without that trade. Nor would they survive without it. But they were also used by the Spartokhoriots. To sit sipping a whisky in a tourist bar was now firmly part of local life. And although the Spartokhoriots had for long been familiar with the ways of the city, in the 1970s they contrasted Athens and the village. They were acutely aware of the village as backward, as lacking the amenities of civilization. In 1994 they still contrasted Athens and the village (it was a lot nicer to be in the village than in Athens), but the comforts and customs of urban life had now come to Spartokhori.

The opening-up of the village, fundamentally a response to tourism, had not, however, affected its demographic decline, nor had the provision of those amenities whose lack was so complained of during my fieldwork: a water supply, a transport system allowing easy access to the island, even the much sought high school, finally built a few years after my departure. In fact easy access to and from the island had probably accelerated its depopulation – if, that is, one counts as its population only those who lived there year-round. In 1980 people had to make a choice: to live most of the time in Athens, or to remain on Spartokhori. With the car ferries, people could live where they worked (Athens, Patras, Preveza, even Lefkadha) confident that they could return to the island whenever they had a free weekend or a couple of days off. If Spartokhori had become a tourist resort, it had also become even more than in 1980 a holiday and second home for its own emigrant population. As far as I could judge (and I could not reduplicate in a matter of weeks data that had taken me over two years to compile) only a handful of families now lived permanently in the village. The high school, demanded in 1980 as a means of halting the island's depopulation, had a total of only twenty-one students from all three of Meganisi's villages, while Spartokhori's primary school had closed for want of children, and Katomeri's, now serving the entire island, had only forty-eight students. There had, however, been some immigration. Two families of *Arvanites*, of refugee 'Albanians', had moved into Spartokhori and were doing (as Albanians are now doing throughout Greece) whatever manual work was available. If their children married in the village, perhaps they would one day become Spartokhoriots.

Depopulation might, of course, have proceeded even without easier communications and simply as a result of economic factors. Agriculture had gone further into decline as the ageing population of farmers and pensioners gradually died out. At the same time, most Spartokhoriots I spoke to assured me that work on the ships, too, had become a thing of the past. There were only a half a dozen sailors still living in the village, and no young men were going to sea. All of them 'knew letters' and worked in the city. Tourism offered some scope for local employment, and those families who owned restaurants appeared to be doing well, but the work was seasonal and the number of people employed was not great. On the whole, Meganisi no longer had a local economy (even an offshore one) to sustain a permanent population. Significantly, a number of young men who did work seasonally in the tourist trade had shifted their place of residence to Lefkadha, from where they could commute to Meganisi, and where there was more opportunity for year-round casual employment. All three high-school teachers similarly lived in Lefkadha and commuted to the island, and Andonis, the builder, had also returned to Lefkadha, and came across to Meganisi when and if there was work for him. What local economy existed was now integrated into Lefkadha's. The only other forms of employment available on the island were those created by the island's reconstitution as a *dhimos*. I have already mentioned the local bus, which employed a Spartokhoriot driver. But the municipality was also providing new services, and Spartokhori now had a garbage collection. This was staffed by a number of younger villagers whom I had known during my fieldwork, and as I watched the village 'garbos' at work, I realized that the class structure which had begun to form in 1980 had now been perfected. A Spartokhoriot, a doctor, had become Lefkadha's member of parliament; other Spartokhoriots had become the local rubbish-collectors. How easy it would be to continue to say 'We're all one family' and 'We're all just *anthropi* (human beings)' seemed to me doubtful.

But whether a Spartokhoriot community had ceased to exist in the terms that I have described it in this book was not entirely clear. There were plans, I was told, to turn Spartokhori's disused primary school into a museum and cultural centre, celebrating the island's folklore and history. A certain Dhimos Tselios, the Meganisiot kleft who took part in the Greek War of Independence (Tertsetis 1967), had been promoted to official local hero. Someone had been doing their homework. Perhaps the idea of community, self-conscious, historicized, folklori-cized, romanticized, was replacing the practice of community amongst an educated and urbanized generation now celebrating their village roots rather than living out a village existence. That shift had been under way even in 1980, but it seemed to have considerably progressed by 1994. But at the very least, a strong attachment to place remained. And then, on Sunday 16 October, Greece held its first local government elections. The village, which was largely deserted during the first few days I was there, began to fill as ferry-loads and car-loads of Spartokhoriots returned in order to vote on the island where they continued to be registered. As I watched and listened to candidates try to whip up support in the restaurants and coffee-shops, the same appeals to kinship and family that I remembered were again exercised. One young woman, a PASOK party member, was going the rounds, talking to group after group. No one really seemed to know her. No one had seen her before. She lived in Lefkadha, she explained, as did her parents. But at each encounter she gave a careful account of her genealogy. She was the daughter of so-and-so who had married so-an-so, whose brother was old 'uncle' so-and-so, and thus forth. And as she explained this, Maria, the now elderly wife of the coffee-shop proprietor in whose room I had lived, got up from her seat and stroked her on the cheek. They were family, after all. She was not a stranger. She was one of 'our people', one of *dhiki mas*. Some things – at least for some people – seemed to be the same.

Nevertheless, the situation and the events that I have described in this book are now nearly twenty years old. Like most anthropologists, like most travellers, perhaps just like most people, I cannot help occasionally feeling that what I witnessed on fieldwork was the end of an era; that I saw and knew in Spartokhori and Meganisi a way of life that has now gone. In a sense that is true. Things have changed. But I have also listened to too many 'old hands' (British archaeologists, for the most part) telling me 'You should have seen Greece before the war', 'You should have seen Greece in the 1950s', 'You should have seen Greece in the 1960s', not to realize that the sense of an era is largely provided by the observer. What frames a period of time, what gives it coherence, what makes it a unit, is the fact that it was a relatively discrete (and for most ethnographers, extremely important) period of one's own life. History itself does not come in chunks, and I have tried to provide in this book enough of Meganisi's history to show that things there were always changing. It does not worry me at all that the results of my fieldwork must now be read as history (that is the common fate of ethnography). It would, however, worry me greatly if they were not read *historically*, as a particular moment in a continual process of change, but as the account of a vanished way of life.

References Cited

Allen, Peter S. 1973. 'Social and Economic Change in a Depopulated Community in Southern Greece'. PhD dissertation, Brown University. Ann Arbor, Michigan: University Microfilms

―― 1976. 'Aspida: a depopulated Maniot community', in M. Dimen and E. Friedl (eds), *Regional Variation in Modern Greece and Cyprus: Toward a Perspective on the Ethnography of Greece*, 168–98. New York: Annals of the New York Academy of Sciences 268

―― 1979. 'Internal migration and the changing dowry in Modern Greece', *Indiana Social Studies Quarterly* XXXII (1): 142–56

―― 1980. 'What isn't wrong with Athens', *The Athenian*, October 1980: 30–45

―― 1986. 'Positive aspects of Greek urbanization. The case of Athens by 1980'. *Ekistiks* 318/319. May–June/July–August 1986: 187–94

Anderson, Benedict. 1983. *Imagined Communities. Reflections on the Origins and Spread of Nationalism*. London: Verso

Andromedas, John N. 1957. 'Greek kinship terms in everyday use', *American Anthropologist* 59: 1086–8

Ansted, D.T. 1863. *The Ionian Islands in the Year 1863*. London: Wm. H. Allen & Co

Ardener, Edwin 1987. ' "Remote areas" – some theoretical considerations', in A. Jackson (ed.), *Anthropology at Home*, London: Tavistock

―― 1989a. 'Language, ethnicity and population', in M. Chapman (ed.), *Edwin Ardener. The Voice of Prophecy and Other Essays*, 65–71. Oxford: Blackwell

―― 1989b [1971]. 'The new anthropology and its critics', in M. Chapman (ed.), *Edwin Ardener. The Voice of Prophecy and Other Essays*, 45–64. Oxford: Blackwell

Aschenbrenner, Stanley. 1976. 'Karpofora: reluctant farmers on a fertile land', in M. Dimen and E. Friedl (eds), *Regional Variation in Modern Greece and Cyprus: Toward a Perspective on the Ethnography of Greece*, 207–21. New York: Annals of the New York Academy of Sciences 268

―― 1986. *Life in a Changing Greek Village. Karpofora and its Reluctant Farmers*. Dubuque, Iowa: Kendall/Hunt

Barnes, John A. 1962. 'African models in the New Guinea highlands', *Man* 52: 5–9

Barth, Fredrik. 1969. 'Introduction', in F. Barth (ed.), *Ethnic Groups and Boundaries. The Social Organization of Cultural Difference*, 9–38. London: George Allen and Unwin

―― 1978. 'Conclusions', in F. Barth (ed.), *Scale and Social Organization*, 253–73. Oslo: Universitetsforlaget

Baumann, Gerd. 1996. *Contesting Culture. Discourses of Identity in Multi-Ethnic London*. Cambridge: Cambridge Unversity Press

Baxevanis, John. 1972. *Economy and Population Movements in the Peloponnesus of Greece*. Athens: National Centre of Social Research

Bender, D.R. 1967. 'A refinement of the concept of household: families, co-residence and domestic functions', *American Anthropologist* 69 (5): 441–59

Bennett, Diane O. 1988. 'The poor have much more money', *Journal of Modern Greek Studies* 6: 217–43

Benton, Sylvia. 1934. 'The Ionian islands', *Annual of the British School at Athens* 32 (1931–2): 213–46

Bestard-Camps, Joan. 1985. 'Que hay en un pariente?' Thesis, University of Barcelona: Barcelona

—— 1991. *What's in a Relative? Household and Family in Formentera*. Oxford: Berg

Bialor, Perry. 1976. 'The northwestern corner of the Peloponnesos: Mavrikion and its region', in M. Dimen and E. Friedl (eds), *Regional Variation in Modern Greece and Cyprus: Toward a Perspective on the Ethnography of Greece*, 222–35. New York: Annals of the New York Academy of Sciences 268

Bloch, Maurice. 1971. 'The moral and tactical meaning of kinship terms', *Man* n.s. 6: 79–87

Blok, Anton. 1974. *The Mafia of a Sicilian Village*. Oxford: Blackwell

Boissevain, Jeremy. 1975. 'Introduction: towards a social anthropology of Europe', in J. Boissevain and J. Friedl (eds), *Beyond the Community: Social Process in Europe* 9–17. The Hague: Department of Educational Science of the Netherlands

—— 1979. 'Towards a social anthropology of the Mediterranean' (published with 'Comments' by Aceves, Beckett, Brandes, Crump, Davis, Gilmore, Griffin, Padiglione, Pitt-Rivers, Schonegger, Wade, and a 'Reply' by Boissevain), *Current Anthropology* 20 (1): 81–93

—— 1991. 'Ritual, play and identity: changing patterns of celebration in Maltese villages', *Journal of Mediterranean Studies* 1(1): 120–34

—— 1992. *Revitalizing European Rituals*. London: Routledge

—— 1994. 'Towards an anthropology of European communities?', in V. Goddard, J.R. Llobera and C. Shore (eds), *The Anthropology of Europe. Identities and Boundaries in Conflict*, 41–56. Oxford: Berg

Boissevain, Jeremy and John Friedl (eds) 1975. *Beyond the Community: Social Process in Europe*. The Hague: Department of Educational Science of the Netherlands

Bondelmonti, Christopher. 1824. *Librum Insularum Archipelagi*. Lipsiae et Beroloni

Bory de Saint-Vincent, M. Le Colonel. 1823. *Histoire et Description des Iles Ioniennes etc.* Paris

Bourdieu, Pierre. 1984. *Distinction. A Social Critique of the Judgement of Taste*. Trans. Richard Nice. Cambridge, MA: Harvard University Press

—— 1990. *The Logic of Practice*. Trans. Richard Nice. Cambridge: Polity Press

Bragadin, Pietro. 1703. Manuscript of edict (in Venetian). Lefkadha Archives

Brandes, Stanley. 1980. *Metaphors of Masculinity*. Philadelphia, PA: University of Philadelphia Press

Buck Sutton, Susan. 1983. 'Rural–urban migration in Greece', in M. Kenny and D. Kertzer (eds), *Urban Life in Mediterranean Europe. Anthropological Perspectives*, 225–49. Urbana: University of Illinois Press

—— 1986. 'Family and work: new patterns for village women in Athens', *Journal of Modern Greek Studies* 4(1): 33–49

—— 1988. 'What is a "village" in a nation of migrants?', *Journal of Modern Greek Studies* 6: 187–215

Burgel, Guy. 1976. *Athens: the development of a Mediterranean capital*. Athens: Exantas

Campbell, John K. 1963. 'The kindred in a Greek mountain community', in J. Pitt-Rivers (ed.), *Mediterranean Countrymen*, 73–96. Paris: Mouton

—— 1964. *Honour, Family and Patronage: A Study of Institutions and Moral Values in a Greek Mountain Community*. Oxford: Clarendon Press

—— 1983. 'Traditonal values and continuities in Greek society', in R. Clogg (ed.), *Greece in the 1980s*, 184–207. London: Macmillan

Carsten, Janet. 1997. *The Heat of the Hearth. The Process of Kinship in a Malay Fishing Community*. Oxford: Clarendon

Carsten, Janet and Stephen Hugh-Jones. 1995. 'Introduction', in J. Carsten and S. Hugh-Jones (eds), *About the House. Lévi-Strauss and Beyond*, 1–46. Cambridge: Cambridge University Press

Cattastico de' Benni tutti ch'esistono nel Scolgio di Mega Nisi, formato per Pubblico Comando nell'anno 1720. Manuscript (in Venetian). Lefkadha Archives

Chapman, Malcolm. 1978. *The Gaelic Vision in Scottish Culture.* London: Croom Helm

—— 1992. *The Celts - The Construction of a Myth.* London: Macmillan

—— 1993. 'Copeland: Cumbria's best-kept secret', in S. Macdonald (ed.), *Inside European Identities. Ethnography in Western Europe,* 194–218. Oxford: Berg

Clark, Mari H. 1988. 'The Transformation of Households on Methana, Greece, 1931–1987', PhD thesis, The University of North Carolina at Chapel Hill

Clogg, Richard (ed.) 1976. *The Movement for Greek Independence 1770–1821.* London: Macmillan

—— 1979. *A Short History of Modern Greece.* Cambridge: Cambridge University Press

Cohen, Anthony P. (ed.) 1982. *Belonging: Identity and Social Organisation in British Rural Cultures.* Manchester: Manchester University Press

—— 1985. *The Symbolic Construction of Community.* London: Tavistock

Corbin, John R. and Marie P. Corbin. 1983. *Compromising Relations.* Farnborough: Gower

—— 1987. *Urbane Thought.* Farnborough: Gower

Corbin, M. and P. Stirling. 1973. *A Computer Analysis of Community Census Materials in the Comarca of Ronda.* Report to SSRC, Cyclos, UKC

Couroucli, Maria. 1985. *Les Oliviers du Lignage.* Paris: Maisonneuve et Larose

—— 1987. 'Dot et société en Grèce moderne', in G. Ravis-Giordani (ed.), *Femmes et Patrimoine dans les sociétés rurales de l'Europe méditerranéenne,* 327–48. Paris: Editions du Centre National de la recherche scientifique

Cowan, Jane K. 1990. *Dance and the Body Politic in Northern Greece.* Princeton: Princeton University Press

Crump, Thomas. 1975. 'The context of European anthropology: the lesson from Italy', in J. Boissevain and J. Friedl (eds), *Beyond the Community: Social Process in Europe,* 19–28. The Hague: Department of Educational Science of the Netherlands

Cutileiro, Jose. 1971. *A Portuguese Rural Society.* Oxford: Clarendon

Dakin, Douglas. 1972. *The Unification of Greece, 1770–1923.* London: Ernest Benn

Danforth, Loring M. 1984. 'The ideological context of the search for continuities in Greek culture', *Journal of Modern Greek Studies* 2: 53–85

—— 1989. *Firewalking and Religious Healing: The Anastenaria of Greece and the American Firewalking Movement.* Princeton: Princeton University Press

—— 1991. 'The resolution of conflict through song in Greek ritual therapy', in P. Loizos and E. Papataxiarchis (eds), *Contested Identities: Gender and Kinship in Modern Greece,* 98–113. Princeton: Princeton University Press

—— 1995. *The Macedonian Conflict. Ethnic Nationalism in a Transnational World.* Princeton: Princeton University Press

Davis, John. 1973. *Land and Family in a South Italian Town.* London: Athlone

—— 1977. *People of the Mediterranean: An Essay in Comparative Social Anthropology.* London: Routledge and Kegan Paul

Davy, J. 1842. *Notes and Observations on the Ionian Islands and Malta etc.* (2 vols). London: Smith, Elder & Co

de Bosset, C.P. Lieut.-Col. 1821. *Parga and the Ionian Islands: Comprehending a Refutation of the Mis-statements of the Quarterly Review of Lieut.-Gen. Sir Thomas Maitland etc.* London: John Warren

Delamont, Sara. 1995. *Appetites and Identities. An Introduction to the Social Anthropology of Western Europe.* London and New York: Routledge

Dimen, Muriel. 1979. 'The state, work, and anthropology: contradictions in a Greek village', *Michigan Discussions in Anthropology* 9(2): 102–35

—— 1986. 'Servants and sentries: women, power, and social reproduction in Kriovisi', in J. Dubisch (ed.), *Gender and Power in Rural Greece,* 53–67. Princeton: Princeton University Press

Douglas, Mary. 1963. *The Lele of the Kasai.* Oxford: Oxford University Press

Driessen, Henk. 1992. *On the Spanish-Moroccan Frontier. A Study in Ritual, Power and Ethnicity*. Oxford: Berg

du Boulay, Juliet. 1974. *Portrait of a Greek Mountain Village*. Oxford: Clarendon Press

—— 1976. 'Lies, mockery and family integrity', in J.G. Peristiany (ed.), *Mediterranean Family Structures*, 389–406. Cambridge: Cambridge University Press (in association with the Social Science Research Centre, Cyprus)

—— 1983. 'The meaning of dowry: changing values in rural Greece', *Journal of Modern Greek Studies* 1: 243–70

—— 1984. 'The blood: symbolic relations between descent, marriage, incest prohibitions and spiritual kinship in Greece', *Man* n.s. 19: 533–56

—— 1986. 'Women – images of their nature and destiny in rural Greece', in J. Dubisch (ed.), *Gender and Power in Rural Greece*, 139–68. Princeton: Princeton University Press

—— 1989. 'La mariée et sa belle-mère. Aspects du rituel du mariage dans un village de Grèce', in J.G. Peristiany and M.-E. Handman (eds), *Le Prix de l'Alliance en Mediterranee*, 379–94. Paris: Editions du CNRS

Dubisch, Jill. 1977. 'The city as resource: migration from a Greek island village', *Urban Anthropology* 6: 65–81

—— 1991. 'Gender, kinship, and religion: "reconstructing" the anthropology of Greece', in P. Loizos and E. Papataxiarchis (eds), *Contested Identities: Gender and Kinship in Modern Greece*, 29–46. Princeton: Princeton University Press

Dumont, Louis. 1970. *Homo Hierarchicus. The Caste System and its Implications*. London: Weidenfeld and Nicolson

—— 1986. *Essays on Individualism*. Chicago: Chicago University Press

—— 1991. *L'idéologie allemande*. Paris: Gallimard

Dumont, Louis and David Pocock. 1957. 'Village studies', *Contributions to Indian Sociology* 2: 23–41

Evans-Pritchard, Edward Evans. 1976. 'Some reminiscences and reflections on fieldwork', in *Witchcraft Oracles and Magic among the Azande*, abridged by Eva Gillies, 240–54. Oxford: The Clarendon Press

—— 1940. *The Nuer. A Description of the Modes of Livelihood and Political Institutions of a Nilotic People*. Oxford: The Clarendon Press

Evelpidis, Chryssa. 1968. 'L'exode rural en Grèce', in J.G. Peristiany (ed.), *Contributions to Mediterranean Sociology: Mediterranean Rural Communities and Social Change*, 127–40. The Hague: Mouton

Fabian, Johannes. 1983. *Time and the Other: How Anthropology Makes its Object*. New York: Columbia University Press

Farsoun, S.K. 1970. 'Family structure and society in modern Lebanon', in E. Sweet (ed.), *Peoples and Cultures of the Middle East*, Vol. 2, 257–307. New York: National History Press

Faubion, James D. 1993. *Modern Greek Lessons. A Primer in Historical Constructivism*. Princeton: Princeton University Press

Firth, R., J. Hubert and A. Forge 1969. *Families and their Relatives: Kinship in a Middle-Class Sector of London*. London: Routledge and Kegan Paul

Fog Olwig, Karen and Kirsten Hastrup. 1997. 'Introduction', in K. Fog Olwig and K. Hastrup (eds), *Siting Culture. The Shifting Anthropological Object*, 1–14. London: Routledge

Foster, George M. 1963. 'The dyadic contract in Tzintzuntzan, II: patron-client relationship', *American Anthropologist* 63: 1173–92

Foucault, Michel. 1972. *The Archaeology of Knowledge*. London: Tavistock

Freeman, Derek. 1968. 'On the concept of the kindred', in P. Bohannan and J. Middleton (eds), *Kinship and Social Organization*, 255–72. New York: The Natural History Press

Freeman, Susan T. 1973. 'Introduction' to 'Studies in rural European social organization', *American Anthropologist* 75: 743–50

Friedl, Ernestine. 1959. 'The role of kinship in the transmission of national culture to rural villages in mainland Greece', *American Anthropologist* 51: 30–8

264 References Cited

—— 1964a. *Vasilika: A Village in Modern Greece*. New York: Holt, Rinehart & Winston

—— 1964b. 'Lagging emulation in a post-peasant society', *American Anthropologist* 66: 569–86

—— 1976. 'Kinship, class and selective migration', in J.G. Peristiany (ed.), *Mediterranean Family Structures*, 363–87. Cambridge: Cambridge University Press (in association with the Social Science Research Centre, Cyprus)

Galani-Moutafi, Vasiliki. 1993. 'From agriculture to tourism: property, labor, gender, and kinship in a Greek island village (part one)', *Journal of Modern Greek Studies* 11: 241–70

—— 1994. 'From agriculture to tourism: property, labor, gender, and kinship in a Greek island village (part two)', *Journal of Modern Greek Studies* 12: 113–31

Gallant, Thomas. 1988. 'Greek bandits: lone wolves or a family affair', *Journal of Modern Greek Studies* 6: 269–90

—— 1990. 'Peasant ideology and excommunication for crime in a colonial context: the Ionian Islands (Greece), 1817–1864', *Journal of Social History* 23(3): 485–512

Geertz, Clifford. 1973. 'Thick description: toward an interpretive theory of culture', in C. Geertz, *The Interpretation of Cultures*, 3–30. New York: Basic Books

Gellner, Ernest. 1983. *Nations and Nationalism*. Oxford: Basil Blackwell

Gilmore, David. 1980. *The People of the Plain: Class and Community in Lower Andalusia*. New York: Columbia University Press

Gilsenan, Michael. 1973. 'The vital lie', Cyclo, paper for 1973 ASA conference

Goddard, Victoria A. 1994. 'From the Mediterranean to Europe: honour, kinship and gender', in V. Goddard, J.R. Llobera and C. Shore (eds), *The Anthropology of Europe. Identities and Boundaries in Conflict*, 57–92. Oxford: Berg

Goddard, Victoria, Josep R. Llobera and Cris Shore. 1994. 'Introduction: the anthropology of Europe', in V. Goddard, J.R. Llobera and C. Shore (eds), *The Anthropology of Europe. Identities and Boundaries in Conflict*, 1–40. Oxford: Berg

Goodisson, W. 1822. *The Ionian Greeks; A Historical and Topographical Essay upon the Islands of Corfu, Leucadia, Cephalonia, Ithaca and Zante etc.* London: Thomas and George Underwood

Goody, Jack (ed.). 1958. *The Developmental Cycle in Domestic Groups*. Cambridge: Cambridge University Press

Grillo, R.D. (ed.) 1980. *'Nation' and 'State' in Europe. Anthropological Perspectives*. London: Academic Press

Gudeman, Stephen. 1975. 'Spiritual relationships and selecting a godparent', *Man* n.s.10: 221–37

Gutenshwager, Mary C. 1971. 'Nea Aeolia: Persistence and Tradition in an Urban Greek Community'. PhD thesis, University of North Carolina at Chapel Hill

Hammel, Eugene A. 1968. *Alternative Social Structures and Ritual Relations in the Balkans*. New Jersey: Prentice-Hall

Handman, Marie-Elisabeth. 1983. *La Violence et la Ruse. Hommes et Femmes dans un Village Grec*. La Calade, Aix-en-Provence: Edisud

Harris, Christopher C. 1990. *Kinship*. Milton Keynes: Open University Press

Hart, Laurie Kain. 1991. *Time, Religion, and Social Experience in Rural Greece*. Lanham, MD: Rowman and Littlefield

Hastrup, Kirsten. 1985. *Culture and History in Medieval Iceland: An Anthropological Analysis*. Oxford: Oxford University Press

—— 1990. *Nature and Policy in Iceland, 1400–1800: An Anthropological Analysis of History and Mentality*. Oxford: Oxford University Press

Herzfeld, Michael. 1980. 'Honour and shame: problems in the comparative analysis of moral systems', *Man* n.s.15: 339–51

—— 1982a. *Ours Once More: Folklore, Ideology, and the Making of Modern Greece*. Austin: University of Texas Press

—— 1982b. 'When exceptions define the rules: Greek baptismal names and the negotiation of identity', *Journal of Anthropological Research* 38: 288–302

—— 1983. 'Interpreting kinship terminology: the problem of patriliny in rural Greece', *Anthropological Quarterly* 56: 157–66

—— 1985. *The Poetics of Manhood: Contest and Identity in a Greek Mountain Village*. Princeton: Princeton University Press

—— 1986. 'Within and without: the category of "female" in the ethnography of Modern Greece', in J. Dubisch (ed.), *Gender and Power in Rural Greece*, 215–33. Princeton: Princeton University Press

—— 1987a. *Anthropology through the Looking-Glass: Critical Ethnography on the Margins of Europe*. Cambridge: Cambridge University Press

—— 1987b. '"As in your own house": hospitality, ethnography, and the stereotype of Mediterranean society', in D. Gilmore (ed.), *Honor and Shame and the Unity of the Mediterranean*, 75–89. Special publication of the American Anthropological Association 22

—— 1991. *A Place in History: Social and Monumental Time in a Cretan Town*. Princeton: Princeton University Press

—— 1992. *The Social Production of Indifference: Exploring the Symbolic Roots of Western Bureaucracy*. Chicago: University of Chicago Press

—— 1997. *Cultural Intimacy. Social Poetics in the Nation-State*. London: Routledge

Hirschon, Renée. 1976. 'The Social Institutions of an Urban Locality of Refugee Origin in Piraeus'. DPhil thesis. Oxford.

—— 1978. 'Open body/closed space: the transformation of female sexuality', in S. Ardener (ed.), *Defining Females*, 66–88. London: Croom Helm

—— 1981. 'Essential objects and the sacred: interior and exterior space in an urban Greek community', in S. Ardener (ed.), *Women and Space. Ground Rules and Social Maps*, 72–88. London: Croom Helm

—— 1983. 'Under one roof: marriage, dowry and family relations in Piraeus', in M. Kenny and D. Kertzer (eds), *Urban Life in Mediterranean Europe. Anthropological Perspectives*, 299–323. Urbana: University of Illinois Press

—— 1989. *Heirs of the Greek Catastrophe: The Social Life of Asia Minor Refugees in Piraeus*. Oxford: Clarendon Press

Hobsbawm, Eric. 1959. *Primitive Rebels. Studies of Archaic Forms of Social Movement in the 19th and 20th Centuries*. New York: Norton

Hoffman, Susannah M. 1976. 'The ethnography of the islands: Thera', in M. Dimen and E. Friedl (eds), *Regional Variation in Modern Greece and Cyprus: Toward a Perspective on the Ethnography of Greece*, 328–40. New York: Annals of the New York Academy of Sciences 268

Holy, Ladislav. 1996. *Anthropological Perspectives on Kinship*. Chicago: Pluto

Ipouryion Esoterikon (Ministry of Internal Affairs).1872. *Statistiki tis Elladhos. Plithismos 1870. (Statistics of Greece. Population 1870)*. Athens

Jamous, Raymond. 1981. *Honneur & Baraka. Les Structures Sociales Traditionelles dans le Rif.* Cambridge: Cambridge University Press

Jervis-White Jervis, Henry. 1852. *History of the Island of Corfu and of the Republic of the Ionian Islands*. London

Just, Roger. 1988a. 'A shortage of names: Greek proper names and their use', *Journal of the Anthropological Society of Oxford* 19: 140–50

—— 1988b. 'Anti-clericism and national identity: attitudes towards the Orthodox Church in Greece', in W. James and D.H. Johnson (eds), *Vernacular Christianity. Essays in the Social Anthropology of Religion Presented to Godfrey Lienhardt*, 15–30. Oxford: JASO

—— 1992. 'Ethnicity and the village; the "them" and "us" of family and state', in J. Burke and S. Gauntlett (eds), *Neohellenism*, 113–40. Canberra: Humanities Research Centre Monograph No. 5, Australian National University

—— 1995a. 'Public certainties and private doubts', in W. James (ed.), *The Pursuit of Certainty*, 285–308. London: Routledge

—— 1995b 'The Meganisiot fishing system', in S. Damianakos, M.-E. Handman, J. Pitt-

266 References Cited

Rivers and G. Ravis-Giordani (eds), *Brothers and Others. Essays in Honour of John Peristiany*, 241–52. Athens: Centre National de Recherches Sociales

Kaklamanaki, Roula. 1984. *I Thesi tis Ellinidhas. Stin Ikoyenia. Stin Kinonia. Stin Politia.* (The Position of the Greek Woman. In the Family. In Society. In the State). Athens: Ekdosis Kastanioti

Kalafati-Papagalani, Irene. 1985. 'En fouillant les testaments. . . La loi et son application à Aghios Petros, île de Leucade, du xiii au milieu du xx siècle' in C. Piault (ed.), *Familles et Biens en Grèce et à Chypre*, 213–34. Paris: L'Harmattan

—— 1989. 'Femme sujet, femme objet: se marier à Aghios Petros de Leucade', in J.G. Peristiany and M.-E. Handman (eds), *Le Prix de l'Alliance en Méditerranée*, 355–78. Paris: Editions du CNRS

Karakasidou, Anastasia, N., 1997. *Fields of Wheat, Hills of Blood. Passages to Nationhood in Greek Macedonia, 1870-1990.* Chicago: University of Chicago Press

Karp, Ivan. 1978. 'New Guinea Models in the African Savannah', *Africa* 48: 1–17

Kayser, Bernard. 1968. 'Les migrations intérieures en Grèce', in J.G. Peristiany (ed.), *Contributions to Mediterranean Sociology: Mediterranean Rural Communities and Social Change*, 191–200. The Hague: Mouton

Kayser, Bernard, Pierre-Yves Pechoux and Michel Sivignon. 1971. *Exode Rurale et Attraction Urbaine en Grèce.* Athens: Centre for Social Science Research

Kendrick, Tertius. 1822. *The Ionian Islands. Manners and Customs; Sketches of Ancient History.* London: James Haldane

Kenna, Margaret. 1971. 'Property and Ritual Relationships on a Greek Island'. PhD thesis, University of Kent

—— 1977. 'Greek urban migrants and their rural patron saint', *Ethnic Studies* 1: 14–23.

—— 1983. 'Institutional and transformational migration and the politics of community: Greek internal migrants and their migrants' association in Athens', *Arch. European Sociology*, XXIV: 263–87

—— 1993. 'Return migrants and tourism development: an example from the Cyclades', *Journal of Modern Greek Studies* 11: 75–95

Khouliarakis, Mikhail. 1973. *Yeografiki Dhiikitiki ke Plithismiak: Ekseliksis tis Elladhos, 1821–1971 (Geographical, Administrative and Demographic Development of Greece, 1821–1971).* Athens: *Ethnikon Kentron Kinonikon Erevnon*

Khuri, Fuad I. 1976. 'A profile of family associations in two suburbs of Beirut', in J.G. Peristiany (ed.), *Mediterranean Family Structures*, 81–100. Cambridge: Cambridge University Press (in association with the Social Science Research Centre, Cyprus)

Kolodny, Emile. 1974. *La population des îles de la Grèce. Essai de géographie insulaire en Méditerranée orientale* (3 vols). Aix-en-Provence: *Edisud*

Kouniakis, D.A. 1974. *O Kolokotronis ke ta Eptanisia* (Kolokotronis and the Septinsulars). Athens.

Kouniakis, Panos Th. 1937. *I Sinkhronos Lefkas, 1890–1936. (Contemporary Lefkas, 1890–1936).* Patras

Kuper, Adam. 1988. *The Invention of Primitive Society.* London: Routledge

Lacroix, M. Louis. 1853. *Iles de la Grèce.* Paris

Laslett, Peter. 1972. 'Introduction: the history of the family', in P. Laslett and R. Wall (eds), *Household and Families in Past Times*, 3–89. Cambridge: Cambridge University Press

Leach, Edmund. 1951. 'The structural implications of matrilateral cross-cousin marriage', *Journal of the Royal Anthropological Institute* 81: 23–55

—— 1961. *Pul Eliya. A Village in Ceylon.* Cambridge: Cambridge University Press.

Leekley, Dorothy and Robert Noyes. 1975. *Archeological Excavations in the Greek Islands.* Park Ridge, New Jersey: Noyes Press

Lévi-Strauss, Claude. 1949. *Les Structures élémentaires de la Parenté.* Paris: Presses universitaires de France

—— 1983a. *The Way of the Masks.* Trans. S. Modelski. London: Jonathan Cape

—— 1983b. 'Histoire et ethnologie', *Annales* 38(2): 1217–31
—— 1984. *Paroles données*. Paris: Plon
—— 1987. *Anthropology and Myth: Lectures 1951–1982*. Oxford: Blackwell
—— 1991. 'Maison', in P. Bonte amd M. Izard (eds), *Dictionnaire de l'ethnologie et de l'anthropologie*. Paris: Presses universitaires de France
Lineton, Michael J. 1971. *Mina. Past and Present. Depopulation in a Village in Mani, Southern Greece*. PhD thesis, University of Kent
Llobera, Josep R. 1986. 'Fieldwork in Southern Europe: anthropological panacea or epistemological straitjacket?', *Critique of Anthropology* 6(2): 25–33
—— 1987. 'Reply to critics', *Critique of Anthropology* 7(2): 101–18
—— 1994. 'Anthropological approaches to the study of nationalism in Europe. The work of Van Gennep and Mauss', in V. Goddard, J.R. Llobera and C. Shore (eds), *The Anthropology of Europe. Identities and Boundaries in Conflict*, 93–112. Oxford: Berg
Loizos, Peter. 1975a. *The Greek Gift: Politics in a Cypriot Village*. Oxford: Blackwell
—— 1975b. 'Changes in Greek property transfer among Greek Cypriot villagers', *Man* n.s. 10: 503–23.
—— 1981. *The Heart Grown Bitter: A Chronicle of Cypriot War Refugees*. Cambridge: Cambridge University Press
—— 1992. 'User-friendly ethnography?', in J. de Pina-Cabral and J.K. Campbell (eds), *Europe Observed*, 167–87. Basingstoke: Macmillan
Loizos, Peter, and Evthymios Papataxiarchis. 1991. 'Introduction. Gender and kinship in marriage and alternative contexts', in P. Loizos and E. Papataxiarchis (eds), *Contested Identities: Gender and Kinship in Modern Greece*, 3–25. Princeton: Princeton University Press
McDonald, Maryon. 1989. '*We are not French!': Language, Culture and Identity in Brittany*. London: Routledge
—— 1993. 'The construction of difference: an anthropological approach to stereotypes', in S. Macdonald (ed.), *Inside European Identities. Ethnography in Western Europe*, 219–36. Oxford: Berg
—— 1996. 'Unity in diversities: some tensions in the construction of Europe', *Social Anthropology*, 4(1): 47–60
Macdonald, Sharon. 1993. 'Identity complexes in Western Europe: social anthropological perspectives', in S. Macdonald (ed.), *Inside European Identities. Ethnography in Western Europe*, 1–26. Oxford: Berg
—— (ed.) 1993. *Inside European Identities. Ethnography in Western Europe*, 1–26. Oxford: Berg
McKechnie, Rosemary. 1993. 'Becoming Celtic in Corsica', in S. Macdonald (ed.), *Inside European Identities. Ethnography in Western Europe*, 118–45. Oxford: Berg
McNeill, William H. 1978. *The Metamorphosis of Greece since World War II*. Oxford: Blackwell.
Mahairas, K. 1951. *I Lefkas epi Enetokratias, 1684–1797 (Lefkas during Venetian Rule, 1684–1797)*. Athens
Makris, Julie. 1992. 'Ethnography, history and collective representations: studying vendetta in Crete', in J. de Pina-Cabral and J.K. Campbell (eds), *Europe Observed*, 56–72. Basingstoke: Macmillan
Malakasis, Dhimos. 1982. *To Khroniko ton Emboroktimation tis Ayias Mavras 1820–1920* (The Period of the Merchant-Landowners of Santa Maura 1820–1920). Athens
Maronitis, D.N. 1993. 'Meganisi', *To Vima*, 25 April
Meganisiotiki Andilali (Meganisiot Echoes). 1980. 4:17. Athens
Mintz, S. and E. Wolf, 1950. 'An analysis of ritual co-parenthood (compadrazgo)', *South West Journal of Anthropology* 6: 341–68
Modanio, Mario. 1982. 'Greece abolishes male supremacy', *The Times*, December 1: 8
Moore, Henrietta L. 1988. *Feminism and Anthropology*. Cambridge: Polity Press
Morosini, Antonio. 1720. Manuscript of edict (in Venetian). Lefkadha Archives

Morosini, Francesco. 1684. Manuscript of edict (in Venetian). Lefkadha Archives

Moustaka, C. 1968. 'Attitudes towards migration', in J.G. Peristiany (ed.), *Contributions to Mediterranean Sociology: Mediterranean Rural Communities and Social Change*. The Hague: Mouton

Mouzelis, Nicos P. 1978. *Modern Greece: Facets of Underdevelopment*. London: Macmillan

Nader, L. 1965. 'Communication between village and city in the Modern Middle East', *Human Organization* 24: 18–24.

National Statistical Service of Greece. 1979. *Statistical Yearbook of Greece 1978*. Athens

—— 1985. *Statistical Yearbook of Greece 1984*. Athens

—— 1994a. *Statistical Yearbook of Greece 1990–1*. Athens

—— 1994b. *Greece in Figures 1994*, Athens

Needham, Rodney (ed.). 1971. 'Introduction', in R. Needham (ed.) *Rethinking Kinship and Marriage*, xiii–cxvii. London: Tavistock

New Piloting Directions for the Mediterranean Sea etc. 1831. London: J.W. Norrie & Co

O'Neill, Brian J. 1987. *Social Inequality in a Portuguese Hamlet: Land, Late Marriage and Bastardy, 1870–1978*. Cambridge: Cambridge University Press

Ott, Sandra. 1981. *The Circle of Mountains. A Basque Shepherding Community*. Oxford: Clarendon Press.

Palmos, Kostas. 1992. *Meganisiotika*. Athens: Aghrambeli

Panayotopoulos, Basile. 1985. 'Dimension et composition de la famille péloponnesienne aux environs de 1700: quelques remarques', in C. Piault (ed.), *Familles et Biens en Grèce et à Chypre*, 29–44. Paris: L'Harmattan

Pandazi-Tzifa, Konstandina. 1984. *I Thesi tis Yinekas stin Elladha (The Position of Women in Greece)*. Athens: Nea Sinora

Panourgia, Neni. 1995. *Fragments of Death, Fables of Identity. An Athenian Anthropology*. Madison, WI: University of Wisconsin Press

Papataxiarchis, Evthymios. 1991. 'Friends of the heart: male commensual solidarity, gender, and kinship in Aegean Greece', in P. Loizos and E. Papataxiarchis (eds), *Contested Identities: Gender and Kinship in Modern Greece*, 156–79. Princeton: Princeton University Press

—— 1998. 'The devolution of property and kinship practices in late- and post-Ottoman ethnic Greek societies', *Mélanges de L'Ecole Française de Rome* 110(1): 217–41

Parkin, Robert. 1997. *Kinship. An Introduction to the Basic Concepts*. Oxford: Blackwell.

Partsch, Joseph. 1889. *Die Insel Leukas. Eine Geographische Monographie*. Gotha: Justus Perthes

Peletz, Michael J. 1995. 'Kinship studies in late twentieth-century anthropology', *Annual Review of Anthropology*: 343–72

Peristiany, John G. 1963. 'Introduction to a Cyprus highland village', in J.G. Peristiany (ed.), *Mediterranean Sociological Conference. Mediterranean Rural Communities and Social Change* , 75–96. Athens

—— 1965. 'Honour and Shame in a Cypriot highland village', in J.G. Peristiany (ed.). *Honour and Shame. The Values of Mediterranean Society*. 173–90. London: Weidenfeld and Nicolson

Peristiany, John G. (ed.) 1968 (1963). *Contributions to Mediterranean Sociology: Mediterranean Rural Communities and Social Change*. Athens: Social Science Centre. First published in cyclostyle form, 1963, as *Mediterranean Sociological Conference. Mediterranean Rural Communities and Social Change*

Peters, Emrys Lloyd. 1972. 'Shifts in power in a Lebanese village', in R. Antoun and I. Hayek (eds), *Rural Politics and Social Change in the Middle East*, 165–97. Bloomington: Indiana University Press

—— 1976. 'Aspects of affinity in a Lebanese Maronite village', in J.G. Peristiany (ed.), *Mediterranean Family Structures*, 27–80. Cambridge: Cambridge University Press (in association with the Social Science Research Centre, Cyprus)

Phidhalion.1976. *The Rudder of the Orthodox Catholic Church, containing all the sacred and divine Canons of the Eceumenical and Holy Synods of the Undivided Church, etc. according to the 3rd edition of S. Raftanis, 1864.* Athens: Astir

Pina-Cabral, Joao de. 1989. 'The Mediterranean as a category of regional comparison', *Current Anthropology* 30 (3): 399–406

—— 1992. 'The primary social unit in Mediterranean and Atlantic Europe', *Journal of Mediterranean Studies* 2(1): 25–41

Pitt-Rivers, Julian. 1954. *The People of the Sierra.* Chicago: University of Chicago Press

—— 1965. 'Honour and social status', in J.G. Peristiany (ed.), *Honour and Shame. The Values of Mediterranean Society,* 21–95. London: Weidenfeld and Nicolson.

—— 1976. 'Ritual kinship in the Mediterranean: Spain and the Balkans', in J.G. Peristiany (ed.), *Mediterranean Family Structures,* 317–34. Cambridge: Cambridge University Press (in association with the Social Science Research Centre, Cyprus).

—— 1977. 'The moral foundations of the family', in J. Pitt-Rivers, *The Fate of Schechem or the Politics of Sex. Essays in the Anthropology of the Mediterranean,* 71–93. Cambridge: Cambridge University Press

Radcliffe-Brown, A.R. 1950. 'Introduction', in A.R. Radcliffe-Brown and D. Forde (eds), *African Systems of Kinship and Marriage.* Oxford: Oxford University Press

Rondoyiannis, P.G. 1980. *Istoria tis Nisou Lefkadhos (History of the Island of Lefkadha)* Vol. A. Athens: Society of Lefkadhiot Studies

—— 1982. *Istoria tis Nisou Lefkadhos (History of the Island of Lefkadha)* Vol. B. Athens: Society of Lefkadhiot Studies.

Salamone, S.D. and J.B. Stanton. 1986. 'Introducing the *nikokyra*: ideality and reality in social process', in J. Dubisch (ed.), *Gender and Power in Rural Greece,* 97–120. Princeton: Princeton University Press

Sant Cassia, Paul and Constantina Bada. 1992. *The Making of the Modern Greek Family. Marriage and Exchange in 19th Century Athens.* Cambridge: Cambridge University Press

Saulnier-Thiercelin, Françoise. 1985. 'Principes et pratiques du partage des biens: l'exemple crétois', in C. Piault (ed.), *Familles et Biens en Grèce et à Chypre,* 47–64. Paris: L'Harmattan

Schein, Muriel Dimen. 1970. 'Change and Continuity in a Greek Mountain Community'. PhD thesis, Department of Anthropology, Columbia University. Ann Arbor: University Microfilms

—— 1974. 'Stratification in a Greek village', in A. La Ruffa et al. (eds), *City and Peasant,* 488–95. New York: New York Academy of Sciences

Schneider, David M. 1984. *A Critique of the Study of Kinship.* Ann Arbor: University of Michigan Press

Schneider, Jane and Peter Schneider. 1976. *Culture and Political Economy in Western Sicily.* New York: Academic Press

Schweizer, Thomas and Douglas R. White (eds). 1998. *Kinship, Networks and Exchange (Structural Analysis in the Social Sciences).* Cambridge: Cambridge University Press

Seremetakis, Nadia M. 1991. *The Last Word. Women, Death, and Divination in Inner Mani.* Chicago: University of Chicago Press

Siegel, Bernard. 1973. 'Cultural mediation in Greece', in K. Weibust (ed.), *Kulturvariation I Sydeuropa,* 35–48. Copenhagen: NEFA Forlag

Silverman, Sydel. 1975. *Three Bells of Civilization: the Life of an Italian Hill Town.* New York: Columbia University Press

Simvoulio Isotitas ton Dhio Filon (Council for the Equality of the Two Sexes), n.d., *Ikoyeniako Dhikeo* (Family Law)

Skouteri-Dhidhaskalou, Nora. 1984. *Anthropoloyika yia to Yinekio Zitima* (Anthropological Issues for Feminism). Athens: O Politis

Smyth, Rear-Admiral W.H. 1854. *The Mediterranean: a Memoir, Physical, Historical and Nautical.* London: John W. Parker and Son

Stato Annuale di Battezzati, Sposati, Morti, nella Citta e Isola de Santa Maura dal 1 Gennajo al 31 Dicembre for the years 1831, 1832, 1833 and 1834. Lefkadha Archives

270 References Cited

Stewart, Charles. 1988. 'The role of personal names on Naxos (Greece)', *Journal of the Anthropological Society of Oxford* 19:151–9
—— 1991. *Demons and the Devil: Moral Imagination in Modern Greek Culture.* Princeton, New Jersey: Princeton University Press
Stone, Linda. 1997. *Kinship and Gender: An Introduction.* Boulder, Colorado: Westview Press
Stott, Margaret E. 1985. 'Property, labor and household economy: the transition to tourism in Mykonos, Greece', *Journal of Modern Greek Studies* 3(2): 187–206
Strathern, M. 1981. *Kinship at the Core: an Anthropology of Elmdon, Essex.* Cambridge: Cambridge University Press
—— 1982. 'The place of kinship: kin, class and village status in Elmdon, Essex.' In A.P. Cohen (ed.), *Belonging. Identity and Social Organisation in British Rural Cultures*, 73–100. Manchester: Manchester University Press
Sutton, David E. 1998. *Memories Cast in Stone. The Relevance of the Past in Everyday Life.* Oxford: Berg
Sutton, Susan. 1978. 'Migrant Regional Associations: An Athenian Example and its Implications'. PhD thesis, University of North Carolina at Chapel Hill
Svoronos, Nikos G. 1940a. '*Hii prosfiyes en Lefkadhi* (Hiot refugees in Lefkadha)', in *Afieroma is Konstantinon Amandon* (Tributes to Konstantinos Amandos), 197–220. Athens
—— 1940b. '*Engrafa anaferomena is tous en Lefkadhi kleftas ke armatolous* (Documents relating to the klefts and armatoli in Lefkadha)', *Epeteris tou Meseonikou Arhiou, A (1939).* (Yearbook of the Mediaeval Archives, Vol. A, (1939)), 105–23
—— 1985. *Episkopisi tis Neoellinikis Istorias* (An Overview of Modern Greek History). Athens: Themelio
Tertsetis. 1967. '*Aftografika Apomnimonevmata tou Dhimou Tseliou*' ('Autobigraphical Memoirs of Dhimos Tselios') in G. Baletas (ed.), *Tertseti Apanda, Tomos* B (Complete Works of Tertsetis, *Vol. 2*), 20–21. Athens: Christos Yiavanis Publications
Torgovnick, M. 1990. *Gone Primitive. Savage Intellects, Modern Lives.* Chicago: Chicago University Press
Tsaoussis, D.G. 1976. 'Greek Social Structure', in M. Dimen and E. Friedl (eds), *Regional Variation in Modern Greece and Cyprus: Towards a Perspective on the Ethnography of Greece*, 429–41. New York: Annals of the New York Academy of Sciences 268
Turner, Hilary Louise. 1987. 'Chios and Chrisopher Buondelmonti's Liber Insularum', *Dheltion tis Istorikis ke Ethnoloyikis Eterias tis Elladhos* (Bulletin of the Historical and Ethnographic Society of Greece) 30: 47–71
Tzannatos, Zafiris. 1986. 'Comment on women's status and changing position in Greece', in Z. Tzannatos (ed.), *Socialism in Greece*, 108–13. Aldershot, Hants: Gower
Vacalopoulos, Apostolos. 1976. *The Greek Nation.* New Brunswick: Rutgers University Press
Vermeulen, Cornelis. 1970. 'Families in Urban Greece'. PhD thesis, Cornell University
—— 1976. 'Development and migration in the Ceres Basin', in M. Dimen and E. Friedl (eds), *Regional Variation in Modern Greece and Cyprus: Towards a Perspective on the Ethnography of Greece*, 59–70. New York: Annals of the New York Academy of Sciences 268
Vermeulen, Hans. 1983. 'Urban research in Greece', in M. Kenny and D. Kertzer (eds), *Urban Life in Mediterranean Europe. Anthropological Perspectives*, 109–32. Urbana: University of Illinois Press
Vernier, Bernard. 1991. *La Genèse Sociale des Sentiments. Aînés et cadets dans l'île grecque de Karpathos.* Paris: Editions de l'Ecole des Hautes Etudes en Sciences Sociales
Vgenopoulos, Costas. 1985. *Growth and Unemployment. The Case of Greek Post-war International Emigration.* Athens: Exantas
Vivlion Ay. Yeoryiou, Meganision (Book of [the church of] St George. Meganisi). n.d. Folder of eighteenth-century baptismal records (in several hands). Lefkadha Archives
Ware, Kallistos. 1983. 'The Church: a time of transition', in R. Clogg (ed.), *Greece in the 1980s*, 208–30. London: Macmillan

Yotopoulos-Marangopoulos, Alice. 1986. 'Some aspects of the legal status of Greek women', in Z. Tzannatos (ed.), *Socialism in Greece*, 89–98. Aldershot, Hants: Gower

Zakhos, Emmanouil. 1981. *Leksiko tis Piatsas* (Dictionary of Slang). Athens: Kaktos

Zinovieff, Sofka. 1991. 'Hunters and hunted: *kamaki* and the ambiguities of sexual predation in a Greek town', in P. Loizos and E. Papataxiarchis (eds), *Contested Identities: Gender and Kinship in Modern Greece*, 203–20. Princeton: Princeton University Press

Index

prohibition and, 101; marriage and, 118; overlapping nature of, 98-9, 104, 115, 121, 180; *soi* and, 100, 123

Kinship terminology 103-110, 184; affines, for, 104-110; bilateral nature of 103-4, 110, 121; cousins, for, 104

Kinship (see also Family) affinity and 109, 253; agnatic, 99-100, 244; bilateral, 98-100, 122-8 *passim*, 244; business ventures, as basis of, 170-2, 173; and migration, 172-4; category confusions within, 146; classificatory problems of, 99-100, 123-8 *passim*; community, as basis of, 37-8, 40-43, 94-5, 102, 109, 112-4, 153-4, 178, 188, 246, 258; cooperation, as basis of, 168-77 *passim*, 177, 180, 188; extensiveness of, 102, 109, 110, 112-15, 121, 154, 183-4; friendship and, 175, 181, 182, 184, 241; godparenthood and, 130-2, 134, 135, 136, 142-4, 147, 148-9; Greek, varieties of, 96-8; household and, 101; idiom of, 177-85; importance of, 1, 5-7; marriage, acquired through, 42, 52; as moral system, 94-5, 109, 155, 168, 171, 175, 181-2, 183, 184-5, 246; obligations of, 130, 175, 185, 244; patronage and, 174-5; politics and, 178-80, 185, 258; Spartokhoriot, general features of, 98-9; strategically invoked, 155, 184-5; studies of, 95-6

Klefts 47 *and notes 20-3, 49 n.24*
Kolokotronis 44, *47 n.20, 49 n.24*
Kseni (see also Foreigners) *12 n.3, 39, 41 and n.3, 42, 94, 110, 115, 154, 156, 162, 172, 186, 248, 253, 254*; incoming brides as, 241; non-family as, 220

Land: acquisition of 57, 60, 67, 73, 219; amounts of, 219; division of, 211, 212, 218; dowry as, 219-20, 221-2; landlessness and, 177; migration and, 174; ownership of, 52, 54, 56 *and n.44*, 57, 59, 60, 61, 70, 75, 209, 211; sons, reserved for, 222; wealth, as, 54, 58, 61 *and n.57*, 70

Landlords, absentee *54 n. 37*, 56-8 *and note 46*, 60

Leach, Edmund 6 *and n.3*, 127, *134 n.9*
Lévi-Strauss, Claude *96 n.3*, 134 *and n.9*, 192, 193 *and n.5*, 199, 245
Lineages 96 *and n.3*, 99-100, 123, 125, *126 n.18*, 127
Llobera, Josep R. 24 *and n.21, 25 n.22*
Loizos, Peter *21 n.15*, 95-100 *passim*, 182
Love 237-9 *passim*; marriage, as basis for, 217, 218, 224, 227, 230; ideological importance of, 226, 230; meaning of, 228-9, 232; traditional antipathy towards, 228; individual choice and, 239

Macdonald, Sharon 37
Mahairas, K. *45 notes 12-14, 57 n.46*
Malakasis, Dhimos *56 n.45, 60 n.55*

Marriage 99, 217-44 *passim*; affines, between, 119-21; ages of, 198, 202, 235-40; arranged, 66, 72, 97, 112, 170, 217, 228-30, 253; bride, transferred at, 241, 242; changes in attitude towards, 224, 226, 239; economic change and, 238-40; forbidden between agnates, 134; godparenthood, as analogue of, 134-5, 142, 148-9, 153; godparenthood, incompatibility with, 134, 136, 146, 150-3; incest prohibition and, 101, *105 n.8*; integration into community through, 38, 42, 51-2 *and n.32*, 59, 109, 110-11, 115; order of, 198; prohibitions on, 115-19; relatives by, 104-5; residence and, 98; *soi*, and, 123; sponsorship of, 130, 132-4; 137-41, 144-6; strategies of, 199; village endogamy and, 110-12, 234-5

Matriliny 191, 222
Mediterranean anthropology, history of 20-28
Migration 1-2, 21-3, 26-9 *and notes 25, 27 & 30*, 35-6, 38, 41-3, 45-53 *and n.33*, 58, 59-61 *and notes 51 & 52*, 62 *and notes 58 & 59*, 63 *and n.1*, 64, 67, 71-92 *passim and n.9*, 93, 111, 114, 115, 152, 170-1, 173-4, 182, 195-6, 200, 203, 204, 257; endogamy and, 111-12, 235; baptism and, 140; family, assisted by, 172-4; inheritance and, 191, 196, 197, 199, 200, 203-4; dowry and, 217-18, 220, 221-2; remittances and, 220; daughters and, 243
Mobility of population (see also Migration) 32, 38, 41, 43, 44, 79-80, 93
Modernization *62 n.59*, 76, 218, 226, 229, 230
Morality, public 155-9 *passim*, 160, 161, 166-7, 175, 235
Morosini, Antonio *46 n.17*
Morosini, Francesco *45 n.11, 46 n.15*
Mothers-in-law and daughters-in-law 210, 243
Mouzelis, Nikos P. 26 *and notes 23 and 26, 59 n.51, 62 n.59*

Naming, patterns of 131 *and n.3*; and baptism, 131-2
Needham, Rodney 5-6
Neolocal residence 89, 200, 202, 204, 205, 209, 210, 215, 221-2, 241, 243, 244
Nicknames 122, 124, 125
Nuer 5, *216 n.14*

Occupations (historical) 57-8
Ott, Sandra *192 n.4*
Ottomans (and Ottoman rule) 45-6 *and n.19*, 49

Palmos, Kostas *42 n.4, 57 n.48, 58-9 and n.50, 66 n.4*
Panourgia, Neni *24 n.19*
Papandreou, Andreas *55 n.42*, 226
Papataxiarchis, Akis *39 n.1*, 95-100 *passim*
Parkin, Robert 6 *and n.2*

Partsch, Joseph 50 *and n.29*, 52
Pastoralism 50-4 *passim and n.34*, 64
Patrigroups 99-100, 122-8 *passim*
Patriliny (see also Agnation) 121-8 *passim*
Patronage 174-7 *passim*; godparenthood and, 148, 176-7; kinship and, 174-5, 179
Peletz, Michael J. *6 n.2*
Peristiany, John 3, 5, *25 n.22, 26 n.25*, 95 *and n.1*, 100
Pina-Cabral, Joa de *144 n.18*
Piracy 44-49 *passim and notes 10 & 21*, 50, 52
Pitt-Rivers, Julian 135-6 *and n.13*, 143-4 *and n.17, 148 n.21, 149 n.23, 159 n.3*, 96
Politics 178-9; family and, 178-80
Population Spartokhori and Meganisi, of, 44-53 *passim and notes 27, 28 & 29*, 59, 80-92 *passim*, 188, 200-2, 257-8; Athens of, 27-8 *and n.28*; Greece of, 22-3
Poverty 56, 63, 71, 202, 210, 226
Private world 157, 159, 160, 161, 163, 166-8, 186-8, 236; men and women and, 187, 236
Proksenia (see also Marriage, arranged) 228-30
Public world 155-61 *passim*, 166-8, 175, 185; men and women, of, 186, 187, 234, 236; morality of, 234, 235, 240, 241

Radcliffe-Brown *6 n.3*
Remoteness 1, 11, 12, 19, 20, 21, 26, 29, 33-4, 36, 79, 225
Respect 158, 159, 176, 204-8 *passim*, 210, 241, 242
Rondoyiannis, P.G. *45 notes 12 & 14, 48 n.23, 54 n.36, 56 n.45, 64 n.2, 60 n.55*
Roukha 224 *and notes 1 and 2*
Rural communities: Meganisi and Spartokhori as 12-20, 29-31; study of: 1-3, 5, 20-28, 33-7, 44, 45-6 *and notes 39 and 40*

Sailors 2, 28, 29, 31, 37, 57-8, 63-92 *passim*, 130, 148; economic position of, 209, 217, 219, 221, 222, 225, 238, 257; marriages of, 238-40 *passim*
Salamone S.D. and J.B. Stanton *224 n.3*
Sarakatsani 26 *and n.24*, 96, 99 *and n.4*, 101, 122, 127
Saulnier-Thiercelin, Francoise *214 n.12*
Secrecy 163-4, 164-6 *passim*, 189
Shame 177, 207, 209, 213, 217, 224, 225, 240, 254
Shepherds 16, 30, 53, 57; population growth and, 51-2 *and n.31*, 59
Ship-owners 70, 161, 166, 170, 175-6
Shipping (and seafaring) 28, 29, 31, 51, 56 *n.46*, 59, 62, 63-4, 257; history of, 64-71 *and notes 2 & 4*
Shore, Cris *25 n.22*
Silverman, Sydel 16 *and n.6*, 55
Simpetheros: as term for go-between 229 *and n.6*
Smyth, William Henry 49

Soi (see also Agnation and Kindred): as bilateral 100, 101, *102 n.6*, 122; as agnatic 121-8 *passim*
Sons: division of *spiti* and 192-3, 210; relations between fathers and, 205-9, 209-12 *passim*, 239, 240, 241, 244; relations between parents and, 242-3
Spiti (see also House and Household): basic village unit, as 188, 191; composition of, 193, 197-9; continuity of, 192, 212; definition of, 190, 197-8; division of, 191-3, 195-9 *passim*, 209-10, 212, 213-4; historical composition of, 199-202; household and, 100-3 *passim*; inheritance and, 126 ; private, as, 155, 159; solidarity of, 155, 193, 210-11, 244
Sponsors 129-54 *passim*; baptismal, 31, 130, 132; financial obligations of, 132; marriage, 130, 132; naming and, 131-2; origins of, 153; patronage and, 147-8; types of, 133
Stewart, Charles *21 n.15, 24 n.21, 30 n.33*
Strathern, Marilyn 5
Students 29, 32, 78, 82, 85, 86, 91, 92, 178, 206, 231-2, 235; young women as, 240

Tourism (and tourists) 3, 4, 12, 14, 247-51, 253, 254, 257
Tradition 2, 4, 6, 26, 30, 31, 33, 76: dowry as, 226; oral, 44, 52, 58
Tselios, Dhimos 44, 258
Turks and Turkish rule (see also Ottoman) 45 *and notes 9 & 11*, 46 *notes 16 & 19*
Turner, Hilary Louise *43 n.6*

Urban studies 20-28
Urbanization 1-2, 27 *and n.29*, 28, 34-7, 38, 71-88 *passim*

Valaoritis, Aristotelis *56 n.46*
Venice and Venetian rule 45-7 *passim and notes 11, 12, 13, 14, 15, 16, 17, 19 & 21*
Vermeulen, Hans 20 *and n.13*, 25, *26 n.23*
Vernier, Bernard *29 n.31, 116 n.12*, 191
Vgenopoulos, Costas *62 n.59*
Village studies 1-2, 20-8
Village: contrasted with city 2, 34-7, 257; family and, 34, 37, 41, 42, 102, 112-5 *passim*, 155, 156, 159, 167, 168, 235, 246; solidarity of, 42, 130, 136, 154, 156, 157, 159, 161, 167, 168, 253-4
Virtues, commonly expressed 40, 166, 253

Ware, Kallistos *131 n.2*
Wealth (and wealthy) 203, 212, 220, 244; attitudes of wealthy, 225-6, 229-30; emigration, from, 63, 72; inequalities of, 55-6, 58, 61, 70, 71, 92, 176, 180; shipping, from, 28, 64, 69, 70; younger generation, of, 218, 221, 222, 225, 238
Wine-making 168-9, 170, 180